Self-Experience

Self-Experience

Essays on Inner Awareness

Edited by
MANUEL GARCÍA-CARPINTERO AND
MARIE GUILLOT

OXFORD
UNIVERSITY PRESS

Great Clarendon Street, Oxford, OX2 6DP,
United Kingdom

Oxford University Press is a department of the University of Oxford.
It furthers the University's objective of excellence in research, scholarship,
and education by publishing worldwide. Oxford is a registered trade mark of
Oxford University Press in the UK and in certain other countries

© the several contributors 2023

The moral rights of the authors have been asserted

First Edition published in 2023

Impression: 1

All rights reserved. No part of this publication may be reproduced, stored in
a retrieval system, or transmitted, in any form or by any means, without the
prior permission in writing of Oxford University Press, or as expressly permitted
by law, by licence or under terms agreed with the appropriate reprographics
rights organization. Enquiries concerning reproduction outside the scope of the
above should be sent to the Rights Department, Oxford University Press, at the
address above

You must not circulate this work in any other form
and you must impose this same condition on any acquirer

Published in the United States of America by Oxford University Press
198 Madison Avenue, New York, NY 10016, United States of America

British Library Cataloguing in Publication Data

Data available

Library of Congress Control Number: 2022947386

ISBN 978–0–19–880539–7

DOI: 10.1093/oso/9780198805397.001.0001

Printed and bound in the UK by
Clays Ltd, Elcograf S.p.A.

Links to third party websites are provided by Oxford in good faith and
for information only. Oxford disclaims any responsibility for the materials
contained in any third party website referenced in this work.

Contents

List of Contributors   vii

1. Introduction: Views about Self-Experience   1
   Manuel García-Carpintero and Marie Guillot

PART I. DOUBTS AND QUESTIONS ABOUT SELF-EXPERIENCE

2. Conscious Experience: What's in It for Me?   27
   Léa Salje and Alexander Geddes

3. Four Impediments to the Case for Mineness   50
   Tom McClelland

4. Transparency and Subjective Character   77
   Robert J. Howell

5. Mineness, Deflation, and Transparency   99
   Gianfranco Soldati

6. Mineness and Introspective Data   120
   Wayne Wu

7. The Sense of Body Ownership: What Are We Studying?   142
   Krisztina Orbán and Hong Yu Wong

PART II. PUTTING SELF-EXPERIENCE TO WORK

8. The Three Circles of Consciousness   169
   Uriah Kriegel

9. Experiencing Subjects and So-Called Mine-Ness   191
   Martine Nida-Rümelin

10. The Phenomenal Concept of Self and First-Person Epistemology   223
    Marie Guillot

11. The Bounded Body: On the Sense of Bodily Ownership and the Experience of Space   250
    Carlota Serrahima

vi CONTENTS

12. The Phenomenology of Bodily Ownership   269
   Frédérique de Vignemont

13. Emotions of Mineness   291
   Richard Dub

14. What Is It Like to Lack Mineness? Depersonalization as a
   Probe for the Scope, Nature, and Role of Mineness   314
   Alexandre Billon

15. The Ownership of Memories   343
   Jordi Fernández

Analytic Index   363

List of Contributors

Alexandre Billon is Associate Professor in philosophy at the University of Lille. He is working on the articulation of our subjective and our objective points of view. He has published a book of poetry and some articles on happiness, the paradoxes of self-reference, and many others on self-consciousness and psychopathology.

Frédérique de Vignemont is a CNRS Senior Researcher in philosophy. She is the Deputy Director of the Jean Nicod Institute (ENS-PSL University-EHESS-CNRS). Her major current works focus on bodily awareness, self-consciousness, and social cognition. Her recent book, *Mind the Body: A Philosophical Exploration of Bodily Awareness* (Oxford University Press, 2018), provides the first comprehensive treatment of bodily awareness and of the sense of bodily ownership, combining philosophical analysis with recent experimental results. She has also edited two interdisciplinary volumes: *The Subject's Matter* (2017, MIT Press, with A. Alsmith) and *The World at Our Fingertips: A Multidisciplinary Exploration of Peripersonal Space* (forthcoming, Oxford University Press, with A. Serino, H.Y. Wong and A. Farnè).

Richard Dub received his doctoral degree in philosophy from Rutgers University and is currently a Visiting Assistant Professor of Philosophy at Clarkson University. He has previously been a postdoctoral researcher with the Swiss National Science Foundation and with the Swiss Centre for the Affective Sciences in Geneva, Switzerland. His research concerns the role of affect in delusion formation and other philosophical issues at the intersection of emotion and psychosis.

Jordi Fernández is an Associate Professor of Philosophy at the University of Adelaide. His teaching and research interests are in philosophy of mind, epistemology and metaphysics. He is the author of *Transparent Minds: A Study of Self-Knowledge* (2013), and *Memory: A Self-Referential Account* (2019).

Manuel García-Carpintero is Professor of Philosophy at the University of Barcelona, Spain. He has been a Fellow at the Center for the Advanced Studies in the Humanities (Edinburgh, 2001), and he has been appointed Visiting Professor at the University of Lisbon (2013–onwards). His main interests are in philosophical logic, the philosophy of language, the philosophy of mind and related epistemological and metaphysical issues.

Alexander Geddes is a Research Associate at KCL, on the ERC-funded project Better Understanding the Metaphysics of Pregnancy, and Stipendiary Lecturer at Exeter College, Oxford. Prior to that, he was a Research Fellow at the University of Southampton and a Postdoctoral Researcher at the Centre for Philosophical Psychology, University of Antwerp.

Marie Guillot is a Senior Lecturer at the University of Essex. Her research focuses on issues in the philosophy of mind and the philosophy of language, especially subjectivity,

viii LIST OF CONTRIBUTORS

self-consciousness, phenomenal consciousness, indexicality, and the ethics and politics of speech acts.

Robert J. Howell is Professor of Philosophy at Southern Methodist University and is the author of *Consciousness and the Limits of Objectivity* (Oxford University Press, 2013). He is also co-author with Torin Alter of *A Dialogue on Consciousness* (Oxford University Press, 2009) and *The God Dialogues* (Oxford University Press, 2011).

Uriah Kriegel is Professor of Philosophy at Rice University. He is the author of *Subjective Consciousness: A Self-Representational Theory* (Oxford University Press, 2009), *The Sources of Intentionality* (Oxford University Press, 2011), *The Varieties of Consciousness* (Oxford University Press, 2015), *Brentano's Philosophical System: Mind, Being, Value* (Oxford University Press, 2018), as well as a number of articles on for-me-ness and mine-ness.

Tom McClelland specializes in philosophy of mind and has published on topics including consciousness, mental action, perceptual experience, cognitive phenomenology, the self, introspection and the significance of teapots. He also works in aesthetics and has a special interest in how insights from psychology and philosophy of mind can shed light on our experience of art. Before becoming a Lecturer at the University of Cambridge, Tom previously held posts at the Universities of Warwick, Manchester, and Glasgow, and gained degrees from the Universities of Sussex, York, and Cambridge.

Martine Nida-Rümelin studied philosophy, psychology, and mathematics at the University of Munich. Since 1999, she is Full Professor at the University of Fribourg (Switzerland). Her research focuses on issues in the intersection of philosophy of mind and metaphysics concerning the ontological status of conscious beings and their identity and of experiential properties. Further topics in the center of her research are: pre-reflective self-awareness and self-reference; agency and the capacity of being active in human and non-human animals. She aims at developing a version of subject-body dualism which avoids the weaknesses of traditional substance dualism. In 2019 she has been awarded the Jean-Nicod-Price for her work in philosophy of mind.

Krisztina Orbán is a Postdoc at the Department of Philosophy and CIN Philosophy of Neuroscience Group at the University of Tübingen, Germany. Her research interests centre around first person reference, the self, and animal cognition. She is currently exploring the notion of self-directed action.

Léa Salje is a philosopher of mind at the University of Leeds. She received her PhD from University College London. Her primary research interests are first person thought and bodily self-awareness. In addition to these topics, she has published on the format of thought, second person thought, the significance of non-indexical thought, and immunity to error through misidentification.

Carlota Serrahima is currently a postdoctoral researcher at the University of Barcelona within the ERC-funded project "Rethinking Conscious Agency." She has previously held postdoctoral positions at the Institut Jean Nicod in Paris and the Center for Philosophical Psychology at the University of Antwerp. Her research focuses on issues in the philosophy of mind and phenomenology, specially bodily awareness, self-consciousness, and their relation to phenomenal consciousness.

Gianfranco Soldati works on phenomenology, mind and knowledge. Among other things he is interested in problems related to perception, action, reason, self-knowledge, and in the philosophical analysis of experience. He holds the chair of modern and contemporary philosophy at the Philosophy Department of Fribourg University and is a member of EXRE. He was editor of *Dialectica* and a member of the scientific council of the Swiss National Science Foundation.

Wayne Wu holds a PhD in philosophy and an MA in molecular and cell biology from the University of California, Berkeley. He is interested in philosophy of mind, action, perception as well as philosophy of science, with focus on psychology and neuroscience.

Hong Yu Wong is Professor of Philosophy and Head of the CIN Philosophy of Neuroscience Group at the University of Tübingen, Germany. His research interests centre around action, perception, and the body. His monograph *Embodied Agency* is forthcoming with Oxford University Press.

1

Introduction

Views about Self-Experience

Manuel García-Carpintero and Marie Guillot*

Recent debates on phenomenal consciousness have shown renewed interest for the idea that experience generally includes an experience of the self—a *self-experience*—whatever else it may present the self with. When a subject has an ordinary experience (as of a bouncing red ball, for example), the thought goes, she is not just phenomenally aware of the world as being presented in a certain way (a bouncy, reddish, roundish way in this case); she is also phenomenally aware of the fact that it is presented to *her*. This view, associated with historical figures such as William James, Husserl, Merleau-Ponty, and Sartre, is attracting a new surge of attention at the crossroads of phenomenology, analytic philosophy of mind and the philosophy of cognitive science, but also intense controversy. This book explores some of the questions running through the ongoing debate on the putative subjective dimension of experience: *Does it exist?*, the *existence* question; *What is it?*, the *essence* question; *What is it for?*, the *function* question; and *What else does it explain?*, the *explanation* question. The remainder of this Introduction dwells mostly on the first two questions, before giving a brief presentation of the chapters to follow.

1. Subjective Character and Phenomenal Consciousness

1.1. Phenomenal Consciousness

It is sometimes assumed that some topics addressed in philosophy are "natural kinds" endowed with relatively hidden, to that extent objective "real essences,"

---

* The editors are equal co-authors of the book, listed alphabetically. Financial support was provided by the DGI, Spanish Government, research project FFI2016-80588-R, the award "ICREA Academia" for excellence in research, 2018, funded by the Generalitat de Catalunya, a Juan de la Cierva fellowship (Spanish Government), n°JCI-2012–13921, and the Marie Skłodowska Curie project PHENOSELF, FP7-IEF-622127. This Introduction received helpful comments from Mohan Matthen, Miguel Ángel Sebastián, and Carlota Serrahima. Many thanks to the audiences of the two Barcelona Mineness conferences in 2015 and 2017 for stimulating discussion. Thanks to Carlota Serrahima for preparing the Index, and to Peter Momtchiloff, our editor, for his encouragement and patience. Thanks finally to Michael Maudsley for the grammatical revision.

Manuel García-Carpintero and Marie Guillot, *Introduction: Views about Self-Experience* In: *Self-Experience: Essays on Inner Awareness*. Edited by: Manuel García-Carpintero and Marie Guillot, Oxford University Press.
© Manuel García-Carpintero and Marie Guillot 2023. DOI: 10.1093/oso/9780198805397.003.0001

2 INTRODUCTION

worth theorizing about.[1] Phenomenal consciousness and the features of conscious experiences we are aware of when in a phenomenally conscious state, *qualia*, are a good case in point.[2] It is often a crucial part of whatever illumination philosophy can provide in addressing its topics to agree on a minimal characterization, making sure we are all on the same page in engaging them.[3] Such a characterization should only use uncontroversial notions, and it should be neutral among the different accounts of the topic that can be provided—including the sceptical view that rejects the just stated ontological assumption, contending instead that the phenomenon is a "grue-like" one, lacking any objective explanatory nature.

A possible strategy for the consciousness case is suggested by Hill's *meta-problem* proposal (Hill 2009, 19–22; cf. Kriegel 2015, 52–3, Chalmers 2018): *qualia* are properties such as pains, orgasms, colours, or tastes, which *it is reasonable to think of* as fully graspable only from the perspective of the conscious subject, so that such and such *prima facie* compelling arguments (here specific examples are mentioned, like those in Kripke (1980) or Jackson (1986)) have been advanced to argue for their irreducibility to the physical.

A more traditional strategy for this case in contemporary analytic philosophy has been to use Nagel's (1974) *what it is like* characterization: *qualia* are features of experiences such that there is something it is like for a subject in virtue of having them. Now, one of us once had a teacher—a laureated poet engaged as a philosopher, unsympathetic to what he called "positivism"—who used to complain that analytic philosophers do philosophy that doesn't translate well from English. This may be a case in point; Nagel's title is translated into Spanish as "¿Cómo (qué) es ser un murciélago?," but the phrase 'cómo (qué) es...' lacks in Spanish connotations suggestive of phenomenal states and their contents; the same is true of the French translation "Quel effet cela fait-il…." In fact, Snowdon (2010) has examples indicating that this may be true in English too, which is in part what motivates the alternative characterization mentioned above. Stoljar (2016) provides a detailed semantic analysis, arguing that Nagel's phrase has, at least pragmatically (perhaps also in Spanish and French then), the required intimations. As he summarizes his proposal:

---

[1] Here we *don't* use 'natural' in opposition to 'social', but rather to refer to properties and kinds in Lewis' (1983) "sparse" (as opposed to "abundant") sense. Natural kinds in this sense might well be "social constructs," definable by social rules. "Natural" properties and kinds are those that play substantive explanatory roles, and hence have a "hidden nature" which only reveals itself after theorizing. This might just be philosophical, armchair-like; but it should be unifiable with empirical theorizing along standard lines.

[2] Cf. Shea (2012) for elaboration and justification.

[3] Cf. the illuminating discussion Taylor (2018, §2–4) provides as a prelude to his minimal characterization of another traditional philosophical topic, *indeterminacy*.

'what it is like'-sentences express relations of a certain kind—I call them *affective relations*—that hold between individuals and events; to a first approximation, an affective relation holds between an individual and an event just in case the individual is affected in a particular kind of way by the event. In many contexts, but not in all, the affective relations expressed by 'what it is like'-sentences will be of a certain special kind I call *experiential* relations...an experiential relation holds between an individual and an event just in case the individual feels a certain way in virtue of the event.   (Stoljar 2016, 1162)

As Stoljar points out, Nagel's characterization has suggested to many "a reflexive or self-representational theory, according to which an individual is in a conscious state if the individual represents or is aware of (in some sense) their being in that state" (1162); he quotes a crisp statement of the suggestion by Levine (2007, 514):

the very phrase that serves to canonically express the notion of the phenomenal— 'what it's like for x to...'—explicitly refers to the phenomenal state in question being 'for' the subject. The way I would put it...is: Phenomenal states/properties are not merely instantiated in the subject, but are experienced by the subject. Experience is more than mere instantiation, and part of what that 'more' involves is some kind of access.[4]

Stoljar goes on to persuasively show that, on his analysis, no reflexivity is entailed by Nagel's minimal characterization: it just follows from S being in a phenomenally conscious state that S *feels some way* by being in it, which *prima facie* doesn't require that S *represents* or be *aware* of the state, or of herself being in that state.[5] The question, as he grants, is whether there are good reasons to think that this "feeling some way" common to phenomenal states is such that the individuals in them are "in some sense" aware of their being in them—and what that sense is.

1.2. From Phenomenal Consciousness to Subjective Character

In a classical paper trying to isolate the phenomenal character of conscious states, Block (1995, 235) suggests that phenomenal states "often seem to have a 'me-ishness' about them, the phenomenal state often represents the state as 'a state of me'."[6] Debates whether this is so, and how it should be understood if so, have

---

[4] But cf. Levine (2019) for his more nuanced recent position, which grants, we think, Stoljar's objection.

[5] Cf. Byrne (2004, 214–16), Siewert (2013, 238–41), Guillot (2017, 35), Stoljar (2021, §6). We argue below for the need to make significant distinctions in the relevant "senses" of awareness and self-awareness alluded to here.

[6] Cf. also Rosenthal (1986, 344–5).

4 INTRODUCTION

proliferated in the past decade. They have a long pedigree, going back to Aristotle (Caston 2002).[7] The present collection of chapters, originating in a workshop the editors organized in Barcelona in 2015 with a 2017 follow-up, explore the theme in depth.

Conscious states have distinctive features, distinguishable in them or across them, those "ways" their subjects "feel" by being in them. These are the aforementioned *qualia*, and their study has occupied philosophers for the past decades. Beyond such *determinates*, the current issue minimally concerns a *determinable* common to all phenomenally conscious states in some accounts, to most or some in others. This would thereby have claims to be considered the essence of consciousness, or a crucial feature thereof (Zahavi & Kriegel 2016, 50); to that extent, our topic overlaps with the main target of philosophical theories of consciousness (Smith 2020, §3, Siewert 2021, §7). Gallagher & Zahavi (2021, §1) put it thus:

> There is something it is like to taste chocolate, and this is different from what it is like to remember what it is like to taste chocolate, or to smell vanilla, to run, to stand still, to feel envious, nervous, depressed or happy, or to entertain an abstract belief. All of these different experiences are, however, also characterized by their distinct first-personal character. The what-it-is-likeness of phenomenal episodes is properly speaking a what-it-is-like-*for-me*-ness. This for-me-ness doesn't refer to a specific experiential quality like sour or soft, rather it refers to the distinct first-personal givenness of experience. It refers to the fact that the experiences I am living through are given differently (but not necessarily better) to me than to anybody else.[8]

In their introduction to a recent journal issue on our topic, Farrell & McClelland put thus the contrast: "When we perceptually experience the sunset we have an outer awareness of the scene before us but we also have an inner awareness of that very experience, or of something associated with it" (Farrell & McClelland 2017, 2).[9]

As the quoted passages show, a first thing that is confusing about the issue is the terminology itself; there is a bewildering variety of terms that have been used to capture the notion, from Block's 'me-ishness' and Kriegel's 'inner awareness' to Gallagher & Zahavi's 'for-me-ness' and 'mineness'.[10] This in turn has contributed to some ambiguities. (In particular, it is not always clear in the debate whether the relevant awareness is turned towards the subject, as in Block's quotation above, or towards the conscious state she is in, as in the last two quotations, or both. More

---

[7] Cf. Frank (2004) and Zahavi (2005) for other strands in the history of the notion.

[8] Cp. the feature of conscious experience that Merlo (2021), following James, calls *feltness*, and the *ontological* problem of other minds he develops on its basis.

[9] The term 'inner awareness' comes from Kriegel (2009).

[10] This is just a small sample; cf. Byrne (2004, §3), Guillot (2017, 25).

on this below.) In previous influential work, Zahavi (2005) borrowed from the phenomenological school (which, as he shows, intensively discussed the topic) the descriptively accurate 'pre-reflective self-awareness'. In the rest of this section, we fix on Levine's (2001, 6–7) still evocative but less unwieldy terms, contrasting 'qualitative character' and '*qualia*' with 'subjective character' and 'subjectivity'. We use "self-experience" pre-theoretically, in the title and elsewhere, as a synonym.

1.3. Deflationary and Robust Views about Subjective Character

We should distinguish subjective character from introspection, by which we will understand a conscious judgment about features of one's mental life. Let's consider a perceptual state, visually experiencing a red disc in front of one. We could introspect the perceptual state and its features, its perceptual mode (discriminating it from a visual imagining, perhaps with the same content), the reddishness in it, whether the diameter that the disc appears to have is smaller than the distance at which the disc appears to be, and so on; this would be a further conscious state. The subjective character of the perceptual state is supposed to be a feature that it has, whether or not it becomes the target of such an introspective state. It is also a feature that, by being conscious, the introspective state itself has, even if it itself is not the target of a further, second-order introspection.

In a previous quote, Gallagher & Zahavi deny that subjective character is a *specific* experiential quality, but a few paragraphs below they conclude that on their view the self "is an integral aspect of conscious life, and involves this immediate experiential character." They thus set apart the most deflationary view, on which subjectivity is just a feature of something that is in fact an experience, from more robust views on which it, by itself, makes a distinctive additional contribution to phenomenal character, to what it is like for its subject to have that conscious experience. Here Zahavi & Kriegel make this distinction:

> The for-me-ness of experience still admits of two crucially different interpretations. According to a deflationary interpretation, it consists simply in the experience *occurring* in someone (a 'me'). On this view, for-me-ness is a non-experiential aspect of mental life—a merely metaphysical fact, so to speak, not a phenomenological fact. The idea is that we ought to resist a no-ownership view according to which experiences can occur as free-floating unowned entities. Just as horse-riding presupposes the existence of a horse, experiencing presupposes a subject of experience. In contrast, a non-deflationary interpretation construes for-me-ness as an experiential aspect of mental life, a bona fide *phenomenal* dimension of consciousness. On this view, to say that an experience is *for me* is precisely to say something more than that it is *in me*.
>
> (Zahavi & Kriegel 2016, 36)

6 INTRODUCTION

They go on to make a further distinction in the non-deflationary camp, among those who take subjective character to be universal and those who take it to be absent in some conscious states, see fn. 12 below.

Minimally understood, thus, subjective character consists in the ontological fact that phenomenally conscious experiences are not "free-floating" eventualities like raining or lightning but require a subject—which does appear to be implied by Nagel's characterization—plus the epistemological fact that they are available for introspection. Robustly understood in contrast, as Howell & Thompson (2017, 106) put it, subjective character should make some contribution to the overall phenomenal character of a conscious state, and it should in some way present the subject of that state.[11]

O'Conaill (2019, 331–2) helpfully enumerates the features that subjectivity should have:

> Inner awareness is *pre-reflective*: each subject is aware of her own experiences prior to reflecting on them. It is *non-voluntary*: one will be aware of whatever experience one is currently having, regardless of what one tries to do. It is *ubiquitous*: each subject is aware of each of their occurrent experiences in this way. It is *direct*: one is not aware of having an experience in virtue of being aware of anything else. It is *non-inferential*: one does not need to [*sic*] evidence or a chain of reasons to be aware of one's experience. It is *non-attentive*: in inner awareness one does not focus one's attention on the experience one is having.[12]

One might be sceptical about the robust view, sticking to the minimal view by claiming that it is only through introspection that we gain a conscious awareness of ourselves:[13]

> Being possessed of the first-person conceptual capacity always, or at least for the most part, puts one in a *position* to know immediately about one's own conscious mental life as one's own. This "privileged" position is exploited if and when the capacity for reflective self-consciousness is exercised. But it does not follow from the ever present *availability* of taking up a distinctively first-personal relation to one's own conscious experience that there is an *actual* consciousness

---

[11] Or just the state itself (Wilford 2015).

[12] Cf. also Zahavi & Kriegel (2016, 49). The *ubiquity* feature should be qualified if there might be atypical or abnormal cases in which subjectivity is absent, which some authors support (McClelland 2015, 2486; Billon, 2016; Guillot 2017, §§4.1, 4.2; Duncan 2019). This is debated in some of the chapters compiled here, see below.

[13] Stoljar (2021) offers a thorough examination of extant arguments for robust accounts of subjectivity and questions them all, in support of a minimalism like the one that Shear and Howell & Thompson advance in the quotes that follow—see also Siewert (2013, 250) and Giustina (forthcoming) for a reply. Stoljar (2018) has a good account of the relation between phenomenal states and introspection consistent with sceptical views.

of oneself that, *experientially*, always accompanies one's conscious experience of the world. (Schear 2009, 98)

Despite the fact that experiences on the unreflective level don't have mineness, we can gain a sense of mineness in reflection…In reflection we lay claim to our experiences, and the mineness is a product—not a condition of—that attitude.
(Howell & Thompson 2017, 120)[14]

Hume's famous incapacity to find himself in experience provides a phenomenological motivation for the deflationary position. Here is an often-quoted passage to that effect from Sartre, reminiscent of Moore's also often quoted passage on the transparency of experience:

When I run after a streetcar, when I look at the time, when I am absorbed in contemplating a portrait, there is no *I*. There is consciousness of the streetcar-having-to-be-overtaken, etc. I am then plunged into the world of objects…but *me*, I have disappeared…There is no place for me on this level. And this is not a matter of chance, due to a momentary lapse of attention, but happens because of the very structure of consciousness. (Sartre 1957, 48–9)

The moment we try to fix our attention upon consciousness and to see what, distinctly, it is, it seems to vanish: it seems as if we had before us a mere emptiness. When we try to introspect the sensation of blue, all we can see is the blue: the other element is as if it were diaphanous. (Moore 1903, 450)

It is worth noticing that neither Moore nor Sartre embraced the sceptical position the texts suggest: Moore assumes in the quoted passage that "the other element" is there nonetheless, appearances notwithstanding, and Sartre takes pre-reflective self-consciousness to be an essential ingredient of the "structure of consciousness." But some theorists of consciousness rely on the intuitive impressions that Sartre and Moore helpfully describe. "First-order" representational theories along the lines of those developed by Dretske or Tye are influential views that stress those intuitions. These views accept a notion that has become recently somehow controversial, for which Block (2015) offers compelling considerations; namely, that there are unconscious states with representational features, perhaps the very same had by conscious states.[15] What makes the difference? Consistent with the deflationary view of subjectivity just outlined, first-order theorists invoke dispositional or functional features; thus, for instance, Tye (2002, 62) speaks of their being "poised," their standing "ready and available to make a direct impact on beliefs and/or desires."

---

[14] Cp. however Howell (2019) for a slightly less deflationary view, and his contribution to this volume.

[15] Cf. also Quilty-Dunn (2018).

8   INTRODUCTION

Many philosophers have argued for some robust view of consciousness that posits occurrent phenomenal features.[16] Sticking to representational views, this is upheld by "higher-order" theories developed by Armstrong, Carruthers, Lycan, or Rosenthal, on which the conscious character of a state is fixed by a concurrent higher-order awareness of it, a perception or a further thought—to prevent a regress, ultimately unconscious.[17] This is compatible with *phenomenism*, which some of those philosophers also endorse—the view that conscious states have essential intrinsic features beyond their representational ones, which don't supervene on them. Such "mental paint" (Block 2003) affords by itself an alternative account of consciousness, in terms of real (as opposed to merely intentional) relations of familiarity or acquaintance between the subject and those features.

Proposals along such lines have been made about subjectivity; in Schear's (2009, 96) happy turn of phrase, subjective character turns out to be on those views "a kind of implicit acquaintance with oneself, or background self-familiarity." In previous work, one of us (cf. Guillot 2017) makes a three-part classification of schemas for philosophical theories of subjective character, which several contributors to this volume among others have found helpful.[18] As Guillot puts it,

> 'subjective character' is not merely a label for the metaphysical fact that experiences are had by subjects, in the sense that they occur in them. It is intended to capture a further, epistemic fact, namely that subjects are aware of their experiences; and, more demandingly still, a phenomenological fact, namely that this awareness is experiential, and registers as a certain "way it feels" to the subject.
>
> (Guillot 2017, 27)

She then goes on to distinguish three increasingly more demanding views on the role of the subject in subjective character, three "grades of subjective involvement" as we might call them in a Quinean vein: she might appear, (i) "as one of the two *relata* in the relation of phenomenal awareness to her experiences, i.e. as the one who is *appeared to*," which Guillot labels 'for-me-ness'; (ii) "as also *appearing* to herself in being aware of the other relatum (the experience)," 'me-ness'; and (iii) "as appearing to herself as *the owner* of the experience" (27), 'mineness'. Guillot

---

[16] The dispositions posited by dispositional accounts are of course themselves occurrent properties, but the explanatory features in them (the introspecting, in our cases) are merely iffy. (We find it difficult to classify McClelland's (2015, 2489) "affordances" account on the deflationary-robust scale, because we are unsure about his views on dispositions.)

[17] Cf. Siewert (2013), Stoljar (2017), and Williford (2019) for discussion on whether a regress is thereby successfully prevented, and Weisberg (2019) for a recent defense of the Higher-Thought account of subjectivity.

[18] Cf. Barbieri (2021) for a finer-grained taxonomy, and Stoljar (2021, §§4–5) for a coarser characterization of the debated claims, both consistent with Guillot's.

contends that the three notions are conceptually different, and this seems to be borne out by the *prima facie* differences among progressively more committed accounts of subjectivity to be found in recent literature.

Thus, for instance, on Kriegel's (2009) view, subjectivity consists in the fact that phenomenally conscious states peripherally represent themselves, in addition to whatever other representational features they may have. O'Conaill (2019) defends a related view, on which the relevant self-representational feature of conscious states is claimed to be a generic kind of *mode*, like the mode distinguishing conscious visual perceptual states from conscious visual imaginings, but with a more general character. Williford (2015) offers yet another variant, a view on which the self-presentation of the state is not an intentional relation but a real one, an acquaintance relation. On these three views, subjects are just the entities to whom these self-representings or self-manifestings of conscious states occur, but they are not what is primarily represented or manifested; these are instead the states themselves. Hence these all count as views of type (i), on which subjective character is just for-me-ness.

Zahavi (2018, 706–8) takes his own view to be one of this kind. He rejects a taxon for type (ii) views because, on his account of what selves are, and what is required to be aware of them, consciously presenting a conscious state (which is what all conscious states do for themselves, according to him, given their essential nature) suffices to present the subject bearing that conscious state. Hence, *for-me-ness* equals *me-ness*. But Guillot (2017, 35–7) grants that this might be so; it might be that the best metaphysical account of selves is one along such minimal lines, as defended for instance by Strawson (2009). However, as she points out, to establish this requires substantive metaphysical argument. This might be an *a priori* affair in some sense; but Guillot is only claiming a conceptual difference among the views, and this, we take it, merely requires the *prima facie* conceivability of the discriminability of her distinctions, which is compatible with their *ultima facie* collapse.

In contrast, other theorists have provided accounts of subjective character that, as such and without the need for independent metaphysical assumptions about the nature of selves or consciousness, appear to go beyond for-me-ness. Sebastián (2012, 2019) for one argues that conscious experiences include a *de se* representation of their subjects. On the face of it, this looks like a proposal to characterize subjectivity as me-ness. Duncan (2018) in his turn argues for an acquaintance view on which we are not just acquainted with our conscious states, but also with ourselves, and also with our bearing or ownership relation to them. This looks like a view on which subjectivity is mineness.

At this most robust end of the scale, where presentations or representations of the self as such are invoked to characterize subjectivity, proposals would be further clarified, we suggest, from addressing a related issue: which links subjectivity has, if any, with bodily self-awareness (cf. de Vignemont (2020)). Thus, there is a debate on whether the perspectival character of some perceptual experiences should be accounted for by positing at that level a first-personal representation of the subject bearing that perspective (cf. Schwenkler (2014), Richardson (2017), Alsmith (2017), Gallagher & Zahavi (2021, §4)). There is a distinct debate on whether interoception—the perception of the body from within—contributes to a coherent and stable self-model (cf. Allen and Tsakiris (2018)). We could thus further ask whether there is any connection, constitutive or otherwise, between such self-representations and subjectivity; the more robust views just outlined might get further support from a positive answer (cf. Gallagher (2019)). In any case, this, we think, is another topic that merits further research.

1.4. How the Debates Are Conducted

Which arguments could decide among these views on subjective character, or others than might be canvassed? Four types of arguments have, to date, attracted the most discussion. First, both sceptics and robust theorists have invoked phenomenological data in support. As McClelland (2015) points out, however, this very fact makes it doubtful that such evidence can be decisive. Second, robust theorists have invoked clinical research on pathological forms of experience such as depersonalization, thought-insertion, somatoparaphrenia, or delusion of control. Absent, aberrant or mislocated subjective character in those cases has been used as a contrast case for normal consciousness. Contributions to this book show however that a consensus on how such conditions should be interpreted is still missing. Third, more controlled empirical data are emerging from lab experiments on typical subjects; the rubber-hand illusion (Botvinick and Cohen 1998) and drug-induced ego-dissolution (Millière 2017) are two central illustrations. Finally, various explanatory roles have been ascribed to different forms of subjective character. A critical examination of such roles can, in an abductive spirit, lend support to the existence of subjectivity. Of particular significance, in this respect, is what Zahavi (2018, 711, 716) takes to be a transcendental argument, with strong roots in different philosophical traditions; versions of the argument develop the idea that subjective character is a precondition for full-fledged *de se*, first-personal representations proper of introspective states:

> I can be first-person authoritative with respect to the mental states I consciously live through because these mental states are characterized by a subjective presence. Now, the claim is not that first-personal givenness in and by itself amounts to authoritative first-person knowledge (or critical self-deliberation), nor is the suggestion that we should obliterate the difference between the two, but the

suggestion is that the former provides an experiential grounding of any subsequent self-ascription, reflective appropriation, and thematic self-identification.

(Grünbaum & Zahavi 2013, 229)

Most of the essays in this compilation aim to make an impact on this debate about the existence and robustness of subjective character, from perspectives that run the full gamut we have presented in previous pages. The book covers a range of interrelated questions—some of them also already mentioned above—including the following.

How is subjective character distributed? Is it present in all conscious states, by virtue of an *a priori* connection with the concept of phenomenal consciousness (Kriegel), or can it sometimes be absent—or at least attenuated or altered—for instance in some abnormal conscious states, such as disowned memories (Fernández), or the pathological experiences typical of depersonalization, somatoparaphrenia, and thought insertion (Billon, Dub)?

If there is such a thing as subjective character, is it a *sui generis* phenomenal quality, or is it reducible to other kinds of phenomenology—whether sensory, agentive, cognitive, or affective (Billon, Dub, Serrahima, de Vignemont)? Is it a phenomenal *quale* at all—discrete, separable—or rather a "substantive commonality" shared by all *qualia* (Kriegel)?

Can subjectivity be explained in terms of operations of the mind that are not exclusively or even preferentially turned inwards, such as judgment (Wu), epistemic seemings (Fernández), or emotions (Dub)?

Is subjective character best understood as a *property* of experience, and as a contribution to its phenomenal character, as assumed in this Introduction; or are alternative models needed for characterizing the pre-reflective self-awareness at issue (Nida-Rümelin, Soldati)?

Are there special issues raised by self-directed aspects of phenomenology in specific forms of experience, such as the sense of bodily ownership (de Vignemont, Serrahima, Orbán & Wong, Wu); the sense of oneself as a bounded object located in space (Serrahima); the sense of one's own movement (de Vignemont, Orbán & Wong, Wu); the sense of agency (Orbán & Wong, Wu); the sense that my memories are mine (Fernández)?

What biological function, if any, could subjective character conceivably serve in a human organism (McClelland, Billon, Dub, de Vignemont, Orbán & Wong)?

What explanatory role, if any, should subjective character play in accounts of the "first-person perspective" (Nida-Rümelin); of the transparency of self-knowledge (Soldati); of the concept of self and the capacity for explicit self-attributions (Guillot); of the epistemology of self-attributions (Guillot, Salje & Geddes); of the metaphysics of experiencing subjects (Nida-Rümelin)?

12 INTRODUCTION

We will now summarize the contributions that readers will find in the pages that follow. Part I of the book gathers more deflationary views, Part II more robust ones.

2. The Chapters

2.1. Part I: Doubts and Questions about Self-Experience

In their "Conscious Experience: What's in It for Me?," **Léa Salje & Alexander Geddes** articulate a deflationary perspective on our topic. Like some of the other authors in the first part of the book, they have doubts about the very characterization of what is being debated about. They start with a discussion of what the "intended feature" (as they put it, meaning, we take it, subjective character robustly understood) of experiences is supposed to be. After making some distinctions—related in interesting ways that we will not go into here to those by Guillot (2017) we have been relying on—they settle on the property of *being an experience that is present or given to its subject*. They then go on to critically examine the view that this is a universal feature of conscious experiences. They first take up explanatory considerations in favour of a robust understanding of subjectivity, and then descriptive considerations. By the latter they mean the intimations of subjectivity that some writers, as we mentioned above, find in Nagel's *what it is like* pre-theoretical characterization of consciousness. They grant that the characterization suggests that in conscious experience something is "present" to a conscious "perspective," but (along the lines that Howell develops in the transparency argument in his own chapter, see below) they contend that the worldly items that conscious states made accessible to subjects are quite enough to account for that—no presence of the experience itself or its intrinsic features being required for it. When it comes to arguments for robust subjectivity that rely on its alleged explanatory significance, they discuss, and dismiss, explanations on that basis of *immunity to error through misidentification*, the epistemic asymmetry between first-personal and third-personal knowledge of conscious states, and the easiness of introspective judgments and introspective reports. We refer readers who are not familiar with the first issue to their chapter, which provides a characterization as clear and simple as any we could offer here. Their critical discussion of the second alleged explanatory virtue of robust subjective character nicely complements Soldati's related discussion, while that of the third complements Shear's (2009), mentioned in §1 above. At the very least, the arguments pose a serious challenge to supporters of robust subjective character to articulate significant roles for it.

Assuming Guillot's three-part classification, in "Four Impediments to the Case for Mineness" **Tom McClelland** focuses on the third, most robust "grade of subjective involvement"—what Guillot calls mineness. He distinguishes three versions, relative to how widespread it is claimed to be: a universalist view that finds it in any conscious state, one that posits it only in normally functioning subjects, and a minimal one closer to sceptical views that finds it only in those states that are targets of conscious reflection. He assumes that sceptics like those we have mentioned above have at least shown that no compelling case for mineness has so far been made, and then he raises four difficulties for making such a case for it. The first is epistemological: if there were such a thing as mineness, it would be elusive. This is mostly due to the centrality of the method of *phenomenal contrast* (Siegel 2007) to discern features of phenomenology. It is a clear difficulty for universalists—what could we possibly contrast subjective character with, if it is ubiquitous?—but McClelland shows that it may also pose difficulties for the two other views. The second problem is created by the assumption that the self-presentation posited by the mineness thesis is a form of representation, given that representations are supposed to be possibly inaccurate while this doesn't seem to be an option in the mineness case. The third has to do with finding a plausible functional role for mineness, analogous to the ones that can be clearly ascribed to a sense of ownership for one's own actions or one's own body. The final one complements the latter two, by critically engaging proposals that have been made by non-universalists on mineness like Billon and others, which construe some pathological cases as evidence of malfunction of the sense of mineness. McClelland's arguments here overlap with Howell's and Wu's (see below), although the three authors develop their critiques in different ways.

In the first part of his contribution "Transparency and Subjective Character," **Robert J. Howell** rehearses in some detail the dialectics confronting sceptics and robust theorists of subjective character outlined above. He then goes on to offer an argument against the form of the latter that posits a near-universal distinct self-presenting component in the phenomenology of the conscious experiences of normal, non-pathological subjects. The argument appeals to the Moorean datum of transparency, quoted above; to ground the argument, Howell first elaborates on how transparency should be understood for his purposes, in illuminating ways. Howell finally considers whether a "mode" version of subjective character, not unlike the one in O'Conaill (2019), already mentioned, might elude his transparency argument. He voices two concerns: "there is a real question about what makes it subjective character (me-ness), versus 'present character' (nowness). There is also the worry that if there were such a thing we would have no clear way of apprehending it, because it would be ever-present, leaving us with no contrasting experiences." One might consider whether the "natural kind" approach that Shea (2012) recommends might help to address the second worry; this, we suggest, is an interesting research question to pursue, although Shea himself (309) is sceptical that the methodology might be applied to the determinable *subjective character*, as opposed to the *qualia* determinates. Howell concludes by

14   INTRODUCTION

critically examining whether pathological cases provide a good argument for robust subjectivity, as argued by Billon in his contribution to this volume and elsewhere, and by others. He offers an alternative model of the relevant pathologies, compatible with deflationary views, and with Wu's proposal in this collection (see below). On that model, what accounts for the pathological cases is not the absence or attenuation of a phenomenal trait (subjectivity), but rather the presence of novel phenomenal features.

Gianfranco Soldati's "Mineness, Deflation, and Transparency" adds to the sceptical arguments mounted by Salje & Geddes, Howell, and McClelland. The chapter develops another epistemological "impediment," based on an epistemological variation on the transparency data that Howell uses as an argument against the very existence of subjective character robustly understood. Soldati puts aside such ontological concerns and limits himself to using transparency considerations to argue for the epistemological inadequacy of subjective character for making a distinction between first-personal and third-personal access to the mind. Soldati first argues that subjectivity cannot play any evidential role in self-knowledge; he offers a sort of regress argument for that claim. Subjectivity theorists might perhaps complain that accounts of introspection along the lines of the one offered by Gertler (2012) have the resources to stop the regress; this is one more issue that merits future research. Soldati then moves to offer a transparency account of self-ascription of mental states, understanding 'transparency' in a familiar epistemic sense developed by Evans, McDowell, and others. The idea is that one judges that one judges that p on the grounds of the very same worldly reasons that lead one to judge that p in the first place. Soldati confronts objections to this account which our topic highlights. First, are the reasons for making the first-order judgment enough for making the second-order one, or does one rather need the conscious awareness thereof—which would bring subjective character back into the picture? Second, can the transparency account be generally applied to conscious states? Here Soldati discusses in detail the case of intentions and desires, suggesting ways to extend to them a transparency view.

Wayne Wu's "Mineness and Introspective Data" raises a further challenge for advocates of a robust subjective character. Wu focuses on appeals to what he calls "mineness" as an *explanans* in interpretations of empirical data. His examples (the rubber hand illusion and schizophrenic delusions of control) concern specifically bodily sensations and action, but the general shape of his case is more general. The chapter raises a methodological question about the introspective reports from clinical and experimental subjects that many empirically-informed, robust accounts of mineness use as their primary data. Some of those reports are broadly of the form "I feel like (or it seems like) this mental state, limb or action is (or isn't) mine." Should we take those words at face-value? While proponents of subjective character often pay close attention to the precise wording of introspective reports and read a phenomenological datum off of them (as Billon, Dub, de Vignemont, Serrahima, and Fernández do in this volume and elsewhere), Wu argues that there is reason for caution. First, the words "seem" and "feel" are multiply ambiguous; they can sometimes express an epistemic assessment rather than a phenomenological given. Second, a parsimony principle invites us to look for rationalizations of the reports that, where possible, only depend on uncontroversial phenomena. Wu claims that there are sufficient resources in our phenomenology, mineness aside, for explaining why subjects make the reports that they do. He goes on to propose parsimonious interpretations of two sets of empirical data, one experimental and the other one clinical: the reports of "positive mineness" in the rubber hand illusion, and of "negative mineness," or alienness, in schizophrenic delusions of control. In so doing, Wu raises the question whether introspective reports are really a basis for a form of inference to the best explanation concluding in the presence of mineness (as Billon argues in this volume), and he challenges a key source of evidence relevant to the *existence question*.

Krisztina Orbán & Hong Yu Wong's chapter, "The Sense of Body Ownership: What Are We Studying?," is also devoted to clarificatory and methodological issues. Its focus is the sense of bodily ownership, which has generated intense philosophical, clinical, and experimental research, but also, as the authors argue, much confusion and talking at cross-purposes. Given the lack of a commonly-accepted definition of the object of study, Orbán & Wong propose that competing accounts should at least ensure that they can accommodate three sets of data-points—concerning the ordinary experience of embodiment, pathologies of bodily awareness, and lab-induced reports of bodily ownership. The authors go on to try to disentangle the debate by distinguishing five different questions it could aim to answer: the "Constitutive Question" (what does the sense of bodily ownership consist in?), the "Phenomenological Question" (what does it feel like to have it?), the "Causal Question" (what is its cause?), the "Functional Question" (what is its function?), and the "Mereological Question" (what is the relation between the sense of ownership as targeting individual body parts, and that as extended over the body as a whole?). Equipped with these distinctions, Orbán & Wong go on to critically review some of the most influential accounts of the sense of bodily ownership, teasing apart the various explanatory projects that their authors can be understood to pursue in the light of their five questions, charting various ways in which those questions are interrelated, and assessing the empirical adequateness of the different positions.

2.2. Part II: Putting Self-Experience to Work

In "The Three Circles of Consciousness," **Uriah Kriegel** elaborates on the account of subjective character he has already defended in previous work. Here he uses 'for-me-ness' to refer to it, and characterizes it as "the substantive commonality

16 INTRODUCTION

among all phenomenal characters." He contends that this "might be the least committal way to home in on it; we can later debate the exact profile of this substantive commonality." However, he understands it in a robust enough way that goes beyond what we assumed above, for he says that "although for-me-ness is just a commonality among phenomenal characters, and cannot constitute a phenomenal character all by itself, it does have a substantive nature, one that makes a specific *contribution* to (every) phenomenal character," which "is an *occurrent, categorical* property"; this is at odds with the deflationary view described by Zahavi & Kriegel (2016) in a quotation above.[19] Relying on arguments provided in previous work, he distinguishes three different components of phenomenal character: content, attitude, and for-me-ness, and he offers a model that captures the crucial co-occurrence relations among them. The chapter includes a discussion of transparency, offering a way for friends of robust subjectivity to confront Howell's and Soldati's arguments in their own chapters here. It would be a valuable research project to critically come to terms with the relevant considerations in their respective contributions.

Martine Nida-Rümelin explores in depth in her "Experiencing Subjects and So-Called Mine-ness" the conceptual landscape we presented in the previous section. She makes distinctions roughly corresponding to those made above between the minimal understanding of subjective character ('subjectivity$_1$' in her terms), Guillot's for-me-ness ('subjectivity$_2$') and Guillot's me-ness ('subjectivity$_3$'). She agrees that these are conceptually distinct, but she goes on to provide an ontological argument to show that they are ultimately necessarily coextensive. (This perhaps explains why she refrains from describing the claim that subjective character just is subjectivity$_1$ as "deflationary," see her fn. 1.) The argument depends on a "subject property framework" she has previously argued for and goes on to outline here, which, opposing a contrasting "experience property framework," contends that phenomenal properties are primarily instantiated by subjects. Nida-Rümelin finally considers Guillot's "mineness" category. She argues that, to the extent that we understand the relevant awareness of the belonging relation as something missing in some pathological cases, it has little to do with the topic of subjective character—along lines that have been discussed by others, including Grünbaum & Zahavi (2013) and Zahavi & Kriegel (2016).

Marie Guillot devotes "The Phenomenal Concept of Self and First-Person Epistemology" to the *explanatory question*. The chapter defends the hypothesis that self-experience—which Guillot defines as the phenomenal awareness a subject has of herself, *as* herself, in experiencing other objects—serves as the anchor for the ordinary concept of self. The best model for that concept, she argues, is that of phenomenal concepts. That model, in turn, helps explain the

---

[19] Kriegel is here assuming that the view earlier described as deflationary doesn't offer a minimal characterization of subjective character but just rejects it, which is of course also legitimate.

special epistemological behaviour of judgments in the first person. Guillot takes as her starting point Coliva (2003), and its diagnosis that the property of immunity to error through misidentification (IEM), historically studied in connection with first-personal judgments, has often been conflated with two other epistemic properties: the alleged impossibility of a split between speaker's reference and semantic reference in the case of "I," and what Coliva calls the "Real Guarantee." Understanding the concept of self on the model of phenomenal concepts, Guillot argues, casts further light on this diagnosis and on first-person epistemology. The approach can explain each of the three epistemological properties distinguished by Coliva, in terms of their common source in self-experience and in a phenomenal concept of self, as well as the fact that they are so often conflated in the debate. These explanatory benefits, in turn, give some support to the existence of self-experience.

Carlota Serrahima's chapter, "The Bounded Body: On the Sense of Bodily Ownership and the Experience of Space," focuses on the sense of bodily ownership, defined as the sense that the *body* one experiences in bodily sensations is one's own (as distinguished from a sense of ownership over the bodily *sensations* themselves). She starts from a taxonomy of views within the literature on the sense of bodily ownership. Phenomenal Accounts, on which she concentrates here, propose that the awareness of a body as one's own is grounded in the phenomenal character of bodily experiences (rather than in judgments of ownership, as Cognitive Accounts claim). These Phenomenal Accounts come in inflationary and deflationary variants, with the former positing, and the latter rejecting, a *sui generis* "mineness" *quale* in bodily sensations. Serrahima's contribution has two aims, one constructive and the other negative. The constructive part, which seeks to fill a methodological gap in the literature, is a proposal concerning the *desiderata* that any account of the sense of bodily awareness should satisfy. The negative part is a critique of two versions of a type of deflationary account on which the sense of bodily ownership just is the awareness of the body as a bounded spatial object, as gained *via* somatosensation. Serrahima argues that neither version satisfies the relevant *desiderata*; on her analysis, this type of approach falls short either by being question-begging, or by leaving an explanatory gap unaddressed. In putting pressure on a prominent family of reductive views about the sense of bodily ownership, Serrahima's study also implicitly lends support to more robust views, such as the one defended by de Vignemont in her own chapter.

Frédérique de Vignemont begins her contribution "The Phenomenology of Bodily Ownership" by noting the difference between the two occurrences of the first person in the self-ascription of a bodily experience, *I feel my legs crossed*. The first signals the topic we have so far been discussing, the subjective character of those experiences; the second, bodily ownership. Her chapter concerns the latter—a proper account of which may perhaps require bringing in the former, as suggested in §1 above. She offers a classification of views, which somehow

18   INTRODUCTION

parallels the classifications of views on subjectivity we have discussed, and which is related to, although distinct from, Serrahima's own taxonomy. There is first an eliminativist view, on which there is no experience of bodily ownership as such that grounds self-ascriptions of bodily ownership. There are in addition two non-eliminativist proposals, a deflationary one that aims to account for bodily ownership without positing a specific quality of bodily experience—by grounding it on its spatial features—and several versions of a contrasting account committed to such a specific *quale*. She critically examines the options, by relying on empirical data about dissociations in different pathological and non-pathological illusory experiences. She then elaborates on a non-deflationary proposal—the Bodyguard Hypothesis—she has defended elsewhere, on which the specific phenomenal character has an affective nature. The key idea is that we each have a "protective body map" to track the body which is significant to our survival: namely, what is in fact *our own* body. Representations *via* this body map come with an affective feeling, which de Vignemont characterizes as "narcissistic," in the thin sense that it "aims at securing what is best for the organism"; and it is precisely this affective phenomenology that constitutes the sense of bodily ownership. De Vignemont shows that her proposal makes sense of the pathological cases—explained in terms of malfunctions in the protective body map—where the alternatives fail.

Richard Dub devotes his contribution, "Emotions of Mineness," to the *essence* question. The chapter is a case for the hypothesis that what he calls "mineness"—a super-type encompassing feelings of ownership and authorship over body parts, actions, and mental states—is best understood not just as affective (as de Vignemont also claims), but, more precisely, as a kind of emotion. First, its intentional structure aligns with that of prototypical emotions such as fear, anger, or surprise. Like the latter, mineness has an intentional object (for instance a thought, a body part, or an action), but also a formal object (*being mine* or *being caused by me*). Second, Dub argues that mineness also shares with emotions a pattern of appraisal mechanisms, and an association with distinctive responses. In common with them, it has in particular the ability to generate *delusions*. Just as powerful feelings of jealousy or despair can cause delusional beliefs, so can powerful aberrant feelings of ownership or disownership, authorship or lack thereof, cause delusions of mineness or alienation (e.g., somatoparaphrenia, thought insertion, experiences of alien control, or passivity...). Treating mineness as an emotion thus has the benefit of explaining these various disorders of the self in the light of a more general mechanism, namely the ability of emotions to generate delusions. The chapter ends with a discussion of a possible objection: unlike prototypical emotions, it is unclear whether the feeling of mineness is evaluative. Dub discusses a range of possible responses, including the hypothesis that "being mine" is indeed a value property—roughly, "being worth defending." This suggestion chimes in with ideas defended by Billon and de Vignemont in this volume. As a possible answer to the *function question*, it offers a response to

McClelland's "third impediment" to the case for mineness (also in this book), and it indicates an avenue for further research.

Alexandre Billon's "What Is It Like to Lack Mineness? Depersonalization as a Probe for the Scope, Nature, and Role of Mineness" focuses on depersonalization, a clinical condition affecting subjects who complain of feeling detached or alienated from their mental states, limbs, or actions, as if the latter weren't theirs. Some patients also report feeling as though they were dead or non-existent. Billon argues that depersonalization is a unique source of empirical evidence on "mineness," which stands in his writing for a robust and thick version of subjective character. According to Billon, there is good reason to take seriously the testimony of depersonalized patients, most of whom are not delusional or irrational. Doing so favours an interpretation of depersonalization as consisting in the lack or attenuation of mineness, understood as a phenomenal feature that marks the experiences of a healthy subject as hers. The lessons Billon draws from his analysis of depersonalization, in the light of both historical and contemporary clinical research, concern all four of the main questions addressed by this volume. Depersonalization gives empirical support to a positive answer to the *existence* question: mineness does exist, and it has a very wide scope, being at least *generally* present in a large range of conscious experiences including thoughts, sensations, affects, intentions in action, imaginings, and memories. On the *essence* question, Billon argues that mineness is a phenomenal feature of experiences rather than a discrete experience, and that it forms a *sui generis* psychological kind, irreducible to other types of mental states. His contribution to addressing the *explanation* question includes an outline of how mineness might ground our basic self-awareness and mastery of self-reference, the certainty that we exist, and our ability to imagine or remember "from the inside." The chapter directly discusses McClelland's challenge regarding the *function* question, by suggesting an adaptive biological function for mineness as what makes us feel concerned by what objectively matters to us.

Like Billon, **Jordi Fernández** devotes his chapter, "The Ownership of Memories," to a pathological form of experience, and uses it as negative evidence for the existence of subjective character in non-clinical subjects. Fernández looks at the very rare phenomenon of "disowned memory," where a subject reports both a memory and the feeling that it isn't their own. The best way to make sense of such reports, he argues, is to say that there is "something missing" from the memory: an experience of "mineness" that is, by contrast, present in non-pathological memories. The chapter also uses clinical data to offer an answer to the *essence* question, at least in the case of memory. Arguing against Klein & Nichols (2012), according to whom disowned memories lack a sense that the subject is identical to the person who witnessed the remembered scene, Fernández proposes instead that the feeling of mineness they lack consists in an experience of the memory matching the past. This is what he calls the "endorsement model." To say that the subject *endorses* a memory is to say that it feels to them as though they have reason to regard it as fitting or appropriate (as a memory is when it corresponds to what really happened). Other mental states can be endorsed in that sense, and the last part of the chapter outlines a possible generalization of the model. Looking at other pathological cases—delusions of thought insertion, "made" emotions, "made" impulses, and "made" action—Fernández shows that they, too, can be construed as missing a feeling that the relevant experience is one the subject has reason to have. It would be interesting to see if the approach can be fully generalized to cover, for example, mental states which don't have a clear intentional object (moods, for instance), as well as states such as mere imagining or entertaining, which may not be so straightforwardly constrained by conditions on reasonableness or fittingness. Billon raises in his chapter a potential difficulty for endorsement models which may also lead to further discussion.

References

Allen, Micah & Taskiris, Manos (2018). "The Body as First Prior: Interoceptive Predictive Processing and the Primacy of Self-Models," in Tsakiris, Manos & de Preester, Helena (eds.), *The Interoceptive Mind: From Homeostasis to Awareness.* Oxford University Press.

Alsmith, Adrian J. T. (2017). "Perspectival Structure and Agentive Self-Location," in Alsmith, A. J. T., & De Vignemont, F. (eds.), *The Subject's Matter: Self-Consciousness and the Body.* MIT Press, 263–287.

Alsmith, A. J. T. & De Vignemont, F. (eds.) (2017). *The Subject's Matter: Self-Consciousness and the Body.* MIT Press.

Barbieri, Alberto (2021). "The Debate on the Problem of For-Me-Ness: A Proposed Taxonomy," *Argumenta*, DOI 10.14275/2465-2334/20210.bar.

Billon, Alexandre (2016). "Making Sense of the Cotard Syndrome: Insights from the Study of Depersonalisation," *Mind and Language* 31(3): 356–391.

Block, Ned (1995). "On a Confusion about a Function of Consciousness", *Behavioral and Brain Sciences* 18: 227–247.

Block, Ned (2003). "Mental Paint", in Martin Hahn & B. Ramberg (eds.), *Reflections and Replies: Essays on the Philosophy of Tyler Burge.* MIT Press, 165–200.

Block, Ned (2015). "The Anna Karenina Principle and Skepticism about Unconscious Perception," *Philosophy and Phenomenological Research* 93: 452–459.

Borner, M., Frank, M., & Williford, K. (eds.) (2019). *Senses of Self: Approaches to Pre-Reflective Self-Awareness, ProtoSociology* 36. http://www.protosociology.de/

Botvinick, M. & Cohen, J. (1998). "Rubber Hands 'Feel' Touch that Eyes See," *Nature* 391: 756. doi: 10.1038/35784

Byrne, Alex (2004). "What Phenomenal Consciousness Is Like," in R. Gennaro (ed.), *Higher-Order Theories of Consciousness: An Anthology.* John Benjamins.

Caston, Victor (2002). "Aristotle on Consciousness," *Mind* 111: 751–815.

Chalmers, David (2018). "The Meta-Problem of Consciousness," *Journal of Consciousness Studies* 25(9–10): 6–61.

Coliva, Annalisa (2003). "The First Person: Error through Misidentification, the Split between Speaker's and Semantic Reference and the Real Guarantee," *Journal of Philosophy* 100: 416–31.

de Vignemont, Frédérique (2020). "Bodily Awareness," *The Stanford Encyclopedia of Philosophy* (Fall 2020 Edition), Edward N. Zalta (ed.), https://plato.stanford.edu/archives/fall2020/entries/bodily-awareness/

Duncan, Matt (2018). "Subjectivity as Self-Acquaintance," *Journal of Consciousness Studies* 25(3–4): 88–111.

Duncan, Matt (2019). "The Self Shows Up in Experience," *Review of Philosophy and Psychology* 10: 299–318, DOI 10.1007/s13164-017-0355-2

Farrell, J. & McClelland, T. (2017). "Editorial: Consciousness and Inner Awareness," *Review of Philosophy and Psychology* 8: 1–22.

Frank, Manfred (2004). "Fragments of a History of the Theory of Self-consciousness from Kant to Kierkegaard," *Critical Horizons* 5: 53–136, doi: 10.1163/1568516042653567

Gallagher, Shaun (2019). "The Senses of a Bodily Self," in Borner, M., Frank, M., & Williford, K. (eds.), *Senses of Self: Approaches to Pre-Reflective Self-Awareness*, *ProtoSociology* 36: 414–433.

Gallagher, Shaun & Zahavi, Dan (2021). "Phenomenological Approaches to Self-Consciousness," *The Stanford Encyclopedia of Philosophy* (Spring 2021 Edition), Edward N. Zalta (ed.), https://plato.stanford.edu/archives/spr2021/entries/self-consciousness-phenomenological

Gertler, Brie (2012). "Renewed Acquaintance", in D. Smithies & D. Stoljar (eds.), *Introspection and Consciousness*. Oxford University Press, 93–127.

Giustina, Anna (forthcoming). "A Defense of Inner Awareness: The Memory Argument Revisited," *Review of Philosophy and Psychology*.

Grünbaum, T. & Zahavi, D. (2013). "Varieties of Self-awareness," in K. W. M. Fulford, M. Davies, R. Gipps, G. Graham, J. Sadler, G. Stanghellini, & T. Thornton (eds.), *The Oxford Handbook of Philosophy and Psychiatry*. Oxford University Press, 221–239.

Guillot, Marie (2017). "I Me Mine: On a Confusion Concerning the Subjective Character of Experience," *Review of Philosophy and Psychology* 8: 22–53.

Hill, Christopher (2009). *Consciousness*. Cambridge University Press.

Howell, Robert J. (2019). "Reflecting on Pre-Reflective Self-Consciousness," in Borner, M., Frank, M., & Williford, K. (eds.), *Senses of Self: Approaches to Pre-Reflective Self-Awareness*, *ProtoSociology* 36: 157–185.

Howell, R. & Thompson, B. (2017). "Phenomenally Mine: In Search of the Subjective Character of Consciousness," *Review of Philosophy and Psychology* 8: 103–127.

Jackson, Frank (1986). "What Mary Didn't Know," *Journal of Philosophy* LXXXIII: 291–295.

22 INTRODUCTION

Klein, Stanley & Nichols, Shaun (2012). "Memory and the Sense of Personal Identity," *Mind* 121: 677–702.

Kriegel, Uriah (2009). *Subjective Consciousness: A Self-Representational Theory.* Oxford University Press.

Kriegel, Uriah (2015). *The Varieties of Consciousness.* Oxford University Press.

Kripke, Saul (1980). *Naming and Necessity.* Harvard University Press.

Levine, Joseph (2001). *Purple Haze.* Oxford University Press.

Levine, Joseph (2007). "Two Kinds of Access," *Behavioural and Brain Sciences* 30: 514–5.

Levine, Joseph (2019). "Acquaintance Is Consciousness and Consciousness Is Acquaintance," in J. Knowled & T. Raleigh (eds.), *Acquaintance.* Oxford University Press, 33–48.

Lewis, David (1983). "New Work for a Theory of Universals," *Australasian Journal of Philosophy* 61: 343–377.

McClelland, Tom (2015). "Affording Introspection: An Alternative Model of Inner Awareness," *Philosophical Studies* 172: 2469–2492.

Merlo, Giovanni (2021). "The Metaphysical Problem of Other Minds," *Pacific Philosophical Quarterly* 102(4): 633–664, DOI: 10.1111/papq.12380

Millière, Raphaël (2017). "Looking for the Self: Phenomenology, Neurophysiology and Philosophical Significance of Drug-induced Ego Dissolution," *Frontiers in Human Neuroscience* 11: 245. doi: 10.3389/fnhum.2017.00245

Moore, George (1903). "The Refutation of Idealism," *Philosophical Studies.* Routledge and Kegan Paul, 1–30.

Nagel, Thomas (1974). "What Is It Like to Be a Bat?," *Philosophical Review* 83: 435–450.

O'Conaill, Donnchadh (2019). "Subjectivity and Mineness," *Erkenntnis* 84: 325–341, DOI 10.1007/s10670-017-9960-9

Quilty-Dunn, Jake (2018). "Unconscious Perception and Phenomenal Coherence," *Analysis* 79(3): 461–469, doi:10.1093/analys/any022

Richardson, Louise (2017). "Sight and the Body," in Alsmith, A. J. T. & de Vignemont, F. (eds.), *The Subject's Matter: Self-Consciousness and the Body.* MIT Press, 239–261.

Rosenthal, David (1986). "Two Concepts of Consciousness," *Philosophical Studies* 49: 329–359.

Sartre, Jean Paul (1957). *The Transcendence of the Ego.* The Noonday Press.

Schear, Joseph K. (2009). "Experience and Self-Consciousness," *Philosophical Studies* 144: 95–105.

Schwenkler, John (2014). "Vision, Self-location, and the Phenomenology of the 'Point of View'," *Noûs* 48(1): 137–155. doi:10.1111/j.1468-0068.2012.00871.x

Sebastián, Miguel Angel (2012). "Experiential Awareness: Do You Prefer 'It' to 'Me'?" *Philosophical Topics* 40(2): 155–177.

Sebastián, Miguel Angel (2019). "Subjective Character, the Ego and De Se Representation," in Borner, M., Frank, M., & Williford, K. (eds.), *Senses of Self: Approaches to Pre-Reflective Self-Awareness, ProtoSociology* 36: 316–339.

Shea, Nicholas (2012). "Methodological Encounters with the Phenomenal Kind," *Philosophy and Phenomenological Research* 84(2): 307–44.

Siegel, Susanna (2007). "How Can We Discover the Contents of Experience?," *Southern Journal of Philosophy* XLV: 127–142.

Siewert, Charles (2013). "Phenomenality and Self-Consciousness," in U. Kriegel (ed.), *Phenomenal Intentionality*. Oxford University Press, 235–259.

Siewert, Charles (2021). "Consciousness and Intentionality," *The Stanford Encyclopedia of Philosophy* (Fall 2021 Edition), Edward N. Zalta (ed.), https://plato.stanford.edu/archives/fall2021/entries/consciousness-intentionality/

Smith, Joel (2020). "Self-Consciousness," *The Stanford Encyclopedia of Philosophy* (Summer 2020 Edition), Edward N. Zalta (ed.), https://plato.stanford.edu/archives/sum2020/entries/self-consciousness/

Snowdon, Paul (2010). "On the What-It-Is-Like-Ness of Experience," *Southern Journal of Philosophy* 48: 8–27.

Stoljar, Daniel (2016). "The Semantics of 'What It's Like' and the Nature of Consciousness," *Mind* 125: 1161–1198.

Stoljar, Daniel (2017). "The Regress Objection to Reflexive Theories of Consciousness," *Analytic Philosophy* 59(3): 293–308.

Stoljar, Daniel (2018). "Introspection and Necessity," *Noûs* 52(2): 389–410.

Stoljar, Daniel (2021). "Is There a Persuasive Argument for an Inner Awareness Theory of Consciousness?," *Erkenntnis*, DOI 10.1007/s10670-021-00415-8.

Strawson, Galen (2009). *Selves: An Essay in Revisionary Metaphysics*. Oxford University Press.

Taylor, David E. (2018). "A Minimal Characterization of Indeterminacy," *Philosopher's Imprint* 18(5): 1–25, www.philosophersimprint.org/018005

Tye, Michael (2002). *Consciousness, Color, and Content*. MIT Press.

Weisberg, Joel (2019). "Higher-Order Theories of Consciousness and the Heidelberg Problem," in Borner, M., Frank, M., & Williford, K. (eds.), *Senses of Self: Approaches to Pre-Reflective Self-Awareness*, *ProtoSociology* 36: 340–357.

Williford, Kenneth (2015). "Representationalisms, Subjective Character, and Self-Acquaintance," in T. Metzinger & J. M. Windt (eds.), *Open MIND* 39(T). MIND Group.

Williford, Kenneth (2019). "Self-Acquaintance and Three Regress Arguments," in Borner, M., Frank, M., & Williford, K. (eds.), *Senses of Self: Approaches to Pre-Reflective Self-Awareness*, *ProtoSociology* 36: 368–412.

Zahavi, Dan (2005). *Subjectivity and Selfhood: Investigating the First-Person Perspective*. MIT Press.

Zahavi, Dan (2018). "Consciousness, Self-Consciousness, Selfhood: A Reply to Some Critics," *Review of Philosophy and Psychology* 9: 703–718.

Zahavi, D. & Kriegel, U. (2016). "For-Me-Ness: What It Is and What It Is Not," in Dahlstrom, D. O., Elpidorou, A., & Hopp, W. (eds.), *Philosophy of Mind and Phenomenology: Conceptual and Empirical Approaches*. Routledge, 36–53.

PART I
DOUBTS AND QUESTIONS ABOUT SELF-EXPERIENCE

2

Conscious Experience

What's in It for Me?

Léa Salje and Alexander Geddes

We begin with a familiar quote from Thomas Nagel:

> [T]he fact that an organism has conscious experience *at all* means, basically, that there is something it is like to *be* that organism. There may be further implications about the form of the experience; there may even (though I doubt it) be implications about the behaviour of the organism. But fundamentally an organism has conscious mental states if and only if there is something it is like to *be* that organism—something it is like *for* the organism.
>
> We may call this the subjective character of experience.   (Nagel 1974, p. 436)

Like Nagel, many take this 'something it is like' talk to capture, or at least point to, the central characteristic aspect of conscious experience: its subjectivity or subjective character. And it is now standard to speak of what it is like to have particular experiences, or kinds of experiences, and to refer to this in each case as the phenomenal character of that (kind of) experience.

A number of philosophers claim that sufficient reflection on the character of our conscious lives reveals the involvement of a certain feature whose presence is often overlooked or even denied. The feature they have in mind appears to go by many names: 'for-me-ness', 'mine-ness', 'a sense of mine-ness', 'pre-reflective self-awareness', 'intransitive self-consciousness', 'peripheral inner awareness', 'ipseity', 'first-person givenness', and more besides. So let us speak of *the intended feature* in order to refer to whatever it is that these phrases are intended to pick out. In a moment, we'll look at some natural candidates for what this feature might be. For now, we can simply say that the intended feature is supposed to be, involve, or imply some form of awareness of experiences.

There are debates both over the nature of the intended feature and over its prevalence. Our concern in the present chapter is with the view that it is a universal aspect of conscious experience—that every conscious episode has the intended feature. Call this view *universality*.

Léa Salje and Alexander Geddes, *Conscious Experience: What's in It for Me?* In: *Self-Experience: Essays on Inner Awareness.* Edited by: Manuel García-Carpintero and Marie Guillot, Oxford University Press. © Léa Salje and Alexander Geddes 2023. DOI: 10.1093/oso/9780198805397.003.0002

28   CONSCIOUS EXPERIENCE

This chapter has two central aims. The first is to arrive at a clear and minimal statement of what the intended feature is supposed to be. We do this in §1 by distinguishing between some of the importantly different phenomena that might serve as natural referential candidates for three of the labels standardly used to refer to the intended feature ('for-me-ness', 'mine-ness', and 'a sense of mineness'). We argue that proponents of universality sometimes equivocate between these candidates in their use of these phrases, and that as a result they may be guilty of reading the plausibility of certain relatively modest claims into their more controversial commitments. We end the section by settling on an unambiguous statement of both the intended feature and universality.

Our second aim is to consider—and ultimately debunk—some of the ways in which universality has been motivated in recent analytic work. These motivations fall into two broad camps. First, *explanatory*. Here, the claim is that universality must be accepted because the intended feature explains a range of otherwise puzzling epistemological-cum-psychological phenomena associated with consciousness. Second, *descriptive* or *conceptual*. Here, the claim is that universality must be accepted because an adequate description or conception of conscious experience must represent it as involving the intended feature, prior to any theorizing about it.[1] §2 considers motivations of the first sort; §3 the second.[2]

In all of this we restrict our discussion to the paradigm of conscious experience, namely conscious perception. If universality fails to hold in the domain of conscious perception, then *a fortiori* it fails to hold for conscious experience *per se*.

1. Features of Perceptual Episodes

Here are some things that one might say when speaking about one's perceptual episodes:

I perceive the world; I see things, hear things, and so on. When I do, objects and their properties are present to me. They are present to me in experience. I am the subject of the experiences in which these things are present to me.

So we have before us the notion of things being present to me in experience, or in experiences, of which I am the subject. These ordinary terms are ones of which we all have a grasp. We need not take any of them to be jargon, nor give any of them an implicitly jargonistic reading, in order to make sense of such speech.

---

[1] The distinction between these two kinds of motivation is drawn in Zahavi and Kriegel (2015, 45). We discuss their paper below.

[2] Our aim therefore differs from those who seek to undermine universality via reflection on pathological or marginal cases of conscious experience. (See Billon and Kriegel (2015) for discussion of such strategies.) For we question whether there is a good case to be made for taking the intended feature to be ubiquitous even in ordinary conscious episodes.

FEATURES OF PERCEPTUAL EPISODES   29

Now, the phrases mentioned above—those used to pick out the intended feature—are not like that. They are unfamiliar to most. But they are not *pure* jargon, for they are in fact quite suggestive. And this makes sense: they were selected by those who employ them in part because they were taken to be phenomenologically apt. Still, unlike the ordinary language used in the indented passage above, these expressions require some unpacking if we are to get beyond mere suggestion. In §1.1 we focus on three of these expressions—'for-me-ness', 'mine-ness', and 'a sense of mine-ness'—and in each case ask: what features of perceptual episodes, as just characterized, might these phrases most naturally be used to pick out? The various features we identify are laid out in Table 2.1 (for 'for-me-ness', 'mine-ness'), and Table 2.2 (for 'a sense of mine-ness'). With these in hand, we'll turn in §1.2 to some representative passages from proponents of universality, and ask: which of them, if any, should we take the intended feature to be?

1.1. Three Labels

(i) 'For-me-ness'

What might this phrase pick out? The first thing to note is that it must denote a *property*; that's what the '-ness' gets you. The second is that, in this context, talk of something being 'for me' connotes *presence*, and presence *to me*.[3] It is that on which I have a conscious perspective—that which is present to me—that would most naturally be said to be there for me in a perceptual episode. The most natural denotation of 'for-me-ness' within an experiential situation of mine, then, is what we might call *object for-me-ness*: the property of *being present to me*. This is a property instantiated by the objects of my experiences, whenever they are indeed objects of my experience. So when I see a table, that table instantiates object for-me-ness: it has the property of being present to me.[4]

Another possible denotation for 'for-me-ness', slightly less natural but still reasonable, would be the other side of this coin, as it were. This we can call *experience for-me-ness*: the property of *being that in which something is present to me*, or, more simply, of *presenting something to me*.[5] Within a perceptual episode of mine, this will be instantiated not by objects of my experiences, but by my

---

[3] In what follows, we shift between writing in the first-person plural and the first-person singular, for obvious reasons. We ask that the reader overlook the slightly awkward transitions.

[4] 'Objects of my experiences' is here a quasi-technical term for anything that is indeed present to me in experience, whether it be an object (in the ordinary sense), an event, a state of affairs, a property, or anything else. We make no assumptions about what can figure in experience.

[5] We must be careful with this admittedly very natural transition. The basic notion is that of something being present to one or to one's mind, and it is this same notion that is at work when we speak of an experience *in which* something is present to one. But in speaking instead of an experience *presenting* something to one, we may seem to shift from treating 'present' as something two-place to treating it as something three-place, that is, from taking 'x is present to y' as canonical to taking 'z presents x to y' as canonical. The latter, then, should be understood at this point primarily in terms of the former; that is, as 'z is that in which x is present to y'.

30 CONSCIOUS EXPERIENCE

experiences themselves. These are two sides of the same coin because if there is something that instantiates object for-me-ness—if there is something that is present to me—then there will be an experience that instantiates experience for-me-ness—an experience in which that thing is present to me. And vice versa.

(ii) 'Mine-ness'

Once again, the '-ness' indicates that we ought to be looking for a property. But to speak of something being 'mine' connotes, not presence, but rather *ownership* or *possession* or *belonging* or *having*. One property that it could naturally pick out, then, is what we might call *state/event mine-ness*: the property of *having me as its subject*. This will be instantiated not by the objects of my experience, but by my experiences themselves. (Note, though, that this property is not instantiated *only* by my experiences; it is instantiated by anything that has me as its subject in the relevant sense, including my physical states.)

Another natural denotation for 'mine-ness' would be what we might call *part mine-ness*: the property of *being a part of me / my body*. This, of course, will be instantiated by all and only those things that are part of me or my body.

These four properties are set out in Table 2.1. We have two observations to make about them before we move on.

The first is that all of these are subject specific. *Being present to me* is not the same property as *being present to you*; *presenting something to me* is not the same property as *presenting something to A* (assuming I am not A); and so on. (They are not, though, *first-personal* in any interesting sense, as this way of specifying the properties is intended to be transparent: in A's mouth, 'being present to me' picks out the same property as 'being present to A' does in anyone else's mouth.) Of course, we can also speak of the non-subject-specific properties that will be instantiated whenever one of these subject-specific properties is: *being present to someone, presenting something to someone, having someone as its subject*, and *being a part of someone / someone's body*. Or, indeed, of the relations out of which both the subject-specific and non-subject-specific relational properties are constructed: *being present to, presenting…to, being the subject of*, and *being a part of*.

Table 2.1 '…-Ness'

Phrase	Natural denotations		Instantiated by
'for-me-ness'	object for-me-ness	*being present to me*	objects of my experience
	experience for-me-ness	*presenting something to me*	my experiences
'mine-ness'	state/event mine-ness	*having me as its subject*	my experiences(/states/…)
	part mine-ness	*being a part of me / my body*	my parts / my body's parts

The second observation is that all of these properties must be, rather trivially, universally involved in my episodes of conscious perception. Which is to say, each will be instantiated whenever I consciously perceive something. After all, my consciously perceiving something is simply a matter of something being present to me in experience. So in any episode of it, we have something being present to me, and an experience in which that thing is present that has me as its subject. And whenever I and my body exist, as we must when I perceive, we each will have parts.

We now move on to the third phrase, 'a sense of mine-ness'.

(iii) 'A Sense of Mine-ness'

To speak of 'a sense' of something, we take it, is to speak of awareness of that thing. But awareness of what? Well, in principle, *any* of the properties we have just identified are ones of which I could be aware. So we have the possibility of speaking of 'a sense of' any one of them. And it is clear what the resulting phrases would most naturally pick out: awareness of the relevant kind of thing instantiating the relevant property. 'A sense of mine-ness', then, ought to denote either awareness of state/event mine-ness—of (in the case of perceptual episodes) my experiences having me as their subject—or awareness of part mine-ness—of my parts (or body's parts) being parts of me (or my body). But, equally, we could speak of 'a sense of for-me-ness', which ought to denote either awareness of object for-me-ness—of objects of my experience being present to me—or awareness of experience for-me-ness—of my experiences presenting something to me. (It is perhaps notable that while proponents of universality speak of 'for-me-ness', 'mine-ness', and 'a sense of mine-ness', they do not in fact use the phrase 'a sense of for-me-ness'.) These are laid out on Table 2.2.

There are three important things to note about these awarenesses. The first is that they differ with respect to their targets, not only in that they target different properties, but also in that they target the different things that instantiate those properties. So whereas awareness of object for-me-ness is awareness of an *object* of my experience, and awareness of it having the property of being present to me, awareness of experience for-me-ness and awareness of state/event mine-ness are

Table 2.2 'A Sense of...-Ness'

Phrase	Natural denotation
'a sense of for-me-ness'	awareness of an object of my experience being present to me
	awareness of an experience of mine presenting something to me
'a sense of mine-ness'	awareness of an experience of mine having me as its subject
	awareness of a part of me / my body being a part of me / my body

both awarenesses of an *experience* of mine, in the first case awareness of it having the property of presenting something to me, and in the second case awareness of it having the property of having me as its subject. Awareness of part mine-ness is awareness of something else again, namely awareness of a *part* of me or my body, and awareness of it having the property *being a part of me / my body*.

The second thing to note is that, because the properties in question are subject specific, each form of awareness must be characterized in subject-specific terms. This is not to say that the forms of awareness must be, or must be thought of as, first-personal or *de se* (although that would suffice.) It is just to say that each must be thought of as a form of awareness that in some sense encompasses the identity of a particular subject or individual. Of course, we can also speak of awareness of the non-subject-specific versions of these properties, identified above, and these forms of awareness will be characterized in subject-neutral terms.

The third and perhaps most important thing to note is that none of these forms of awareness is explicitly part of perceptual episodes as characterized at the start of this section. So whereas the properties in Table 2.1 are uncontroversially instantiated whenever there is conscious perception, it is not trivial that any of the forms of awareness in Table 2.2 are instantiated whenever there is conscious perception. And while each of these forms of awareness may well, in one way or another, feature in our mental lives, their universality is not simply a given.

In drawing these distinctions, we do not mean to suggest that all of these properties, or all of these forms of awareness, are independent. There are undoubtedly interesting relations and dependencies that hold between them. But if one speaks in a single breath of more than one of them, and in particular if one wants to shift from speaking of the properties in the first table to the forms of awareness in the second, one should be sure to justify the move.

1.2. Some Quotes

We have seen, then, that the most natural interpretations of the various terms we have been considering diverge. And yet, as we began by noting, they are typically used interchangeably. This invites a suspicion that the terminological profusion reflects a failure to adequately distinguish between what are in fact different aspects of conscious episodes. If that's right, then what should we most charitably take the intended feature to be? In what follows, we consider a number of passages from two leading proponents of universality illustrative of the terminological slippage characteristic of this literature. These examples reveal the potentially distorting effects of such equivocation. We end the section with an explicit characterization of both the intended feature and of universality.

We take as our source material a recent paper by Zahavi and Kriegel (2015) entitled 'For-Me-Ness: What It Is and What It Is Not'.[6] As a clarificatory position statement from two prominent proponents of universality, it is a reasonable place to look to get a sense of when and how the intended feature is invoked. But our observations turn on nothing distinctive about this particular text; parallel points could be made about various other recent discussions.

Zahavi and Kriegel's canonical statement of their view is: "All conscious states' phenomenal character involves for-me-ness as an experiential constituent" (p. 37). We understand this claim as follows. The phenomenal character of an experience is or comprises a range of properties instantiated by that experience, namely those that contribute to (and collectively constitute) what it is like to have that experience. To characterize what it is like to have that experience is to identify and appropriately characterize these properties. Their claim is that the intended feature is among these properties for every conscious experience. But when we look at the way in which they elaborate their thesis, and the way in which they use the various labels that are supposed to refer to the intended feature, we encounter ambiguities and inconsistencies.

By way of illustration, consider the following pair of passages:

(1) Our view is not that in addition to the objects in one's experiential field—the books, computer screen, half-empty cup of coffee, and so on—there is also a *self-object*. Rather the point is that each of these objects, when experienced, is given to one in a distinctively first-personal way, and that this givenness is a pervasive dimension of phenomenal life. (p. 38)

(2) [...] once *anything* occurs consciously, it must be given to the subject and thus exhibit for-me-ness. (p. 38)

In both (1) and (2), Zahavi and Kriegel speak of something being given to a subject. But *what* is said to be given in each case differs. In (1), it is external objects that are said to be given, albeit in a particular way, and it is their being so given that is claimed to be a universal feature of conscious experience. In (2), it is that which 'occurs consciously'—namely, experiences themselves—that are said to be given, and indeed always to be given. And yet in both cases it is the ubiquity of the relevant items' givenness within the domain of conscious experience that is supposed to constitute Zahavi and Kriegel's central thesis. Another pair:

---

[6] Clearly, Zahavi and Kriegel use 'for-me-ness' as their primary phrase for the intended feature. But in this short article alone, we also find them using the phrases 'mine-ness', 'subjective givenness', 'pre-reflective self-consciousness', 'pre-reflective self-awareness', and 'sense of ownership' as alternative names for the feature.

34 CONSCIOUS EXPERIENCE

(3) [...] experience *presents* [...] features, in the sense of making *someone* phenomenally aware of them. To that extent, although all the presented items are worldly items, the presenting itself—presenting to someone—is an aspect of phenomenal consciousness as well. There is thus a minimal dimension of for-me-ness [...] (pp. 40–1)

(4) Regardless of how alienated [a] patient feels vis-á-vis [an] experience, the experience does not manifest itself entirely in the public domain. It continues to be phenomenally present to the patient in a way that is, in principle, unavailable to others. (p. 45)

In (3) and (4), the talk is of presence rather than givenness. But as above, what is said to be present differs. In (3), it is worldly items. In (4), it is experiences themselves. And yet, again, it is in each case the ubiquity of the relevant items' presence that is supposed to constitute the central thesis.

Moreover, the phrase 'for-me-ness', their central label, is being used inconsistently in (3) and (2). While in both passages it is used to denote a property, and the property is being ascribed to experiences themselves, the property differs. In (3), it is (the non-subject-specific version of) what we called 'experience for-me-ness': the property *presenting something to someone*. But in (2), it appears to be the non-subject-specific property *being given to its subject*. (Juxtaposing (2) and (4) suggests that they take 'being given to' and 'being present to' to be equivalent, in which case this is the same property as *being present to its subject*.) But to predicate these properties of an experience is to say something quite different in each case. To say an experience presents something to someone is, at least in the case of perception, to say something relatively trivial; to say an experience is given or present to its subject, however, is to say something substantial.

These complaints may strike some as nitpicking. But there is an important lesson to be drawn from them. For suppose we take 'for-me-ness' as a name for the property *being present / given to someone* (in accordance, perhaps, with (2) above). Then the claim that conscious experience always involves for-me-ness is crucially ambiguous. On the first, relatively uncontroversial, reading, it is the claim that whenever there is a conscious experience, something is given to someone. On the second, more controversial, reading, it is the claim that every conscious experience is itself given to someone. If we fail to clearly and consistently distinguish these claims—something always being present or given in experience and experiences themselves always being present or given—then any plausibility apparent in the former is liable to create an illusion of plausibility for the latter.

Nevertheless, it is clearly the latter, more controversial claim that proponents of universality intend to be advancing. This remains clear despite the fact that the phenomenon of worldly items being given or present to a subject is sometimes offered as illustrating the involvement of the intended feature. The lesson, then, is that we must be careful not to allow such slips to lend universality an unwarranted degree of plausibility. And we would suggest that this is a trap that proponents of universality have not entirely avoided.

So what should we take the intended feature, and universality, to be? There are various options. But ideally, we want to characterize them in such a way that the kind of ambiguity just identified cannot arise. So let us take the intended feature to be the property of *being an experience that is present or given to its subject*.[7] And let us take universality to be the claim that every conscious experience instantiates this property.[8,9]

We are now in a position to evaluate the motivations for universality. Above, we said that these motivations fall into two camps: either *explanatory* or *descriptive/conceptual*. We will address each camp in turn.

2. Explanatory Motivations

An explanatory case for universality must do two things: it must identify a universal property of experiences, and it must show that having this property is best explained by having the intended feature. In this section we consider three interrelated properties that have sometimes been taken to be explained by universality. These concern the immunity to error through misidentification of experiential

---

[7] Zahavi and Kriegel also, at one point, characterize the intended feature as 'a sort of *minimum point* of self-consciousness' (p. 44). (Cf. the phrases 'pre-reflective self-awareness' and 'intransitive self-consciousness' mentioned above.) This might be thought to generate yet another candidate for the intended feature: *being an experience in which the subject of that experience is given to itself*. (Thanks to an anonymous referee for reminding us of this.) We suspect that 'self-consciousness' (or 'self-awareness') here is being used to mean something like 'awareness of experience', rather than 'awareness of subject'—a very common, if potentially misleading, usage. If so, then this characterization does not in fact generate the extra candidate for the intended feature just mentioned, and so there is no extra equivocation here. But even if such equivocation does occur, it seems clear enough that it does not play the same kind of role in generating undue plausibility for universality, and hence is not deserving of the same kind of scrutiny as the uses discussed in the text.

[8] Note that this formulation of the intended feature permits of an ambiguity if universality is not appropriately formulated. For there is a distinction to be drawn between the claim that every conscious experience involves the instantiation of this property and the claim that every conscious experience instantiates this property. The former (in principle) allows that there could be an experience e_1 of an experience e_2 where only e_2 instantiates the intended feature. The latter does not. Even specifying that the intended feature is involved in every experience's phenomenal character, as Kriegel and Zahavi do, does not resolve the ambiguity. For e_1 may present e_2 having the property. There is no way, as far as we can see, to formulate the feature so as to avoid this. As such, universality must always be stated in terms of experiences instantiating the property, not merely involving it. Proponents of universality tend to avoid this ambiguity in their canonical statements, but are not always so careful in discussion.

[9] Despite superficial similarities, this view is to be sharply distinguished from claims of the sort advanced by those who defend higher-order theories of consciousness (see Carruthers 2011 and references therein). While such theorists claim that every phenomenally conscious experience is one of which the subject is 'aware', they adopt a distinct and revisionary notion of awareness from the one at work in the text, according to which a subject can be said to be non-consciously aware of something—aware of something without it figuring in that subject's perspective. Universality is the claim that every experience is one of which the subject is *consciously* aware—that every experience figures in its subject's conscious point of view.

36 CONSCIOUS EXPERIENCE

self-ascriptions, the epistemic asymmetry between first- and third-personal access to experiences, and the ease with which we are able to report on our occurrent experiences. In each case we will grant that the relevant property is universal, but argue that the intended feature is not needed to explain what needs explaining.[10]

2.1. Immunity to Error through Misidentification

Every conscious experience is such that an experiential self-ascription, when made on the sole basis of undergoing that experience, will be immune to error through misidentification relative to its first-personal component. This is the first explanandum we will consider. Immunity to error through misidentification is a modal property of some judgments, conferred onto them by their mode of formation. Specifically, a judgment a is F, made on grounds g, is immune to error through misidentification relative to a just in case it would not be possible in judging that a is F on g to know that *something* is F on those grounds, but make a mistake solely in virtue of being wrong through a misidentification in judging that it is a that is F.[11]

Let's take an example. Suppose that on the basis of a visual experience I judge that I am seeing a canary. My judgment might have gone wrong in all sorts of more or less interesting ways. It can't, however, be wrong in the following way. I can't be right in judging solely on the basis of that experience that *someone* is seeing a canary, but wrong in thinking (on those same grounds) that it's me. This is, of course, only an illustrative example; but we take it that the same will hold of all other experience-based self-ascriptions. So we arrive at the universal claim that any experiential self-ascription made on the sole basis of an experience is immune to error through misidentification relative to its first-personal component. How might universality explain this datum?

One writer who has recently argued that it does is Shaun Gallagher. He suggests that no matter how else an experience might be disrupted, 'I nonetheless have a sense that *I* am experiencing these things' (2012, p. 203), and so claims that 'the true anchor for IEM is the self-specific first-person perspective that characterizes every experience' (p. 211). In less picturesque terms, the idea might be something like this. Episodes of visual perception are open in a number of ways

---

[10] A recent example of someone who has argued along similar lines is Schear (2009).

[11] There are active debates in the literature on immunity to error through misidentification concerning its correct formulation, and the question whether such formulations should be made to respect significant distinctions between different kinds of error through misidentification—for some recent examples of these discussions, see the collected papers in Prosser and Recanati (2012). We take this to be a fairly orthodox formulation based on Shoemaker's original characterization in his (1968), but with the standard revisions of relativization to grounds and framed in terms of judgments rather than statements.

to either pathological distortion or artificial manipulation.[12] According to Gallagher, however, there is one property had by all such episodes, and it is this property that ensures the immunity to error through misidentification of self-ascriptive judgments formed on the sole basis of the related experience. That is, no matter how else a visual experience might depart from a veridical visual perception, the subject *cannot fail to be aware of the experience itself*, and moreover to be *aware of it having herself as its subject*.[13] If this is right, he seems to suggest, then no matter how else a self-ascription of undergoing an experience might be mistaken when made on the sole basis of having the experience—no matter what other experiential disturbances get taken up into the judgment—there is one way in which the judgment is perfectly epistemically secure. The subject cannot be mistaken through a misidentification in judging that it is she herself who is undergoing the experience, since through it all she was aware of the experience as her own.

Thus a particular form of awareness of experiences is taken to explain the universal property of conscious experiences of being such that whenever a subject makes an experiential self-ascription on the sole basis of undergoing an experience, she cannot be wrong solely through a misidentification that she is the experience's subject. To put it in first-personal terms: I can't be wrong under such conditions in judging the experience to be mine, because throughout the experiential episode I am unfailingly aware of it having me as its subject.

The problem with this explanation is that it misses its mark. We will first say why an explanation of the immunity to error through misidentification datum need not appeal to universality. We will then say something about why Gallagher and others might have thought that it does.

What *does* explain the immunity to error through misidentification of all experiential self-ascriptions, if not awareness of experiences? Quite simply, that if I judge anything on the sole basis of ϕ-ing, then I must be ϕ-ing. So I cannot be wrong in judging, on that basis, that I am ϕ-ing. That is, only experiences of mine could form the sole basis for a judgment of mine—so if I form a self-ascriptive judgment on the sole basis of undergoing an experience of some kind, then it is impossible that I could have gone wrong in having judged myself to have undergone an experience of that kind. The only property of experiences we need appeal to, in the terms of §1.1, is state/event mine-ness, the property of *having me as its subject*. We need say nothing about my experiences being present to me to get this explanation off the ground. So Gallagher's explanation misses its mark; it appeals to a stronger claim than is needed to explain what needs explaining.

---

[12] See Gallagher (2012) for some of these varieties of perceptual distortion.

[13] This last qualification makes Gallagher's view more specific than universality as we have defined it, in that he commits to a certain property of every experience being given to that experience's subject. But this claim implies the weaker claim that every experience is given to its subject; it is effectively a stronger version of universality.

38   CONSCIOUS EXPERIENCE

It is nevertheless easy to feel that Gallagher was on to something, and we want to say a few words about why we think this is. The pull of his explanation, we think, comes from a running together of two neighbouring kinds of question. One sort of question we might ask is: is it possible, when an experiential self-ascription is formed on the basis of undergoing an experience, that the judgment could be wrong about who the experiential predicate is known to apply to? This is a bona fide question about immunity to error through misidentification, and we have seen that all we need to answer it is a reminder of the fact that all and only the experiences that I undergo are mine. If I have formed an experiential self-ascription on the sole basis of undergoing an experience, then it is guaranteed that the experience is one of my own. So I cannot be mistaken solely through a misidentification in judging myself to be having the sort of experience I thereby take it to be.

Another sort of question we might be interested in is: when is a subject in a position to make a knowledgeable self-ascription on the basis of undergoing an experience? Or: so long as one forms a judgment about an experience at all, under what conditions could one fail to self-ascribe it?[14] Whatever it is we are asking here, we are not asking about the immunity to error through misidentification of the relevant judgments. These, rather, are questions about our self-ascriptive behaviours, about the production of first-person judgments. And, of course, facts about one's awareness of one's experiences might well be relevant in answering them. But unless there is a universal property of experiences in the vicinity—and we do not see any plausible candidates—then there is no explanatory case here for *universal* awareness of experiences.[15]

We turn now to the second potential explanandum, the phenomenon of epistemic asymmetry.

2.2. Epistemic Asymmetry

A second universal feature of conscious experience is that they are always accessible in a more direct way to their subjects than to anyone else. Something like this

---

[14] There is evidence that Gallagher is, at least sometimes, moved by this second kind of question rather than the first. In comparing his construal of immunity to error through misidentification to the nearby phenomenon of guaranteed self-reference, he writes, 'IEM mirrors guaranteed self-reference, so to speak, but is more basic because it is based on the first-person perspective *that allows me to generate* first-person *as-subject* statements' (2012, p. 204, first emphasis added).

[15] An adjacent diagnostic point concerns the somewhat delicate relation between the state/event mine-ness explanation of universal immunity to error through misidentification of experiential self-ascriptions on the one hand, and facts about our awareness of our experiences on the other. It may well be true that to form an experiential self-ascription on the sole basis of an experience implies awareness of that experience. But that they come together in this way should not mislead us into thinking that the second kind of fact is needed to explain the first.

feature is sometimes taken to be explained by universality. In their joint encyclopedia entry on the topic, for instance, Gallagher and Zahavi write:

> Although two people, A and B, can perceive a numerically identical object, they each have their own distinct perceptual experience of it; just as they cannot share each other's pain, they cannot literally share these perceptual experiences. Their experiences are epistemically asymmetrical in this regard. [...] The subject's epistemic access to her own experience, whether it is a pain or a perceptual experience, is primarily a matter of pre-reflective self-awareness.
>
> (Gallagher and Zahavi 2016, §1)

This passage gestures at an explanatory connection between the intended feature (here called 'pre-reflective self-awareness') and the privileged epistemic access that we each have to our own experiences.[16] In one form or another, we find this connection posited under various guises in Levine, Kriegel, and Zahavi.[17] In what follows we focus on a particular argument by Kriegel given in chapter 2 of *Subjective Consciousness*. The stated aim of Kriegel's argument is the vindication of research programmes targeting phenomenal consciousness. But he does this by giving an explanatory argument for universality.

The explanandum, as Kriegel construes it, is the universal property of conscious experiences of being *access conscious* (in Ned Block's terminology): the property of being 'poised for free use in reasoning and for direct "rational" control of action and speech' (Block 1997, p. 382). So understood, access consciousness gives us a way of characterizing more sharply the asymmetry between my epistemic standing with respect to my experiences and yours; those experiences are poised for free and direct use in reasoning and action in my own case, and not in yours.

Kriegel's argument begins by registering that access consciousness is a dispositional property of experiences. He writes, '[n]othing has actually to happen with a mental state or event for it to qualify as access-conscious: the state or event need not actually be access*ed*; it needs only to be access*ible*' (p. 37). Dispositional properties, however, are not explanatorily basic; they must be grounded in non-dispositional categorical properties. By way of illustration, Kriegel invites us to consider the case of fragility:

> The glass is fragile—it is disposed to break under relatively lax conditions—*because*, or *in virtue of*, its physico-chemical constitution. Its particular constitution is thus

[16] There might seem to be a quick response here for proponents of universality—namely, that the sense in which a subject has special access to her own experiences just is that they are present to her. Notice, though, that this is *too* quick: an explanatory case for universality must identify a universal property *other than the intended feature* that's best explained by it. To put things this way would effectively be to posit universality itself as the explanandum. And nothing explains itself.

[17] See, e.g., Levine (2001); Zahavi (2005 esp. chs. 1 and 5), Levine (2006), Kriegel (2009b ch. 2).

40 CONSCIOUS EXPERIENCE

the *reason for* its fragility—the reason *why* it is fragile. In this sense, the glass's physico-chemical constitution is the categorical basis of the glass's fragility. (p. 37)

Likewise, since access consciousness is a dispositional property we must find a categorical property that will serve as its basis—'[w]hen a mental state is access-conscious, it must also have a categorical property *in virtue of which* it is access-conscious' (p. 37). What could that be? Kriegel offers a candidate:

A natural suggestion is that it is [...] for-me-ness, or subjective character. [...] What makes this suggestion natural is that subjective character seems to play the right explanatory role vis-à-vis access consciousness. The reason why a mental state is poised for the subject's free use in personal-level reasoning and action control, it is reasonable to suppose, is that the subject is already aware of it. (p. 38)

It is because all experiences are already given to their subjects (and to no one else) that they are access conscious within their own subjects' mental lives (and no one else's). The universality of the intended feature thus explains the universality of access consciousness. This is where our present interest in the argument ends, but Kriegel takes it a step further. This conclusion, he thinks, vindicates research into phenomenal consciousness: the intended feature is, on his view, a constitutive component of phenomenal consciousness. This means that a constitutive component of phenomenal consciousness is given as the most plausible categorical basis for access consciousness. Insofar as we are interested in understanding access consciousness, then, it is possible that we will be able to do so by studying phenomenal consciousness.

We think that there are two problems with this argument—the second more serious than the first. The first is a worry about the limited scope of the epistemic asymmetry that emerges from this picture. It is intuitively compelling to think that the range of mental states that forms the first-personal side of the epistemic asymmetry outstrips the realm of phenomenal consciousness. My non-occurrent beliefs, for example, or my dispositional preferences, desires, intentions, and their like, seem to be access conscious. But there is surely nothing it is like for me to believe, without bringing to mind, that it is over 27 miles to Cork, or to be disposed to choose the boot in Monopoly, or to want cake when I see it. These are not phenomenally conscious states. So long as we understand the categorical basis of access consciousness to be a constitutive component of phenomenal consciousness, however, then we will have to let drop these initial intuitions and exclude those states from the reach of access consciousness.[18]

---

[18] Some might claim that such a state is only access conscious when it, or some corresponding cognitive episode, is phenomenally conscious. Such a claim would go well beyond an (already controversial) commitment to the existence of cognitive phenomenology, and we would be highly sceptical

There are at least two ways of responding to this objection, both of which Kriegel seems to incline towards in different places. The first is a bullet-biting response. On the nearby topic of first-person authority, Kriegel and Zahavi insist that, '[e]xperiential for-me-ness *determines* the sphere of what we may have first person authority about' (2015, p. 11); we have first-person authority only over the states that 'we consciously live through' (p. 11). Whatever we make of the relationship between first-person authority and access consciousness, it's clearly open to Kriegel to take a similar stand on access consciousness. Phenomenal consciousness, the idea might be, determines the sphere of access consciousness, so we must simply accept that only the states we consciously live through are access conscious. This position strikes us as implausible, but beyond this point we have little more to offer than intuition-trading.

The second response is to allow for a plurality of categorical bases grounding the phenomenon of access consciousness. Perhaps a constitutive feature of phenomenal consciousness categorically grounds only *some* instances of the dispositional property, and we must look elsewhere to explain others. In *Subjective Consciousness* Kriegel is explicit in allowing this option:[19]

> [T]he functional role occupied by the categorical basis is, like other functional roles, multiply realizable: it allows different occupants to play the exact same role. In similar fashion, access consciousness could readily occur in the absence of its actual categorical basis—if some other categorical properties served as its basis. (p. 42, n.35)

This weakening is surely to be welcomed. There is considerable plausibility to the idea that the explanation of access consciousness will in some cases make mention of the fact that there is something it is like for me to be in the relevant state, even if cases of access consciousness to, say, non-occurrent beliefs are to be explained in other ways. But as soon as we proliferate categorical bases in this way, the argument for the universality of the intended feature begins to look less than complete. If there can be many grounding explanations for the phenomenon of access consciousness, then we will need an extra reason to posit a homogenous explanation for all cases of conscious experience—as we must if this argument is to provide an explanatory case for universality. Perhaps that extra reason could

of a view of this kind. However, we will not engage with this claim in the present chapter. (For discussion of cognitive phenomenology, see the essays in Bayne and Montague 2011.)

[19] It might be noted in other places he seems less open to this option, or at least to take himself to be in the position of needing to be convinced otherwise: 'In the case of access consciousness, it is hard to see what other categorical basis it might have [...]. In any case, until another potential categorical basis is adduced, we should be entitled to proceed on the assumption that subjective character is the *only* categorical basis of access consciousness—that it is not only *a* categorical basis but *the* categorical basis' (Kriegel 2009b, p. 39).

42   CONSCIOUS EXPERIENCE

come from considerations of theoretical virtue: elegance, for example, or parsimony. Our point is only that *something* is now needed to complete the argument.

The second problem with this argument is less easy to shake off. That is, that Kriegel's account of access consciousness doesn't help to explain the broader explanandum of epistemic asymmetry; all it does is push the explanatory demand back a level. All conscious experiences are access conscious to their subjects, for Kriegel, *because their subjects were already aware of them*. This might, strictly speaking, account for the access consciousness of these states—for their free and direct availability in personal-level reasoning and action guidance. But it does so only by appealing to the subjects' *pre-existing* access to those states. So the question is merely moved to an earlier point in the account: what explains the epistemic asymmetry between first-personal and third-personal access to conscious states in the first place? Of course, addressing this broader explanandum was no part of Kriegel's stated aim in the passages we have been discussing. But the worry can be put independently of Kriegel's argument. Generally speaking, how could the intended feature explain the asymmetry between first- and third-personal access to conscious experiences?

The answer cannot be that the intended feature ensures that conscious experiences are always present to their subjects. That is, if you like, a way of describing the nature of the access that subjects have to their experiences. But it doesn't explain what needs explaining, which is why it is that I have that kind of access to these conscious states and not those, and you to those and not these. To explain that asymmetry, we must appeal to the fact that these are *my* conscious experiences, and those are *yours*; we must appeal, in other words, to state/event mine-ness. This is not to say that we might not want to supplement this picture with a characterization of the access that we each have to our own experiences, once we have so divided them between mine and yours using the property of state/event mine-ness. And something like this characterization is what the intended feature supplies. But the point is that it cannot be what explains the initial epistemic asymmetry datum—universality is compatible with epistemic asymmetry, but it cannot be explanatorily motivated by it.

2.3. Ease of Judgment and Reportability

The third explanandum we want to consider is the apparent ease with which experiencing subjects are able to form judgments about, or to report on, the experiences they are occurrently undergoing.[20] There is no question of my having to stop and deliberate if prompted to form a judgment about my current experiences—other things being equal I am always ready to pronounce with ease

---

[20] See (Schear 2009, pp. 102–4) for a different argument against this explanatory motivation.

on what I am experiencing, at least under some description of the experience. The *ceteris paribus* qualification here is included to filter out factors external to the experience itself that could block uptake into a judgment about the experience, such as repressive psychological mechanisms or neuro-physiological abnormalities. We include the 'under some description' qualification to rule out overly demanding readings of this explanandum, on which I am always in a position to judge and to report in full detail on every aspect of my experience. So understood, we think that this is plausibly a universal property of conscious experiences. The question is, is it best explained by universality?

For Zahavi and others, it is. According to universality all experiences are present to their subjects. This means that even before being called upon to form a judgment or report about an experience, the subject is already aware of it. This awareness grants her familiarity with the experience that makes it conspicuously easy, when the time comes, to judge or to say what it is she is experiencing. Thus Zahavi writes: '[I]t is because I am pre-reflectively conscious of my experiences that I am usually able to respond immediately, that is, without inference or observation, if somebody asks me what I have been doing, or thinking, or seeing, or feeling immediately prior to the question' (Zahavi 2005, p. 21). Variations of the argument by different writers come in different strengths and tones. In what we take to be its strongest light the argument has abductive force: the best explanation of the ease with which we are able to form judgments about and to report on our occurrent experiences posits universal awareness of experiences.[21] The problem with explaining this universal feature of conscious experience by appeal to universality, we think, is that such an explanation mislocates the explanatory target. What needs explaining is the ease with which occurrent experiences are taken up into the level of reflective judgment or report. What proponents of the above argument give us is the claim that all experiences are already present to their subjects. But in this they remain silent about how these experiences (that are always present to their subjects) are transformed into self-ascriptive experiential judgments or reports—the ease of which process was what needed explaining. Universality, in other words, is an answer to a different question. Put it this way: we might conceive of creatures whose conscious experiences are stipulatively always given to their subjects, but whose specific cognitive architecture nevertheless makes the transition from conscious experience to experiential self-ascription a psychologically laborious one. To say that experiences are always given to their subjects, even by stipulation, does not answer the question how those experiences are converted into self-ascriptive judgments. And, more importantly, it does not say why the process by which that happens is an easy one.

---

[21] See, e.g., Kriegel (2009a, p. 376) and Gallagher and Zahavi (2016), for examples of different presentations of the argument.

44 CONSCIOUS EXPERIENCE

This is not to say that it is incompatible with the positing of such a mechanism that its operational details—once we know more about them—will require the 'input' experiences to have had the intended feature, but it is also compatible with saying that they won't. It might turn out, for instance, that a proper understanding of the psychological process by which we make these transitions between experience and experiential self-ascription will reveal that our cognitive structures have evolved in a way that permits psychologically fluid transitions between a first-order experience and its self-attribution without any mediation via conscious awareness of the experience.[22] This is just to say that the fact that there must be such a psychological mechanism to explain the ease datum is no evidence yet one way or another on the question whether its input experiences must have already been present to the subject.

Once the details have been worked out it might also turn out that this mechanism will appeal to the fact that the starting experiences are phenomenally conscious. Indeed, we think that much seems likely. But this will not advance proponents of universality very far. A commitment to phenomenal consciousness playing a central explanatory role in an account of a given epistemic or psychological feature of experience moves entirely independently from a commitment to understanding phenomenal consciousness in terms of universal experiential awareness. One can very well accept that phenomenal consciousness will feature essentially in our best explanations of a range of such features without thereby incurring any obligation to understand phenomenal consciousness one way or another. So there is no independent argument here that has (any form of) universality as its conclusion.

To summarize, the basic complaint is that universality—understood in its broadest terms as the claim that all experiences are present to their subjects—falls short of explaining what needs explaining. Even with universality in place, it is a further task to say how conscious experiences are taken up into self-ascriptive experiential judgments or reports. It is worth pointing out, however, that the specific version of universality invoked above by Zahavi admits of a specific version of this problem. We saw in the quote above that the relevant awareness of experiences for Zahavi is 'pre-reflective'. Something similar is true of the versions of universality taken by Kriegel and Gallagher to explain this ease datum too. Gallagher, for instance, writes that:

[W]hat makes my thoughts accessible in reflective introspection is precisely an already operating *pre-reflective* self-awareness that is part of the concurrent structure of any conscious process. (Gallagher 2012, p. 189, emphasis added)

---

[22] Cf., e.g., Evans (1982, §7.4), Peacocke (2001), and Récanati (2007).

And Kriegel that:

[I]ntrospecting feels more like a phenomenologically light shifting around of attention than like a dramatic mental act that produces a completely new awareness. [...] This may be taken to constitute phenomenological evidence that prior to the introspecting, there was already inner awareness of the conscious experience, *albeit peripheral.*   (Kriegel 2009a, p. 376, emphasis added)

where peripheral awareness is to be understood as non-focal awareness.[23]

For these writers the awareness of experiences that explains the ease with which self-ascriptive experiential judgments are formed is pre-reflective or pre-attentive awareness. But to form an introspective judgment about her experiences, a subject must reflect or attend to them—this difference between pre-reflective awareness and introspective awareness of experiences looms large in the accounts of all three of these writers.[24] But the problem can now be put like this. The explanatory datum of this section is the ease with which we are able to move from having experiences to forming reflective judgments about them. If—along with Zahavi, Kriegel, and Gallagher—we posit universal pre-reflective awareness of experiences, then the explanatory response to this datum will be an account of the (easy) process by which pre-reflective experiential awareness is exploited in introspective judgment. Otherwise, our response will be an account of the (easy) process by which our first-order experiences are exploited in introspective judgment. Either way, what is called for is an account of the relevant process. And that call does not prejudge what its inputs will be.[25]

3. Descriptive Motivations

We have argued against several explanatory cases for universality. But it is sometimes claimed that even if universality isn't explanatorily mandatory, it is

---

[23] Kriegel (2009a, p. 360); like Gallagher and Zahavi, Kriegel also elsewhere talks about this awareness as 'pre-reflective'.

[24] See, e.g., Levine (2001, p. 4), Gallagher (2012, p. 189), Kriegel (2009a, §4), Zahavi and Kriegel (2015, p. 40), Gallagher and Zahavi (2016, §1).

[25] The most fully developed account of this process we have found is in Kriegel (2009a): 'introspecting one's current experience does not involve entering a completely new representational state. Rather, it involves reorganizing the center/periphery structure of one's overall experience, by transforming one's peripheral inner awareness of one's current experience into a focal one' (p. 372). This account is given in the service of defending universality against the objection that such universal awareness of experiences would be, but is not, introspectively manifest. On his model of introspection this is to be expected; 'introspecting cannot reveal peripheral inner awareness because it *annihilates* it (by supplanting it)' (p. 373). Although he spends several pages on this point, however, he does not directly address our concern, which is to say *how*—in his terms—the 'center/periphery structure' of one's experience becomes reorganized, and why we should expect this transformation to be effortless. This is hardly surprising given his different focus in these passages.

46 CONSCIOUS EXPERIENCE

nevertheless *descriptively* mandatory. Consider, for instance, the following passage from Zahavi and Kriegel:

> Before we can assess the explanatory potency of any posit, we must have a grasp of some phenomena in need of explanation. Presumably this means that *some* phenomena would have to be accepted as real independently of their own explanatory potency. [...] Given this, rejecting the existence of for-me-ness requires showing not only that citing for-me-ness is useless and/or unnecessary for *explaining* the phenomena, but also that it is useless and/or unnecessary for *describing* the phenomena. But in our opinion, it is impossible to correctly *describe* the structure of phenomenal consciousness without citing for-me-ness.
>
> (2015, p. 45)

In this section we turn to this second kind of motivation for universality. A word first, though, on what such a descriptive—or perhaps conceptual—case amounts to.

Kriegel and Zahavi begin this passage with the idea that inquiry into the explanatory usefulness of a thing must begin with some intuitive grasp of what the inquiry is about, a pre-theoretical conception of the object of inquiry. The passage ends with the claim that when it comes to the phenomenon of conscious experience, a complete articulation of our pre-theoretical conception must include mention of the intended feature. Our naive grasp of conscious experiences represents them as mental items that are present to their subjects. But is this right?

It is widely thought that the best basic articulation of our naive conception of conscious experiences is provided by the Nagelian phrases with which we began—by talk of there being something it is like for a subject to have an experience, or of what it is like for a subject to have an experience. For proponents of universality, the key bit of these phrases—the bit that captures the *subjective character* of experience—is the 'for a subject' bit. What this part of the phrase emphasizes is the idea of a subject's perspective, or point of view—an idea that really does seem to be built into our naive conception of conscious experience. And drawing attention to the importance of the subject's perspective certainly seems to be part of what Nagel takes himself to be doing with these phrases.[26]

Now, the notion of a subject's point of view, we take it, is the notion of a point of view *on something*; it is the notion of something figuring in a subject's conscious perspective. We also take it that for something to figure in a subject's conscious perspective is for that thing to be present to the subject. This is plausibly the basic notion at work in our naive conception of conscious experience. That is, we conceive of a conscious experience as an event of something being present to a

---

[26] See esp. pp. 437–8, 441–5. Cf. Martin (1998, p. 173) and Hoerl (2015).

subject. And this is surely something with which proponents of universality ought to agree. For it is this same basic notion of something being present to a subject that they use to articulate their distinctive interpretation of Nagel's phrases. But their specific claim is that when we speak of 'what it is like for me to undergo an experience', the 'for me' part of this phrase somehow captures the fact that *the experience itself* is present to me. It is only by understanding Nagel's phrases in this way—as implying a subject's point of view on her own experiences—that proponents of universality might hope to vindicate the idea that it is impossible to fully and correctly describe the structure of phenomenal consciousness in line with our pre-theoretical conception of it without citing the intended feature. This, then, is the cornerstone of the descriptive case for universality.

But there is, we think, a missing step here. The step is between the demand for presence, on the one hand, and the demand for presence of experiences, on the other. According to proponents of universality, we do justice to the idea of a subject having a point of view by saying that an experience is present to that subject. But then how can we *fail* to do justice to the idea of a subject having a point of view when we employ the very same notion of presence, but say instead that some *worldly* item is present to that subject? What matters here, what is doing the work, is the notion of presence itself—the relation between the subject and that which figures in their point of view. And our naive conception clearly does not *restrict* what can figure in a point of view to experiences. But given this, there seems to be no conceptual problem or incoherence in the notion of a point of view in which *only* worldly items figure.[27] And so the descriptive/conceptual case for universality fails.

4. Conclusion

We end with three take-home messages. The first is that we need to take particular care, when discussing the nature of consciousness, to use phenomenologically suggestive phrases in clear and consistent ways, so as to avoiding distorting or giving undue plausibility to philosophical claims made in their terms—and proponents of universality have not entirely avoided this danger. The second is that,

---

[27] Levine (2006), while advocating universality, seems to recognize the missing step. In order to motivate the claim that it is experiences that must be present to the mind, he offers a one-paragraph invocation of the argument from hallucination (p. 180). The thought being: *something* must be present to the mind in conscious experience. Because hallucinations are possible, it cannot be anything non-experiential. Therefore experiences are present to the mind in conscious experience. But there are two points to make about this. One is that this is not a *conceptual* motivation for universality. The conceptual motivation will merely be for universal *presence* (of something or other) in conscious experience. The grounds for taking it to be *experiences* will be broadly speaking explanatory. (We do not suggest that Levine thinks otherwise.) And second, it is far from clear exactly what implications the possibility of hallucination should be taken to have. For detailed discussion, see, e.g., Martin (2004, 2006).

given a careful formulation of universality, we find no compelling explanatory case to be made for it. And the third is that, while the notion of something being present to a subject plays an essential role in our naive conception of consciousness, the notion of *experiences* being present does not. What, then, is there 'for me' in conscious experience? Simply: whatever it is that is present to me.

References

Bayne, Tim, and Michelle Montague, eds. 2011. *Cognitive Phenomenology*. Oxford University Press.

Billon, Alexandre, and Uriah Kriegel. 2015. "Jaspers' Dilemma: The Psychopathological Challenge to Subjectivity Theories of Consciousness." In *Disturbed Consciousness*, edited by R. Gennaro, 29–54. MIT Press.

Block, Ned. 1997. On a Confusion about a Function of Consciousness. In *The Nature of Consciousness: Philosophical Debates*, edited by Ned Block, Owen Flanagan and Güven Güzeldere, 375–415. MIT Press.

Carruthers, Peter. 2011. "Higher-Order Theories of Consciousness." In *The Stanford Encyclopedia of Philosophy*, edited by Edward N. Zalta, Fall 2011. http://plato.stanford.edu/archives/fall2011/entries/consciousness-higher/.

Evans, Gareth. 1982. *The Varieties of Reference*. Edited by John McDowell. Oxford University Press.

Gallagher, Shaun. 2012. "First-Person Perspective and Immunity to Error Through Misidentification." In *Consciousness and Subjectivity*, edited by Sofia Miguens and Gerhard Preyer, 187–214. Ontos Verlag.

Gallagher, Shaun, and Dan Zahavi. 2016. "Phenomenological Approaches to Self-Consciousness." In *The Stanford Encyclopedia of Philosophy*, edited by Edward N. Zalta, Winter 2016. http://plato.stanford.edu/archives/win2016/entries/self-consciousness-phenomenological/.

Hoerl, Christoph. 2015. "Writing on the Page of Consciousness." *Proceedings of the Aristotelian Society* 115 (3): 187–209.

Kriegel, Uriah. 2009a. "Self-Representationalism and Phenomenology." *Philosophical Studies* 143 (3): 357–81.

Kriegel, Uriah. 2009b. *Subjective Consciousness: A Self-Representational Theory*. Oxford University Press.

Levine, Joseph. 2001. *Purple Haze: The Puzzle of Consciousness*. Oxford University Press.

Levine, Joseph. 2006. "Conscious Awareness and (Self-)Representation." In *Self-Representational Approaches to Consciousness*, edited by Uriah Kriegel and Kenneth W. Williford, 173–98. MIT Press.

Martin, M. G. F. 1998. "Setting Things Before the Mind." *Royal Institute of Philosophy Supplement* 43: 157–79.

Martin, M. G. F. 2004. "The Limits of Self-Awareness." *Philosophical Studies* 120 (1–3): 37–89.

Martin, M. G. F. 2006. "On Being Alienated." In *Perceptual Experience*, edited by Tamar S. Gendler and John Hawthorne. Oxford University Press.

Nagel, Thomas. 1974. "What Is It Like to Be a Bat?" *The Philosophical Review* 83 (4): 435–50.

Peacocke, Christopher. 2001. "First-Person Reference, Representational Independence, and Self-Knowledge." In *Self-Reference and Self-Awareness*, 215–46. John Benjamins.

Prosser, Simon, and Francois Recanati. 2012. *Immunity to Error through Misidentification: New Essays*. Cambridge University Press.

Récanati, François. 2007. *Perspectival Thought: A Plea for Relativism*. Oxford University Press.

Schear, Joseph K. 2009. "Experience and Self-Consciousness." *Philosophical Studies* 144 (1): 95–105.

Shoemaker, Sydney. 1968. "Self-Reference and Self-Awareness." *Journal of Philosophy* 65 (October): 555–67.

Zahavi, Dan. 2005. *Subjectivity and Selfhood: Investigating the First-Person Perspective*. Bradford Book / MIT Press.

Zahavi, Dan, and Uriah Kriegel. 2015. "For-Me-Ness: What It Is and What It Is Not." In *Philosophy of Mind and Phenomenology: Conceptual and Empirical Approaches*, 36–53. Routledge.

3

Four Impediments to the
Case for Mineness

Tom McClelland

1. Introduction

It has been suggested that we are phenomenally aware of our experiences *as our own*. Many take this sense of 'mineness' to be an essential feature of all experience. Some take this to be a feature of experience that is only absent in certain specific cases of cognitive malfunction. And others take it to be a feature that an experience only acquires when we explicitly reflect on its ownership. Although these three camps disagree on how widespread the sense of experiential ownership is, they are united by the claim that the sense of mineness is a genuine feature of our phenomenology. Although some arguments have been given in favour of this conclusion, it is fair to say that a compelling case has not yet been made for the existence of the sense of mineness. My aim in this chapter is to introduce four impediments that obstruct any such case being made. Rather than coming down for or against the existence of a sense of mineness, I leave it to the reader to decide whether the right arguments could overcome these impediments, or whether they are ultimately insurmountable. Before I introduce the four impediments, some stage-setting is needed.

2. The Varieties of Mineness

As readers of this anthology will no doubt be aware, there are a number of different ways in which one's experience might be taken to be characterized by a sense of mineness. My target is one specific understanding of mineness, so the first task is to distinguish this from other understandings. Following Guillot (2017), a distinction can be made between three ways in which the subject might figure in experience.

Under the pen of different writers, the subject appears variously:

- as one of the two relata in the relation of phenomenal awareness to her experiences, i.e. as the one who is appeared to;

Tom McClelland, *Four Impediments to the Case for Mineness* In: *Self-Experience: Essays on Inner Awareness.*
Edited by: Manuel García-Carpintero and Marie Guillot, Oxford University Press. © Tom McClelland 2023.
DOI: 10.1093/oso/9780198805397.003.0003

- as also appearing to herself in being aware of the other relatum (the experience);
- as appearing to herself as the owner of the experience. (Guillot 2017, p. 27)

Guillot uses the label 'for-me-ness' for the first of these, 'me-ishness' for the second, and 'mineness' for the third. My target is the third sense and I will follow Guillot in using the label 'mineness' to designate it. I will thus understand mineness as follows:

Mineness: An experience of a subject S displays a sense of mineness just in case S experiences herself as the owner of that experience.[1]

It must be remembered that different authors use the same terms in subtly but importantly different ways. Consequently, we will have to look deeper than an author's terminological choices to discern where they stand on the issue of mineness.

Guillot's key insight in making this ternary distinction is that there are not entailment relations between the three features—at least not without the addition of substantive further premises. If a subject is the one to whom an experience is presented, it doesn't follow that the experience is presented *as her own* (also see Howell & Thompson 2017, p. 119). Similarly, if the subject is presented with herself in experience, it doesn't follow that she is presented to herself *as the owner* of her experience. Thus neither the for-me-ness of an experience nor the me-ishness of an experience (if such there are) entail that the experience has mineness. One might think that the entailment does run in the other direction: that if one is phenomenally aware of one's ownership of a conscious state, one must be phenomenally aware of oneself and phenomenally aware of one's experience. However, if we are phenomenally aware of some relation it isn't necessarily the case that our awareness of its relata is itself phenomenal. Thus:

> even if *some form or other* of awareness of the experience, and of myself, is a necessary condition for the *phenomenal* awareness of myself as owner of the experience (mineness), it doesn't follow that an *a priori* relation of implication holds from mineness to for-me-ness (a phenomenal awareness of the experience) and me-ishness (a *phenomenal* awareness of the experiencer).
>
> (Guillot 2017, p. 33)

---

[1] Here I follow many in the literature in supposing that when an experience displays the quality of mineness its subject is *aware* of this quality of their experience. That said, if one wished to hold that experiences can display a quality of mineness that falls outside the scope of a subject's awareness, the worries raised in this chapter will still apply.

Overall then, the claim that we are phenomenally aware of our experiences *as our own* is independent of claims about our phenomenal awareness of our experience and our phenomenal awareness of ourselves. Consequently, questions surrounding the for-me-ness and me-ishness of experience can be bracketed for current purposes.

3. The Mineness Thesis

Having clarified how the sense of mineness is to be understood, we are now in a position to formulate the target thesis of the chapter.

The Mineness Thesis: Experience is characterized by a sense of mineness.

For convenience, I will refer to anyone who supports this thesis as a 'Mineness Theorist'. As it stands, the Mineness Thesis says nothing about *which* experiences are characterized by a sense of mineness. Mineness Theorists have very different views on this matter. I suggest that the main views in the literature are captured by the following three versions of the Mineness Thesis:

Universal Mineness Thesis: All experiences are characterized by a sense of mineness.

Functional Mineness Thesis: All experiences are characterized by a sense of mineness, except in certain cases of cognitive malfunction.

Reflective Mineness Thesis: Experiences are characterized by a sense of mineness when, and only when, the subject reflects on their experience.

The following passages from Zahavi and Block capture the Universal Mineness Thesis:

> When I am aware of an occurrent pain, perception, or thought from the first-person perspective, the experience in question is given immediately, non-inferentially and non-criterially as mine. That is, the experience is given (at least tacitly) as an experience I am undergoing or living through.
>
> (Zahavi 2004, p. 78)

> We may suppose that it is platitudinous that when one has a phenomenally conscious experience, one is in some way aware of having it....Sometimes people say Awareness is a matter of having a state whose content is in some sense 'presented' to the self or having a state that is 'for me' or that comes with a sense of ownership or that has 'me-ishness'....
>
> (Block 2007 quoted in Guillot 2017, p. 25, Guillot's emphasis)

On this view, the sense of ownership is simply built into the nature of experience and there can be no exception to the rule. The Functional Mineness Thesis is a weaker thesis that acknowledges the existence of atypical experiences that lack mineness. Guillot, for instance, holds that 'ordinary experiences of normal subjects exhibit...mineness' (2017, p. 45) but argues as follows:

> Patients who experience depersonalisation, typically as a part of severe depression, report an alteration of their experiences. In many cases, it no longer seems as though the experiences are theirs.   (Guillot 2017, p. 41)

Similarly, López-Silva is sympathetic to the claim that ordinary experiences are characterized by a sense of mineness but argues as follows:

> Zahavi proposes that all experiences include a sense of mineness as a part of the way in which they are given. However, reports of people suffering from different pathologies challenge this idea. From the revision of cases of somatoparaphrenic delusions, alien hand syndrome and thought insertion, among others, we concluded some experiences can lack [a] sense of mineness.
> (López-Silva 2014, p. 221)

The third and final version of the Mineness Thesis is weaker still, and suggests that mineness only rarely features in experience. In ordinary experience, our phenomenology is silent on the ownership of our experience. When we reflect on the ownership of our experience, however, our phenomenology acquires a character of mineness. Thus:

> Despite the fact that experiences on the unreflective level don't have mineness, we can gain a sense of mineness in reflection...In reflection we lay claim to our experiences, and the mineness is a product—not a condition of—that attitude.
> (Howell & Thompson 2017, p. 123)

Howell & Thompson argue that a similar view can be found in the Pali-Buddhist tradition (see Albahari 2010, p. 102) and in Sartre, who they quote as follows:

> Contrary to what has been held, therefore, it is on the reflected level that the ego-life has its place, and on the unreflected level that the impersonal life has its place....   (Sartre 1993, p. 58 quoted Howell & Thompson 2017, p. 124)

Although advocates of all three versions of the Mineness Thesis acknowledge the existence of a sense of experiential ownership, they differ dramatically in how widespread they take this phenomenological feature to be. The three versions of the Mineness Thesis are not intended to be logically exhaustive. One might, for instance, adopt a position somewhere between the Functional Mineness Thesis and the Reflective Mineness Thesis according to which many but not all non-reflective experiences are characterized by mineness. Although my plan is to focus on the three versions of the Mineness Thesis found in the literature, the problems I introduce will likely be faced (in some form or another) by any version of the Mineness Thesis.

4. The Limited Case for Mineness

The project of this chapter must be understood against the backdrop of a certain scepticism about existing arguments for the sense of mineness. Arguing for the existence of an elusive feature of our phenomenology is difficult, and the arguments that have so far been put forward for the Mineness Thesis are far from compelling. Although I will not review these arguments here, I will highlight their two most prevalent shortcomings.

First, many arguments for the Mineness Thesis start from an innocuous claim about experiences having for-me-ness or me-ishness then mistakenly infer that experiences must therefore have the property of mineness (e.g. Zahavi 2004). As discussed above, an experience having for-me-ness or me-ishness does not entail that it has 'mineness' (Howell & Thompson 2017, p. 119). This unwarranted inference often goes unnoticed because of equivocations between different senses of 'mineness' and related terms (Guillot 2017 pp. 47–50).

Second, many arguments for the Mineness Thesis start from an innocuous claim about our *knowledge* that an experience belongs to us, then quickly infer that this knowledge must be explained by a phenomenal quality of mineness that tags our experiences as our own (e.g. Grünbaum 2012). It is wrong, however, to assume that self-knowledge is grounded in features of our phenomenology since, as Howell & Thompson observe, 'Plenty of accounts of self-[knowledge] do not give a central role—at least in any obvious way—to phenomenal consciousness' (2017, p. 115). Furthermore, even if our knowledge that we own our experiences *is* grounded in our phenomenology, this might be explained by phenomenal features besides a specific sense of ownership. Indeed, Howell & Thompson argue that the existence of a sense of ownership would not even be able to explain how we know beyond doubt that our conscious states belong to us, since it would always be possible to doubt whether such a phenomenal tag is veridical (2017, p. 116).

None of this is to say that no good argument for the Mineness Thesis could be found: an absence of compelling arguments should not be mistaken for a compelling argument for absence. My position is simply that *if* a compelling case can be made for some version of the Mineness Thesis, it has not yet been offered. My goal in this chapter is to introduce four impediments to any such case. Each of these four impediments raises a problem that casts doubt on the existence of a sense of mineness. The first is a worry about the epistemic accessibility of mineness, the second is a worry about the content of phenomenal states characterized by mineness, the third is a worry about the function of the sense of mineness, and the fourth is a worry about the absence of cases in which the sense of mineness malfunctions. Much of the chapter is dedicated to the fourth impediment as it requires careful discussion of cases in which the sense of mineness is alleged to be absent: specifically, thought insertion, depersonalization disorder and Cotard's delusion.

Crucially, none of these considerations are knock-down objections: it is an open possibility that a case for the Mineness Thesis can be developed that overcomes all four impediments. My suggestion is that the four considerations I raise should be used as a litmus test by which to judge any case for the Mineness Thesis. As such, I am neutral on whether the Mineness Thesis is true. One might treat the four impediments as obstacles that a compelling case for the Mineness Thesis must navigate. Or one might instead treat the four impediments as strong (if defeasible) indicators that all versions of the Mineness Thesis are false. Either way, all four impediments must be taken seriously.

5. The Epistemic Impediment

We are in a good epistemic position to establish the existence of a phenomenal property if we can contrast experiences that have that property with experiences that do not. Indeed, many arguments for the existence of contentious phenomenal properties rely on phenomenal contrast cases (e.g. Bayne 2009; Siegel 2010). Conversely, if we cannot contrast experiences that have some phenomenal property with experiences that do not, then we are in a bad epistemic position to establish their existence. Kriegel notes that 'It is in general difficult to notice even stimuli that are constant for a relatively short time, such as the hum of the refrigerator pump' (2009, p. 52). When the noise of the pump stops, we notice a change in our phenomenology and recognize that our earlier experience was characterized by a certain auditory phenomenal quality. Had the pump not stopped though, we may never have noticed this auditory quality. If there are phenomenal properties that, for whatever reason, are contrast-resistant, then those properties will be elusive to us. This then entails an epistemic problem: if a phenomenal property is elusive, how can you be confident that it really exists? I suggest that if there were a sense of mineness then it would be a contrast-resistant phenomenal property, and so present precisely the epistemic problem described above.

The three versions of the Mineness Thesis have different implications for the possibility of contrasting experiences with and without mineness. If the Universal Mineness Thesis is true, then it is metaphysically impossible for a subject to undergo an experience that lacks mineness, and thus metaphysically impossible for a subject to experience a contrast between a phenomenal state that has mineness and a phenomenal state that lacks it.

If the Functional Mineness Thesis is true then subjects who are not undergoing a cognitive malfunction will be unable to experience the relevant contrast. Perhaps one can experience the contrast if one undergoes certain kinds of malfunctions viz. malfunctions that remove the sense of mineness from one's experience. But this raises at least two difficulties.

The first difficulty is that the malfunctions thought to extinguish the sense of mineness are far from routine. Most subjects do not, for example, suffer from thought insertion or Cotard's delusion. Perhaps some of the symptoms of depersonalization are more commonplace: there is reason to believe that subjects who are not suffering from any pathology can experience some of the symptoms of depersonalization in circumstances such as drug use, trance, trauma, or extreme fatigue. But the point remains that such subjects will only experience these malfunctions rarely, and that many subjects will never experience them at all. If you only undergo the relevant malfunction rarely, you won't be in a good position to spot the phenomenal contrast, especially since the circumstances in which you undergo the malfunction are all ones in which your mental faculties are impaired. And if you never undergo the relevant malfunction then you can only go on the testimony of those who have undergone it. Inferring the existence of a phenomenal quality from testimony may well be justified, but epistemically it is a poor substitute for experiencing the relevant phenomenal contrast for yourself.

The second difficulty for advocates of the Functional Mineness Thesis is that the malfunctions thought to extinguish the sense of mineness from experience may not do so at all. This means that even subjects who do undergo the malfunctions associated with depersonalization, for instance, won't be undergoing a malfunction that leads them to experience a contrast between the presence and absence of the sense of mineness. I will discuss this in detail when we reach the fourth impediment.

Things may seem a little better for advocates of the Reflective Mineness Thesis. After all, this version of the thesis predicts that subjects will generally enjoy a phenomenology that lacks mineness, and will only experience mineness when they explicitly reflect on the ownership of their experience. But closer examination suggests that even this view may be committed to mineness being contrast-resistant. A phenomenological contrast only reveals the existence of a phenomenal property to us if we notice it. To notice that our experience has changed from lacking mineness to possessing mineness, it is plausible that we would have to be reflecting on our experience. But according to the Reflective Mineness Thesis, reflecting on our experience *causes* it to be characterized by a sense of mineness. So if we reflect on our experience we will never catch ourselves having an experience that isn't characterized by mineness. Trying to do so would be like trying to jump on your own shadow.

This argument only goes through if reflecting on one's experience *always* generates a sense of mineness. If one instead adopted a view according to which reflection generates a sense of mineness only if certain other conditions are met, then it would be possible to spot a contrast between those reflective cases in which it is present and those in which it is absent. However, such a view would have to be argued for and a clear story would need to be told about the circumstances under which a sense of mineness comes about.

My argument here is not that there are no contrast-resistant phenomenal properties. Such properties may well exist but, for the reasons discussed, *knowing* that a particular contrast-resistant property exists is problematic. Furthermore, my argument is not that knowledge of a contrast-resistant property is impossible. Rather, my claim is that such properties are elusive, and that reaching firm conclusions about the existence of elusive properties is difficult. Introspective judgements are prone to error at the best of times (Schwitzgebel 2008) but when we aren't even in a position to use phenomenal contrasts to justify our judgements we should be especially circumspect. This means being circumspect not just about the judgements we might make about the presence of mineness in our own experience, but about the judgements other people make about mineness in their experiences.

A possible response here is to eschew the method of highlighting phenomenal contrasts in favour of the method of highlighting phenomenal commonalities. Zahavi (2005) argues that when we have experiences that have different objects, and that put us in different intentional relations to those objects, we can nevertheless discern a commonality between those experiences. Specifically, 'They are all characterized by what might be called a dimension of for-me-ness or mineness' (Zahavi 2005, p. 58). However, Howell & Thompson observe that even if it's true that we can discern that different experiences have something in common, a further argument would be needed to show that what they share is the sense of mineness (2017, p. 114). Why not, for instance, adopt the more modest view that experiences share for-me-ness?

Overall then, the case for the Mineness Thesis faces an Epistemic Impediment. All three versions of the Mineness Thesis seem to entail that the sense of mineness is contrast-resistant. Contrast-resistant phenomenal properties are elusive, and introspective judgements about the presence of elusive phenomenal properties are insecure. None of this entails that a sense of mineness doesn't exist. But when someone posits the existence of a phenomenal property, the burden of proof is firmly on them to make a convincing case for its existence. The challenge for the Mineness Theorist is to satisfy this burden of proof despite the inevitable elusiveness of the sense of mineness.

6. The Representation Impediment

The second obstacle to a case for mineness is captured by the following argument:

1. If we are phenomenally aware of our experiences as belonging to us, then we phenomenally *represent* them as belonging to us.
2. If we phenomenally represent our own experiences as belonging to us, it would be impossible for such representations to be inaccurate.
3. All representations are such that it is possible for them to be inaccurate.
4. Therefore we are not phenomenally aware of our experiences as our own.

Let me explain why each premise of the argument is at least initially plausible. Premise 1 is based on the claim that if we are phenomenally aware of something *as having some property* then we phenomenally *represent it* as having that property. On this view, to be phenomenally aware of your experience *as yours* entails *representing* your experience as yours. To adopt this representational view of phenomenal states does not entail a commitment to any bolder claims about phenomenology supervening on intentional properties, or intentionality supervening on phenomenal properties. Despite entrenched debates about the exact relationship between phenomenality and intentionality, there is fairly widespread agreement that phenomenal awareness should be understood representationally.

Premise 2 is based on the claim that the only experiences we can experience are our own—we never have other people's experiences. A case might be made for concluding that the very notion of having someone else's experience is unintelligible, thus any experience that presents itself as belonging to the subject can't but be accurate. This applies to any version of the Mineness Thesis. Whether all experiences involve a sense of mineness, or whether only some do, it remains the case that phenomenally representing one's experience as one's own is inevitably veridical.

Premise 3 is based on a widely-supported view of the nature of representation. Neander explains 'a capacity to misrepresent is often thought to be essential for representing: no possibility of misrepresentation, no representing' (Neander 2012). A state is representational only if it is the kind of thing that is assessable for accuracy. If it is intelligible that some state should be accurate, it must also be intelligible that it be inaccurate. Thus a state is a representation only if it is intelligible for that state to be a *mis*representation.

Together the three premises entail that there is no sense of mineness. Although all three premises are credible, the Mineness Theorist has some latitude to respond. Regarding Premise 1, the Mineness Theorist might argue that phenomenal awareness is not *representational* but *presentational* (e.g. Zahavi 2004, p. 74). The key difference between representation and presentation is that when we are presented with something, there is no possibility of error. Being presented with some object or property requires the existence of that object or property. Accordingly, if we are presented with our experience's property of belonging to us, we should expect no possibility of error. The same point might also be put in terms of acquaintance (e.g. Hellie 2007): if the sense of mineness is a matter of being acquainted with the mineness of your experience, then the sense of mineness cannot fail to be veridical. If the Mineness Theorist adopted this response, they would be committed to a presentation-based or acquaintance-based view of phenomenal awareness. This is not necessarily a bad thing, but it is a significant commitment for a case for mineness to take on. It would mean rejecting the prevalent representational approach to the phenomenal and would require the confrontation of a number of difficult questions raised by the notion of presentation, including worries about the naturalizability of such a relation.[2]

Regarding Premise 2, the Mineness Theorist might claim that it is possible for us to be phenomenally aware of an experience as our own *inaccurately*. This would mean offering a metaphysics of consciousness in which it is possible for a subject to undergo experiences that do not belong to them. We could then undergo experiences that are not our own, while phenomenally misrepresenting them as belonging to us. It is implausible, however, that the concept of undergoing an experience and the concept of owning an experience come apart in this way. Although I do not envisage Mineness Theorists pursuing this bold response, it is worth noting that the option is open to them.

Regarding Premise 3, the Mineness Theorist might deny that representation requires the possibility of misrepresentation. As a generalization, it is appropriate to say that representations are such that it is possible for them to be non-veridical, but a space might be carved out to allow exceptions to this rule. For instance, Neander suggests:

> there may be exceptions to the general rule that all representations can misrepresent (e.g., a representation that has the content something or nothing). Misrepresentation is also not possible in every kind of mental context (e.g., in dreaming and, perhaps, desiring). (2012)

If the Mineness Theorist can motivate the conclusion that phenomenal awareness of mineness is an exception to the rule, then Premise 3 could be denied.

Overall, the existence of a sense of mineness is at odds with the conjunction of the three plausible premises described above. To varying degrees, each of these three premises could be challenged, meaning that the argument offered is far from a knock-down objection to the Mineness Thesis. However, the challenge for the Mineness Theorist is to offer a plausible account of where the argument

---

[2] Objections to this non-representational view of consciousness are explored in detail by Kriegel (2009, ch. 4).

60 FOUR IMPEDIMENTS TO THE CASE FOR MINENESS

goes wrong. Denying any of the three premises—whether by adopting a presentation-based/acquaintance-based view of phenomenal awareness, by claiming that subjects can undergo experiences that do not belong to them, or by countenancing representations that can't but be accurate—would be a significant commitment, and could cast significant doubt on the plausibility of the Mineness Thesis. The representation impediment thus presents a serious obstacle to any case for the Mineness Thesis.

7. The Function Impediment

Experience serves to tell us about ourselves and the world, and the way our experience is at a specific time serves to tell us about how we and the world are at that time. As the product of a long evolutionary history, the human mind abhors redundancies. Consequently, if our experiences are characterized by a sense of mineness there must be some use to their being so: the sense of mineness must tell us something helpful about how things are. To appreciate this fact, consider the functions served by our phenomenal awareness of other kinds of ownership, such as our ownership of our actions and our ownership of our body.[3]

Experiencing our actions as our own serves to distinguish things that we have done from things that have been done by other agents, and from things that have occurred non-agentially. It is hard to see how we could make effective decisions about how to act in the world without being able to recognize which actions are ours and which are not. The sense of action-ownership serves to mark that distinction. Accordingly, when a subject fails to experience their actions as their own, as in cases of anarchic hand syndrome, their ability to function in the world is impaired.[4] Parallel points can be made about the sense of bodily-ownership. Experiencing our body parts as our own serves to distinguish those elements in the world that are part of us from those elements in the world that are not. Being aware of this distinction clearly helps guide our actions by, for instance, marking the bounds of the organism that we need to protect. Accordingly, when a subject's sense of bodily-ownership malfunctions, as in cases of somataparaphrenia like alien hand syndrome, their ability to function in the world is impaired.

What function would it serve to be phenomenally aware of our experiences as our own? In the case of action, we perceive both our own actions and the actions

---

[3] Of course, whether our experiences of these things are marked by a sense of ownership is contentious. The point remains, however, that if these phenomenal properties *do* exist, it wouldn't be hard to tell a story about the function they serve.

[4] Like subjects with anarchic hand syndrome, subjects with alien hand syndrome lack a sense of ownership over the actions of their hand. However, unlike subjects with alien hand syndrome, subjects with anarchic hand syndrome generally retain a sense of ownership over the hand itself. Cases of anarchic hand syndrome can thus be understood as specifically involving a deficit in the sense of action-ownership.

THE FUNCTION IMPEDIMENT   61

of others, and need to distinguish between them. Similarly, we perceive both our own bodies and the bodies of others, and again need to distinguish between them. But (as discussed in the previous section) the only experiences we experience are our own. So what value could there be to a phenomenal sense of mineness that tells us that our experiences do not belong to someone else?

This worry applies to all three versions of the Mineness Thesis. It is particularly pronounced for the Universal Mineness Thesis: if it is impossible to have an experience that lacks mineness then there's no way that its presence in experience could function to indicate anything informative about our experience. Much the same holds for the Functional Mineness Thesis: if experiences only lack mineness when they malfunction, then mineness cannot function to mark a useful distinction between different kinds of situation. The problem applies in a slightly different way to the Reflective Mineness Thesis. On this view, mineness is absent in non-reflective experiences. But this isn't because unreflective experiences aren't ours. Rather, our phenomenology only says anything about the ownership of our experience when we explicitly reflect. Since mineness is present *whenever* we reflect, its presence again cannot serve to mark a useful distinction between different kinds of situation.

Two responses are available to the Mineness Theorist here. The first response is to say that the sense of mineness does serve a function after all.[5] Even if the sense of mineness does not conform to the model of distinguishing things that are owned from things that are not owned, it may serve some other kind of purpose. Perhaps a sense of ownership over our experience makes it vivid to us that the contents of our experience are imperative to our decisions. If a pain experience is just a pain experience, we have no imperative to do anything about it, but if a pain experience is *our* pain experience then it motivates us to avoid the painful stimulus. For what it's worth, I do not find this kind of view plausible: a sense of ownership over the body part that is in pain would be enough to drive our action without also needing to have a sense of ownership over our *experience* of the pain. Nevertheless, this example serves to illustrate the kind of response available to the Mineness Theorist here.

The second response is to say that although the sense of mineness serves no function, it is an explicable by-product of processes that do serve some function. Perhaps our awareness of our experiences is such that all the properties of our experience are revealed to us. This helpfully makes us aware of numerous informative properties of our experience, but also makes us aware of properties like *mineness* that it is not useful to be aware of. Or perhaps we have a general

---

[5] One strategy available to advocates of the Functional Mineness Thesis is to look at cases of cognitive malfunction in which the sense of mineness is absent, and to observe what functional impairments these subjects suffer. However, in the next section we will see that it is not entirely clear that such malfunctions exist.

propensity to attribute ownership to things that belong to us. This propensity would have adaptive value because of the kinds of ownership that it is useful to track—such as action-ownership and bodily-ownership—but the sense of mineness is a useless by-product of this useful propensity. I would argue that the claim that all properties of experience are revealed to us is very bold, and that it is psychologically implausible that we have an all-purpose ownership-attribution mechanism. Again though, these suggestions illustrate the kind of position available to the Mineness Theorist.

The availability of these two kinds of response means that the Function Impediment is not a knock-down objection to the Mineness Thesis. That said, it does show that the Mineness Theorist owes us an account of the function of the sense of mineness, or at least an account of why it exists despite its lack of utility. The challenge for the Mineness Theorist is to provide such an account.

8. The Malfunction Impediment

8.1. The Inconsistent Triad

We are now ready to discuss the most complex impediment to a case for the Mineness Thesis. Mental mechanisms malfunction. The mechanisms that underwrite our phenomenology are no exception to this. Presumably every aspect of our experience serves some function for us, and when things go wrong our experience can mislead us. In non-pathological cases these errors might be transient and harmless, but in pathological cases a malfunction can have more serious consequences. If there is such a thing as the sense of mineness, one would expect that the mechanism responsible for this sense would misfire in at least some cases. The problem, I would argue, is that it is far from clear that there are any such cases of the sense of mineness malfunctioning, which in turn casts doubt on whether the sense of mineness exists. The Mineness Theorist thus needs to find a way out of the following inconsistent triad:

I) The sense of mineness performs a function.
II) For any cognitive mechanism that performs a function, there are cases in which it malfunctions.
III) There are no cases in which the sense of mineness malfunctions.

If you deny that subjects are ever phenomenally aware of their experiences as belonging to them, then you can avoid this inconsistent triad. If, on the other hand, you advocate any version of the Mineness Thesis, then you are committed to denying at least one of the three propositions. I will consider the consequences of denying each proposition in turn.

First, the Mineness Theorist might break the inconsistent triad by denying I. On this view, the sense of mineness can't malfunction because it doesn't have any function from which to deviate. However, we saw in the previous section that denying that the sense of mineness has a function is a very uncomfortable commitment. At the very least, the Mineness Theorist would be left with the unenviable task of explaining why we would have developed a sense of mineness if our doing so serves no purpose.

Second, the Mineness Theorist might break the inconsistent triad by denying II. They could claim that although there are many cognitive mechanisms that malfunction, the mechanism responsible for the sense of mineness is an exception to the rule. This line of thought can be developed in one of two ways.

The first is to suggest that it is *impossible* for the mechanism responsible for the sense of mineness to malfunction. The problem with this route is that if there is a neural mechanism that serves some function, then it must be physically possible for that mechanism to undergo changes that prevent it from performing that function successfully. The idea of a physical mechanism that cannot fail is at best implausible, and at worst unintelligible. Mineness Theorists might respond that the mechanism responsible for a conscious state displaying the sense of mineness is bound up with the mechanism responsible for that state being conscious at all. This might entail that any defect in the mechanism responsible for the sense of mineness would thereby prevent one from undergoing a conscious state at all, thus rendering it impossible to have an experience that doesn't display mineness. This kind of response is only available to advocates of the Universal Mineness Thesis, as advocates of the other two theses countenance the possibility of experiences in which the sense of mineness is absent. Although this is an option for advocates of the Universal Mineness Theorist, the burden of proof would be on them to show that this constitutive link exists between a state's being conscious and its displaying the sense of mineness.

This leaves Mineness Theorists with the second route, which is to acknowledge the *possibility* of a malfunction in the mechanism responsible for the sense of mineness, but to deny that this possibility is *actual*. On this view, it is a contingent matter of fact that the mechanism responsible for the sense of mineness has never malfunctioned. It is thus a counter-example to the conditional claim made by II that for any cognitive mechanism that performs a function, there are actual cases in which it malfunctions. The problem with this response is that it risks being *ad hoc*: for any other aspect of our phenomenology, cases can be found in which the mechanism responsible for that aspect misfires, so it is arbitrary to claim that the sense of mineness exists but happens not to malfunction. To appreciate how odd it would be for the sense of mineness not to malfunction, we should consider how the mechanisms responsible for other senses of ownership can go wrong.

The mechanism responsible for the sense of bodily-ownership can be lead astray surprisingly easily. In the rubber hand illusion, a specific combination of tactile and visual signals leads us to experience an inanimate hand as belonging to us (see Metzinger 2009). In 'full-body illusions' we can experience a virtual body as our own. In one study, subjects wearing a head-mounted display were presented with a virtual body. Blanke & Metzinger explain that:

> When the participants saw their body in front of themselves, being stroked synchronously (with their own back), they felt as if the virtual body was their own.
> (2009, p. 12)

Here the mechanism responsible for our sense of bodily-ownership is in good working order, but misfires given a certain unnatural combination of sensory stimuli. As mentioned in the previous section, there are also cases in which the mechanism misfires because it has been damaged. In cases of somataparaphrenia like alien hand syndrome, for instance, subjects with neurological damage lose their sense of ownership over their own hand.

A similar story holds for the mechanism responsible for our sense of ownership over our actions. Metzinger describes a striking experiment by Wegner & Wheatley in which the experimenters:

> led subjects to experience a causal link between a thought and an action, managing to induce the feeling in their subjects that the subjects had wilfully performed an action even though the action had in fact been performed by someone else. (Metzinger 2009, p. 123)

And there are again pathological cases in which the mechanism responsible for the sense of action-ownership is damaged: it seems that subjects who suffer from alien hand syndrome or anarchic hand syndrome do not experience the actions of their hand as belonging to them.

There are thus clear cases—both pathological and non-pathological—in which the mechanisms responsible for specific senses of ownership malfunction. Why, then, would the mechanism responsible for our sense of ownership over our own experiences happen not to malfunction? As things stand, the rejection of II is *ad hoc*. Advocates of the Mineness Thesis wanting to take this route will have their work cut out explaining why the sense of mineness never actually malfunctions.

The Mineness Theorist must deny at least one of three propositions in the inconsistent triad. So far I have shown why rejecting propositions I or II would be unattractive. This leaves the Mineness Theorist with the option of rejecting III; i.e. of saying that there are actual cases in which the sense of mineness malfunctions. However, this option is only available for some versions of the Mineness Thesis. The Universal Mineness Theorist is committed to *all* experiences being characterized by a sense of mineness, so cannot countenance cases in which mineness is absent due to some malfunction. Universal Mineness Theorists are thus forced to reject one of the first two propositions of the triad which, dialectically speaking, is an unfortunate position for them to find themselves in. The Functional Mineness Thesis, in contrast, is specifically tailored to accommodate the possibility of cases in which atypical subjects have experiences that lack a sense of mineness. Similarly, the Reflective Mineness Thesis is quite consistent with the sense of mineness malfunctioning. These two versions of the Mineness Thesis are thus consistent with the rejection of III. But can such a rejection be justified?

Before we look at the putative cases of malfunction put forward by Mineness Theorists, we should reflect on the different ways in which the mechanism responsible for the sense of mineness might go wrong. One suggestion we can rule out right away is a malfunction that leads to subjects being phenomenally aware of someone else's experience as their own. As discussed in connection to the second and third impediments, the only experiences of which we are phenomenally aware are our own, so it is impossible to be phenomenally aware of someone else's experience as belonging to us. As such, if there are malfunctions in the sense of mineness they must be cases in which subjects have an experience but where it does not seem to them that their experience belongs to them. It is important to distinguish the different ways in which a subject might lack the sense of mineness over their own experience. We can differentiate between:

A) Subjects who are phenomenally aware of their own experience as someone else's.
B) Subjects who are phenomenally aware of their own experience as not belonging to them (without being phenomenally aware of them as belonging to someone else).
C) Subjects who are not phenomenally aware of their own experience as belonging to them (without being phenomenally aware of them as not belonging to them, or as belonging to someone else).

The distinctions between options A–C are subtle but important. Cases of type 'A' are characterized by a sense that one's experience belongs to somebody else. This must be distinguished from cases of type 'B' because one's experience might seem not to belong to one without it seeming to belong to some other person. And cases of type 'B' must be distinguished from cases of type 'C' because one might *lack* a sense that one's experience belongs to one without *possessing* a sense that one's experience doesn't belong to one (this is simply an example of the well-known distinction between it 'not seeming that p', and it 'seeming that not-p'). It is worth adding that cases of type 'C' only qualify as malfunctions in the sense of mineness if *normal* subjects are aware of their experiences as their own. If the Mineness Thesis is false and normal subjects lack a sense of mineness, then lacking a sense of mineness would not constitute a malfunction.

66 FOUR IMPEDIMENTS TO THE CASE FOR MINENESS

To understand this three-way distinction, we can again compare mineness with a different kind of ownership. Consider bodily-ownership. Intuitively, there are differences between: being aware of your hand as belonging to somebody else; being aware of your hand as not belonging to you; and not being aware of your hand as your own. These three potential malfunctions in the sense of bodily-ownership would be analogous to malfunctions in the sense of mineness of types 'A', 'B', and 'C' respectively.

This three-way distinction provides a framework with which to understand putative malfunctions in the sense of mineness. Advocates of the Mineness Thesis have tended to focus on cases of *thought insertion* and cases of *depersonalization disorder* and the related phenomenon of *Cotard's delusion*, which I will consider in turn.

8.2. Thought Insertion

In cases of thought insertion, subjects report that their thoughts do not seem to belong to them and, in many cases, report that they seem to belong to some other person. The following are some representative reports cited by Billon (2013, pp. 291–2):

> Thoughts are put into my mind like 'Kill God.' It's just like my mind working, but it isn't. They come from this chap, Chris. They are his thoughts.
>
> (quoted in Frith, 1992, p. 66)
>
> The thoughts of Eamonn Andrews come into my mind. There are no other thoughts there, only his...He treats my mind like a screen and flashes onto it like you flash a picture.   (quoted in Mellor 1970, p. 17)

It is tempting to say that the experiences of these patients are *lacking* a quality that is present in the experiences of neurotypical subjects. Some Mineness Theorists have suggested that the experiences of neurotypical subjects are characterized by a sense of mineness, and that patients suffering from thought insertion have experiences that lack this sense of mineness. This is not to say that the patients do not *experience* their inserted thoughts.[6] The suggestion is that although they do experience their thoughts, they are not phenomenally aware of those experiences *as their own*. Guillot suggests that if we carefully differentiate for-me-ness from mineness, then:

---

[6] Interestingly, Billon (2013) denies that subjects experience their inserted thoughts. He suggests that although patients have first-person access to inserted thoughts, they are not aware of them phenomenally.

it becomes possible to acknowledge that the abnormal thoughts are given to her in a first-personal way (thus exhibiting for-me-ness), while still hypothesising that she might be specifically lacking a sense of owning those thoughts (mineness). (2017, p. 43)[7]

For convenience, I will call this view of thought insertion the 'mineness interpretation'. Metzinger adopts the same interpretation:

the popular principle that your own thoughts always are your *own* thoughts is by no means a necessary precondition of all experience. There are ways of mentally modelling reality in which this presupposition is suspended...Mineness and cognitive subjectivity can be lost, with global coherence and phenomenal experience as such being preserved. (2003, p. 446)

Similarly, López-Silva quotes Smith and Sims as endorsing the same view (2014, p. 215), and himself concludes that:

it is plausible to say that is possible to have experiences with no sense of mineness attached to them.... (2014, pp. 216–17)

Advocates of the mineness interpretation do not always make it clear what *type* of malfunction they think is occurring in cases of thought insertion. Looking at Guillot's statement above, she seems to be regarding it as a type 'C' malfunction in which subjects simply lack a sense of ownership over their experiences. That said, in the two quotations above from patients suffering from inserted thoughts, they report that their thoughts are inserted *by some specific person*. So these reports might be taken to suggest that they are undergoing a malfunction of type 'A' in which they are phenomenally aware of their experiences as belonging to someone else. And consider the report that 'One evening one thought was given to me electrically that I should murder Lissi' (Jaspers 1963, p. 580 quoted in Guillot 2017, p. 43). This might be taken to indicate a malfunction of type 'B' in which the subject is aware of an experience as not belonging to her without being aware of it as belonging to some other person. I think that a fully developed argument for the mineness interpretation would have to paint a clear picture of what kind (or kinds) of malfunction occurs in thought insertion. However, the disjunctive claim that thought insertion involves a malfunction of type 'A', 'B', or 'C' constitutes a suitable target for current purposes. What objections can be raised against the mineness interpretation of thought insertion?

---

[7] I should note that Guillot only presents this interpretation of thought insertion tentatively. Her argument is that it's a *possible* interpretation, and concedes that justifying this interpretation would require careful work.

68 FOUR IMPEDIMENTS TO THE CASE FOR MINENESS

Some have suggested that thought insertion patients still have a sense of mineness, but lack a sense of agency over their thoughts (e.g. Gallagher 2004). I think it's fair to say that this interpretation of thought insertion has been comprehensively rebutted (see, e.g., Billon 2013; López-Silva 2014; Howell & Thompson 2017). In particular, this interpretation is unable to differentiate cases of thought insertion from other cases in which subjects plausibly lack a sense of agency over their thoughts, such as the unbidden thoughts that neurotypical subjects experience routinely, and that subjects with obsessive disorders experience more persistently.

The fact that this objection to the mineness interpretation is raised by advocates of the Universal Mineness Thesis such as Gallagher is worth reflecting on. The mineness interpretation explains thought insertion by making two claims about mineness: (i) that the experiences of ordinary subjects have mineness; (ii) that the experiences of subjects with thought insertion lack mineness. Universal Mineness Theorists are committed to (ii) being false, so argue that the mineness interpretation is wrong because subjects with inserted thoughts do not lack a sense of mineness. In contrast, I am seeking to cast doubt on (i): there are no convincing reasons to think that neurotypical subjects have a sense of mineness, so lacking a sense of mineness would not explain the symptoms of those suffering from thought insertion. With this in mind, I will now offer three objections to the mineness interpretation.

The first objection is that it *appearing* to a subject that their thought is not theirs does not entail that it *phenomenally* appears to them that their thought is not theirs. Perhaps it non-phenomenally appears to neurotypical subjects that their thoughts belong to them. Due to some kind of malfunction, some of the thoughts of the atypical subjects discussed do not appear to belong to them, and may even appear to belong to someone else. This interpretation offers a potential explanation of thought insertion that doesn't require the experiences of neurotypical subjects to have some phenomenal property that the experiences of atypical subjects lack. Although I'm not in a position to argue that this explanation is *better* than the phenomenological explanation offered by the mineness interpretation, it is certainly one that advocates of the mineness interpretation would need to *rule out*. As things stand, those who posit a malfunction in the sense of mineness move too quickly from claims about how things *appear* to subjects suffering from thought insertion to how things are *experienced* by such subjects.[8]

The second objection grants that thought insertion should be understood as some kind of phenomenological disturbance, but questions the assumption that

---

[8] Some reports are explicitly about the reporter's experience, so in cases like this one might have more justification to explain the symptoms specifically in terms of how things phenomenally appear to the subject. Nevertheless, such cases will still face the second objection regarding exactly what kind of phenomenology to posit.

this phenomenological disturbance must be a disturbance to the sense of mineness. Howell & Thompson (2017, p. 117) note that delusions such as thought insertion are standardly understood in terms of a two-factor account. This means that the delusion is a product of an atypical experience combined with an atypical line of reasoning based on that experience. The presence of this second factor makes it difficult to determine *what* is atypical in the patient's experience. Howell & Thompson explain:

> There could be numerous factors that typically characterize our thoughts (or fail to characterize our thoughts) that when missing (or when present) lead some people but not others to beliefs about insertion because of differences in the way the subjects update beliefs in light of that fact...Compare the phenomenon of Capgras' syndrome in which sufferers believe that their family members and others are not the real thing but are perhaps replaced by clones. It is relatively well-accepted that Capgras patients lack some emotional or familiarity response, perhaps due to problems in the limbic system. It seems plausible that this response is connected to representations of the person, but the familiarity response it not itself a representation of "family member" or "brother." Similarly, it seems plausible that the missing ingredient in cases like thought insertion are not themselves representations of the self or "mineness" but nevertheless lead to a delusional sense of impersonalization when they are missing.
>
> (2016, pp. 15–16)

Advocates of the mineness interpretation fail to justify the assumption that thought insertion must specifically be explained by the absence of a sense of mineness, and not by some other atypical phenomenology.

The first and second objections reflect quite general worries about how to draw phenomenological conclusions from pathological reports. The third objection is more specific to the interpretation of thought insertion and cuts a little deeper. Let's grant for a moment that ordinary subjects experience a sense of ownership over their thoughts, and that subjects suffering from thought insertion lack this sense of ownership. What does this have to do with the sense of ownership over *experiences*? It seems that the mineness interpretation confuses felt ownership of the *object* of experience with felt ownership of the *experience itself*. If one subject suffers from alien hand syndrome and another does not, this might suggest that the first subject does not have a sense of bodily-ownership over their hand and that the second subject possesses such a sense of ownership. But this tells us nothing about whether either subject has a sense of ownership over their *experience* of the hand. Perhaps both subjects are phenomenally aware of their hand-experience as belonging to them, or perhaps neither is. The case in question doesn't tell us either way. Analogously, comparing a subject with inserted thoughts to a neurotypical subject might suggest that the first subject does not have a sense of ownership over their thought while the second subject does have such a sense. But this is consistent with both subjects being phenomenally aware of their thought-experiences as belonging to them and, more pertinently, it is consistent with *neither* subject being phenomenally of their thought-experience as belonging to them.[9]

A possible response to this objection is that our experience of a thought is identical with the token thought that is experienced, so lacking a sense of ownership over the thought means lacking a sense of ownership over the experience of the thought. This suggests that my analogy with bodily-ownership is misleading: no hands are identical with a subject's experience of their hand, but some thoughts are identical with a subject's experience of their thought.[10]

I can see two counter-arguments to this response. The first is simply to deny that thoughts are ever identical with our experiences of our thoughts. On many models of phenomenal awareness, the mental state of which we are phenomenally aware must be distinct from our phenomenal awareness of it. Advocates of the mineness interpretation have some latitude here, but claiming that some thoughts are identical with our experiences of them is a substantive commitment that would take significant work to defend.

The second counter-argument is to note that even if some token thought is identical with the experience of that thought, it doesn't follow that a sense of ownership over one's thought entails a sense of ownership over one's experience. Consider the following invalid argument:

1. The subject is phenomenally aware of their mental state M *as their thought.*
2. M is identical with the subject's experience of their thought.
3. Therefore, the subject is phenomenally aware of their mental state M *as their experience.*

What this toy argument highlights is that 'being phenomenally aware of...' is an intensional context. Even if the metaphysics happens to be such that there is a single mental state M that is both your thought *and* your experience of that thought, you can be phenomenally aware of M as yours *qua thought* without being phenomenally aware of M as yours *qua experience.* Cases of thought insertion might suggest that ordinary subjects have the former kind of phenomenal awareness of M, but do not suggest that they have phenomenal awareness of the latter kind. So even granting the substantive metaphysical claim that underwrites this potential response, it remains the case that thought insertion is best understood as a disruption to the sense of ownership over one's *thoughts* and not a disruption to one's sense of ownership over one's *experience* of that thought.

---

[9] Zahavi (2005) is also keen to distinguish the sense of ownership over the object of an experience from the sense of ownership over the experience itself. However, where Zahavi assumes that we are always aware of our experience as belonging to us, I am encouraging the opposite view.

[10] López-Silva (2014, p. 220) raises an objection not dissimilar to this against the claim of Zahavi described in the previous footnote.

8.3. Depersonalization Disorder and Cotard's Delusion

Billon offers the following description of depersonalization:

> Depersonalisation is a complex condition involving a broad modification of experience. Its core, however, is probably the feeling that the self or some of its significant parts are estranged, missing or nonexistent.   (2016, p. 371)

This estrangement from the self seems to underwrite a number of more specific symptoms associated with depersonalization including: it seeming as if body parts do not belong to one; it seeming that mental states—including emotions, perceptions, and imaginings—do not belong to one; and it seeming as if one is dead (see Billon 2016, pp. 371–3).

Crucially, subjects with depersonalization disorder are not delusional: they report that it is *as if* they are in the alarming situations described, but they recognize that these appearances are non-veridical. In contrast, patients with Cotard's delusion accept these appearances as veridical. Many Cotard's patients report, for instance, that they are actually dead. This symmetry between Cotard's and depersonalization leads Billon and others to conclude that 'Cotard syndrome can...be characterised as the delusional form of depersonalisation, depersonalisation being, conversely, the "as if" form of the Cotard syndrome' (Billon 2016, p. 372). I will assume that those suffering from depersonalization and Cotard's have similar kinds of experience, and differ mainly in the beliefs they form on the basis of those experiences. Most pertinent to the current discussion are cases in which patients report an estrangement from their own experience. Consider the following two reports:

> It was as if it was not me walking, it was not me talking, as if it was not me living...I can look at me, I am somehow bothered by my body, as if it wasn't me, as if I lived on the side of my body, on the side of myself if you want. I don't know how to explain.   (Janet and Raymond, 1898)

> When a part of my body hurts, I feel so detached from the pain that it feels as if it were somebody else's pain.   (Sierra and Berrios, 2000)[11]

Some offer a 'mineness interpretation' of these reports, proposing that where the experiences of neurotypical subjects are characterized by a sense of mineness, the experiences of these patients lack a sense of mineness. Given the diversity of reports made by those suffering from depersonalization or Cotard's, it might be overambitious to say that *all* subjects with these disorders undergo experiences that lack mineness. But if just *some* subjects do this would be enough to constitute

---

[11] Both quotations are from (Guillot 2017, p. 419) though she in turn takes both quotations from Billon (2015) and attributes Billon the translation of the first.

72 FOUR IMPEDIMENTS TO THE CASE FOR MINENESS

an example of a malfunction in the sense of mineness. Billon endorses the mineness interpretation:

> even if we do not usually pay attention to it, our experiences normally incorporate a certain subjective feature in virtue of which they seem to be ours to us, [and] this feature is attenuated in depersonalisation. (Billon 2016, pp. 373–4)

He goes on to quote a passage in which Jaspers seems to endorse the same conclusion:

> Every psychic manifestation, whether perception, bodily sensation, memory, idea, thought or feeling carries this particular aspect of 'being mine' of having an 'I' quality, of 'personally belonging', of it being one's own doing. This has been termed personalisation. If these psychic manifestations occur with the awareness of not being mine... we term them phenomena of depersonalisation.
> (1962, p. 121, quoted in Billon 2016, p. 374)

Guillot also endorses the mineness interpretation:

> some depersonalised patients appear to be phenomenally aware of their experiences, but not of the fact that the experiences are theirs....
> (Guillot 2017, p. 41)

The proposal is that subjects with these disorders are not phenomenally aware of their experiences as their own. Guillot reaches the further conclusion that such subjects are not aware of *themselves*, hence their reports that (it is as if) they do not exist. Applying her ternary distinction, Guillot concludes:

> I thus propose to describe the depersonalisation syndrome as a condition in which experience lacks both mineness and me-ishness, but retains for-me-ness.
> (Guillot 2017, p. 42)

As with the mineness interpretation of thought insertion, proponents of this view do not specify what *type* of malfunction to the sense of mineness is meant to be occurring. Unlike thought insertion, neither depersonalization nor Cotard's are associated with subjects reporting that their mental processes belong to someone else, so it is unlikely that subjects are suffering from a type 'A' malfunction in which they are phenomenally aware of their experience as belonging to someone else. This leaves type 'B' malfunctions in which your experience seems not to belong to you, and type 'C' malfunctions in which you lack the sense that your experience belongs to you without specifically being phenomenally aware of it as not-yours. A fully developed defence of the mineness interpretation would have to specify which type of malfunction is occurring. I will assume that advocates of the mineness interpretation support the disjunctive thesis that depersonalization and Cotard's are characterized by malfunctions of either type 'B' or 'C'.

What objections can be raised against the mineness interpretation of depersonalization and Cotard's? I will begin by considering whether any of the three objections raised against the mineness interpretation of thought insertion can be re-applied.

The first objection to the mineness interpretation of thought insertion can be re-applied as follows: even if it *appears* to subjects suffering from depersonalization or Cotard's that their experience does not belong to them, this does not justify the conclusion that it *phenomenally* appears to them that their experiences do not belong to them. Again, advocates of the mineness interpretation can be accused of moving too quickly from claims about appearances to claims about phenomenology.

The second objection also has some traction. As the symptoms of Cotard's delusion are the product of both an atypical experience and an atypical belief-forming process, we cannot assume that subjects' phenomenology directly reflects their reports (see Howell & Thompson 2017, p. 118). In cases of depersonalization, it might be inappropriate to say that subjects have an atypical belief-forming process—after all, they correctly identify that their experiences are not veridical. Nevertheless, the point remains that their reports are the product of an *interpretation* of their experience, and so may not directly reflect the content of the experience itself. According to a classic school of thought (see Billon 2016, p. 362), depersonalization and Cotard's are *affective* disorders in which subjects are estranged from their emotions. If this interpretation is correct, subjects might report that (it is as if) they do not own their experiences because of a disruption to their ordinary affective phenomenology, and not because of a disruption to the putative sense of mineness. The mineness interpretation must rule out any such alternative accounts of the disorders.

The third objection to the mineness interpretation of thought insertion does not re-apply. The objection was that ownership of thoughts should not be conflated with ownership of experiences. Since at least some reports from subjects with depersonalization or Cotard's are explicitly about ownership of experiences, no such conflation is evident. I suggest, however, that there is a further problem that is distinctive to the mineness interpretation of depersonalization and Cotard's.

As discussed above, Guillot suggests that patients suffering from depersonalization and Cotard's lack a sense of me-ishness. That is, subjects lack a phenomenal awareness of the self that neurotypical subjects have in all their experiences. Let us grant that this is true. I suggest that this alone could explain why some patients report that (it is as if) they lack ownership over their experiences. To represent something as belonging to you is to attribute ownership of it to *yourself*. In ordinary cases of self-attribution of ownership you are phenomenally aware of yourself—the entity to whom you are attributing ownership. So if you have a

74   FOUR IMPEDIMENTS TO THE CASE FOR MINENESS

diminished sense of yourself, the normal passage of self-attribution is disrupted. Without a phenomenal awareness of oneself, it would be natural to report that it is as if one doesn't own one's experience. Such reports can thus be explained by positing a disruption to one's experience *of the owner* of one's experience rather than a disruption to the experience *of the ownership relation* that one stands in to one's experiences.[12] Consequently, it would be explanatorily redundant to say that neurotypical subjects have a sense of mineness that is absent in these atypical cases.

I can see two possible responses to this objection. The first is to say that the symptoms in question are explained by both an absence of me-ishness in the patients' phenomenology *and* an absence of mineness. The difficulty with this response is that it renders the appeal to mineness redundant. If the symptom can be explained without positing this second phenomenological disruption, then it should be. After all, advocates of the mineness interpretation are attempting to explain a wide range of symptoms in an economical way. For instance, the report that (it is as if) one is dead is explained in terms of an absence of me-ishness and not in terms of the absence of a phenomenal quality *as of being alive*. If advocates of the mineness interpretation advocate economy in explaining these symptoms, then the same commitment to economy should lead them not to posit a disruption to the sense of mineness. Perhaps an advocate of the Mineness Theorist could counter that we *have* to posit a lack of mineness because if subjects lacked a sense of me-ishness but *possessed* a sense of mineness, then they would not report that it appears that their experience does not belong to them. The difficulty with this response is that it assumes that, in the absence of some malfunction, subjects ordinarily experience mineness. Of course, this is not an assumption I am prepared to grant, so the response is ineffective.

The second response is to concede that symptoms ought to be explained economically, but to claim that the symptoms are best explained by the absence of mineness rather than by the absence of me-ishness. The reports in question are thus explained by a disruption to just one aspect of the patient's phenomenology, which is just as economical as the explanation premised on a disruption to me-ishness. The difficulty with this response is that it does not explain the wider symptoms of depersonalization and Cotard's. Lacking a sense of ownership over your experience doesn't really explain why it would seem as if you did not own your guts, or why it would seem as if you were dead. In contrast, if one lacks a phenomenal awareness *of oneself* then all these symptoms are more readily explained.

Overall, the Malfunction Impediment presents a very serious obstacle to a case for mineness. The challenge for the Mineness Theorist is to find a way out of the inconsistent triad. Advocates of the Universal Mineness Thesis must either deny

---

[12] This is not to say that the absence of me-ishness *entails* that it appears to you that your experiences is not your own. Rather, having an experience that lacks me-ishness makes such an error understandable.

that the sense of mineness performs a function, or reject the principle that for any mental mechanism that performs a function there will be cases in which it malfunctions. Advocates of the Functional Mineness Thesis and the Reflective Mineness Thesis have the option of arguing that the sense of mineness *does* malfunction. Cases of thought insertion and of depersonalization/Cotard's have been interpreted as cases in which the sense of mineness is disrupted. I have argued that such interpretations are not sufficiently justified. This leaves advocates of the mineness interpretation of these disorders with the difficult task of bolstering their interpretation against the objections raised, or of finding different kinds of case that could plausibly be regarded as malfunctions in the sense of mineness. In line with the other impediments discussed, it is an open possibility that advocates of the Mineness Thesis can find a way out of the inconsistent triad. As things stand though, the triad presents a very serious challenge.

9. Concluding Remarks

Existing arguments for the Mineness Thesis are inconclusive, and any future argument for the Mineness Thesis must navigate the four impediments presented in this chapter. The Epistemic Impediment, the Representational Impediment, the Function Impediment, and the Malfunction Impediment each constitute a significant problem for any version of the Mineness Thesis. I have outlined the kinds of move that the Mineness Theorist might make to overcome each of these impediments. For every impediment, the Mineness Theorist has certain options available to her, but each of these options comes with certain theoretical costs. Perhaps the costs entailed by overcoming one or two of these impediments would be tolerable. But the costs entailed by overcoming *all four* of the impediments are likely to be considerable. Mineness Theorists will have their work cut out showing that the advantages of the Mineness Thesis are worth these costs. We should not dismiss out of hand the possibility that such a case for the Mineness Thesis could be made. That said, given the four problems discussed, pessimism about the prospects of such a case being made would not be unfounded.

References

Albahari, M. (2010). 'Nirvana and Ownerless Consciousness', in Mark Siderits, Evan Thompson, & Dan Zahavi (eds.), *Self, No Self? Perspectives From Analytical, Phenomenological, and Indian Traditions*, Oxford: OUP.

Bayne, T. (2009). 'Perception and the Reach of Phenomenal Content', *Philosophical Quarterly*, 59(236), 385–404.

Billon, A. (2013). 'Does Consciousness Entail Subjectivity? The Puzzle of Thought Insertion', *Philosophical Psychology*, 26(2), 291–314.

Billon, A. (2015). 'Why Are We Certain that We Exist?', *Philosophy and Phenomenological Research*, 91(3), 723–759.

Billon, A. (2016). 'Making Sense of the Cotard Syndrome: Insights from the Study of Depersonalisation'. *Mind and Language,* 31(3), 356–391.

Blanke, O. & Metzinger, T. (2009). 'Full-Body Illusions and Minimal Phenomenal Selfhood', *Trends in Cognitive Science*, 13(1), 7–13.

Frith, C. D. (1992). *The Cognitive Neuropsychology of Schizophrenia*. Hove: Lawrence Erlbaum Associates.

Gallagher, S. (2004). 'Neurocognitive Models of Schizophrenia: A Neurophenomenological Critique', *Psychopathology*, 37(1), 8–19.

Grünbaum, T. (2012). 'First-Person and Minimal Self-Consciousness', in S. Miguens & G. Preyer (eds.), *Consciousness and Subjectivity*. Heusenstamm: Ontos Verlag, 297–320.

Guillot, M. (2017). 'For-me-ness, Me-ishness, Mineness: On a Confusion Concerning the Subjective Character of Experience', *Review of Philosophy and Psychology,* 8, 22–53.

Hellie, B. (2007). 'Higher-Order Intentionality and Higher-Order Acquaintance', *Philosophical Studies*, 134, 289–324.

Howell, R. & Thompson, B (2017). 'Phenomenally Mine: In Search of the Subjective Character of Consciousness', *Review of Philosophy and Psychology,* 8, 103–127.

Jaspers (1963). *General Psychopathology*. Manchester: Manchester University Press.

Kriegel, U. (2009). *Subjective Consciousness: A Self-Representational Theory*. Oxford: Oxford University Press.

López-Silva, P. (2014). 'Self Awareness and the Self-Presenting Character of Abnormal Conscious Experience', in A. Gerner & J. Gonçalvez (eds.), *Altered Self and Altered Self-Experience*. Berlin: Norderstedt BoD, 209–224.

Mellor, C. (1970). 'First rank symptoms of schizophrenia: 1. The frequency in schizophrenics on admission to hospital; 2. Differences between individual first rank symptoms', British Journal of Psychiatry, 117, 15–23.

Metzinger, T. (2003). *Being No One*. Cambridge, MA: MIT Press.

Metzinger, T. (2009). *The Ego Tunnel*. New York: Basic Books.

Neander, K. (2012). 'Teleological Theories of Mental Content', *The Stanford Encyclopedia of Philosophy* (Spring 2012 Edition), Edward N. Zalta (ed.), http://plato.stanford.edu/archives/spr2012/entries/content-teleological/

Schwitzgebel, E. (2008). 'The Unreliability of Naive Introspection', *Philosophical Review*, 117(2), 245–273.

Siegel, S. (2010). *The Contents of Visual Experience*. Oxford: OUP.

Zahavi, D. (2004). 'Back to Brentano', *Journal of Consciousness Studies*, 11(10–11), 66–87.

Zahavi, D. (2005). *Subjectivity and Selfhood: Investigating the First-Person Perspective*. Cambridge, MA: MIT Press.

4

Transparency and Subjective Character

Robert J. Howell

A number of philosophers argue that all normal conscious experiences involve not only a qualitative character but also a subjective character. While qualitative character involves the "what it's like" to experience the various objects of a experiences—the diverse sensations involved in tasting blue cheese, feeling pain, or feeling afraid—subjective character is universal and reflects what it is for these experiences to be for me, or mine. There is a good deal of skepticism about subjective character. Some of this skepticism derives from confusion about what it is supposed to be, but in my view the most compelling reason to be skeptical is phenomenological. Normal, unreflective experience seems to be transparent, and the self and the subjective states of the self are not presented as such in unreflective experience. If this is the case, it seems that there is little room for subjective character in unreflective experience.

In this chapter, I explore the tension between subjective character and the transparency of experience. I argue that the phenomenological datum of transparency tells against the existence of subjective character in normal consciousness. I will consider an argument that certain pathological cases—most particularly cases of depersonalization—require us to posit me-ness or subjective character. I will argue that these cases are in fact consistent with transparency and the lack of subjective character, and that ironically they might best be explained by the failure of transparency rather than the disappearance of subjective character.

Since this is a topic that has been fraught with confusion, in section 1, I will explore the notion of subjective character, and consider some distinctions that will help us keep track of the target notion. In section 2, I will do the same for transparency, providing the intuitive phenomenological case on its behalf and making clear which of many possible theses I take myself to defend. In section 3, I will make the argument against subjective character from transparency explicit and consider some replies on behalf of the defenders of subjective character. In section 4, I will consider the argument from depersonalization, which maintains that pathological cases of various sorts provide a strong case for the existence of me-ness. In section 5, I will provide a competing account of the pathological cases which is consistent with transparency and denies subjective character in the

Robert J. Howell, *Transparency and Subjective Character* In: *Self-Experience: Essays on Inner Awareness.*
Edited by: Manuel García-Carpintero and Marie Guillot, Oxford University Press. © Robert J. Howell 2023.
DOI: 10.1093/oso/9780198805397.003.0004

1. Introducing Subjective Character

There is something it is like to have some conscious states. There is something it is like to experience the taste of chocolate that is different from what it's like to experience the taste of blue cheese; there is something it is like to feel a pain that is quite distinct from what it is like to feel an itch. We can say that these experiences have phenomenal character. According to a number of authors, conscious experiences also have what might be called a subjectish phenomenology. There is a mineness or a me-ishness to my experience of chocolate and my feeling of pain. Uriah Kriegel provides a particularly clear presentation of the distinction:

> The bluish way it is like for me has two distinguishable components: (i) the bluish component and (ii) the for-me component. I call the former qualitative character and the latter subjective character....my conscious experience of the blue sky is the conscious experience it is in virtue of its bluishness, but it is a conscious experience at all in virtue of its for-me-ness.   (Kriegel 2009, p. 1)

As we shall see, numerous philosophers seem to agree that there is such a thing as this subjective character that is over and above (though not necessarily separable from) qualitative character. Others, including myself, have a hard time getting a handle on what subjective character is supposed to be, and have serious doubts about its existence.[1] Part of the problem is that authors frequently seem to be talking about different things in different contexts. For example, consider the following, from a couple of the giants of the phenomenological tradition:

Husserl
The Ego appears to be permanently, even necessarily, there, and this permanence is obviously not that of a stolid unshifting experience, or a "fixed idea." On the contrary, it belongs to every experience that comes and streams past, its "glance" goes "through" every actual cogito and towards the object.

(Husserl 1952, p. 156)

Merleau-Ponty
All thought of something is at the same time self-consciousness, failing which it could have no object. At the root of all our experiences and all our reflections,

---

[1] Dainton (2008), Prinz (2012).

we find, then, a being which immediately recognizes itself because it is its knowledge both of itself and of all things, and which knows its own existence, not by observation and as a given fact, nor by inference from any idea of itself, but through direct contact with that existence. Self-consciousness is the very being of the mind in action.   (Merleau-Ponty 1994, p. 371)

It is not obvious that Husserl and Merleau-Ponty are talking about the same thing here, and it is less obvious that they are saying the same thing as contemporary philosophers who have taken up the banner of mineness or me-ishness. Consider:

Zahavi
The mineness refers to the distinct manner, or how, of experiencing. It refers to the first-personal presence of all my experiential content; it refers to the fact that the experiences I am living through present themselves differently (but not necessarily better) to me than to anybody else. When I have experiences, I so to speak, have them minely.   (Zahavi 2014, p. 22)

Block
P-conscious states often seem to have a "me-ishness" about them, the phenomenal state often represents the state as "a state of me."   (Block 1995, p. 235)

Billon
It was early suggested that our experiences all come with a certain phenomenal feature in virtue of which they seem to be ours to us, and that such a feature would be lacking or altered in depersonalized patients....In line with the modern terminology we can call this lacking phenomenal feature "the mark of mineness" or, simply "mineness."   (Billon, Chapter 14, this volume)

Marie Guillot has recently untangled three distinct notions of mineness that often get conflated in these debates.

Much of the debate on the subjective character of experience is affected by a failure to distinguish between three different dimensions one might identify as the invariant phenomenal core across all experiences: that my experiences appear to me (for-me-ness); that I am manifested to myself through them (me-ness); and that they are presented as my own (mineness).   (Guillot 2016, conclusion)

Of these notions, the first—for-me-ness—doesn't seem to describe anything (distinct from qualitative character) that would show up in the phenomenological field. Instead it seems to reflect the fact that all of my experiences appear to me. This is either an epistemic fact, that each subject has a privileged access to his or her own phenomenology, or a metaphysical point that reflects the fact that experiences are had by experiencing subjects. Using different vocabulary, Martine Nida-Rümelin puts the latter point nicely in her Chapter 9 of this volume:

It is therefore a mistake to search for the special 'phenomenal feel' of [subjective character]₁ or [subjective character]₂. It is like something *for* the subject concerned to have the experience and the subject is primitively aware of having the associated experiential properties…To say this is not to attribute a common 'phenomenal feature' to all experiences; it is rather to specify that the event at issue falls into the category of those that are instantiations of experiential properties by experiencing beings; it is to specify its ontological nature.

(Nida-Rümelin, Chapter 9, this volume)[2]

Perhaps this for-me-ness is what defenders want, but since it needn't involve any addition to the feel of conscious states, it is not a very "thick" sense of mineness. There are other ways notions of mineness can fail to be thick, so I suggest the following as conditions for something to count as "thick subjective character":[3]

1) The Phenomenal Condition—Subjective Character must make some contribution to a subject's total phenomenal character; and
2) The Representational Condition—Subjective Character must in some way present, refer to, or concern the self.
3) The Distinctness Condition—Subjective Character must be distinct from Qualitative Character.

The phenomenal condition requires that there be some discernible component of the phenomenal field that corresponds to subjective character. If there is a sense of subjective character that doesn't appear in the phenomenal field, subjective character is more like for-me-ness. It would be a metaphysical or epistemic fact about phenomenology rather than a phenomenal character in itself. It is consistent with this "for-me-ness" view that the phenomenal field is itself impersonal and anonymous. The second, representational condition is meant to specify just what sort of conscious character can serve as subjective character. The quality that distinguishes the painfulness of an experience from the itchiness of the experience isn't the subjective character by anyone's lights. That is the qualitative character. But even if supposing that there is something contributing to the conscious field that is not qualitative character, there must be something that makes it appropriate to call it me-ness or mineness. All of my conscious experiences share a number of characteristics other than being mine. They also appear in the present and at a particular location in the world. They all have nowness, and perhaps hereness. There must be some quality that distinguishes me-ness, and it seems that quality must be representational in some way.

---

[2] I'm not certain that Nida-Rümelin means precisely "for me-ness" by her two subscripted notions of subjective character. She divides the territory a little differently in general. But the point she is making is exactly the one I wish to make about "for-me-ness."
[3] These are adapted from Howell and Thompson (2017).

The representational condition can sound stronger than I intend it, so it is worth clarifying that it does not require that subjective character involve a part of the phenomenal field that explicitly represents the self in the way a part of one's visual field represents an apple. Many, if not most, defenders of subjective character would explicitly reject such a condition.[4] Nevertheless, there must be some sense in which a part of the phenomenal field *concerns* the self at least in the sense that it serves to justify self-attributions of experiences and underwrite a sense of ownership.

The distinctness condition simply insists that subjective character must be something over and above qualitative character. This condition rules out two more plausible views that might otherwise seem to embrace subjective character but are in the end too thin. One view is ultimately epistemic. One could hold the view that we are hard-wired to self-ascribe experiences. Under some accounts of justification, we might then want to say that the qualitative character itself justified the experience's self-ascription. In this case there is only qualitative character but with the addition of the epistemic fact that we are immediately justified in self-ascription of things with qualitative character. A similar view would hold that phenomenally there is only qualitative character, but every experience with qualitative character has as part of its content that it is had by the particular subject who has it. This would be to support the idea of subjective content but not subjective phenomenal character. Both of these views are too thin, since subjective character wouldn't introduce any new aspect of the phenomenal field. There would be nothing about the phenomenology of experience that would tell us these views were true. Since the authors who introduce the notion of subjective character themselves draw attention to its phenomenology and its distinctness from qualitative character, I take it this constraint shouldn't be controversial.[5]

Even if one believes in subjective character, there is a question about how universal it is. Does it characterize every state for every subject, or just some states for some subjects? At one end of the spectrum would be a univeralist who believes subjective character is present in every conscious state for every subject. On the other is a nihilist who thinks that thick subjective character isn't present in any state for any individual.[6] There are, of course, many possible positions in between. One could hold, as Billon does in this volume, that subjective character is universal for the experiences of normal subjects but that some pathological subjects lack it. Or, one could hold that subjective character is only present in reflective

---

[4] Zahavi (2005 and 2014) as well as Zahavi and Kriegel (2015), reject such a view, as does Billon, Chapter 14, this volume).

[5] One might hold the view that there is no phenomenal content that is not discernible in phenomenal character. If this is the case, recognizing subjective content requires that one recognize subjective character. Such a view would satisfy the three conditions for subjective character since it would involve a part of phenomenology over and above qualitative character that presented or concerned the subject.

[6] These categories come from Billon, Chapter 14, this volume.

experiences or when conscious states are the object of a second order thought.[7] Or, one could hold that there is a subset of experiences that lack subjective character—say, for example, perceptual experiences—but that other experiences—like those associated with certain conative or affective states like desiring, willing, and certain emotions—have subjective character. I will not take a stance on these positions here. Instead, I will argue that transparency gives us reason to oppose universalism, as well as the weaker thesis that subjective character is universal in the experiences of normal (non-pathological) subjects.

2. Transparency

The primary reason to doubt the existence of thick subjective character is, ironically, phenomenological. It is oft noted that experience is transparent. Philosophers in the phenomenological tradition have taken this so seriously that they have made extraordinary claims in its name. Jean-Paul Sartre claimed, among other things, that the ego is a transcendent entity and not within consciousness at all, because "if it existed...it would slide into every consciousness like an opaque blade" (Sartre 1957, p. 40). Purging consciousness of the ego, meanwhile, "recovers its primary transparency. In a sense, it is a nothing, since all physical, psycho-physical, and psychic objects, all truths, all values are outside it; since my me has itself ceased to be any part of it" (Sartre 1957, p. 93). When I am involved in the world, not reflecting but engaging, I am fully occupied with the objects of experience. Not only is my self not in view, colors, sounds, and tastes appear to be out there, on or radiating from the objects. Sartre's odd notion of consciousness as a nothing is echoed in Harman's famous remarks:

> When Eloise sees a tree before her, the colors she experiences are all experienced as features of the tree and its surroundings. None of them are experiences as intrinsic features of her experience. Nor does she experience any features of anything as intrinsic features of her experience. And that is true of you too.
>
> (Harman 1990, p. 31)

These sorts of observations seem to support something like the following transparency thesis:

Unreflective Phenomenological Transparency: when we are not reflecting on our mental states, but are engaging with the world, we are not aware of our selves or our sensory states but of the qualities and things in the world.

---

[7] Sartre (1957), Howell and Thompson (2017).

This is the sort of thesis that is usually defended by Sartre.

G.E. Moore famously observed that even when we are attending to consciousness, trying to take it as an object, it slips through our fingers.

> Though philosophers have recognized that something distinct is meant by consciousness, they have never yet had a clear conception of what that something is...The moment we try to fix our attention upon consciousness and to see what, distinctly, it is, it seems to vanish: it seems as if we had before us a mere emptiness. When we try to introspect the sensation of blue, all we can see is the blue: the other element is as if it were diaphanous. (Moore 1903, p. 450)

This suggests that experience is transparent even when we are reflecting on it. Hume, of course, says something similar about self-awareness—when he introspects he doesn't find a self, but instead finds the "particular perceptions" of heat or cold or whatever it is he is perceiving (Hume 1978, p. 251).[8]

These two sorts of observations suggest the following thesis:

Reflective Phenomenological Transparency: one is not aware of one's self or own experiences in reflection.

Contemporary philosophers who endorse this thesis—and incidentally Moore is not one of them—tend to emphasize "experience transparency", the view that we are never aware—at least directly—of our experiences. Authors who support this include Dretske (1995, p. 62), Tye (2000, 113:51–2), and many others who are attracted to representationalist views of perception. They are often less explicit about self-transparency, but the phenomenological data seem similar.[9]

Perhaps the most important, and most overlooked ambiguity in these theses arises because it is possible to be aware of something, and even attend to it, without being aware of it as the thing that it is. When we are looking at a movie on television, we are aware of pixels, but not as pixels; when playing a game with a VR headset we are aware of the screen, but not as such. If we are trying to spot something, we might well attend very closely to an area of the screen. But we are not aware of it as a screen.[10] It is conceivable that we are aware of our sensations

---

[8] Hume seems to think that he does find "impressions and ideas", which might suggest a lack of transparency. Considering the fact that he denies we are aware of objects apart from such things, I suspect the difference here is located not in the phenomenology but in the epistemology and views about mental content.

[9] Thanks to Marta Jorba who helped me recognize the need to add "self-transparency" to my argument.

[10] Note that we are not misperceiving or miscategorizing the screen. We are aware of it, but we are arguably not perceiving it or categorizing it at all. Our awareness of it presents what it represents, not the screen itself.

in the same way, and are in fact attending to them, only without being aware of them as sensations.

These considerations suggest a further disambiguation of the transparency thesis that cuts across both reflective and non-reflective transparency:

Deep Transparency: We are not aware of our experiential states (and selves), not only as experiential states, but at all.

Naive Transparency: We are not aware of our conscious experiential states as experiential states, and we are not aware of our selves as our selves.

This, then, gives us four different transparency theses: Deep Unreflective Transparency, Deep Reflective Transparency, Naive Unreflective Transparency, and Naive Reflective Transparency. Though some might wish to argue for stronger theses, phenomenology comments most unequivocally on the weakest thesis: naive unreflective transparency. Perhaps we are always in some sense aware of our sensations. And, perhaps reflective episodes or perceptual anomalies lead us to be aware of the subjective face of our experience. But in the normal and untheoretical approach to the world, our sensations do not call attention to themselves as subjective experiences. They usher our attention to the world and the things they represent.[11]

3. The Conflict

Naive unreflective transparency conflicts with the claim of the existence of universal thick subjective character. If there is thick subjective character, our experiences not only have an outwardly pointing representational component, they must also have a phenomenologically discernible component that refers to or concerns the self. The way in which they refer to the self will depend on whether they are supposed to have "me-ness" or "mineness." If they are supposed to have "mineness" it seems that they must announce themselves as belonging to a subject. This implies they have to announce themselves as subjective experiences, which conflicts with experience transparency. If they have "me-ness" it would seem that they must have a phenomenal component that represents the self itself, which conflicts with subject transparency. Even if one disagrees with Hume that

---

[11] Martine Nida-Rümelin has suggested, in Chapter 9 of this volume and elsewhere (Nida-Rümelin 2017 and 2018) that we have a primitive awareness of our experiences that is non-conceptual but is nonetheless awareness of it as an experience. On this view, naive transparency would be false as stated but true if it means that we don't conceptualize our experiences as experiences. For this view to be phenomenologically adequate, it would have to be the case that we can be aware of experiences as experiences (in this sense), have the concept of experience, and yet not apply the concept to those experiences in most of the cases in which we have experiences. Perhaps there is a sense in which that is true, but I'm inclined to believe that this is a very special and thin sense of "being aware of x as F" that is not really in conflict with my argument here.

we don't find the self in introspection, it is surely true that we don't have a phenomenal representation of it in every experience. Even if one did think that there was such a representation of the self, one wonders what properties visual experiences, say, would represent the self as having. The most plausible view—and the one that seems most in keeping with the advocates of phenomenal character—is that it would represent the self as having those experiences. Once again, in that case our experiences would have to be salient as experiences. Experience transparency strongly supports, and perhaps even entails, subject transparency.

This gives us the following argument against subjective character:

1. When subjects are unreflective their sensations and selves are not salient as sensations or selves.
2. If sensations had subjective character either they should be salient as sensations in unreflective experience, or selves should appear as selves in unreflective experience.
∴. Sensations don't have subjective character.

One could respond to this argument by denying premise 2. We are aware of sensations and their qualities, after all, without being aware of them as sensations. Why couldn't we be aware of their mineness but not as mineness? The most natural way to hold such a view is to say that we project the phenomenal character of our sensations onto the world. Phenomenologically, at least, the redness of the car appears to be a modification of the car. So, sensations can have phenomenal characters that represent the way the world is but that do not call attention to their status as sensations as such. So, perhaps the defender of subjective character can say that their view is similarly consistent with transparency. Perhaps our sensations have a thick subjective character that doesn't announce itself, just as the character of red sensations doesn't announce itself.

The problem with this view, though, is that while it seems to make sense to project the phenomenal character of redness onto a car—so that the subjective features of redness don't appear subjective but appear as a modification of the car—it doesn't seem plausible that we project the subjectivity of sensations. What would it be, after all, to project the mineness of a sensation? Is it that something out there—like the redness of the car—presents itself as belonging to me, or even some random conscious subject? This is implausible. We don't seem to perceive such personalized properties. Since projection is implausible about subjective character, and non-projected me-ness would have to draw attention to sensations as such, subjective character is incompatible with naive unreflective transparency.[12]

---

[12] It might be plausible that we can perceive ourselves as ourselves, and perhaps in such cases we project a kind of me-ishness onto the object in the world that is us. I'm skeptical, but in any case this is not the projection that the defender of subjective character needs. If even experiences of the redness of the car also project a phenomenal "mineness," even when we do not perceive ourselves, the mineness must modify something else in the world. That is implausible.

The argument from unreflective naive transparency against thick subjective character can thus be put as follows:

1. If there is thick subjective character, its phenomenal aspect must either be projected as a modification of what experiences represent, or it must modify the experiences themselves.

2. If subjective character modifies the experiences themselves, then in unreflective experience we will have to be aware of our experiences as experiences or our selves as selves.

3. In unreflective experience we are not aware of our experiences as experiences or our selves as selves.

4. If subjective character is projected in unreflective experience, then perceived objects and properties of objects should appear to have a property of mineness, or the self should somehow be found in the world.

5. Perceived objects and properties of objects don't appear to have a property of mineness and the self isn't to be found in the world.

:. There is no thick subjective character.

Put much more succinctly, if there is subjective character in unreflective experience it should either show up as characterizing our subjective states or the world the states represent, but in fact it does neither. In unreflective experience both our experience and the world has no discernible feature that corresponds to mineness. As Sartre puts the point:

> I am then plunged into the world of objects...but me, I have disappeared; I have annihilated myself. There is no place for me on this level. And this is not a matter of chance, due to a momentary lapse of attention, but it happens because of the very structure of consciousness. (Sartre 1993, p. 49)

A natural objection to Sartre and this approach to transparency is to say that there is something in principle wrong with the way we are trying to discover subjective character. By focusing on unreflective experience, it might be thought we are frustrating our investigation at the start. If we aren't reflecting on experience, how are we to know anything about it? It is hardly telling, the objection goes, if we don't find a particular property in consciousness when we aren't attending to conscious experience. When I'm returning a serve, I'm unlikely to be attending to my opponent's face but that hardly means it's not there.

Sartre himself considers something like this objection. The answer is ultimately to distinguish between the lived, unreflective moment and the attentive investigation of that moment in retrospect. Though experiences might not present themselves as experiences in a moment, at a later time one can become aware that one was having experiences, and one can attend to the details of those experiences. One can realize that though one was having experiences one wasn't aware of them as such, and one can realize that the experiences one was having didn't come with a subjective tag. And, one can realize, that this is part of why the experiences allowed one to become absorbed in the world in the first place.

This point about phenomenological methodology helps to head off a reply Kriegel makes to the transparency objection. Kriegel argues that subjective character is peripheral. As such, it is not surprising that it disappears when it becomes focal. Kriegel argues that "peripheral inner awareness is phenomenologically manifest, yet not introspectible" (Kriegel 2009, p. 372). He argues:

> My claim is that this model predicts that peripheral inner awareness is not introspectible. On this model, introspection cannot reveal peripheral inner awareness, because it supplants it. Introspecting one's current experience is a matter of having focal inner awareness of it. But once one enters the state of focal inner awareness, the state of peripheral inner awareness that existed prior to the introspecting has gone out of existence; or rather, it has "graduated" to focal awareness.... Thus introspecting cannot reveal peripheral inner awareness because it annihilates it (by supplanting it).

Kriegel's response doesn't touch our argument from the unreflective transparency thesis since that thesis is not based on introspecting one's current experience to see if there is subjective character present. Rather, it is to attend to an unreflective moment to see what was there—in the periphery or otherwise. Kriegel's response assumes that the transparency thesis is only a thesis about what we find in reflection and introspection, and indeed most transparency theorists do claim that we don't find intrinsic characters of experience in reflection. But they are claiming that we don't find them *even* when we introspect, not only when we introspect.

Even aside from the details of our approach, there is a problem with Kriegel's response. He argues that since inner awareness is peripheral, it becomes annihilated when it becomes focal. But that doesn't follow. In general, something that is in the periphery isn't annihilated when it becomes focal, it just is no longer peripheral. If Kriegel means, however, that this is a feature of consciousness that always disappears on attention—that it is essentially out of grasp—we have an extreme version of the methodological worry raised by McClelland in Chapter 3, this volume. The principal source of evidence for subjective character— phenomenology—becomes highly questionable since our principle access to it— through introspection—is said to annihilate subjective character. We are asked instead to rely on what we might think we can catch out of the corner of our mind's eye. This method is unlikely to reliable. By claiming this is the only source of data for subjective character, and that it is unconfirmable by the sorts of introspection and attention defenders of self-knowledge typically recommend, the phenomenological case for subjective character can confer precious little justification for belief in its existence. Meanwhile, the persistent impression of unreflective transparency continues to suggest that it doesn't exist on that level.

Another response to the transparency argument will maintain that instead of using the wrong approach to find subjective character, we are looking for the wrong sort of thing. This response maintains that me-ness deniers have been treating subjective character as if it were qualitative character, or just another qualitative feature of experience on par with painfulness and the sensation of red. Most defenders of subjective character insist that it should not be thought of in this way. Dan Zahavi is particularly clear about this:

> Some might object that there is no property common to all my experiences, no stamp or label that clearly identifies them as mine. But this objection is misplaced in that it looks for the commonality in the wrong pace. The for-me-ness or mineness in question is not a quality like scarlet, sour or soft. It doesn't refer to a specific experiential content, to a specific what, nor does it refer to the diachronic or synchronic sum of such content, or to some other relation that might obtain between the contents in question. Rather it refers to the distinct givenness or how of experience. It refers to the first-personal presence of experience. It refers to the fact that the experiences I am living through are given differently (but not necessarily better) to me than to anybody else. It could consequently be claimed that anybody who denies the for-me-ness or mineness of experience simply fails to recognize a constitutive aspect of experience.
>
> (Zahavi 2005, p. 59)

Further, in a recent article Zahavi and Kriegel have maintained that subjective character is not a detachable "self quale that one could introspect in isolation from any other content of consciousness, but rather an experiential feature of all phenomenal episodes that remains constant across them and that constitutes the subjectivity of experience" (Zahavi and Kriegel 2015, p. 39).

I suspect that in these responses the authors are simply shifting to a thin notion of subjective character that is more akin to what Guillot calls for-me-ness. This, I think, is supported by the fact that Zahavi and Kriegel claim that this "experiential feature...constitutes the subjectivity of experience." It would be quite odd that a phenomenological feature of experience itself constituted the subjectivity of experience. Something that is itself in the content or character of consciousness presupposes consciousness and subjectivity; it cannot constitute it. In the claim that there is "an experiential feature...that constitutes the subjectivity of experience," "experiential feature" is ambiguous. It might be a feature that shows up in experience, such that it is a feature of one's phenomenological field, or it might just be a characteristic of the experience—perhaps an essential one—that is not itself *in* the experience. As we noted before when discussing for-me-ness, there are important ontological features of experience such that an experience is always an experience of a subject, and no two subjects share experiences. If defenders of subjective character have this metaphysical fact in mind, we should agree whole-heartedly. But these ontological features don't require anything subjective showing up in, or being a salient aspect of the phenomenal field. Perhaps this is what defenders of me-ness really have in mind. But if so, it is a little misleading to suggest, as Kriegel does, that "the bluish way it is like for me has two distinguishable components: (i) the bluish component and (ii) the for-me component" (Kriegel 2009, p. 1). After all there are many, many other experiential features in this metaphysical sense. There is a temporal component, a neural component, as well as many metaphysical components that explain its modal features. We should admit there are such things, but it's a stretch to say they form part of the character of the experience.

The most promising version of subjective character, and thus the most promising response to the above argument, maintains that it marks a sort of mode of apprehension of sensations. Even if one believes in transparency, one should acknowledge the difference between perceiving that p and remembering that p, or hoping that p and believing that p. These states differ in respect to a certain mode of thinking about p, but not in their content. Could there not then be a universally present feature of all modes of thinking and feeling which is in some sense self-ascriptive or self-referential? If so, perhaps this would be consistent with transparency, much as hoping, doubting, and remembering are.[13]

This is an interesting suggestion, but I'm inclined to reject it for more or less the same reasons already presented. It is true that this "subjective mode" strategy preserves a sort of transparency in that the subjective character isn't modifying the presentation of the content of the unreflective state. Nevertheless, it seems that if it is to make a phenomenological appearance at all it should still draw attention to the subject or the subject's mental states. It's hard to know what it would be otherwise. The modes of entertaining like fearing and remembering are modes of entertaining certain contents of my experiences or thoughts—I am remembering La Sagrada Familia, while months ago I was perceiving it. I am hoping for impeachment of the U.S. President, not fearing it. These modes affect how I am approaching the content of my thought, which in unreflective cases is out there in the world. But subjective character would, I take it, affect the way we approach our experiences. (It would be part of the explanation why we self-ascribe them, for example.) This is an important disanalogy between modes of entertaining like fearing and remembering and the supposed subjective mode. What's more, it seems that preserving any serious analogy would again require that we be aware of sensations or the subject in unreflective experiences, because it's not coherent to say that we have a mode of awareness of something that we are not aware of.

---

[13] Thanks to Martine Nida-Rümelin, Manuel Garcia-Carpintero, and Matheus Valente for pushing me to consider this possibility more explicitly.

The best version of a "subjective mode" view is one according to which there is a subjective mode of apprehending sensations and experiences *in reflection*. That is, when we actually are reflecting on our experiences, and they are the objects of our thoughts and (second-order) mental states, we are apprehending them in a certain way that asserts ownership or possession of them. In my view, this is not implausible and it preserves the analogy with other modes of entertaining in that the mode affects how one is entertaining the object or contents of the relevant state. It might well be a form of subjective character. But it is not one that modifies all conscious states—instead, it is only present in reflection.[14]

If one takes the view, however, that there is something phenomenological present in unreflective experience, when sensations and the self are not salient, there is a real question about what makes it subjective character (me-ness), versus "present character" (nowness). There is also the worry that if there were such a thing we would have no clear way of apprehending it, because it would be ever-present, leaving us with no contrasting experiences. There is, however, an argument which might answer these concerns, thus providing much needed aid to the phenomenological case for subjective character. To this we now turn.

4. The Argument from Depersonalization

At the end of the previous section, I argued that even if there is a phenomenological feature of experience that hums along in the background, accompanying all of consciousness, there would be little reason to call it "subjective character" if it didn't in some sense represent or refer to the self. Pair this with the argument from transparency and there is a compelling reason to doubt the existence of subjective character. There is, however, empirical evidence that might seem to push strongly in the other direction. Pathological cases, including thought insertion, depersonalization, and Cotard's Syndrome might well provide contrast cases that support the existence of thick subjective character. If there is something phenomenological that is present in normal cases but absent in these pathological cases, then it has a good claim to be subjective character even if there is no explicit representation of the self. That phenomenological element would be subjective character (as opposed to temporal character) because it explained the typical grasp of the self that the self-challenged subjects lack.

In his contribution to this volume, Alexandre Billon provides a compelling defense of this argument. In this section, I will summarize his argument. In the section that follows, I will suggest an alternative model of the pathological cases and their relation to the normal case. The alternative account will be consistent

---

[14] This sort of view is hinted at in Howell (2006 and 2010) and Howell and Thompson (2017). Thor Grunbaum also gestures toward such a view in Grunbaum (2012).

with naive unreflective transparency and will open a path to rejecting thick subjective character altogether.

Before I summarize Billon's argument, however, it should be noted that not all defenders of subjective character want the help he is providing. Philosophers such as Zahavi and Kriegel think that subjective character is a *sine qua non* of consciousness. Kriegel (2009) builds an account of consciousness out of it, and Zahavi (2014) insists that the mineness at issue is an essential part of consciousness. So unless they are willing to say that inserted thoughts and depersonalized experiences are not conscious, they must say that what is missing in these cases is not the mineness at issue.[15] Zahavi is explicit about his stance on these cases:

> regardless of how alienated or distanced the patient feels from the experiences, the experiences do not manifest themselves entirely in the public domain. They continue to be phenomenally present to the patient in a way that is in principle unavailable to others. This is what their first-personal character amounts to, and this is why even the pathological experiences under consideration retain their mineness and for-me-ness. (Zahavi 2014, p. 41)

One suspects that Zahavi is just indicating that he really isn't talking about thick subjective character at all. It is likely that he has something like for-me-ness (in Guillot's sense) in mind.[16] Nevertheless, the arguments from depersonalization do seem to be arguing for thick subjective character. They involve substantial alterations in the phenomenal field, and those alterations seem to have a significant effect on patients' sense of subjectivity.

Depersonalization generally involves a deep sense of alienation from what normal people take to be some of the most intimate and essential features of themselves. A compelling patient description is offered by Sierra:

> I feel some degree of 'out of it' all the time...I can sit looking at my foot or my hand and not feel like they are mine. This can happen when I am writing, my hand is just writing, but I'm not telling it to. It almost feels like I have died, but no one has thought to tell me. So, I'm left living in a shell that I don't recognize any more. (Sierra, 2009, p. 27; quoted in Billon, Chapter 14, this volume)

Billon groups these depersonalizations into four general kinds. Depersonalization of the first sort involves being alienated from one's own mental states. Pains feel

---

[15] It's worth noting that Billon (2011) is willing to bite the bullet and claim that inserted thoughts and experiences of depersonalized patients are not conscious. It's difficult to see how he can say this while insisting, as he must, that we have to take the patients' reports at face value.

[16] He might well have the subjective mode view in mind. He would insist, I take it, that such a mode cannot but be present in conscious experience. On such a view, one might say that the mode is that we are entertaining p "consciously." Then, the only question is whether this sort of subjective character amounts to anything more than the recognition that all conscious states are conscious.

like pains, but they are not compelling—it is as if they were someone else's. The same can happen for thoughts, emotions, and perceptual states. Billon calls this *dementalization*. Patients can also be alienated from their body parts, displaying what Billon calls *desomatization*. Some patients complain of being alienated from their own actions—they are doing things, but they feel like they are the actions of an automaton rather than themselves. Billon calls this *deagentivation*. The final involves complaints of death or even non-existence. Patients feel in some sense removed from the world. (For these descriptions and patient reports of these feelings, see Billon, Chapter 14, this volume.)

Billon argues that the best explanation of these reports is that these patients lack mineness or subjective character. As Billon puts it:

• *Dementalization* would result from mental states lacking their normal mineness and feeling accordingly alien or lacking. A lack of mineness for pains, emotions and thoughts in general would explain why they feel alien.

• *Deagentivation* would result from intentions-in-action lacking their normal mineness, making the action feel alien.

• *Desomatization* would result from bodily sensations lacking their normal mineness, making the bodily part "in" which they occur seem alien (see de Vignemont (2007, 2014) for a precise account of how an alteration of bodily sensations' mineness can lead to the feeling that some bodily parts are alien).

• *Death and nonexistence complaints* would result from a substantial and global attenuation of mineness. Such attenuation would estrange the patient from all his experiences, leading to the impression that *he* really has no experience and that he is phenomenally dead. It would ultimately even estrange him from himself, leading to the impression that he is not there, he is not himself, or that he does not exist (see Billon 2015, 2014 ... for details).

(Billon, Chapter 14, this volume)

Given the explanatory value of positing a lack of mineness to account for the patient's reports, we should, according to Billon, believe that normal subjects in normal conditions have this mineness. This is why we aren't alienated from our actions, bodies, pains, and agency. Those who deny the existence of this mineness are either not noticing it because it is so universally and unproblematically present, or they are looking for something like a qualitative sensation which is the wrong thing to be looking for.

5. Conscious Abnormality

When I'm sick I'm inclined to say that I don't feel well, that I lack energy, or that I don't feel like myself. After recovering, I might say that I feel well for the first time in weeks. But is there a phenomenal character that all healthy people have but that people who are sick lack? If we take the statements of sick people on face value, it can look that way. It's notable, though, that people don't go around saying that they feel this feeling of wellness. If they are asked how they feel, they are likely to say they feel "good" or "well," but this is likely to be automatic and unreflective. But even if we take their reports seriously, their feeling well isn't a matter of there being something in their phenomenal field corresponding to wellness. Even when I say "I feel well for the first time in weeks," I'm not really reporting on a phenomenal feel that will endure so long as I am well. It's rather that I'm reporting on a certain lack—the lack of the soreness of muscles, the shortness of breath, the nausea, the feeling of effort it takes to perform the simplest tasks. There is a collection of symptoms that bring with them phenomenal discomfort, and feeling well is precisely not having those. The conscious experience of being unwell, of course, needn't involve only the addition of phenomenally conscious feelings that indicate a lack of health. It might instead involve a lack of a feeling that normal people feel. One might, for example, no longer feel one's legs. Of course the feeling that one lacks is not the feeling of health, it's the feeling one usually has of one's legs and lacking that leads to a sense of being unwell. The picture, then, is of feeling unwell involving a deviation from the normal states of consciousness that are a result of good health.

We can call this account of well-feeling a "conscious abnormality" account because it doesn't posit a positive feeling for wellness but instead posits a sense of unwellness resulting from deviations from the normal feelings of a healthy person. Some of these deviations involve the introduction of feelings that indicate the lack of health, and some involve the loss of feelings that are typical of good health. There needn't be, and there likely isn't, a single type of phenomenal feeling that is present when one is healthy or unhealthy. Nevertheless, the various unusual conscious states of a sick person are unified by what they indicate about the patient's lack of health. This lack, though indicated by phenomenal abnormalities, is not a matter of something phenomenal missing. It is a matter of the improper functioning of the body that constitutes poor health.

I suggest a similar story can be told about mineness and the pathological cases. There are a number of things that must be working well for us to feel like ourselves, agents in control and possession of our bodies and thoughts. But there needn't be any single type of phenomenal state that comes with that. When certain connections fail, psychological abnormalities manifest themselves in phenomenal abnormalities that lead to a feeling of alienation. The phenomenal abnormalities that generate this feeling of alienation are apt to be diverse. When my leg doesn't seem like my leg, it might well be because there are a number of conditions that must obtain for my leg to work correctly and when those don't occur there might be a number of things—conscious and otherwise—that lead me to say that it seems to me the leg isn't mine. There might well be a number of different things that need to happen for me to feel emotions like a normal person.

If those things are missing, or other peculiar conscious states are added, I might be led to say the emotions don't feel like they are mine. This doesn't imply that they lack me-ness—it's rather that they lack or possess a certain characteristic (perhaps conscious, perhaps not) that typifies the emotions and bodies of normal subjects, and this deviation from the norm leads to a sense of alienation.

We can see this sort of situation at work in other breakdowns of subjectivity. Consider the feeling of controlling an avatar in a video game. Most of us are familiar with the frustrating process of figuring out the controls, pushing thumbs this way and that as the guy on the screen jumps around like a fool. We are painfully aware of our hands and thumbs, and the avatar is just a character on the screen, comical in its ineptness. After a while, though, our thumbs and hands fade into the background and a certain transparency sets in. If we become involved enough, there is an almost mindless flow as we dodge axes and jump tree trunks. The character becomes ours. There is no single sort of phenomenal state that marks this transition. There is simply an unperturbed fluency. If, however, there is an increase in the latency of the network connection, generating a slight lag between movements on the controller and actions in the game, one can feel strangely disassociated from the avatar. There is a sense of non-responsiveness, a frustration with the fact that the avatar is escaping one's control. The controller becomes salient as do one's hands on it. If there is a bug in the game, leading to random departures from expected avatar behavior, one can disassociate from the character altogether and the spell is broken. This is not to say that there is a lost feeling of mineness. It is rather that one feels estranged from the avatar because of a breakdown in normal functioning.

The cases of health and video games are, of course, mere analogs for what is going on in depersonalization. But they can help us reflect on the phenomenology of cases that might well be similar. In these cases one might well report the sudden loss of something—health, agency, control—without its being the case that there was a positive feeling that accompanied normal health, agency, or control. In these cases we report a lack, but it is precipitated by a feeling of a lack, not the lack of a feeling.

The conscious abnormality account is very close to a view Billon considers, that depersonalization is explained by a new feeling of alienation rather than a lost feeling of mineness. In previous work with Kriegel, he seems willing to countenance this sort of explanation when it comes to thought insertion (Billon and Kriegel 2015). But he doesn't think the case can be extended to cases of depersonalization. He argues that in depersonalization "patients explicitly complain that a certain feeling or impression that they used to have is lacking." In support of this he cites Janet who "even coined the term 'feeling of incompleteness' ('sentiment d'incomplétude') to designate the core of depersonalization's experience" (Billon, Chapter 14, this volume). Janet's term, though, is completely consistent with—and perhaps even supports—the view that what is possessed is a feeling of a lack, not a lack of a feeling. The patient reports Billon mentions in this context are similarly consistent with the view. For example, according to Sierra (2009, p. 8) "they claimed they could think clearly and properly about everything, but the essential was lacking, even in their thoughts." Something essential might indeed be lacking. But instead of there being a feeling that is lacked, the lack of something normal might be designated by an abnormal feeling. Some patient reports, admittedly, are suggestive of a missing sensation. For example, according to one report, "The functions and acts of ordinary life, it is true, still remain to me; but in every one of them there is something lacking. That is, the sensation which is proper to them" (Sierra 2009, p. 8). Even these sorts of reports are quite consistent with the account I am giving, though. There might well be sensations that typify normal experience, which lead the subject to a certain sort of ownership is lacking. That sensation need not be mineness, however. Just as the presence of an abnormal feeling might indicate a lack of health or normal subjectivity, so too the absence of a normal feeling might indicate a lack of health or normal subjectivity. Consider again an analogy with sickness. When I don't feel well, my senses of smell and taste are typically dulled. Food doesn't taste the way it should. Those sensations that are absent indicate that something is wrong—that I am sick—but it is not plausible that the normal crisp taste of the food should be regarded as a wellness feeling. I'm inclined to say that the patients' own reports suggest this sort of reading. Notice that the patient here says ordinary things lack "the sensation which is proper to them." That suggests that there is something that is proper to various things—just as tastes are proper to various foods. It doesn't suggest that there is some sensation that all "owned" states have that is missing. It's quite plausible that there are a number of conscious qualitative features that help the subjective system calibrate itself with both internal and external states of affairs, and the loss or disruption of these would precipitate this sense of a lack.

The view I am suggesting argues that instead of positing a single experience of "mineness" that is normally present but that goes missing with depersonalization, there might be a range of abnormalities that flag a breakdown of normal subjectivity. These might take the form of positive sensations that indicate a lack of normal functioning, or they might take the form of a lack (or alteration) of sensations that accompany normal experience. It might be objected that this account lacks the explanatory unity of Billon's account, and Billon goes to some length (in section 5.3 of Chapter 14) to argue that since depersonalization is a unified disorder it should receive a unified psychological explanation. This is persuasive, but a psychological explanation of a disorder can be unified without appealing to something phenomenal that unifies it. On my view the disorder is not explained by the various phenomenal abnormalities, it is explained by the psychological abnormality indicated by these phenomenal signs. The nature of that explanation will presumably reveal itself to psychological investigation into the mechanisms of agency, many of which operate below the level of consciousness but have effects on consciousness when they fail.[17]

In response to views that deny that depersonalization really lacks mineness, Billon encourages us to take patient reports seriously, and not to think them a result of irrationality or confusion. There is no evidence, he says, to suppose that these patients are poor phenomenologists. But the account I am offering needn't posit such confusions or irrationalities. Or, in any case, we needn't think the patients are any more confused than we are when we say we aren't feeling well. True, if one wants the structure of one's statement to accurately represent the presence or absence of qualitative states, it might be more accurate to say that we're feeling unwell. But we're not wrong, confused, or irrational when we say we aren't feeling well. Similarly, it's not being uncharitable to these patients to say that their reports are accurate even though they don't track the distinction between the lack of a feeling and the feeling of a lack, or between the lack of a feeling of normality and the feeling of abnormality. We are being as charitable to these patients as we should be, given our reports in similar cases.

I'm inclined to think, actually, that the view I am advancing is in the end more charitable, because it takes seriously the reports of all of us who don't find a feeling of mineness in unreflective experience even when we are trying to be careful phenomenologists. In my view, we should take these people's reports very seriously, since they are actually attending to the relevant distinctions and are in many cases people who are practiced at attending to phenomenological differences. Of course even professionals can get things wrong, and most of us haven't had experiences as extreme as depersonalized patients. But given the conscious abnormality account, we needn't say anyone is wrong. The depersonalized patients are truly reporting the abnormality of their phenomenology and the resulting sense of estrangement, and the phenomenologists who endorse transparency are correct that subjective character is missing in unreflective experience.

6. Transparency and Conclusion

I have argued that unreflective experience is transparent in such a way that leaves no room for phenomenal mineness on that level. This view is challenged by

---

[17] Since I am suggesting that there is a cluster of phenomenal abnormalities that characterize depersonalization, why not call the lack of this cluster phenomenal mineness or subjective character? First, in some of these cases the lack of the elements in this cluster would involve nothing positive to serve as subjective character. Second, even in the cases in which there is something phenomenal lacking in depersonalization, what is lacking is a certain sort of qualitative character to experience. But subjective character is supposed to be distinct. Just as it seems wrong to say that the vivid taste of food that I lack when I'm sick is a feeling of wellness, it seems incorrect to say of certain qualitative sensations possessed by normal people but lacked by depersonalized subjects "mineness."

reports of depersonalization, but I have suggested a natural way to account for those reports that reconciles them with unreflective transparency. In normal experience there is no feeling of mineness. Depersonalization cases involve abnormal phenomenology that indicates that the psychological processes underpinning subjectivity are abnormal. Things like the execution of action are less automatic, perhaps, and responses to stimuli are distorted and strange. In fact, I suggest that instead of indicating a missing subjective character, this abnormal phenomenology might well involve the emergence of a sort of self-consciousness— processes that are normally untroubled and under the radar suddenly make an appearance in consciousness and present the subject with himself. It is precisely this that is alienating. Another way to put this is that in these pathological cases transparency itself begins to fail. Our thoughts and sensations no longer take us directly to the exigencies of the world they present, and our limbs no longer operate as automatic and unproblematic executors of our will. In depression and depersonalization an opacity is introduced into the heart of consciousness, and we begin to make a sort of appearance to ourselves. Unfortunately, though, this appearance does not reveal us as vibrant subjects but as tiresome objects whose proper place in the world is in question. If this is correct, the irony is that it is precisely the lack of me-ness and mineness that is characteristic of the healthy, non-depersonalized individual. The moment our sensations and bodies appear to be in need of mineness, the moment they lose their transparency and become salient, they lack the connections to our subjectivity that make them most ours.

References

Billon, Alexandre. 2011. "Does Consciousness Entail Subjectivity? The Puzzle of Thought Insertion." *Philosophical Psychology* 26 (2): 291–314.

Billon, Alexandre. 2014. "Why Are We Certain That We Exist?" *Philosophy and Phenomenological Research* 89 (2).

Billon, Alexandre and Uriah Kriegel. 2015. "Jaspers' Dilemma: The Psychopathological Challenge to Subjectivity Theories of Consciousness." In R. Gennaro (ed.), *Disturbed Consciousness*. MIT Press. pp. 29–54.

Block, Ned. 1995. "On a Confusion about a Function of Consciousness." *Brain and Behavioral Sciences* 18 (2): 227–247.

Dainton, Barry. 2008. *The Phenomenal Self*. Oxford University Press.

Dretske, Fred. 1995. *Naturalizing the Mind*. MIT Press.

Guillot, Marie. 2016. "I Me Mine: On a Confusion Concerning the Subjective Character of Experience." *Review of Philosophy and Psychology* (online May 27 2016).

Harman, Gilbert. 1990. "The Intrinsic Quality of Experience." *Philosophical Perspectives* 4: 31–52.

Howell, Robert J. 2016. "Perception from the First-Person Perspective." *European Journal of Philosophy* 24 (1): 187–213.

Hume, David. 1978. *A Treatise of Human Nature*. Ed. L.A. Selby-Bigge. Oxford University Press.

Husserl, E. 1952. *Ideas: General Introduction to Pure Phenomenology*. New York: Macmillan. (Original work published 1913.)

Kriegel, Uriah. 2009. *Subjective Consciousness: A Self-Representational Theory*. Oxford University Press.

Merleau-Ponty, Maurice. 1994. *The Phenomenology of Perception*. Routledge and Kegan Paul.

Moore, G.E. 1903/1965. "The Refutation of Idealism." *Philosophical Studies*. Littlefield, Adams & Co., 1–30.

Nida-Rümelin, Martine. 2017. "Self-Awareness." *Review of Philosophy and Psychology* 8 (1): 55–82.

Nida-Rümelin, Martine. 2018. "The Experience Property Framework: A Misleading Paradigm." *Synthese* 195 (8): 3361–3387.

Prinz, Jesse. 2012. "Waiting for the Self." In Liu, JeeLoo, ed., *Consciousness and the Self*. Cambridge University Press.

Sartre, Jean-Paul. 1957/1993. *The Transcendence of the Ego: An Existentialist Theory of Consciousness*. Octagon Books.

Sierra, M. 2009. *Depersonalization: A New Look at a Neglected Syndrome*. Cambridge University Press.

Tye, Michael. 2000. *Consciousness, Color, and Content*. MIT Press.

Zahavi, Dan. 2005. *Subjectivity and Selfhood: Investigating the First-Person Perspective*. MIT Press.

Zahavi, Dan. 2014. *Self and Other*. Oxford University Press.

Zahavi, Dan and Uriah Kriegel. 2015. "For Me-Ness: What It Is and What It Is Not." In D.O. Dahlstrom, A. Elpidorou, and W. Hopp, eds., *Philosophy of Mind and Phenomenology*. London: Routledge.

5

Mineness, Deflation, and Transparency

Gianfranco Soldati

1

Gilbert Ryle famously argued that there is no «difference in kind between a person's knowledge about himself and his knowledge about other people» (Ryle, 1949, p. 181). He especially opposed the «theory that minds must know what they are about, because mental happenings are by definition conscious, or metaphorically self-luminous» (Ryle, 1949, p. 161). Ryle did not accept the idea that there is something in our experiences being conscious that plays a role in the explanation of the distinctiveness of self-knowledge.[1] He had qualms both about consciousness being luminous and about self-knowledge being *sui generis*.

Less than thirty years later Donald Davidson proudly announced that «Ryle was wrong» (Davidson, 1987, p. 441). Davidson argued that Ryle «stoutly maintained that we know our own minds in exactly the same way we know the minds of others, by observing what we say, do, and paint» (Davidson, 1987, p. 441). Contrary to this, Davidson suggested that «it is seldom the case that I need or appeal to evidence or observation in order to find out what I believe; normally I know what I think before I speak or act» (Davidson, 1987, p. 441).

Davidson went on developing his own account of self-knowledge, concentrating on one of its central aspects, namely epistemic authority. He did not really wonder whether there was something about the conscious features of experience that would play a role in the explanation of self-knowledge. On the contrary, Davidson emphasized that the authority of self-knowledge can be fully accounted for without relying on anything as experiences, understood as mental objects that are directly given to the mind. In spite of the declared disagreement, Davidson was disregarding the conscious features of experience in his account of self-knowledge just as plainly as Ryle did. They both opposed the Cartesian tradition,

---

[1] Self-knowledge is knowledge of a subject about herself as a subject. It is typically expressed by utterances containing the first-person pronoun. As such, self-knowledge can be about any fact concerning the subject. In this chapter, I shall restrict myself to self-knowledge concerning experiences, i.e. knowledge in the first person about one's own experiences. Unless explicitly stated, the expression 'self-knowledge' will be used with such a restriction.

Gianfranco Soldati, *Mineness, Deflation, and Transparency* In: *Self-Experience: Essays on Inner Awareness.*
Edited by: Manuel García-Carpintero and Marie Guillot, Oxford University Press. © Gianfranco Soldati 2023.
DOI: 10.1093/oso/9780198805397.003.0005

which was said to attribute a special role to the conscious and subjective character of experience.[2]

But what exactly does it mean to attribute a special role to the conscious character of experience in one's account of self-knowledge? There are various answers to that question. In this chapter, I am interested in one such answer. It is the answer that says that a proper account of self-knowledge needs to consider a special feature of conscious experience, namely the fact that each experience comes with a feeling of first-personal ownership, sometimes called phenomenal mineness. I shall try to understand what exactly is meant by this sort of mineness and then elucidate its potential in playing a role in an account of self-knowledge. I shall argue that phenomenal mineness is not required for a proper account of first-personal knowledge of one's own experiences.

In *section 2*, I shall introduce the notion of mineness as it is used in some recent writings by Kriegel and Zahavi. It will appear that it is related to the idea that an experience *is given* in the first person in a special way, different from the way it is presented in the third person. I shall assume that the expression 'to be given in a certain way' can be interpreted epistemologically, thus referring to a way one can come to know something. To say that an experience is given to the subject in a special way is thus to say that there is a special way a subject can come to know her own experience. I shall focus on the claim that there is a direct relation between phenomenal mineness and first-personal knowledge of one's own experiences. The claim under scrutiny will be that one cannot accept the idea that there is a special way a subject can come to know her own experience and yet reject the presence of phenomenal mineness. I shall label this contention the *mineness link*. In the following sections of the chapter, I shall argue against it and propose an alternative. An argument against the mineness link is not as such an argument against phenomenal mineness. In this perspective, the present chapter pursues a different goal than Howell's and McClelland's contributions in this volume. They both aim at confronting the advocates of phenomenal mineness with arguments challenging its reality. The present project might thus be understood as arguing for the epistemological inefficiency of mineness, rather than for its psychological unreality.

In *section 3*, I discuss deflationist accounts of self-knowledge and mineness. These are different forms of deflationism, but they are related. Deflationism about self-knowledge (*epistemological deflationism*) says that an account of the specificity of self-knowledge does not rest on introspective evidence. Deflationism about mineness (*phenomenal deflationism*) says that there is nothing more to the mineness of an experience than the fact that it occurs in me, a subject. Kriegel and Zahavi reject the latter form of deflationism and argue that we must accept a phenomenological fact involving mineness in addition to the mere fact that an

---

[2] See also (Davidson, 1988).

experience occurs in a subject. I show that their argument fails to speak for the link between mineness and self-knowledge. We do not need to accept a phenomenological fact involving mineness in order to explain the specificity of self-knowledge. This being so, epistemological deflationism about self-knowledge is still in the running. It might still be the case that a proper explanation of the specificity of self-knowledge does not need to appeal to any phenomenal mineness.

Section 4 introduces the notion of transparency that is often used by epistemological deflationism. Kriegel and Zahavi argue that mineness is compatible with transparency. There are various forms of transparency. I start by introducing a notion of transparency (as characterized by M. Boyle) that is meant to be general enough to cover various variants. According to such a general notion of transparency, there is a route to first-personal knowledge about one's own experiences that does not rely on any inner or introspective warrant. Instead of saying that my experience is given to me in a different way than it is given to you, we should say that the world is given to me—when I want to find out something about my own experience—in a different way than it is given to you—when you want to find out something about my experience.

Before returning to the issue about compatibility with mineness, we need to enquire into the roots of transparency. *Section 5* focuses on the case of judgement and argues for a rationalistic account of the transparency of judgement: when one judges that p one has a reason to judge that one judges that p because the reason to which one is responding by the first-order judgement rationally commits one to the second-order belief. This result is presented as a consequence of the fact that rationality does not only require one to avoid having contradicting beliefs, or to form the beliefs that are appropriately commanded by the reasons one has, but that it also demands a cogent sensitivity to the reasons one has.

Section 6 summarizes the argument and presents the conclusion that if there is a sense of phenomenal mines that is compatible with transparency, it is far from involving the sort of phenomenological fact Kriegel and Zahavi are arguing for.

Section 7 sketches the main lines of an extension of the rationalistic account presented in section 5 to conative states, such as desires.

2

The idea that conscious experiences come with a sense of ownership which plays a role in the explanation of the way we come to know about them in the first person is not new. It was articulated by a number of authors belonging to the tradition of German Idealism.[3] I shall, however, concentrate on a more recent

---

[3] See (Frank, 2002) and the influential (Henrich, 1967).

102   MINENESS, DEFLATION, AND TRANSPARENCY

proposal, made by Dan Zahavi and Uriah Kriegel, in part separately and in part in a common publication.[4] In this section, I shall quote some passages in order to extract the central claims. I shall later look more closely at some of the arguments.

Let me start with a passage from Dan Zahavi:

> Imagine a situation where you first see a green apple and then see a yellow lemon. Then imagine that your visual perception of the yellow lemon is succeeded by a recollection of the yellow lemon. [...] If we compare the initial situation [...] with the final situation [...], there has been a change of both the object and the intentional type. Does such a change leave nothing unchanged in the experiential flow? Is the difference between the first experience and the last experience as radical as the difference between my current experience and the current experience of someone else? We should deny this. Whatever their type, whatever their object, there is something that the different experiences have in common. [...] The different experiences are all characterized by the same fundamental first-personal character. They are all characterized by what might be called a dimension of for-me-ness or mineness.   (Zahavi, 2010, p. 58)

This passage contains a claim and a terminological suggestion. The claim is that there is something common to all the experiences of one and the same subject, independently of their content and mode (or «intentional type», as Zahavi calls it). It remains constant in the flow of experience and it is something none of those experiences shares with experiences of another person. The terminological suggestion is to call this fundamental first-personal character, *for-me-ness* or *mineness*. I shall use the second term.

Most people who think that we have conscious experiences might be prepared, *pace* Ryle, to endorse the claim that those experiences are given to their owner in a way that is very different from the way somebody else's experiences are given. But Zahavi has an opponent in mind who goes further, maintaining that «there is no property common to all my experiences, no stamp or label that clearly identifies them as mine» (Zahavi, 2010, p. 59). To such a contender he responds as follows:

> this objection is misplaced in that it looks for the commonality in the wrong place. The [...] mineness in question is not a quality like scarlet, sour, or soft. It doesn't refer to a specific experiential content, to a specific *what* [...]. Rather, it refers to the distinct *givenness* or *how* of experience. [...] It refers to the fact that the experiences I am living through *are given* differently [...] to me than to anybody else.   (Zahavi, 2010, p. 59, my emphasis)

---

[4] I shall assume there is one view at stake, although I suppose that each of them might distance himself from some of the claims accepted by the other.

Which is to say, as Kriegel and Zahavi put it:

> What-it-is-like-ness is properly speaking what-it-is-like-for-me-ness.
> (Kriegel and Zahavi, 2015, p. 36)

The issue then does not concern so much the asymmetry between first- and third-personal access to one's experience, but the status of the feature common to all experience of one and the same person. We are told that it «does not refer» to an experiential content, a *what*, but to a givenness or *how*, which is now called "what-it-is-like-for-me-ness."

These are technical terms that are meant to point to something that, I suppose, cannot easily be described with a more mundane terminology. One important point is that one should not think of mineness along other common phenomenal qualities, such as those related to colours, tastes, or smells. It is rather something all experiences of one and the same subject have in common. But what does it mean to say that it is a *how* rather than a *what*? The distinction between what (or that) and how is often used in order to oppose theoretical to practical knowledge. To know how to do something is not the same as to know what is the case, or to know that such and such is the case. But mineness is not announced as characterizing some sort of knowledge. The distinction might rather concern different aspects of experiences. There is something one experiences, this is *what* one experiences, and there is the way one experiences it, this is *how* one experiences. But when an apple appears round, red, and sweet, is it not right to say that sweet is the *way* the apple tastes and that red is the *way* is looks? We certainly say things like this: "*How* does the apple taste? It tastes sweet." The distinction between how and what is not straightforwardly helpful for setting mineness apart from other phenomenal features of experience. We should probably wait for more information in order to settle the point. Let us agree for the moment that mineness is a feature common to all experiences of one and the same subject and that no experience of another subject can share it.

Such a claim obviously needs clarification in order to be properly evaluated. If it is read as meaning that the common phenomenal feature A's experiences share with nobody else's experiences is constituted by the simple fact they are A's experiences and not anybody else's experiences, then it will be difficult to find any contender. Zahavi is indeed happy to make a stronger point. He declares that «anybody who denies the [...] mineness of experience simply fails to recognize an essential constitutive aspect of experience. Such a denial» he insists, «would entail the view that my own mind is either not given to me at all—I would be mind- or self-blind—or present to me in exactly the same way as the minds of others» (Zahavi, 2010, p. 59). This is the contention that one cannot endorse the idea that my own mind is present to me, or *is given to me*, in a different way than it is present or given to you, and yet reject the claim that experiences all have the common feature of phenomenal mineness.

Let us consider the supposedly Rylean *reductionist claim*: my experience is given to me in the same way as your experience is given to me. Much depends on what is meant by the locution 'given to'. A first guess would be that the locution is used in this context in order to characterize *ways of acquiring knowledge*. Among the different ways one can obtain knowledge, some are distinguished by the fact that they offer an epistemic warrant. So the reductionist claim under this interpretation denies that there is a fundamental distinction between first-personal and third-personal warrant for knowledge of one's experiences. This comes indeed close to what Ryle seems to have had in mind, or at least to what Davidson took him to have said. Zahavi's contention would then be that one cannot endorse the idea that there is any asymmetry between first-personal and third-personal warrant for knowledge of one's experiences, and yet reject the claim that a subject's experiences have the common feature of mineness. This establishes an explicit relation between mineness and self-knowledge.

If this is the right interpretation, then Zahavi's claim would reject not only reductionist positions like Ryle's, but also more conciliatory positions, like Davidson's, who accept an asymmetry between first- and third-personal access to one's own mind without supposing any experiential mineness. The issue, in this sense, is not whether one should accept mineness, but whether one must accept it in order to make a distinction between first-personal and third-personal access to the mind. To maintain that there is such an obligation means to maintain that there is a strict link between self-knowledge about one's own experiences and mineness. Let me call this the *mineness link*.

In what follows I shall inquire with more details into the precise relation between mineness and self-knowledge about one's experiences, and into some arguments that might be taken to speak in favour of the mineness link.

3

Deflationist accounts of self-knowledge may generally be characterized by the fact that they aim at providing an account of the specificity of self-knowledge that does not rest on any introspective evidence.[5] As such they do not need to deny the mineness link. They might simply reject the idea that mineness plays a role in a proper account of self-knowledge by virtue of being introspectively accessible. If at all, the mineness link would have to obtain by virtue of some other feature.

Zahavi and Kriegel think that deflationist accounts ought to be rejected. They write:

---

[5] Cf. (Soldati, 2014).

The for-me-ness of experience still admits of two crucially different interpretations. According to a deflationary interpretation, it consists simply in the experience *occurring* in someone (a 'me'). On this view, for-me-ness is a non-experiential aspect of mental life—a merely metaphysical fact, so to speak, not a phenomenological fact. In contrast, a non-deflationary interpretation construes for-me-ness as an experiential aspect of mental life, a bona fide *phenomenal* dimension of consciousness. On this view, to say that an experience is *for me* is precisely to say something more than that it is *in me*. It is to state not only a metaphysical fact, but also a phenomenological fact.

(Kriegel and Zahavi, 2015, p. 36)

According to a deflationist following Kriegel and Zahavi's interpretation, mineness of experience can be reduced to the fact that the experience is 'in' a subject. They call this a metaphysical fact (I find this terminology awkward, but I shall adopt it for the sake of the argument) and they oppose it to a phenomenological fact, which would contain more than just the fact that an experience belongs to, or is the property of a subject.

We have two forms of deflationism here. Deflationism as I defined it above is silent about phenomenal mineness and about the mineness link. It simply insists on the fact that mineness cannot play any evidential role in self-knowledge. Let me call this *epistemological deflationism*. Deflationism in Kriegel and Zahavi's conception goes further. It reduces the phenomenological fact involving mineness of experience to a metaphysical fact about ownership of experience. Call this *phenomenal deflationism*. The latter implies the former. If there is no genuine phenomenological fact involving mineness, then mineness cannot play any role, let alone any evidential role, with respect to self-knowledge. By rejecting phenomenal deflationism one has not yet rejected epistemological phenomenalism. One must reject phenomenal deflationism, however, in order to question epistemological deflationism. One must establish that experiences have phenomenal mineness if one intends to show that mineness plays a role, whether evidential or other, in self-knowledge.

We saw above that on Kriegel and Zahavi's view there is a link between self-knowledge and phenomenal mineness. If they think that the relation is not evidential, then they owe us an alternative account. I shall simply assume that they would minimally agree that mineness plays a role in determining the specific warrant for self-knowledge.[6] In this section, I intend to show that the phenomenological fact is not better suited to explain the epistemological peculiarity of self-knowledge than the metaphysical fact. From this it will be possible to

---

[6] As I said above, I take this to be implied by the idea that there is a specific way one's own experiences are given to oneself, which I understand as meaning that there is a specific way one comes to know one's own experiences.

conclude that a rejection of phenomenal deflationism cannot be used as a starting point for an argument against epistemological deflationism.

Let us assume that the metaphysical fact we are considering is the fact that, for any singular experience, it necessarily belongs to (occurs in the flow of consciousness of) one and only one subject. No two subjects can share one and the same experience. Does this fact contribute to an understanding of self-knowledge? Much depends, of course, on what one generally requires for an attribution of knowledge. But the necessity of p does not generally suffice for one's belief that p to qualify for knowledge, let alone self-knowledge. Even if I believe that I want an ice-cream, and if this present desire is necessarily mine, this does not suffice for me to know that I want an ice-cream. One would typically require my desire to offer me a reason for believing that I want an ice-cream. So, the metaphysical fact that my experiences are necessarily mine might contribute to self-knowledge, but it does not suffice to explain its specificity.

Does the phenomenological fact fare any better in this respect? Unfortunately, it does not. The phenomenological fact, we are told, contains mineness as a *bona fide* phenomenal dimension. Whatever that may be, it seems safe to say that there is a difference between the metaphysical fact that this experience is necessarily mine and the intended phenomenological fact involving mineness. Let us call this phenomenological fact an f-fact ('f' may thus be short for 'experienced mineness'). Consider now the following peculiar argument. (i) We suppose that we all have our own, personal f-facts. I have my own f-facts and you have your own f-facts. (ii) My f-facts are given to me in a different way than they are given to you. (iii) So, I know that I have an f-fact in a way you cannot come to know. But why is this so? (iv) It can't be so just because my f-facts are necessarily mine (see argument above). (v) So, there must be something about f-facts that accounts for the fact that I come to know them in a way you cannot come to know them. (vi) Call this feature 'hyper mineness', a super-phenomenological feature that explains the asymmetry. (vii) And so on.

The argument is odd, but its peculiarity is not easily removed. For instance, it is not a matter of first-order *vs* second-order beliefs, or of pre-reflexive against reflexive consciousness. The mineness of my experience may be given pre-reflexively, or in a first-order belief (the two claims are not equivalent): the argument would still go through. There is simply a problem with the idea that the obtaining of a special phenomenological fact, in addition to what Kriegel and Zahavi call the metaphysical fact, would help to make any progress.

It is rather common at this point to appeal to perspectival, subjective facts. Again, much depends on what such facts are supposed to be. One rather common interpretation is that perspectival facts are facts whose nature prevents them from being known from any perspective but one. Suppose that f-facts are such facts. They can be known only from the perspective of the subject they are about. Only

I can know my f-fact, and only you can know your f-fact. One may arguably wonder why such an asymmetry should apply to f-facts at all. If I can know that you are having a pain, why should I not be able to know that you are experiencing your pain as yours and not mine? But even apart from that, it is unclear how the perspectival character of experiences is related to the alleged mineness which constitutes the f-fact. The perspectival character of experiences is often explained by emphasizing the way the first person would attribute them to herself—namely by using the first-person pronoun. No other person can do so in order to state the same fact—indeed the *same* fact: the fact that one is having a certain experience. There is no obvious need to introduce mineness in order to explain that kind of perspectival difference. It certainly is a difference that applies to the self-attribution of experience just as much as to the self-attribution of any other property. You, but not me, can express the fact that you are alive by using the first-person pronoun. But this does not require the fact that you are alive to contain some sort of mineness. So f-facts being perspectival does not show that they are so in virtue of involving some phenomenal mineness.

The above argument is certainly not meant to show that a subject having an experience cannot be a perspectival fact. Quite to the contrary. It is rather meant to show that if we do not understand what makes the fact I am having an experience perspectival, then adding the phenomenal property of mineness to the very same fact won't bring any substantial progress. Special phenomenological facts are not suited to explain the specificity of self-knowledge. If the introduction of those special facts was supposed to offer an alternative to a deflationist conception of self-knowledge that would reject phenomenal mineness, then the point was misguided. The upshot is not that the deflationist must be credited with a convincing argument against phenomenal mineness, but that phenomenal mineness does not deliver a contribution to a better understanding of the specificity of self-knowledge.

4

One central argument in deflationist accounts of self-knowledge uses an introspective feature often called 'transparency'. Transparency has many facets, but there seems to be a core idea that has suitably been characterized by Matthew Boyle as follows:

> I can *know* various aspects of the nature, content and character of my own mental states by attending in the right way, not to anything 'inner' or psychological, but to aspects of the world at large. Indeed, it seems that [...] all there is for me to contemplate in my sensation of blue is the (apparent) blueness of some

worldly thing, and all there is for me to attend to in my belief that P is the (apparent) fact that P. Various questions about my own present mental state are thus normally 'transparent' for me to questions about the world at large.

(Boyle, 2011, pp. 225–6, my emphasis)

Kriegel and Zahavi wonder whether transparency speaks against phenomenal mineness. They argue that:

phenomenal consciousness does not only represent but also *presents* something (to someone). Compare a conscious perceptual experience of the color and shape of a yellow lemon and a subliminal or blindsighted representation of the same color and shape. Both represent the same distal features [...]. But only the experience *presents* those features, in the sense of making *someone* phenomenally aware of them. To that extent, although all the presented items are worldly items, the presenting itself—presenting to someone—is an aspect of phenomenal consciousness as well. There is thus a minimal dimension of for-me-ness without which we cannot distinguish consciousness from unconscious representations of the same environmental features. This minimal for-me-ness is fully consistent with the contention that *once* a state of a subject presents something to the subject, it *is necessarily* [*my emphasis*] some putative environmental feature that it presents [...]. If we interpret the transparency claim as exhausted by this contention, we can appreciate that *transparency is compatible with for-me-ness* [*my emphasis*].   (Kriegel and Zahavi, 2015, pp. 40–1)

There are four central steps in this argument. First, it is assumed that both a conscious and an unconscious (perceptual) experience *represent* some features of the external world. It is then argued that in a conscious representation those features are further *presented to someone*. This expression is taken to mean that one is phenomenally aware of those features. In a conscious experience one is phenomenally aware of the represented features. But now, third step in the argument, this very phenomenal awareness is taken to be equivalent to for-me-ness. So, conclusion of the argument, what distinguishes conscious from unconscious representations of the world is something (phenomenal mineness) that cannot be reduced to a represented feature of the world. Transparency is compatible with the acceptance of phenomenal mineness, if it is understood as implying that one does not find mineness among what is represented, or consciously presented, neither by looking inside nor by looking outside—simply because mineness itself is an aspect that is never presented *to* the mind.

What is the relation between Kriegel and Zahavi's notion of transparency and the notion Boyle has been using in the passage quoted above? In what follows I shall first inquire into the mechanics of the sort of transparency Boyle has described above. I shall then come back to the compatibility claim made by Kriegel and Zahavi.

If mineness is an aspect of experience that is supposedly compatible with transparency, then transparency in Boyle's sense would entail that I can come to know that aspect by attending to aspects of the world at large. What does that mean? Remember that we were wondering about how mineness impinges on an account of the specificity of self-knowledge. We were asking what role mineness plays in the explanation of the asymmetry between first-personal and third-personal knowledge of one's own mental states. If we apply Boyle's notion of transparency, the difference between my way of knowing my own experience and your way of knowing my experience should not be accounted for in terms of me attending to something other than to aspects of the world at large. The asymmetry between first-personal and third-personal knowledge should then be accounted for in terms of which aspects of the world we would be attending. In order to find out something about my experience I should attend to aspects of the world that are somehow different from the aspects you would attend to in order to find out something about my experience. Instead of saying that my experience is given to me in a different way than it is given to you, we should say that the world is given to me (when I want to find out something about my own experience) in a different way than it is given to you (when you want to find out something about my experience). This is the recipe for the application of Boyle's transparency. We intend to establish whether it is compatible with phenomenal mineness. But before doing so, we must understand how its application can be supported. What kind of considerations speak in favour of transparency *à la* Boyle?

Boyle's transparency is typically applied to acts of judging. Suppose you deliberate about what to do tomorrow. You look at the weather forecast and judge on its basis that it will snow tomorrow. By applying transparency in Boyle's sense to this act of judging, we obtain the claim that you can come to know aspects of your own judging by attending in the right way, not to anything 'inner' or psychological, but to aspects of the world at large. You come to know that you judge that it will be snowing not by looking inside, but by looking into the world. If mineness is supposed to be an aspect of your act of judging, and if transparency in our sense is supposed to be applicable to it, then you ought to attain knowledge about it by attending to some aspect of your environment. Indeed, it has often been argued that a subject may come to know that she judges that *p* by attending to the world in order to find out whether *p*.[7] Why is that so?

---

[7] (Evans, 1982, p. 225) is often quoted for this idea. More recent versions of the notion can be found in (Moran, 2001, p. 66), (Moran, 2012), and (Byrne, 2011). There are differences between the different usages of the notion of transparency. I have discussed the differences, and presented the epistemological version of transparency I am using in this chapter in (Soldati, 2014).

5

Here is a diagnosis of this form of transparency. The issue concerns the relation between the judgement that p (Bp), and the judgement that one judges that p (BBp).[8] It appears that the reason one has for judging that p suffices, in the first person, for the self-attribution of the very same judgement. In other words: if I wonder whether I am judging that p the reason I find for judging that p settles the question as to whether I am judging that p. By virtue of what does this transmission of reason obtain? In this section, I shall contemplate some options and argue for an account that paves the way for an alternative understanding of the relation between mineness and self-knowledge.

One might first take the relation between Bp and BBp to be simply inferential.[9] But that would indeed be peculiar. There is no logical relation between p and Bp. The fact that it is raining does not entail that I judge that it is raining. We should rather look for an alternative. One such alternative uses the notion of rationality as a relation between different attitudes of one and the same subject. It is irrational for instance to believe that p and to believe that p is not the case. If one finds oneself in such a situation, one should aim at resolving the conflict. The rationality requirement offers a reason to drop one of the two beliefs. But it does not suffice to decide which of the two beliefs one ought to drop. One needs to look for independent reasons speaking in favour of one of the two beliefs. The situation in our case is of a similar kind, with important differences.

There is something incoherent in me believing that p and believing that I do not believe that p, although the two beliefs do not contradict each other. The irrationality of the situation becomes manifest when a subject expresses that doxastic state by declaring: 'p, but I do not believe that p'.[10] We surely expect a subject caught in such a predicament to adopt an alternative set of beliefs. Why is that so although there is no contradiction between Bp and $B\neg Bp$?

One might point out that Bp speaks in favour of BBp and against $B\neg Bp$. This is certainly right, but it can't be the whole story. It is not *just* a question of Bp speaking against $B\neg Bp$. A belief is not irrational simply by virtue of there being a fact speaking against it. The belief might simply be mistaken. So even if the fact that one believes that p speaks in favour of attributing the belief to oneself, it does not suffice as such to establish the irrationality of doing the opposite. One might naturally respond that Bp and BBp do not stand in the same relation as p and Bp.

---

[8] I use the symbol 'B' although I speak of acts of judging for simplicity. I shall occasionally use the term 'belief' for stylistic reasons in what follows, but I mean acts of judging, not the disposition or tendency to do so.

[9] See (Byrne, 2008).

[10] This of course is related to what is often called Moore's paradox (see Moore, 1993, p. 209). The idea that the paradox has something to do with rationality is expressed for instance in (Shoemaker, 1995, p. 225.) and (Moran, 1997, p. 144). More about my view on this in (Soldati, 2014, p. 175 ff).

After all: by judging that p one is not simply creating a reason for attributing the belief to oneself. One *holds* that very reason. It might indeed be argued that if I *have* a reason to judge, then I am rationally required to judge (or for that matter: to act) on its basis. To have a reason to judge that p means to see (to be aware of the fact; to have reflective access to the fact) that one ought to judge that p. One should thus feel the obligation to do so.

This might be accepted. But the kind of incoherence that becomes manifest in the assertion of 'p, but I do not believe that p' cannot be fully explained in those terms. Contrast our case with the case of one perceiving that p and believing that p on its basis. If one's perceptual experience provides a reason for judging that p, then by perceiving that p one is rationally required to judge that p. That reason can nevertheless be trumped by considerations speaking against it. This alone does not modify the nature of the perceptual experience.[11] But precisely this happens in our case. It is not possible for one to wholeheartedly judge that p and yet find a reason to doubt that one judges that p. If one finds a reason to doubt that one is judging that p, then it cannot further seem to one that one is judging that p. Consider an example.

Suppose I am standing on the peak of a mountain and I feel the pouring rain sliding down my shoulders. I see and feel the falling rain. In the light of this experience I judge that it is raining. My belief is formed in response to my full appreciation of the fact that it is raining. Can I come to judge that I do not judge that it is raining while fully appreciating the fact that it is raining? It seems that the only way for me to form that second-order belief is that I somehow stop to fully appreciate the fact I am experiencing. But if I do that, then my first-order judgement will sag as well. I simply cannot wholeheartedly embrace a reason for judging that p and find a reason to doubt that I judge that p. The conjunction of Bp and $B\neg Bp$ is unstable in face of fully appreciated evidence.

The root of the incoherence under consideration rests neither in the simple fact that the belief that p speaks in favour of the belief that one believes that p, nor in that fact that by believing that p one acquires a reason to form the belief that one believes that p. The alternative hypothesis is that by believing that one believes that p one ought to be responding to the very same reason to which the first-order belief is sensitive. In the conjunction of Bp and $B\neg Bp$ one reacts to one and the same reason by taking incompatible commitments. This is a specific form of irrationality. It is not the case of having beliefs with contradicting contents. Nor is it the case of having a reason and not forming the belief it commands. It is rather the case of having conflicting attitudes towards one and same reason. Rationality

---

[11] This is sometimes glossed by saying that the fact that one can find grounds for doubting that p does not remove the possibility of it perceptually seeming to one that p. I think that this is not the proper way of describing the situation, since I do not think that perceptual experiences have correctness conditions as usually understood.

does not only require one to avoid having contradicting beliefs, or to form the beliefs that are appropriately commanded by the reasons one has, it also demands a cogent sensitivity to one's reasons.

The difference between these various rational requirements becomes manifest when one considers the routes of their fulfilment. Consider first the rational instability generated by the conjunction of Bp and $B\neg p$. We saw that rationality demands to revise one of the two beliefs, but rationality alone does not determine which of the two contradicting beliefs one ought to drop. One *needs* to look for further reasons. This is different in the case of one having a reason speaking in favour of a belief. If one is offered a ground for forming a belief one would rather not have, one cannot reason from the undesirability of the belief to the absence of the ground. The fact that I'd rather not believe that I just lost my front tooth does not discredit the fact that it appears to be missing when I look at myself in the mirror. One can, however, flood the perceptual experience with evidence speaking against its authority. This undermines the reason provided by the experience without modifying the experience itself. The relation between Bp and BBp is like the latter in the sense that simply by judging that p one has all one needs to be rationally required to judge that one judges that p. One cannot reason from the absence or undesirability of BBp to the rejection of Bp. Contrary to the case above however, one cannot discredit the reason provided by the first-order judgement without corroding that very judgement. If one has enough reasons to doubt that one is judging that p, then one is not only questioning the authority of the judgement, one is spoiling the judgement itself.

When one judges that p one has a reason to judge that one judges that p not simply because one judges that p, but because the reason one is thereby responding to rationally commits one to the second-order belief. This is the source of the transmission of the reason from one's judgement that p to the judgement that one judges that p.

6

We were wondering what conclusions one can draw about the nature of phenomenal mineness from the application of transparency. I said that if mineness is an aspect of experience, then transparency would entail that I can come to know that aspect by attending to aspects of the world at large. I can thus come to know that my act of judging is mine, i.e. that I am judging, by attending to aspects of the world at large. The asymmetry between first-personal and third-personal knowledge should not be accounted for in terms of the first person attending to something other than to aspects of the world, but rather in terms of which different aspects of the world she would need to be attending.[12]

---

[12] In his chapter in this volume Howell writes that «while it seems to make sense to project the phenomenal character of redness onto a car—so that the subjective features of redness don't appear

In the light of the considerations made above about the sources of transparency, we may now conclude that the difference between first-personal and third-personal knowledge about one's own experiences lies in the fact that the experiences themselves belong to the aspects of the world one must take into consideration in order to attain third-personal knowledge, but not so in the case of first-personal knowledge. The same point can be expressed by saying that the experience itself constitutes evidence for the attribution of the experience in the third person, but not so in the first person. The experience delivers a reason for the self-attribution, but it is not itself the reason one responds to in self-knowledge.

On this understanding of transparency, phenomenal mineness might simply be understood as the kind of rational commitment one acquires through an experience. In this sense Kriegel and Zahavi's compatibility claim would be confirmed. For this to be the case, however, we do not need a phenomenological fact in addition to the metaphysical fact Kriegel and Zahavi were rejecting. On the contrary. The idea that we should accept an additional phenomenological fact in order to explain the asymmetry between first- and third-personal knowledge about one's own experiences is a symptom of the fact that one looks for further evidence after having realized that the simple presence of the experience did not suffice. The mistake was there from the beginning: it is the consequence of not having properly appreciated the rational roots of transparency.

7

The rationalistic account sketched so far is generally confronted with an objection concerning its applicability to experiences that appear not to respond to reasons. We seem to be able to attribute such experiences to ourselves, but the rational mechanics described above would not apply to them. Should we then concede that at least for those cases the mineness link applies?

A proper reply to such an objection would obviously need an argument that goes far beyond the scope of the present chapter. Let me however indicate the two main directions such an argument might go. One ought to consider first the fact that the realm of consciousness that is responsive to reason is wider than one might think. Second, one might arguably distinguish between experiences that constitute the core self, which are sensitive to reasons, and experiences that are attributed to the self in the light of their relation to the core self. I shall leave the

---

subjective but appear as a modification of the car—it doesn't seem plausible that we project the subjectivity of sensations. What would it be, after all, to project the mineness or for meness of a sensation? Is it that something out there—like the redness of the car—presents itself as belonging to me, or even some random conscious subject? This is implausible». In the case of sensations, the point may seem plausible. It is less plausible in the case of beliefs. The judgement that p presents p as my reason to attribute the judgement to myself.

discussion of the second point for another occasion. In what follows I shall sketch the main lines of the first one.

Let us thus consider the extent to which consciousness is responsive to reasons. We dealt above with the case of judgement which might be taken as a prototype of an attitude that is responsive to reasons. What about intentions to act, desires, and other conative attitudes? In judging that p one naturally responds to something in the light of which p appears to be true. The reason for judging that p is provided by one's awareness of something speaking in favour of p's truth. Similar considerations apply, *mutatis mutandis*, to intentions to act and to desires. In forming the intention to act, one naturally responds to something in the light of which the action ought to be performed. The reason for intending to do something is provided by one's awareness of something speaking for the importance, the utility, or simply the value of the action. A desire is not simply a brute urge for an action. It involves a sense for the desirability of the latter's outcome. In desiring p one forms an attitude in the light of p's desirability. There is something about p that constitutes one's reason to desire p.[13]

These are some initial characterizations of the way desires and intentions to act respond to reasons. Many more details would be needed in order to provide the beginning of a proper account. One might urge, however, that even granting these initial characterizations, there is a fundamental difficulty that prevents the extension of the rationalistic account to conative states. The point concerns the fact that conative states, contrary to cognitive states, cannot be true or false. Transparency, it might thus be expected, cannot be applied to them in the same way as it applies to judgements.

Let me concentrate on the case of desire. P's desirability speaks in favour of the *belief* that p is desirable by letting the belief that p is desirable appear true. The relation of p's desirability to the desire itself cannot be of the same kind. There is another relation instead. P's desirability speaks for the desire for p not by letting the desire appear true, but by letting it appear appropriate, or fitting. In desiring p one experiences p as having the kind of features that make it seem right for one to desire it. To desire p is to experience p under the guise of the good, however bad one may judge p to be under a different light. To experience p under the guise of the good is not to experience p's being good under the guise of the true. If this is right, if the reason of one's desire doesn't speak for its truth, then one may wonder how it could speak for the truth of its self-attribution. The point can be made in more general terms. Consider a situation where one desires p (Dp) and judges that one desires p (BDp). For the rationalistic account of transparency to apply, the reason provided by Dp should somehow be transmitted to BDp. But if the

---

[13] For reasons of simplicity, I shall assume that one typically desires p, where the latter is some fact or state of affairs. Nothing in what follows should depend on this specific assumption, as opposed to the view that one can (also) desire a particular.

reason for *Dp* doesn't speak for the truth of *Dp*, how could it possibly speak for the truth of *BDp*? If at all, one might surmise, it could speak for the appropriateness of *DDp*.

A further but related problem appears to threaten the application of transparency to conative states. Remember the point we made above about belief. I argued that by maintaining *Bp* and *B¬Bp* one reacts to one and the same reason by taking incompatible commitments that manifest the absence of a cogent sensitivity to reasons. If one has enough reasons to doubt that one is judging that *p*, then one is not simply questioning the authority of the judgement, one is spoiling the judgement itself. We contrasted the case of belief with the case of perception, by showing that one can undermine the perceptual experience with evidence speaking against its authority without modifying the experience itself. Desire resembles perception in this perspective. One certainly feels the pressure to adjust one's desire when one finds it unfitting. But one may be sceptical about the reasons that seem to make one's desire appropriate without thereby destroying it. One does not need to suppose an instance of amorality in order to acknowledge the phenomenon.

There is one central point where the analogy appears to limp. When a desire presents *p* under a positive light, it typically does so with respect to some, but not all its features. These are *evaluative features*, features that are responsible for the evaluative response, whether conative or cognitive. The desire to smoke a pipe presents smoking under a positive light with respect to the taste of tobacco, or with respect to the stimulating effect of nicotine. The belief that smoking is not desirable is typically formed in the light of considerations concerning health hazards. The positive light the desire sheds on smoking bears on features that are not at stake when one judges that smoking is undesirable. In such cases the tension between desire and belief is generated by the fact that the features in the light of which *p* is desired are not identical to those in the light of which it is judged to be contemptible. Let us call this a situation of *external tension* between desire and belief. One is forced to deliberate between conative evaluative features of one kind and cognitive evaluative features of another kind.

When we find a desire inappropriate, we may wonder how it can be sustained. The desire may indeed respond to a feature we are not able to articulate. One may desire *p* without being able to say what one finds desirable about *p*. The apparent incoherence might here be rooted in the fact that we simply do not know the feature in the light of which *p* is desired. We may know that *F* makes *p* undesirable, but we do not know in the light of what we desire *p*. Confronted with a person who desires some *p* we take to be disagreeable, we naturally wonder which features of *p* she experiences as valuable. This is only confirmed by the fact that the discovery of the features that make *p* desirable is generally prompted by the desire, rather than the reverse. We experience the desire as an indication of there being something desirable in *p*, even if we don't know what it is.

The question can now be raised as to the proper description of a situation where one judges that p is repulsing in the light of the very same evaluative features under which it is desired. Can one both desire to smoke in order to enjoy the taste of tobacco and sincerely judge that the taste is repulsing?[14] One may naturally judge that being F makes p desirable and yet fail to desire p even in the light of its F-ness. The issue concerns the possibility of one wholeheartedly judging that F makes p undesirable, and yet experiencing one's desire as appropriate with respects to p's F-ness.

This situation should again be distinguished from the case of one desiring p for the very sake of its badness. Perversion may be the condition that is required for such a desire to be possible. It is the satanic case of one desiring p in the light of the evil rather than the good.[15] Even if conceptually possible, we have a clear sense of the deep disturbance of such a conative frame of mind. I shall ignore this case in what follows. It needs a separate treatment.

Let us then concentrate on the situation where one's desire presents p's F-ness in the light of the good and one yet judges it to be bad in the light of the very same features. It is a situation of *internal tension* between belief and desire. The situation ought to be distinguished from the simple presence of contradictory evaluative judgements, such as the judgements that F-ness makes p good and the judgement that it makes it bad. The central difference concerns the available procedures one may adopt in order to solve the tension. In the case of contradicting evaluative beliefs, the standard assumption would be that one of the two beliefs must be false. One would thus look for further reasons speaking for one of the beliefs and against the other. (Or alternatively look for different standards of evaluation). The evaluative judgements respond to reasons by making them available for deliberation. Suppose for instance that one ends up believing both that p is good and p is bad. This is a flat contradiction. Unless one of the beliefs is simply false, the default assumption is that the contradiction can be solved by finding distinct features that speak for both beliefs.

This is not what happens in the case of desire. One does not typically look for a reason speaking for or against one's desire. One rather experiences one's desire as providing one with a reason for the corresponding evaluative judgement. The case is particularly vivid in situations of internal tension. If I desire p I may wonder about the feature under which p appears desirable. I may wonder why I want to smoke and find that it is the taste of tobacco which makes smoking desirable.[16] But to experience one's desire for p as fitting with respect to p's F-ness is simply to have a reason to believe that there is something good about p—its F-ness. To

---

[14] As mentioned above, I am assuming that the desire to smoke is not a sheer pull and that it is not fundamentally concealed to one's conscious awareness.

[15] Cf. (Velleman, 1992).

[16] I might thus describe the taste of the tobacco as being the reason of my desire.

desire p and to judge that p is bad, with respect to one and the same evaluative feature, would be to deliberately form a belief in flat opposition to the only available reason.[17]

Can a desire be questioned in the light of considerations speaking against its authority without spoiling the desire itself? The considerations above have shown that this is possible when there is an external tension between desire and evaluative belief. It is much less obvious that this can happen in case of an internal tension. In order to question the authority of one's desire for p, one must find a feature in the light of which p is judged to be bad. This would inevitably transform the internal tension into an external one.

The considerations above offer a first basis for a rationalistic account of the self-attribution of desire. The self-attribution of a desire and of the corresponding evaluative judgement respond to the same evaluative features. The same reason is used in both cases. The relevant difference between the evaluative judgement and the corresponding desire lies in the way they respond to evaluative features. The judgement makes them available for deliberation, the desire does not. This has consequences for their self-attribution. According to the rationalistic account, in judging that I judge that p is good I respond to the same reasons to which I respond in judging that p is good. Reasons against attributing the judgement to myself jeopardize the judgement itself. The application of the rationalistic account to desires starts from the assumption that the desire responds to the same reason as the corresponding evaluative judgement. The distinctive feature of desire is that it presents that reason in a way that leaves no room for deliberation. I thus attribute a desire to myself when I am presented with a conclusive evaluative reason. There is transmission of reason in the sense the very reason to which my desire responds is used in the self-attribution of the desire. The desire itself does not constitute additional evidence. To experience a conclusive evaluative reason in a desire is enough for one to attribute the desire to oneself. It should be clear that the claim that a desire presents a conclusive evaluative reason does not imply that one cannot deliberate about one's desires. The point is that such a deliberative process involves a move from an internal to an external tension. It must concern different evaluative features.

The suggested account faces various objections. Some are internal to the account. One may wonder, for instance, whether the present account leads to a view that treats desires as if they were perceptions of evaluative facts. I think that there is something to this idea. Desires and perceptions are both instances of one being directly aware of a fact. They should not be analysed in representational terms. In both cases one should distinguish the fact one is aware of from the way

---

[17] One may doubt that such a belief can be formed at all. If, all things considered, the desire for p offers the only available reason for the belief that p is good, then one would have to *decide* to believe that p is bad. It is doubtful that this corresponds to a psychological possibility.

the fact is articulated in belief. Errors in the conceptual articulation must not be attributed to the nature of the awareness. Both perception and desire offer conclusive reasons. Desires, in opposition to perceptions, deliver evaluative reasons. Both perceptions and desires are attributed to oneself not on the basis of their phenomenal mineness, but on the basis of the way they make reasons available to the subject.

A different sort of objection would insist on the idea that some desires are experienced as sheer pull. One fully acknowledges that it is bad to φ, but one still fells a pull to φ. I am supposing that this is not a case of experiencing φing under some positive light. As such, I would rather not call it a desire. It is more like an urge to scratch one's head. If this is what is meant, then I would suggest treating such experiences along with other experiences, such as itches, that are only derivatively attributed to oneself. I attribute them to myself by virtue of their relation to experiences I can directly attribute to myself. But this, as I said, is a topic for another occasion.[18]

References

Boyle, M. (2011) 'Transparent Self-Knowledge', *Aristotelian Society Supplementary Volume*, 85(1), pp. 223–241.

Byrne, A. (2008) 'Knowing that I Am Thinking', in Hatzimoysis, A. E. (ed.) *Self-Knowledge*. Oxford University Press.

Byrne, A. (2011) 'Transparency, Belief, Intention', *Aristotelian Society Supplementary Volume*, 85(1), pp. 201–221.

Davidson, D. (1987) 'Knowing One's Own Mind', *Proceedings and Addresses of the American Philosophical Association*, 60, pp. 443–458.

Davidson, D. (1988) 'The Myth of the Subjective', in Benedikt, M. and Burger, R. (eds.) *Bewußtsein, Sprache und die Kunst*. Verlag der österreichischen Staatsdruckerei, pp. 45–54.

Evans, G. (1982) *The Varieties of Reference*. Oxford University Press.

Frank, M. (2002) *Selbstgefühl. Eine historisch-systematische Erkundung*. 2nd edn. Suhrkamp Verlag.

Henrich, D. (1967) *Fichtes ursprüngliche Einsicht*. Klostermann.

Kriegel, U. and Zahavi, D. (2015) 'For-Me-Ness: What It is and What It is Not', in Dahlstrom, D.O., Elpidorou, A. and Hopp, W. (eds.) *Philosophy of Mind and Phenomenology*. Routledge, pp. 36–53.

Moore, G. E. (1993) *Selected Writings*. Edited by T. Baldiwn. Routledge.

---

[18] I should like to thank two anonymous referees. Their comments have been greatly helpful.

Moran, R. (1997) 'Self-Knowledge: Discovery, Resolution, and Undoing', *European Journal of Philosophy*, 5, pp. 141–161.

Moran, R. (2001) *Authority and Estrangement*. Princeton University Press.

Moran, R. (2012) 'Self-Knowledge, "Transparency", and the Forms of Activity', in Smithies, D. and Stoljar, D. (eds.), *Introspection and Consciousness*. Oxford University Press, pp. 211–238.

Ryle, G. (1949) *The Concept of Mind*. Hutchinson & Company.

Shoemaker, S. (1995) 'Moore's Paradox and Self-Knowledge', *Philosophical Studies*, 77(2–3), pp. 211–228.

Soldati, G. (2014) 'Prospects of a Deflationary Theory of Self-Knowledge', in Hügli, A. and Horn, A. (eds.), *Die anthropologische Wende*. Schwabe Verlag (Studia philosophica), pp. 169–188.

Velleman, J. D. (1992) 'The Guise of the Good', *Noûs*, 26(1), pp. 3–26.

Zahavi, D. (2010) 'The Experiential Self: Objections and Clarifications', in Siderits, M., Thompson, E., and Zahavi, D. (eds.), *Self, No Self? Perspectives from Analytical, Phenomenological, and Indian Traditions*. Oxford University Press, pp. 56–78.

6

Mineness and Introspective Data

Wayne Wu

1. Introduction

Many philosophers claim that there is a phenomenal sense of mineness in various mental phenomena: bodily sensations, thoughts, perceptual experiences, and the experience of action. Call this feature *phenomenal* mineness or *mineness* for short. Relatedly, mineness is sometimes lost yielding phenomenal *not-mineness.* We can speak of *positive* and *negative* mineness where the latter can be construed either as the absence of positive mineness or the presence of something different, an additional phenomenology we might call *alienness.* These features are often said to be *felt*: X feels like mine or does not. A growing philosophical and empirical literature focuses on explaining such phenomena in mundane and abnormal experience (this volume) though there is dissent, those who question in different ways this phenomenology (this volume).

I join the dissent by questioning how we have dealt with the primary data, namely introspective reports. If a subject reports the presence of mineness, proponents of mineness often take these reports at face value. This yields a *face value inference* to postulating a phenomenal property of mineness in the experience. This is sometimes taken as an inference to the best explanation of the report (Billon this volume). I question the inference. Introspective data is complicated, and we theorists of consciousness have not always treated that data rigorously. Mineness brings this out.

In any scientific domain, data is worked up so it can support good inference. Introspective data is, as we shall see, raw yet not worked up. I will unpack "working up" by example but what it is to systematically process introspective reports is a matter that requires philosophical discussion. Further, what makes for the best explanation is complicated, but *parsimony* is a plausible factor. Consider an approach where we agree on a set P of phenomenal or psychological properties not including mineness. P can provide a neutral set of explanatory materials for discussions where mineness is in dispute. A *parsimony principle* holds that if we can explain *reports* of mineness by appeal to P, namely why the subject generates them, then we should not further attribute phenomenal mineness because there is no reason to. P suffices. In many cases, those who posit mineness unnecessarily

---

Wayne Wu, *Mineness and Introspective Data* In: *Self-Experience: Essays on Inner Awareness.*
Edited by: Manuel García-Carpintero and Marie Guillot, Oxford University Press. © Wayne Wu 2023.
DOI: 10.1093/oso/9780198805397.003.0006

expand P.[1] In this essay, I shall apply the parsimony principle to question the face value inference for mineness. My main goal is to bring to the fore a set of methodological issues regarding data for consciousness that we have too often skipped over.

In central cases, the face value inference from introspective reports is not appropriate. First, I show that the reliability of introspective reports on its own does not always license inference back to phenomenology because the process of generating those reports can be complex, not a simple "reading off" of phenomenology. Second, I raise doubts about the status of some of the core empirical data. I examine the rubber hand illusion, but the lessons generalize: we need to work up introspective reports more carefully. Finally, I urge the importance of exploring detailed, empirically grounded alternative models when claiming that mineness provides the best explanation. Failure to do this might lead to erroneous claims of providing the best explanation. I explicate this response by focusing on loss of mineness in action in schizophrenic delusion of control. We have strong reason to be suspicious of attributions of phenomenal mineness as a distinct sensory phenomenal feature.

2. What Are We Trying to Explain?

In general, if scientists dispute conclusions, they go back to the data.

Since the relevant phenomenal properties are in dispute, we cannot begin with a neutral description of mineness, so we must return to the data of mineness *reports*. The reports have two forms:

- *Positive Mineness*: X seems to be mine
- *Negative Mineness*: X does not seem to be mine[2]

Let us note some clarifications. It is not necessary that subjects use the precise terminology of "being mine/not mine." For example, in delusion of control (see sections 5–6), subjects often say that their action belongs to a specific entity, say some external agent A, but as a report, I shall construe this provisionally as an expression of negative mineness and not assume that it identifies a further phenomenology, the *being-of-A-ness* (say, being of the devil). If you are disinclined to speak of a phenomenal being-of-A-ness in delusion of control, this is due to implicit application of the parsimony principle. In general, every theorist of

---

[1] In general, many philosophical accounts of experience expand P via introspective reports. An alternative approach is to endorse mineness but to *reduce* it, namely to show that it is *nothing more than* some subset of P. This is arguably Mike Martin's approach (Martin 1992).

[2] Guillot (2016) identifies three senses of mineness/ownership. The sense at issue here comes closest to her third notion of "mineness." See p. 31 of her article for discussion and representative quotes.

consciousness applies the parsimony principle at some point to introspective data: it is not the case that for every "F" in a subject's report that they *feel F* that one posits a specific phenomenal *for-Fness* to experience. Where to draw the boundary for parsimony is what is in question.[3]

"Seem" in these schemas stands for a variety of experiential verbs, say "feels." "X" can stand for psychological states or events, the body and its parts, and actions, mental or bodily. In the case of the rubber hand illusion, "X" extends to inanimate objects (Botvinick and Cohen 1998). Depending on the context, such claims can be utterly mundane or strikingly odd. If a friend holds up her hand and says, "This seems to be mine," there is nothing to deny. The visible hand is a part of her body. Now consider when, through proprioception, the individual says of her hand, "This feels to be mine." On the face value inference, the subject is taken to introspectively attend to a phenomenal property reflecting how her hand feels at that moment. Does the report support that attribution?

Introspection is doing heavy lifting, but I myself do not find any distinctive phenomenal mineness. For example, proprioception reveals how my body feels in a way that is not currently available to you: you cannot proprioceptively feel my body. I have a distinctive way of experiencing my body as an extended entity in space, namely in terms of an *egocentric* spatial presentation. If this egocentricity is all that is meant by mineness, then I have no objection. This is consistent with the parsimony principle: mineness is a label for the egocentric spatial content of proprioception and somatosensation (this strikes me as close to Martin's position (Martin 1992)). I find nothing over and above that. Others differ on this, and this means that we disagree on what introspection reveals. Unfortunately, we have no way of calibrating introspection to adjudicate this clash (but see Spener (2015)). How then should we deal with introspective data? Well, it's complex.

3. Not Feeling Myself

Let us begin with a report that seems *prima facie* reliable and mundane: reports of feeling *like myself* or feeling not like myself. That is, reports of positive and negative *myselfness*. Such reports can indicate underlying illness or discomfort, a difference in thought and behavior, and these reports are useful in social and medical contexts. I shall apply the parsimony principle to undercut the face value inference from these reports to a phenomenal *feeling-myself* or *not-feeling-myself*. The point is that while the reports are accurate in that they identify a property of one's

---

[3] Some of the reluctance to run the face value inference will depend on the relevant sense of "feel" or "seem." In the equivalent "look," we distinguish between epistemic, phenomenal, and comparative uses (Jackson 1977). Indeed, these nuances will come to the fore in discussing the Rubber Hand Illusion where "feel" is ambiguous in ways that complicate introspective reports as data.

experience (as we shall see, a relational property), it does not seem fruitful to speak of such properties as *phenomenal* properties. In this case, there isn't, in the phenomenal sense, a *feeling*-myself.

Regarding the phenomenal, it is often said that appearance is reality, yet the inference from *seems X* to *is X* is either trivial or fallacious. It is trivial if "seems" is read in a phenomenal sense, for it effectively affirms that seemings are seemings. The reality of the phenomenal is that it is phenomenal. The inference is substantive if "seems" is read in its epistemic sense, but then the inference is not valid. Certainly, if the report of an epistemic seeming does capture the phenomenal, then how an experience seems, i.e. how I take it to be, is how it is. One accurately represents the phenomenal. Yet that something seems to me to have a certain phenomenal character does not guarantee that it does have that character (see Schwitzgebel (2011) for a variety of cases). In respect of parsimony, the issue is that a subject can reliably report that an experience has a certain property Φ and yet there is good reason not to add Φ to P for the extant members of P can on their own account for why the subject reports Φ.[4]

"I feel not like myself," is something many of us have expressed when tired, ill, or having acted abnormally (see Howell, this volume, for discussion of a similar case). It expresses what it is like for us, inviting concern, not perplexity. Consider also the report: "I feel like myself again. Thank goodness!" "Feel" is a perceptual verb, but like "seem," it can signal an epistemic attitude of cognitively taking or entertaining things to be. Is there a specific phenomenal feature of *phenomenal feeling-myself* or a *phenomenal feeling-not-myself* that introspection locks onto allowing the subject to read-off phenomenology? If so, we can make the face value inference.

Earlier, I worried about when raw introspective data licenses appropriate inferences. Concerned questioning in effect works-up data about myselfness by uncovering the subject's basis for her judgment, and this does not suggest a special phenomenal feature: *myselfness*. We can ask, "What's wrong? What feels off?" The subject responds that her actions feel (are taken to be) off kilter. Normally patient, she has been short-tempered with loved ones; generally frugal, she has spent extravagantly at every opportunity; frequently agreeable, she has expressed contrary opinions vehemently. Alternatively, a subject might feel an unfamiliar pressing on the shoulders that leads to discomfort, a feeling that movements are slower than normal, that thoughts are not as snappy as is their wont. Not feeling like oneself is multiply realizable, and what grounds the judgment is a recognized contrast between a (statistical) norm and one's current state, a difference that one can recognize and express to those who are concerned. Once this line of thinking

---

[4] It does not follow where the extant members of P can explain reports that an experience seems Φ that Φ is *reducible* to P. Someone can appeal to explanatory parsimony with respect to Φ without committing themselves to reducing it. They might, after all, be *eliminativists* about Φ.

is brought forward, the not-oneself judgment is perfectly intelligible. Indeed, this new data discourages positing distinct phenomenal properties of *myselfness*. The subject notices a difference: Normally (typically) I feel a certain way and, now, I feel differently. That is not how I normally am. I feel not my (normal) self. The next day, when things seem normal, the subject can now report: "Thank goodness! I feel like myself again." This is not the announcement of the return of a missing phenomenal property but the elimination of a noticeable difference.

The contrast proposal draws on differences that the subject can introspect, focusing on mundane phenomenal features that on their own do not fix a specific phenomenal feature of myselfness. We can track the underlying properties, say that of pain or other uncomfortable feelings that track illness or bodily unease, or our salient attitudes or our actions "from the inside" and on the basis of tracking and comparing, notice that we are not our normal selves. It is hard to deny that, *sometimes*, judgments of not-feeling-myself are based on reliable introspective contrast regarding elements that are antecedently familiar. This contrast explains the report and there is no need to posit a special phenomenal property over and above what is in P, the neutral features we (and others) can discern that explain the contrast. I shall draw on this capacity to detect contrast in experience in what follows, something that I think is quite mundane.

No doubt, someone can press the point: yes but couldn't there be a phenomenal *myselfness* in these cases? That is to reject parsimony, something I assume is not an attractive option in the current case.[5] In any event, any attempt to reject parsimony for myselfness would have to show that parsimony provides a *worse* explanation and, as things stand, it is not clear that it does. So, the face value inference does not provide an inference to the best explanation. In the case of myselfness, we can see introspective reports as accurate in picking up a relational contrast in one's current experience but not as licensing the positing of a distinctive phenomenal property.

4. *Mineness* in the Rubber Hand Illusion

Proponents of mineness often point to the rubber hand illusion (RHI) as robust empirical evidence for "feelings of mineness." Yet there are issues regarding the primary data and the parsimony principle applies. I recognize that a specific interpretation of RHI has become entrenched among certain theorists, and that the presumption is that it demonstrates the presence of mineness in somatosensory experience (for a compelling recent defense, see (de Vignemont 2013); de

---

[5] If you find yourself tempted to posit a phenomenal feeling-myself, then find another example where you think phenomenology can be reducible (is nothing over and above) a set of phenomenal features that you take to be uncontroversial posits.

Vignemont's considered view is that RHI is importantly *affective*). Yet the data is complex. I ask the reader's indulgence to look at the data with fresh eyes and to see how the parsimony principle applies here to return a more complex interpretation.[6] What we can agree on is that the effect is reproducible, and that it points to how subjects "experience" the rubber hand. In the end, I shall specify the likely complexity of the experience, but in identifying what contributes to the "feeling of mineness," it will turn out that there is no need to posit new sensory phenomenal properties beyond those already familiar to us. There is no sensory feeling of mineness.

The central data concerns reports revealed in answers to questionnaires after inducing the RHI.[7] Take the original published report (Botvinick and Cohen 1998). Often, the RHI is induced by one's feeling the touch of a paintbrush stroking one's unseen right hand while looking at the synchronous stroking of a rubber hand touched in the analogous location. There is a shift in the experience as incongruent visual spatial information is integrated with somatosensory information (this is a familiar multisensory effect, perhaps most saliently seen in ventriloquism). After experiencing the illusion, subjects are asked to rate on a scale from −3 to +3, 0 being neutral, how strong their agreement is to the following statement: "I felt as if the rubber hand were my hand." Subjects are strongly inclined to affirm this claim. Some of the original data is presented in Figure 6.1.

The data is not exactly perspicuous (NB: the title of the original paper is "Rubber hands feel touch that the eyes see"). Let us begin with the uncontroversial result, the neutral point that provides for the relevant explanatory element in

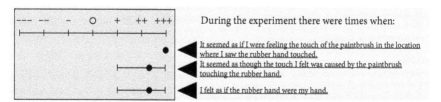

Figure 6.1 A portion of the questionnaire to which subjects respond, from −3 (three "pluses") indicating strong disagreement to + 3 (three "pluses") indicating strong agreement. Claims 1–3 as discussed in the text are arrayed top to bottom. Mean response is indicated by the point while the response range is indicated by the bars. Reprinted by permission from: Springer Nature, *Nature*, "Rubber hands 'feel' touch that eyes see," Matthew Botvinick and Jonathan Cohen, 1998.

---

[6] I'm grateful to Matt Longo and Bigna Lenggenhager for constructive discussions about the experimental data regarding RHI and for good-naturedly tolerating my philosophical skepticism.
[7] Some researcher use the correlated phenomenon of *proprioceptive drift* to track the RHI but as that result on its own wouldn't have motivated talk of feeling as if the rubber hand is one's own, I will focus on the questionnaires. Proprioceptive drift involves subjects mislocating their hand as closer to the rubber hand during RHI.

126   MINENESS AND INTROSPECTIVE DATA

P, where the data is consistently most robust, namely the evidence for a somatosensory *spatial* illusion: one *feels a touch to be* where one sees the tip of the paintbrush, namely on the rubber hand.[8] "Feel" here is a sensory verb expressing the tactile sensation of pressure from a brush. The illusion requires multimodal integration of spatial information between touch and vision, and this secures the importance of the illusion for empirical study: It illustrates an interesting interaction between two sensory modalities (well, three, including proprioception, but let's keep things simple). Let this first data point identify the relevant member of *P* namely somatosensory spatial phenomenology. This is an initial neutral point for applying parsimony.[9]

Claim 3 has become the central datum, and its affirmation by subjects is taken to be strong evidence (a) that there is a phenomenal feature of mineness, (b) it is a property of perceptual experience of our body (c) and mineness can extend to nonstandard objects. I am skeptical about the exact import of the report, but Frederique de Vignemont responds to skeptics thus: "what reasons does one have for not taking the participants at their words when they claim that they experience the rubber hand as their own? The statements describe appearances ('it seemed like')" (de Vignemont 2013, p. 646). In fact, I think there are several reasons.

As noted earlier, "feel" need not refer to a phenomenal appearance. It has an epistemic sense operative in statements such as "I feel as if the world is coming to an end; I feel as if you do not respect me; I feel as if the situation will go south" and so on. Here, the function of "feel" need not be to indicate belief, but something weaker, a gradable attitude of agreement toward a proposition (I feel strongly as if / that…"). In "I do not feel like myself today," one can understand "feel" to register a recognition, and not a sensation, that there is a difference between how I normally feel and how I currently feel (indeed, "feel like myself" suggests a *comparative* sense that fits with the comparative basis of making such a judgment).[10] Interestingly, the one spontaneous report Botvinick and Cohen provide is: "I found myself looking at the dummy hand *thinking* it was actually my

---

[8] As Zina Ward pointed out to me, even Claim 1 is ambiguous for one can read it as a check on whether one feels a touch on one's own hand that corresponds to the analogous location of the rubber hand also being touched (that was how she initially read the claim, as did other students in a seminar on introspection I recently taught).

[9] This spatial illusion is plausibly tied up with a behavioral measure, proprioceptive drift where reports of the location of the subject's unseen hand show a bias toward the rubber hand during conditions of illusion. I do not claim that there is a simple relation between that measure and the experience of multimodal spatial distortion and it would be a mistake to think that there should be a simple relation (e.g. that proprioceptive drift should precisely match reported experience). The importance of the RHI is precisely that it provides an experimentally tractable paradigm to explore multimodal integration of spatial information. That, and not mineness phenomenology, is why it is important.

[10] Shivam Patel emphasized the comparative sense in this context in conversation. It is not clear that this sense will aid proponents of the RHI so I will set aside the reading here as it is the phenomenal sense of sensory verbs that is central to their case (thanks to Shivam Patel for emphasizing the comparative sense).

own" (1998; my emphasis). If this is a restatement of the subject's affirmation of Claim 3, then it reflects the epistemic and not sensory sense of "feel." Yet the interest in the RHI for our purposes is how things *feel* in the sensory sense. This is why the illusion is described as a *perceptual* illusion (Ehrsson 2009).

It is worth noting how entrenched a specific understanding of Claim 3 has become. In a recent BBC documentary on the RHI, a woman undergoing the illusion reports spontaneously, "It's like you're touching my hand with that one [the rubber hand]," a statement that is neutral regarding mineness and which is closest to Claim 2, a claim that does *not* entail Claim 3 understood as reporting a sensory experience qualified by mineness. The experimenter, however, immediately reinterprets her report with the standard interpretation, "So it feels like this [the rubber hand] is your hand that I am touching"—hardly a neutral work up of a subject's report—to which the woman immediately answers, "Yes." If Claim 2 and 3 are distinct, with only the latter expressing mineness, then one possibility is that she does not endorse Claim 3's content but simply, in the quick give and take of marking assent to verbal claims, takes the interrogator's expression of Claim 3 as restating her claim, Claim 2. Data must be approached with care.[11]

Let us expand on the meaning of "feel" which takes at least four readings: two tied to experiences involving the body, an epistemic reading and an affective reading. In other words, "feel" is multiply ambiguous, and this enjoins us to look more carefully at subjective reports in the primary data. Indeed, when theorists speak simply about feeling or experience, they carry over the relevant ambiguity. I claim that none of the four readings supports the standard interpretation that mineness is a phenomenal property qualifying somatosensory experience of our bodies. I shall agree that there is a tactile spatial component to the experience, that subjects think there is something to be said for Claim 3, and that they have affective responses anchored, even if briefly, to the rubber hand during RHI. None of this points to mineness as a distinctive phenomenal property of sensory feeling of one's body.

If mineness is attributed to how the body feels, this assumes a sensory reading but on those readings, it is plausibly inappropriate or false to speak of the rubber hand's feeling as one's own. Consider two sensory uses of "feel." One use is ruled out, namely the *tactile* sense that applies when one feels the rubber hand by touching it. One can speak of an object's feeling like one's own hand because it has a similar felt texture or other tactual quality. This does not apply in the RHI since the subject never touches the hand. On the tactile reading, Claim 3 is false or its

---

[11] The clip is available as a YouTube video with the exchange occurring at 1:12 (though the sequence begins at 0:20 and it is worth noting all the leading descriptions provided by the person inducing the illusion in the subject. Still, despite this, the subject endorses not Claim 3 but Claim 2). In a recent informal attempt to induce the illusion among graduate students, three reported that Claim 2 best captured what they were experiencing. https://www.youtube.com/watch?v=sxwn1w7MJvk

presupposition should be rejected. That is, one should report disagreement with Claim 3, or at least, one should not agree with it.

The other sensory notion of "feel" is tied to proprioceptive experience, as earlier when we imagined a friend saying of her arm, "This feels like mine." Call this the *proprioceptive* sense of "feels." Yet it is also clear that the proposition, the rubber hand proprioceptively feels like mine, makes no sense or again it is false, for no artifact can proprioceptively feel that way because no artifact can be proprioceptively felt. Recall the friend who holds up her hand and says, "This [hand] feels like mine." That expresses the proprioceptive sense, but it would be at the very least odd to say in the same sense, "The rubber hand feels like mine." It does not. We have an interpretive dilemma, namely that on the two sensory readings of "feel" the subjects should disagree with Claim 3 or at least not agree. So how do subjects understand Claim 3 when their answers deviate from what they should say on the two sensory readings of "feel"? Yet the sensory readings provide the standard interpretation for the face value inference to attributions of mineness to somatosensory experience.

One can maintain that subjects experiencing RHI are in fact having a proprioceptive experience as of the rubber hand even if subjects think that actual proprioception of objects that are not their body parts is impossible. Still, I find it hard to proprioceptively imagine what such an experience would be like because I find it plausible that in trying to imaginatively experience that situation, I am just imagining my own hand somehow being where the rubber hand is. In such cases, I imagine feeling my hand as where the rubber hand is (e.g. if it were somehow superimposable on the rubber hand while still allowing me to feel my hand). This would not be to imagine feeling the rubber hand as mine, but feeling my hand to be where the rubber hand is (this comes close to Claim 1).

We can bring out the issue by consider the epistemic sense of "feel" that takes the content: the rubber hand is mine. While appeal to mineness in the somatosensory readings of "feel" suggests a phenomenal property, the natural reading of "mine" in the epistemic reading is not phenomenal. Rather, "mine" is understood as signaling something similar to property ownership as when one says, "That car is mine." This is not to suggest that we think of our bodies as *merely* property (see below on affect, but also de Vignemont (forthcoming)), but mineness here is closer to the property notion than anything phenomenal, and that is the central point. When subjects report *thinking* that the rubber hand is theirs (as in the one subjective report Botvinick and Cohen cite), mineness is *all in the thought*. Still, the subjects know that the rubber hand is not part of their body, and this knowledge should preempt any inclination to *believe* that it is. So subjects again should dissent from Claim 3 since the hand is not theirs. We again have the interpretive problem: how to make sense of the report affirmed since three natural ways of understanding "feel" in Claim 3 suggest that subjects should deny it. What is going on?

It is possible to indicate some level of agreement with a proposition you do not believe or where you believe the opposite. Consider walking out of your home and finding a gleaming red Porsche parked in your driveway, keys in the ignition, next to your olive Subaru, the car you know you own. On reflection, you say what you believe: that Porsche is obviously not mine. Still, throughout the day, no one has called for it and the police have not come knocking. A couple of days later, as it sits there glistening and still undriven, you might say: I believe the car belongs to someone else and, yet, I'm starting to feel as if the car is mine. Months later, you might still believe deep down that it is not yours and yet say: I really feel as if (think) it is mine. Perhaps you sometimes absentmindedly get into it or wash it carefully on weekends, more lovingly than your lonely Subaru.

Indeed, one could say without the air of Moorean paradox: I don't believe it's mine, but I (strongly) feel as if it is mine. One is not speaking of "feeling" in a sensory sense but as indicating an attitude toward the proposition (the other possibility is "feel" in an affective sense to be discussed in what follows). Why is this cognitive sense of "feel" appropriate? Because there's some reason to think the car is one's own. The point is that you can draw on evidence that points to features that one would expect if an object's being one's own (mine) were genuine but in a way that does not entail that you believe it. You can recognize that there is evidence that speaks for a proposition but does not incline you to belief.

The previous example does not provide a perfect analogy, but it illustrates how we can draw on relevant evidence to modulate agreement to a proposition we might not believe. We see something to what is being said. Return to Claim 3. If we consider evidence that might speak in favor of one's owning the rubber hand in the sense of the rubber hand being one's body part, then the phenomenon expressed in Claim 1, the neutral point, can be interpreted as saying something in favor of Claim 3. That is, (A) given the strong spatial illusion of feeling a touch *there* where the rubber hand visibly is, and (2) given that any felt touches are proprietary to one's experience of one's body, these points might incline one to assent to Claim 3 even where one does not believe it.

This assent need not require explicit reasoning, but simply weighing of evidence in contexts of perception-based decision making. Consider recognizing that an oncoming car is approaching too fast to allow one to safely make a turn in front of it. This recognition involves weighing information appropriately, even if one cannot make explicit the factors one weighs. One can in fact report the fact that the car is coming too fast, as when one is sitting in the passenger seat instructing one's teenage child who is learning to drive. In RHI, one approach is to model the illusion as the result of an inference about the cause of the perceptual signals (Samad, Chung, and Shams 2015). The model weights spatial and temporal information from vision, touch, and proprioception to compute a

130 MINENESS AND INTROSPECTIVE DATA

posterior probability of a common cause.[12] So, to explain assent to Claim 3, it is enough to note the spatial distortion in one's experience of one's own body and understanding Claim 3 as an invitation to consider whether there is something to be said for the idea that the rubber hand is one's own.

Let us raise two further questions: (1) can the spatial distortion hypothesis explain other data associated with RHI? And (2) is denying the existence of a distinctive sense of ownership sufficient to explain all phenomena tied to the RHI? These are complex issues and this essay is not the place to hash them out, so let me make preliminary comments.[13] Two robust pieces of data seem to be explainable as a function of the spatial distortion hypothesis, namely proprioceptive drift (the subject's tendency to indicate that their hand position is closer to the rubber hand than it actually is, when subject to RHI) and affective responses to threats to the rubber hand, as when a subject pulls the stimulated hand back when a knife is plunged into the rubber hand. If the subject's own sense of the location of their body is in the direction of the rubber hand, it is a plausible hypothesis that the spatial representations underlying report of hand location would also be similarly distorted. Thus, where a threat occurs close to the felt position of one's body, one might respond by removing that body from the felt position (think of how one turns one's body away from a perceived threat).

Still, one might wonder whether spatial distortion is enough to explain affective responses. The spatial distortion hypothesis can be supplemented with the data from a fourth sense of "feel" tied to affective responses as when we say, *I feel sad, disgusted, afraid, and so on*, or in more complex emotional responses, *I feel like you are my son, that the Porsche is mine, etc.* In the latter cases, certain objects can be targets of affection and be tied to strong bodily and protective responses

---

[12] De Vignemont (see this volume) has emphasized the syndrome of somatoparaphrenia as providing difficulties for non-inflationary accounts. The basic syndrome involves the denial of bodily ownership against a background of asomatoangosia, of which somataoparaphrenia is a special case. A key step is to note that in certain patients, there is "normal" bodily awareness conjoined with bodily disownership. I think the claim that there is "normal" bodily awareness is not substantiated even if, *on certain performance measures*, patients are indistinguishable from controls. In a review of the reported cases of somatoparaphrenia, *all* reported patients exhibit some form of abnormality in motor control, somatosensation, and/or position sense (Vallar and Ronchi 2009, table 1). All that is required is a difference along a salient dimension that triggers reflection leading to judgments that a body part is disowned. Later assertions that a felt body part is not theirs might simply draw on that belief, not on further introspection of ownership or its lack. See also Billon (this volume, Chapter 14) and Howell (this volume, Chapter 4 for a reply).

[13] For (2), consider reports that during RHI, the histamine level in the body increases (Barnsley et al. 2011) and the temperature of the hand being stroked goes down (Moseley et al. 2008). It is very unclear how to understand the etiology of these effects, and postulation of phenomenal mineness hardly explains them. Indeed, it is unclear how the theory of phenomenal mineness in experience of the body would *predict* these effects and I would challenge any theorist of RHI to show why the theory should predict this in an empirically grounded way. Indeed, one might predict that if there is an immune response to the "other" limb that the temperature of that limb should go *up* (think of immune response to infections).

even if none of the items are part of one's body. Material property can induce strong responses. Imagine receiving as a surprise gift, a beautiful but fragile item at a party and how one feels when the guests ask to see the object and begin passing it around, perhaps not too carefully (or consider mistakenly giving one's new smart phone to one's young children at a party who promptly run off with it). One's anxiety can go up, with reflexive behaviors kicking in when one of the passes is fumbled, and substantial emotional responses elicited when the item is dropped and breaks. A colleague reports that when she replicates the RHI with the stabbing in her class, it is not just the subject undergoing the illusion who has a strong response, but the entire audience. The point is that there is something to (affectively) feeling such that we can speak of feelings as if X is one's own (again, consider the jumping audience). This gestures at a familiar, if not uniform, set of responses that gravitate around an object's being literally *owned* (property). Of course, our own body parts anchor more complex affective responses than artifacts that we own, but to acknowledge this, even in the RHI, is not to thereby identify mineness in somatosensory or proprioceptive experience of one's body. It is to register that certain objects can anchor a network of affective responses. What is surprising in RHI is not that an inanimate object can be the focus of such responses, but that a spatial illusion can induce them. But then so can a birthday gift in the right context.

I have noted that the introspective data, measured by assent to Claim 3, is equivocal given the ambiguity of "feel." Where the "feel" implicates sensory awareness of the body, I argued that those claims are patently false or at least of the sort that a normal subject should disagree with Claim 3. I have suggested that where "feel" implicates an epistemic or affective reading, then we have identified plausible elements of the subject's response to the RHI, but that when we unpack those responses, there is no need to posit a phenomenal sense of ownership distinct from familiar phenomena of acknowledging evidence or having affective inclinations. This goes against the grain of much work that interprets Claim 3 to point to a perceptual phenomenon, specifically a way we sensorily experience our bodies as *ours*. The RHI shows that we can treat a non-body part as ours, but this need be nothing more than familiar cognitive and affective responses that do not expand the set *P*.

No doubt, the previous discussion will evoke controversy and I do not expect it to be decisive. Still, if we recognize the ambiguity of "feel" which on its own should raise warning flags about what subjects mean in their introspective reports when assenting to Claim 3, we should recognize that there is complexity in the meaning of those claims that might in fact reflect the actual complexity of the subject's experience in the RHI. On the view suggested here, there are at most three components to RHI experiences: (1) a tactile/proprioceptive spatial distortion; (2) a cognitive attitude that recognizes something to talk of a rubber hand's being one's own; and (3) affective responses that are anchored to objects of concern. There is no additional phenomenal sense of mineness in sensory experience of the body. In a clear sense, we do not feel a rubber hand as our own.

5. Loss of Mineness in Action: Delusion of Control

The previous sections have argued that just because one reports feeling Φ, the face value inference concluding that an experience exemplifies Φ as a phenomenal property is not always warranted. If so, we need to look more carefully at the data, as we did regarding the RHI. I want to conclude this discussion by also locating posits of mineness against the larger theoretical backdrop of any phenomenon for which mineness is being tacked on. I close this discussion by examining a prominent case where one might think positing mineness, specifically its loss, provides the best explanation of a conscious phenomenon. It is not clear that it does.

Delusion of control challenges those who posit mineness as providing the best explanation of our sense of our actions *as belonging to us*. We can all agree that positing phenomenology should connect to extant theories of the mechanisms invoked in the domain in question. Such mechanisms, if widely accepted, are already present in P, our set of uncontroversial psychological capacities and phenomenal features, so do they explain the reports? I shall argue that a prediction mechanism that has been widely postulated to explain delusion of control is not connected to talk of mineness and that it provides an explanation of the abnormality of experience that seems no worse than simply invoking mineness.[14] Yet that explanation is widely accepted and provides a strong counterproposal.

Theorists agree that there must be something abnormal about the experience of action in delusion of control. One explanation appeals to the loss of mineness, for in contrast to normal experience, mineness disappears in delusions of control. In contrast, the alternative explanation I present appeals to two components: (a) the failure of sensory prediction which leads to an error signal that due to resulting phenomenal upshots (b) allows the action performed to grab the subject's attention. This second explanation does not postulate mineness but relies on a mechanism endorsed by most theorists working on schizophrenia.

Everyone can agree that delusion of control involves a loss of normal mineness inherent in intentional action in the neutral sense that normally, when asked, you recognize your actions as your own. Accordingly, we can think of research on delusion of control as probing the normal basis of such mineness in action in individuals who appear to have lost it, so let us begin with understanding how

---

[14] For criticisms of the talk of the sense of agency to which I am sympathetic, see (Mylopoulos 2015). For similar concerns about comparator models and phenomenology in respect of auditory verbal hallucination, see (Cho and Wu 2013).

action mineness can be lost, and then work back to how it is normally present. In delusions of control, agents report that their actions are not theirs but are someone else's. Specifically: they attribute the action to another. Thus, their reports exemplify negative mineness, and for present purposes, I shall work with the parsimonious explanation that treats patients as noticing the *absence* of mineness.[15] Here is a characteristic report from a schizophrenic patient experiencing delusion of control:

> When I reach my hand for the comb it is my hand and arm which move, and my fingers pick up the pen, but I don't control them...I sit there watching them move, and they are quite independent, what they do is nothing to do with me...I am just a puppet who is manipulated by cosmic strings. When the strings are pulled my body moves and I cannot prevent it. (Mellor 1970, p. 18)

Such reports are typically understood as pointing to an oddity in the underlying experience. Let us then provide the following *mineness explanation*: the *absence* of normal mineness phenomenology is noticed by subjects and because it is missing, the subject has experiential grounds for reporting that the experience is not hers. Perhaps subjects notice the *difference* in agentive experience, a capacity we have already encountered (not-myselfness; section 2).

It is important to note that the full story of delusion of control cannot be driven just by phenomenology. Patients not only deny that the actions they perform are theirs but further attribute them to specific entities. If a subject claims to experience her action as controlled by the devil, one could take the face value inference and posit a *being-controlled-by-the-devil* experiential phenomenology but I suspect no one wishes to take this route. Rather, one applies the parsimony principle, drawing on a smaller set of phenomenal properties in P, and then explains the specificity of the report by appeal to additional cognitive factors and propensities. This leads to a two-factor account of delusion where cognitive processes grapple with abnormal experiences (see e.g. (Davies et al. 2001)). On any theory of how agentive *experience* changes in delusion of control, at some point the gap between phenomenology and report is closed by cognitive factors. The task is to first explain what is abnormal about experience.

The mechanisms appealed to in delusion of control can be understood in the first instance as computational mechanisms realized by relevant areas of the brain. We can call these *neurocomputational* mechanisms, namely mechanisms

---

[15] As noted earlier, that subjects report that their actions belong to specific individuals does not tempt us to posit a special phenomenal feeling of being-of-a-specific-individual. Rather, if there is phenomenology beyond the changes brought about by the absence of normal mineness, it would be what is referred to as *alienness*. If proponents of mineness find this unnecessary, then the perspective they are taking with respect to alienness is what I am taking with respect to their view.

that attribute a computational function to a neural network. In delusion of control, the issue concerns areas of the brain that subserve keeping track of actions as one's own. A widely-held model postulates a defect in so-called *self-monitoring* mechanisms that keep track of an agent's own bodily actions (see (Blakemore, Wolpert, and Frith 2002) for a succinct overview).

Self-monitoring is thought to rely on a *corollary discharge* signal that carries information about a motor command. The basic idea goes back to Helmholtz's attempt to explain why the world visually appears stable despite frequent saccadic eye movements (one to three times a second) that shifts the world's projected image onto the retina. Because of eye movement, the retinal image is an ambiguous signal: a shift of the image across the eye could be due to a movement in the world or a movement of the subject's body. What explains the difference between experiencing the world as spatially stable versus as moving? Helmholtz's insight was that the visual system could resolve the ambiguity if it had information from the will, namely information that allowed it to distinguish between changes internally generated and those externally generated (see (Wurtz 2008; Hall and Colby 2011) for reviews of the relevant neural mechanisms and (Wu 2014) for an explanation of visual spatial constancy).

Consistent with Helmholtz's original idea, contemporary theorists deploy corollary discharge to explain visual spatial constancy during eye movement. In motor control theory, corollary discharge has been fruitfully invoked to explain error correction in the on-line generation of accurate movements. It allows the motor system to predict and correct movements even before sensory feedback. In what follows, I focus on the discussion of the mechanism in motor control due to Daniel Wolpert and colleagues (Wolpert and Ghahramani 2000). On this approach, corollary discharge is a signal carrying information regarding an impending movement to neural mechanisms that use that signal to predict sensory and motor consequences of the action. One could say that the mechanisms perform a computation about what the subject is causally responsible for. When the mechanism functions correctly, keeping track of one's movement is partly *predicting* the movement's consequences. In computational terms, the mechanism *compares* the predicted signal carrying information about what will happen to the actual signal carrying information about what has happened, namely incoming sensory information regarding changes in the environment. We can think of this comparison as subtraction of two signals (or, better, the absolute value of the subtraction), and the difference between the signals is the *prediction error*. Where prediction is accurate, the error will be low. When the error is high, that error signal is used to adjust the predictive model as part of fine-tuning action production.

Subjects' reports in delusion of control seem to express their losing track of themselves in action. Feinberg (1978) was perhaps the first to suggest that corollary discharge processing defects might underlie positive symptoms, and the general approach continues to be widely endorsed among theorists of schizophrenia (influentially, (Frith and Done 1988)).[16] There is a body of evidence that suggests that patients with schizophrenia exhibit motor control defects consistent with an underlying defect in self-monitoring (for an influential early set of studies, see (Robert C. Malenka et al. 1982; Robert C. Malenka et al. 1986)). How should we adapt Helmholtz's original idea to explain delusion of control?

Let's begin with the idea that prediction in self-monitoring seems to have phenomenal upshots. Prediction involves the comparison of a predicted with actual signal with the subtraction of signals during comparison resulting in attenuation in the intensity of that signal. If the prediction concerns a sensory consequence, the predicted consequence is compared with the actual perceptual signal. Where the prediction is accurate, then the perceptual signal is attenuated (subtraction). Signal attenuation might then lead to *sensory* attenuation, muting the perceptual sensation.

Is there evidence for such attenuation due to prediction? Certain results are consistent with the hypothesis, such as the phenomenon of self-tickling. Self-tickling is noticeably less ticklish than being tickled by another, and the underlying cause is postulated to be the predictability of the sensory signal in the first case as opposed to the second. When one tickles oneself, the corollary discharge of the tickling movement is used to predict sensory consequences accurately and, hence, in comparing predicted and actual sensory signals, attenuating the latter yields attenuated sensations. Since no such prediction is made when tickled by another, there is no corresponding sensory attenuation. As a result, self-tickling is less ticklish relative to other-tickling. This leads to a prediction: if self-tickling can be made less predictable, sensory attenuation will be diminished and self-tickling should become more ticklish.

Evidence for this was obtained in a study by Blakemore et al. (2000). Using a mechanical device that allowed subjects to tickle themselves, Blakemore et al. induced temporal or spatial distortions in the applied tickle either (1) by introducing a temporal lag between when the subject initiated self-tickling with the device and when the device delivered the stimulation; or (2) by introducing a distortion in the direction of tickling by the device as against the direction of the subject's actual movement. Either distortion should disrupt prediction and, by hypothesis, sensory attenuation. As observed, subjects reported increased ticklishness when prediction was disrupted. Interestingly, for schizophrenia patients experiencing positive symptoms, self-tickling is reported to be as ticklish as when being tickled by others relative to normal subjects and patients in remission, a

---

[16] Predictive coding and Bayesian approaches to explaining delusions have become popular (see e.g. (Fletcher and Frith 2009)). I do not deal with that approach here for several reasons: (a) the approach is less well confirmed for the domains at issue (e.g. motor control and schizophrenia) and (b) one aspect of the approach is the explaining away of *hypotheses*, but in effect, in arguing about the phenomenology we are arguing about what the relevant hypotheses are.

result that is consistent with the postulated defect in self-monitoring. Similar qualitative differences were obtained using a force-matching paradigm where subjects had to match a felt force delivered to their hand either directly or using a mechanical device (Shergill et al. 2005).[17]

With the basic mechanism in view, let us return to the explanation of the *report* of delusion of control. Remember that the first task is to specify how experience is abnormal leading to abnormal reports and responses. One explanation of such reports is to invoke the absence of mineness: an experience of agency is abnormal because the experience lacks the normal feeling of mineness and subjects note the absence. Yet now that we have an additional causal mechanism explaining delusion of control, how do mineness and self-monitoring defects mesh?

Returning to the normal case where prediction is functional and agents thereby keep track of their actions, how should we link prediction in motor control to the normal phenomenology of mineness, when by hypothesis, one experiences one's action to be one's own? Admittedly, we confront one of the challenges of explaining consciousness, namely providing a clear linking principle that connects the brain to phenomenology, or in this case, the self-monitoring neurocomputation to mineness. A plausible first pass on such a principle adapts Chalmers' (2000) notion of a content neural correlate: the contents of conscious experience should correlate with the contents of its underlying neural basis. A simple link then would tie the content of consciousness, say one's experiencing X to the neural basis of the experience as representing X. For example, in looking for the neural content correlate of visually experiencing a face, we look for visual neural representations of faces. Let's work with this simple bridge principle. To simplify, we will assume that the neural realization of any self-monitoring computation is (part of) the neural basis of the experience of mineness in action.

If self-monitoring is the neural basis of normal experience of mineness, then the contents should be correlated. That is, low prediction error should correlate with the experience of mineness and high prediction error with the absence of that experience. The problem for self-monitoring approaches is that prediction error is used in many domains that do not involve mineness. It is part of an explanation of accurate correction of motor movements, even before proprioceptive signals are received (for a detailed review of corollary discharge mechanisms throughout the animal kingdom, see (Crapse and Sommer 2008)). In visual spatial constancy, the issue is phenomenology, but not the phenomenology of mineness but rather that of spatial constancy. Further, the model also explains the intensity of tickling sensations (Blakemore, Wolpert, and Frith 2000), something phenomenal but still not involving mineness. The self-monitoring mechanism and prediction error correlate with too many phenomena, some related to

---

[17] See also work of Simone Schütz-Bosback, e.g. (Desantis et al. 2012).

phenomenology, some not. Indeed, correlation can fail: when one makes a mistake, prediction error can be high and yet one does not feel that the action is not one's own but, rather, one is angry that one's own action came off so badly. If stable correlations are needed to provide the grounds for an explanation of mineness, then prediction error does not provide an obvious correlate.

The initial argument against postulating mineness phenomenology in delusion of control is this: the explanatory adequacy of mineness requires that it integrate with other explanatory theories in the relevant domain, but mineness does not clearly do so in delusion of control. It is then hard to accord it the status of best explanation if it fails to integrate with self-monitoring mechanisms that are widely invoked to explain delusion of control. The next step is to see how well self-monitoring mechanisms explain mineness reports.

6. A Simple Explanation of Reports of Abnormal Experience in Delusion of Control

Each theory of delusion of control aims to identify what makes the experience abnormal. How might we explain abnormality without mineness? Here are three pieces, each supported by evidence independent of introspective reports:

A. A capacity for comparing two signals as postulated in prediction.
B. Failure of prediction can lead to failure of sensory attenuation.
C. Unpredicted sensations can capture attention (bottom-up attention).

If we grant that there is a defect in self-monitoring of motor actions, then where actions are not predicted, this will generate an atypical signal, a large error. This signal can come from a subpersonal mechanism (A), but the hypothesis is that should the error be salient (B), it will lead to the capture of attention (C) (see (Fourneret and Jeannerod 1998) for a vivid example of this). When a normal subject is in the middle of an automatized task but something goes wrong, the subject's attention is captured. One's attention (thought) is then directed at the action that one is performing and one can reflect about that action. In other words, we begin with the mechanism of self-monitoring and the phenomenal upshots of attenuating or failing to attenuate a sensory signal underwriting the somatosensory feelings tied to movement. In delusion of control, the failure of prediction could lead to a larger than normal somatosensory sensation due to failure of attenuation and this grabs the subject's attention: they notice that the action literally *feels* atypical. After all, most actions are in the background and do not grab our attention unless something goes wrong. Once attention is grabbed, we have a case similar to not-myself judgments based on a difference between how actions normally feel and how they now feel. Should this difference persist and remain

138 MINENESS AND INTROSPECTIVE DATA

salient, then how the patient responds with the seemingly "abnormal action" is dependent on cognitive factors that every theory of delusion of control must appeal to.

The proposed account applies the parsimony principle, for we stick to uncontroversial phenomenal and psychological features that are widely accepted, namely the three pieces noted earlier.[18] There is no doubt that it remains mysterious why subjects conclude that their actions are under the control of external forces, often specific agents and any adequate account of the symptom must bridge that gap. Still, we must begin with the oddity of action experiences, and the explanation offered in neurocomputational terms does not invoke talk of mineness but meshes with extant explanatory accounts. Accordingly, this approach is not worse than positing mineness and its absence. Indeed, given its integration with current explanations of delusions of control, it might be a *better* explanation in that (a) it is parsimonious and (b) it meshes with current theories concerning the causes of schizophrenia symptoms.

The upshot is that we need to explore concrete alternative explanations to the various syndromes that yield reports of mineness and its loss. I worry that we are too quick to posit phenomenology when there is no clear need to. The introspective reports point to mental matters of interest, but the face value inference is not always valid, and the underlying mechanisms and processes are often much more complex than we give the mind credit for.

7. Conclusion

The route to mineness is paved with introspective reports, and from these, we have often applied a face value inference from talk of mineness as experienced to phenomenal mineness in experience. In this essay, I have questioned the appropriateness of this inference in three ways. First, I have argued that not all reports warrant the face value inference. Second the data of introspective reports is often ambiguous and must be carefully worked up if it is to provide a solid ground for inferences, yet in a salient central case (RHI), it is not clear that the data supports a face value inference to phenomenal mineness. Finally, claims of inference to the best explanation need to be set in a broader empirical context, but then, it is likely that we will be able to find alternative explanations that are equally plausible without positing phenomenal mineness.

The central message of this discussion is that introspective reports of mineness are a tricky thing. The face value inference has been part of the theorist of consciousness's took kit for a long time now: we begin with introspective reports and

---

[18] A different story will have to be told regarding thought insertion, but for a theory that I am sympathetic to that draws on the subject's drawing a contrast, see (Pickard 2010).

walk back to the underlying phenomenology, conceiving of introspection as a reliable way to read out what experience is like. But reports are data, and indeed just a subset of relevant data, that we should carefully work up. When we do, our view of consciousness and its phenomenal character might be drastically altered. This is, I think, precisely the case regarding phenomenal mineness.

References

Barnsley, N., J. H. McAuley, R. Mohan, A. Dey, P. Thomas, and G. L. Moseley. 2011. "The Rubber Hand Illusion Increases Histamine Reactivity in the Real Arm." *Current Biology* 21 (23): R945–6. doi:10.1016/j.cub.2011.10.039.

Blakemore, S. J., D. Wolpert, and C. Frith. 2000. "Why Can't You Tickle Yourself?" *Neuroreport* 11 (11): R11–16.

Blakemore, S. J., D. M. Wolpert, and C. D. Frith. 2002. "Abnormalities in the Awareness of Action." *Trends in Cognitive Sciences*, January.

Botvinick, M., and J. Cohen. 1998. "Rubber Hands' Feel'touch that Eyes See." *Nature* 391 (6669): 756–6.

Chalmers, David J. 2000. "What Is a Neural Correlate of Consciousness." In *Neural Correlates of Consciousness: Empirical and Conceptual Questions*, edited by Thomas Metzinger. MIT Press. 17–40.

Cho, Raymond, and Wayne Wu. 2013. "Mechanisms of Auditory Verbal Hallucination in Schizophrenia." *Schizophrenia* 4: 155. doi:10.3389/fpsyt.2013.00155.

Crapse, T. B, and M. A Sommer. 2008. "Corollary Discharge across the Animal Kingdom." *Nature Reviews Neuroscience* 9 (8): 587–600.

Davies, Martin, Max Coltheart, Robyn Langdon, and N. Breen. 2001. "Monothematic Delusions: Towards a Two-Factor Account." *Philosophy, Psychiatry and Psychology* 8 (2–3): 133–58.

de Vignemont, Frederique 2013. "The Mark of Bodily Ownership." *Analysis* 73 (4): 643–51. doi:10.1093/analys/ant080.

de Vignemont, Frederique. Forthcoming. "Agency and Bodily Ownership: The Bodyguard Hypothesis." In *The Subject's Matter: Self Consciousness and the Body*, edited by de Vignemont, Frederique and Adrian Alsmith. MIT Press.

Desantis, Andrea, Carmen Weiss, Simone Schütz-Bosbach, and Florian Waszak. 2012. "Believing and Perceiving: Authorship Belief Modulates Sensory Attenuation." *PLoS ONE* 7 (5): e37959. doi:10.1371/journal.pone.0037959.

Ehrsson, H. 2009. "Rubber Hand Illusion." In *The Oxford Companion to Consciousness*, edited by Bayne Tim, Cleeremans Axel, and Wilken Patrick, 531–73. Oxford University Press.

Feinberg, I. 1978. "Efference Copy and Corollary Discharge: Implications for Thinking and Its Disorders." *Schizophrenia Bulletin* 4 (4): 636–40.

140 MINENESS AND INTROSPECTIVE DATA

Fletcher, Paul C., and Chris D. Frith. 2009. "Perceiving Is Believing: A Bayesian Approach to Explaining the Positive Symptoms of Schizophrenia." *Nature Reviews: Neuroscience* 10 (1): 48–58. doi:10.1038/nrn2536.

Fourneret, P., and M. Jeannerod. 1998. "Limited Conscious Monitoring of Motor Performance in Normal Subjects." *Neuropsychologia* 36 (11): 1133–40.

Frith, C. D., and D. J. Done. 1988. "Towards a Neuropsychology of Schizophrenia." *The British Journal of Psychiatry* 153 (4): 437.

Guillot, Marie. 2016. "I Me Mine: On a Confusion Concerning the Subjective Character of Experience." *Review of Philosophy and Psychology* 1: 1–31.

Hall, N. J., and C. L. Colby. 2011. "Remapping for Visual Stability." *Philosophical Transactions of the Royal Society B: Biological Sciences* 366 (1564): 528.

Jackson, F. 1977. *Perception: A Representative Theory*. Cambridge University Press.

Malenka, Rorbert C., Ronald W. Angel, B. Hampton, and Phillip A. Berger. 1982. "Impaired Central Error-Correcting Behavior in Schizophrenia." *Archives of General Psychiatry* 39 (1): 101–7.

Malenka, Robert C., Ronald W. Angel, Sue Thiemann, Charles J. Weitz, and Philip A. Berger. 1986. "Central Error-Correcting Behavior in Schizophrenia and Depression." *Biological Psychiatry* 21 (3): 263–73. doi:10.1016/0006-3223(86)90047-8.

Martin, M. G. F. 1992. "Sight and Touch." *The Contents of Experience*, 196–215. Cambridge University Press.

Mellor, C. S. 1970. "First Rank Symptoms of Schizophrenia. I. The Frequency in Schizophrenics on Admission to Hospital. II. Differences between Individual First Rank Symptoms." *British Journal of Psychiatry* 117: 15–23.

Moseley, G. Lorimer, Nick Olthof, Annemeike Venema, Sanneke Don, Marijke Wijers, Alberto Gallace, and Charles Spence. 2008. "Psychologically Induced Cooling of a Specific Body Part Caused by the Illusory Ownership of an Artificial Counterpart." *Proceedings of the National Academy of Sciences* 105 (35): 13169–73. doi:10.1073/pnas.0803768105.

Mylopoulos, Myrto I. 2015. "Agentive Awareness Is Not Sensory Awareness." *Philosophical Studies* 172 (3): 761–80. doi:10.1007/s11098-014-0332-x.

Pickard, Hanna. 2010. "Schizophrenia and the Epistemology of Self-Knowledge." *European Journal of Analytic Philosophy* 6 (1): 55–74.

Samad, Majed, Albert Jin Chung, and Ladan Shams. 2015. "Perception of Body Ownership Is Driven by Bayesian Sensory Inference." *PLOS ONE* 10 (2): e0117178. doi:10.1371/journal.pone.0117178.

Schwitzgebel, Eric. 2011. *Perplexities of Consciousness*. MIT Press.

Shergill, Sukhwinder S., Gabrielle Samson, Paul M. Bays, Chris D. Frith, and Daniel M. Wolpert. 2005. "Evidence for Sensory Prediction Deficits in Schizophrenia." *American Journal of Psychiatry* 162 (12): 2384–86. doi:10.1176/appi.ajp.162.12.2384.

Spener, Maja. 2015. "Calibrating Introspection." *Philosophical Issues* 25 (1): 300–21.

Vallar, G., and R. Ronchi. 2009. "Somatoparaphrenia: A Body Delusion. A Review of the Neuropsychological Literature." *Experimental Brain Research*, January. http://www.springerlink.com/index/HN50718V8455714X.pdf.

Wolpert, D. M., and Z. Ghahramani. 2000. "Computational Principles of Movement Neuroscience." *Nat Neurosci* 3 (Suppl.): 1212–17.

Wu, Wayne. 2014. "Against Division: Consciousness, Information and the Visual Streams." *Mind and Language* 29 (4): 383–406.

Wurtz, R. H. 2008. "Neuronal Mechanisms of Visual Stability." *Vision Research* 48 (20): 2070–89.

7

The Sense of Body Ownership

What Are We Studying?

Krisztina Orbán and Hong Yu Wong

1. Introduction

Our bodies and our sense of embodiment are critical to our sense of ourselves as material beings (Evans 1982, Cassam 1997). James (1890: 291) wondered: 'our bodies themselves, are they simply ours, or are they *us*?' Whatever the answer is, we have an intimate relation to our body. We take it to be our body. It is the only object one can feel 'from the inside'. For example, one can feel that one's legs are crossed or that one is upside down. It is also the only object one can directly control. Thus the body has a distinctive phenomenological and functional status: one's body is the only body one feels sensation in and acts directly with (O'Shaughnessy 1980; Wong 2018).

But what it is like to be an embodied subject seems to go beyond this. One not only feels one's body 'from the inside', but one has a sense of ownership over that body: one's body *feels* to be one's own. When one is aware of an itch traversing one's back, one feels the itch to move within the boundaries of one's body. In everyday experience, the question as to whether such located bodily sensations can be felt to be located outside of these boundaries—or in a body that does not feel to be mine—does not even arise. Yet this sense of body ownership can be compromised in illness and, surprisingly, can also be induced, so that one feels artificial limbs to be one's own.

The convergence of the philosophical, experimental, and clinical literatures on the sense of body ownership has generated much excitement (Bermúdez et al. 1995, Roessler and Eilan 2003, Tsakiris 2010, Blanke 2012, de Vignemont and Alsmith 2017, de Vignemont 2018). But in approaching the extant literature, one can't help but feel that the phenomenon is elusive. In part this is because of disciplinary differences in the favoured methods, the starting point, and central focus. Philosophers often start with and focus on the normal case. Clinicians study pathologies. Experimentalists have primarily been concerned with the rubber hand illusion (RHI) paradigm. It would appear that these disciplines are all studying the sense of body ownership. But when one looks more carefully, it is not

Krisztina Orbán and Hong Yu Wong, *The Sense of Body Ownership: What Are We Studying?* In: *Self-Experience: Essays on Inner Awareness*. Edited by: Manuel García-Carpintero and Marie Guillot, Oxford University Press. © Krisztina Orbán and Hong Yu Wong 2023. DOI: 10.1093/oso/9780198805397.003.0007

entirely clear whether these diverse disciplines are trying to answer the same question. What exactly is the sense of body ownership? What are we studying when we claim we are studying body ownership?

2. Three Anchor Points for the Sense of Body Ownership

In order to be clear on what we are studying, we have to know the major 'data points' with which we have to be concerned. What are these?

First, aspects of the sense of body ownership are reflected in ordinary experience of one's body. Our normal experience of embodiment is hard to articulate. However, the phenomenology of located bodily sensation provides a clue. When I feel a located bodily sensation, such as an itch or a pain, I don't only feel it to be located, but feel it to be located in a part of *my* body (O'Shaughnessy 1980, Martin 1995). There are bodily sensations which are unlocated, such as nausea, or sensations which are located across the whole body, such as fatigue. But focally located bodily sensations in everyday experience always seem to be located in a body part (or, at least, in a seeming body part, as in cases of phantom sensations) that is part of one's body.

Second, we have pathologies of the sense of body ownership. Though the sense of body ownership is seldom at the focus of one's daily experience, its presence can be brought out by considering cases when it is lost. In cases of somatoparaphrenia, which is associated with extensive right hemispheric lesions, patients report that a limb feels alien and deny ownership of it, often ascribing it to someone else (Vallar and Ronchi 2009). Another example comes from deafferented patients who report at the beginning of their neuropathy, when they have lost proprioception and touch, that their bodies feel alien (Cole 1992, Cole and Paillard 1995). A third case is that of neurological patients who experience 'autoscopic phenomena', such as out-of-body experiences and heautoscopic experiences (Lopez et al. 2008, Blanke 2012). These patients have illusory visual experiences of their own body in extracorporeal space and experience a sense of body ownership over the illusory body double. These pathologies of embodiment demonstrate that the sense of body ownership can be disturbed. If you were unconvinced that there is a sense of body ownership, these cases should at least convince you that there is a sense of body *dis*ownership.

Third, we can artificially induce the sense of body ownership. The possibility of direct experimental studies of the sense of body ownership emerged with the RHI. In the standard RHI setup, a subject sits with her arm resting on a table but hidden behind a screen. A rubber hand is placed in front of the subject, in a position anatomically congruent with the subject's hidden hand; and both the rubber hand and the subject's hidden hand are stroked synchronously. A large portion of subjects then report that (1) they feel the touch to be where they see it (on the rubber hand)—and that (2) they feel that the rubber hand is part of their body. These experiential reports are correlated with two implicit measures: propriceptive drift of the position of the subject's affected hand towards the position of the rubber hand (but see Rohde et al. 2011) and an increased affective response to threats to the rubber hand (Ehrsson et al. 2007). In contrast, this is not the case when the stroking is asynchronous. Thus the RHI is thought to arise from multisensory integration in combination with internal models of the body (Tsakiris 2010, Ehrsson 2012). This paradigm has also been extended for inducing full body illusions, where illusory ownership is induced over a whole body (or an avatar) and not only isolated body parts (Ehrsson 2007, Leggenhagger et al. 2007, Blanke 2012). The experimental induction of the sense of ownership over foreign bodies would seem to provide an existence proof for a sense of body ownership.

In order to be clear about what we are studying when we study the sense of body ownership we need to consider all the three families of data points above. Having these anchor points allows us to peg down the phenomenon under investigation. Any adequate account of a sense of body ownership must explain and must fit these three families of data points.

3. What Are We Studying? Five Questions about the Sense of Body Ownership

Once we accept that any account of the sense of body ownership will have to consider these three anchor points, we have some sense of the target of explanation. In the philosophical literature, one can't help feeling that there is some talking past each other and some ensuing confusion.[1] Whilst some of this is no doubt due to this area of research being relatively new, we suggest that part of the reason behind these issues is that different theorists are actually asking and answering different questions. To remedy this, we propose that we should distinguish five major questions about the sense of body ownership:

    a. *The Constitutive Question*: What is it?
    b. *The Phenomenological Question*: What is it like?
    c. *The Causal Question*: What mechanisms underlie it?
    d. *The Functional Question*: What does it do?
    e. *The Mereological Question*: How do the senses of ownership of the whole body and of body parts relate?

---

[1] We are not the only ones who are protesting. See also Guillot (2017), Bermúdez (2019), and Wu (Chapter 6, this volume).

These questions are all related but distinct. The debate has suffered because these questions have sometime been run together. Distinguishing the questions allows us to see clearly what a theory can explain.

In this chapter, we will explore the interplay between the different questions. In recognising the different projects marked by these different questions, we will re-examine the major philosophical accounts of the sense of body ownership in light of the different questions. Our aim is to use this to develop some morals for studying the sense of body ownership.

Before launching into the discussion, let us introduce our terminology and state some key assumptions. First, just which sense of the sense of body owner-ship are we interested in? We are only concerned here with the sense of experi-encing one's body as one's own. Guillot (2017) distinguishes between three non-equivalent, but sometimes conflated, senses of ownership. We are only con-cerned with one of them—how a subject experiences herself as the owner of an experience, which she labels 'mineness'—in its application to one's body. There are difficult questions about how different forms of ownership (e.g. of bodies, thoughts, experiences, actions, etc.) relate and whether a unified account of own-ership is available.[2] We shall remain neutral on this.

Second, we distinguish between the fact, the experience, and the judgement of ownership (following Dokic 2003). The fact of ownership is the fact about which body is actually mine (assumed to be determined biologically). In somatopara-phrenia, a hand felt to be alien in fact belongs to its subject. Conversely, in the RHI, a subject does not in fact own the rubber hand and does not judge it to belong to her body, but experiences it as hers. Thus, the fact, the experience, and the judgement of ownership can dissociate.

Third, the term 'the sense of body ownership' as introduced here and as it is used in the scientific and clinical literature is neutral on whether it consists of experiences of ownership and/or judgements of ownership. This means that we are leaving it open whether the sense of body ownership has a distinctive phe-nomenology. Our use of the term commits us to there being a core phenomenon which covers the three core anchor points above.

Let us now turn to the five questions. The first question is the Constitutive Question: What is the nature of the sense of ownership over one's body? It is hard to say exactly what giving an account of the nature of a thing involves ahead of giving a successful constitutive account (Burge 2010, Wong 2014). Two things are important here: a constitutive explanation will elucidate the nature of the sense of body ownership and why it is attributable to the whole organism (and not some part of it).

The Constitutive Question is a metaphysical question. Generally metaphysical and phenomenological questions are distinct. Characterising the phenomenology

---

[2] See Dokic (2003), Billon (2017), and Bermúdez (2019).

of some phenomenon does not provide a metaphysical explanation of the nature of that phenomenon or vice versa. So unless the phenomenon is essentially phenomenological, the phenomenological explanation is distinct from the constitutive explanation. Yet some theorists will feel uncomfortable at our distinguishing between the Phenomenological and the Constitutive Questions. Their thought is that once one characterises the phenomenology of body ownership, one *ipso facto* provides a constitutive account. This need not be the case. While it may be that there is a close connection between the phenomenological and constitutive questions about ownership, the differences should be kept in view. Consider the same questions concerning, for example, proprioception—the internal sense of the position and movement of one's body parts. What is it like to proprioceive? A plausible answer is that it is to experience and know the position of one's limbs 'from the inside' non-inferentially without employing the standard exteroceptive senses. Does this provide a constitutive account of proprioception? No, since much proprioception is unconscious. We take our remarks here not to preclude accounts where answers to the phenomenological and constitutive questions are linked or even identical, but simply to suggest that the *questions* should be distinguished.

The second question is the Phenomenological Question: What is it like to have a sense of ownership over one's body? The phenomenological question is about having an experience of body ownership. Key sub-questions include: Is there a *sui generis* phenomenology of body ownership? If not, is there a phenomenology of body ownership or is there only a phenomenology of bodily awareness together with judgements of body ownership? Are there components of the phenomenology of body ownership? If so, what are these? How does the experience of body ownership relate to the judgement of body ownership? Furthermore, how do the phenomenology of body ownership and body disownership relate? Is there a phenomenology of ownership which accompanies our everyday perception of our own body?

The third question is the Causal Question: What mechanisms underlie the sense of ownership over one's body? This is what scientists and clinicians are primarily concerned with. Some theorists who uphold the distinction between the Phenomenological and Constitutive Questions would reject a distinction between the Constitutive and Causal Questions. Compare the same questions posed for visual perception. On one picture (McDowell 1994), the constitutive account of visual perception is simply the subject being in touch visually with the world. This involves the proper functioning of the sub-personal visual system. But the latter need not tell us what the nature of visual perception is. Causal and constitutive questions are traditionally considered separate. This is marked in the distinction between enabling as opposed to constitutive conditions (McDowell 1994), where the typical reading of this distinguishes causal dependence from constitutive dependence. This is not to say that a constitutive account could not allude to aspects of the underlying mechanisms in elucidating the nature of the phenomenon (Wong 2014).

The fourth question is the Functional Question: What is the function of having a sense of ownership over one's body? It has rarely been broached. The causal question obviously connects to the functional question; and the phenomenology may or may not reflect the function. Intuitively the constitutive and functional questions are distinct. Of course, if one is a functionalist and individuates mental phenomena in terms of their causal role (Shoemaker 1981), then the functional and constitutive questions coincide. However, at this stage of inquiry, when we have no clear idea about the function of the sense of body ownership, these two questions flag different directions of inquiry.

The fifth question is the Mereological Question: How does ownership of the whole body and of body parts relate? This question is clearly distinct from the other questions. It arises because it is in principle possible that the account of ownership of the whole body isn't additive—it may not be the case that one owns a body if one owns all parts of that body. When we think about owning or disowning one's whole body it does not seem to be the same as owning or disowning part of the body. Note that while the scholarly discussion seems to be generated by an interest in the subject's owning or disowning her whole body, it has been mostly restricted to discussions of owning or disowning parts of the subject's body.

Having introduced our five questions and discussed possible connections and distinctions, let us now turn to examining how they bear on the major philosophical accounts of ownership.

4. Major Philosophical Accounts of the Sense of Body Ownership

Our aim is not to provide a comprehensive review of the extant debate but to present an opinionated review of some major positions through the lens of our five questions.[3]

4.1. The Spatial View

4.1.1. Special Access to a Bounded Space
Philosophical reflection on the sense of body ownership predates recent clinical and empirical developments and arose independently. The point of departure is

---

[3] Other notable philosophical discussions include Alsmith (2014) and the essays in Bermúdez et al. (1995), Roessler and Eilan (2003), de Vignemont and Alsmith (2017), among others.

148 THE SENSE OF BODY OWNERSHIP

Martin's account of bodily awareness, rooted in his phenomenological investigation of contrasts between the spatial structure of vision, touch, and bodily awareness (1992, 1993, and 1995). When one experiences one's body in sight, one's body is given as one among many other possible objects of perception. In contrast, in bodily awareness one can only be aware of one's body. Martin exploits a modal contrast between spatial awareness in bodily awareness as opposed to touch. His starting point is a phenomenological observation about how the spatial content of bodily sensations is related to how one's body feels to be bounded. The phenomenology serves as a springboard for revealing the structure of ownership. And this structure allows Martin to work out a constitutive explanation of ownership. His strategy is to use the phenomenological question to answer the constitutive question.

Martin (1995) makes three claims. The first concerns bodily awareness as a sole object faculty:

Sole Object: Bodily awareness is a perceptual capacity that allows the subject to perceive only her body and its parts.

The second concerns the phenomenology of located bodily sensations:

Ownership Phenomenology: Located bodily sensations are always felt to be in one's body (or a seeming body part).

How is this ownership phenomenology explained? This distinctive phenomenology of located bodily sensations always feeling to fall within one's apparent body is derived from the spatial content of bodily sensations, in particular, of how one's body feels to be bounded.

Sense of Boundedness: There is a sense of boundedness inherent in bodily spatial experience, which derives from the modal contrast between bodily awareness and touch.

Martin's claim is that any sensation felt through bodily awareness feels to fall within the boundaries of one's body, yet these sensations feel to be in a space that extends beyond the space that I can currently feel 'from the inside'—the latter being something that I grasp through touch or kinaesthesia, when I move my arm through different positions. The spatial content of bodily awareness thus gives us a sense of our bodily boundaries, a sense of boundedness. If we couple this to the sole object claim, we see that this is a bounded space that one has special access to. This is supposed to provide for a sense that the located bodily sensations are always felt to be in one's apparent body.

4.1.2. Boundedness and Connectedness

Bermúdez has drawn on his account of the distinctive spatial structure of bodily awareness (1998 and 2005) to develop a position on the sense of body ownership (2011, 2015, 2017, 2019). He proposes a constitutive account based on what he takes the phenomenology to be. Let us focus on what he takes to be the distinctive spatial content of bodily awareness that licenses judgements of body ownership. He has two key claims:

Boundedness: "Bodily events are experienced within the experienced body (a circumscribed body-shaped volume whose boundaries define the limits of the self)." (2019: 269)

Connectedness: "The spatial location of a bodily event is experienced relative to the disposition of the body as a whole." (2019: 269)

The idea behind Connectedness is that located bodily sensations and proprioceptive experiences are experienced within a holistic postural frame. For example, part of experiencing resting one's hands behind's one's head is to experience the flexion in one's shoulders and elbows. Boundedness and Connectedness bring out different aspects of the spatial content of bodily awareness. Boundedness captures the sense of a limited space that bodily awareness has access to, whilst Connectedness captures the distinctive holistic spatial frame—given in terms of current posture—of bodily awareness. By contrast, no exteroceptive perceptual capacities are characterised by either of these conditions.

Bermúdez further suggests that Boundedness and Connectedness are explained by how bodily space is represented in conscious bodily awareness. Unlike exteroceptive perception, bodily awareness is not centred on a single origin. Bermúdez has argued for a multiple origin view on which the spatial content of bodily awareness is centred on more than one origin (the hinges of the body).[4] Instead bodily sensations and locations are mapped onto a body map in two ways, which he labels 'A-positions' and 'B-positions'. The body map captures the body as a "relatively immoveable torso connected by joints to moveable body parts" (Bermúdez 2019: 270). A-locations are given by locating a sensation or body part on the body map, whereas B-locations convey further information about the dynamic relation between various body parts (in terms of joint angles) based on current posture.[5]

---

[4] Another option is the no origin view (Orbán 2018), on which bodily awareness does not have any origin because sensations are mapped to a somatosensory-based body map and this spatial mapping does not involve an origin.

[5] Compare O'Shaughnessy's (1980) characterisation of the location of bodily sensations on the long-term body image vs. the short-term body image.

150 THE SENSE OF BODY OWNERSHIP

How is this supposed to explain the sense of body ownership? Bermúdez (2019: 270) writes:

> The body-parts that we take to be our own are the body-parts that fall within the experienced body—the body-parts within which bodily events can be A-located. At the same time the B-location dimension of bodily experience reflects the way in which a constant awareness of the disposition of the body as a whole is a background part of bodily experience, and hence a powerful basis for taking one's body to be one's own.

Like Martin, Bermúdez sees the phenomenology of the experiences which grounds judgements of body ownership as exhausted by the spatial content of bodily awareness. But unlike Martin, he is an eliminativist about the sense of body ownership. He denies that there is a phenomenology of body ownership beyond bodily awareness and judgements of body ownership licensed on that basis.[6]

4.1.3. Problems with the Spatial View

We can agree with both Martin and Bermúdez that the spatial structure of bodily awareness provides for a sense of boundedness. But it is unclear that with boundedness one *ipso facto* arrives at a sense that this bounded space is *mine*. So while we can agree that there is an asymmetry in terms of this special structural property, it is unclear that what we have is a sense of body ownership. Perhaps one claim is that the phenomenology in normal embodiment simply is that of the presence of the structural property. We will return to this later.[7]

Whatever the case there, the boundedness view appears to face counterexamples. We can find cases with the boundedness property without a sense of body ownership. The first case is that of somatoparaphrenia (first raised by de Vignemont 2007). Somatoparaphrenic patients report that a limb feels alien and deny it belongs to them, often ascribing it to a relative or even the experimenter. In some of these cases, patients have some preserved touch and bodily awareness. Patients can feel touch or bodily sensation in the affected limb, yet deny that the limb belongs to them (e.g. Bottini et al. 2001). Thus, we have the spatial content of boundedness and special access to that limb without a sense of ownership of the limb where the sensation falls within.

A second novel case comes from considering an intermediate stage of the RHI. The RHI isn't a counterexample to the boundedness view, since feeling touch

---

[6] For eliminativism, compare Wu, Chapter 6, this volume. We will not consider Bermúdez's (2011) negative argument against the sense of body ownership; but see de Vignemont (2013) and Bermúdez (2015) for an exchange.

[7] See also Serrahima (Chapter 11, this volume) for a discussion on this.

PHILOSOPHICAL ACCOUNTS OF THE SENSE OF BODY OWNERSHIP 151

on the rubber hand comes together with an illusory sense of ownership over the rubber hand. Martin's claim is that located bodily sensations are always felt to be in one's body or a seeming body part—the rubber hand is felt to be part of the subject's apparent body and so does not present a counterexample. However, an intermediate stage of the RHI is problematic. During this stage, one feels the touch to be where one sees it to be—on the rubber hand—without feeling the rubber hand to be a seeming body part.[8] In that case, it seems that I feel touch in a limb that does not delimit part of my boundary. How does this challenge the boundedness property? The sensation does not remain within a bodily boundary that defines the boundary of the space that I feel from the inside.

The third problem case is patients who experience 'autoscopic phenomena'. There are cases of ownership which do not intuitively fulfil the of boundedness criteria. Patients have illusory visual experiences of their own body in extracorporeal space and experience a sense of body ownership over the illusory body double. For example, one is resting on a bed while she is experiencing a body above herself which is looking at herself and taking this body to be hers. We will return to this when we will discuss the impact of the Mereological question in section 5.

What do these counterexamples show? They show that the structural property, boundedness, doesn't exhaust ownership and that there is a further component. Connectedness does not help. Somatoparaphrenia, in particular, suggests this component is partly affective, since patients appear to have an altered affective response to the body parts felt to be alien. They reject these limbs felt to be alien.[9]

4.2. The Qualia View

One response to counterexamples such as somatoparaphrenia is to suggest that there is an irreducible *quale* of 'mineness' in normal embodiment. On this picture, the phenomenology of body ownership is due to an intrinsic, first-personal phenomenal quality that is present in normal embodiment and absent in pathologies of embodiment, such as somatoparaphrenia and depersonalisation syndrome. Gallagher (2005) and Billon (2017) defend this position on the sense of mineness as it applies to all conscious experience and not only body ownership. We shall be concerned here only with the position as it pertains to body ownership.

The Qualia View relies on the assumption that the constitutive question can only answered by phenomenological data gathered from phenomenological

---

[8] This intermediate stage is well known to scientists running RHI experiments. Of the roughly 20% of subjects who do not experience the RHI, some experience this intermediate stage of touch referral.

[9] The view that an affective component is involved has been defended by de Vignemont recently (2018, Chapter 12, this volume) and by Damasio (1999) earlier.

152 THE SENSE OF BODY OWNERSHIP

observation of different cases. This strategy assumes that there is a phenomenology of ownership and that this phenomenology is accessible to the subject. Differences in ownership judgements will be explained by differences in the phenomenology of the ownership or disownership experience.

The Qualia View secures the first-personal content of body ownership by taking this to be a primitive feature of the experience of normal embodiment. What is less clear is whether we are entitled to posit such primitive phenomenal qualities based on the argument from pathology. There are three challenges to such as view. First, it does not follow from there being a sense of body disownership in pathologies of embodiment that there is a sense of body ownership in normal embodiment. There are at least two possibilities: (A) It may be that there is a sense of body ownership in normal embodiment, and that this goes missing in the pathologies of embodiment. On this picture, the sense of disownership is the absence of the normal sense of ownership. (B) It may be that there is a sense of body disownership when things go wrong, but no phenomenal quality of mineness in the normal case. This is consonant with observations in the empirical literature on agency that the sense of agency is particularly strong when I experience the loss of control in some way (see e.g. Frith 2005). Perhaps the sense of body ownership is this way too—it only reveals itself in disease or in unusual experimental situations, such as the RHI. As long as the Qualia Theorist hasn't settled why we should prefer the first over the second interpretation, it is unclear why one should think of body ownership in terms of the Qualia View.[10]

Second, we may question whether pathologies of disownership are best interpreted as the Qualia View proposes. On the leading account of monothematic delusions (Langdon and Coltheart 2000, Davies et al. 2001), there are two factors in delusions: (1) there is a weird experience and (2) there is unusual rationalisation of the weird experience. If we only had the first factor without the problems with rationalisation, one wouldn't necessarily have the disownership delusion. This suggests that the unusual rationalisation is partly constitutive of the disownership delusion. But if this is the case we cannot read off a phenomenology of disownership simply by alluding to weird experiences, because the weird experience may not be some *quale* that is the presence or absence of some ownership quality.

Billon (2017 and Chapter 14, this volume) responds to the points above by arguing that, at least in the case of depersonalisation, patients characteristically claim that some feature is absent, rather than some further feeling of disownership. He urges that we should take their reports at face value unless we have reason not to. In particular, in the case of depersonalisation patients, they are not delusional (unlike patients suffering from somatoparaphrenia or Cotard's

---

[10] See Dub (Chapter 13, this volume) and McClelland (Chapter 3, this volume) for further discussion of the difference between cases (A) and (B), and their respective implications.

syndrome) and there is no evidence that their rational capacities are impaired. However, it is methodologically problematic to use an unusual negative experience as a reliable source for understanding normal experience, especially if we only have introspective report. There are simpler explanations available, for example the absence of affect. So it is unclear why a primitive phenomenal quality of mineness in the normal case provides the best explanation (see Wu, Chapter 6, this volume).

Finally, we do not have sufficient phenomenological evidence of the primitive feeling of body ownership in everyday experience. If the Qualia View were correct then either the experience of ownership should be manifest in ordinary experience or it should have a recessive character. It does not appear to be present in everyday experience, so it has to be recessive. But if it were recessive, it would be unclear that we have phenomenological grounds for positing this primitive phenomenal quality in experience, so the grounds must be theoretical. But we have already argued that the theoretical grounds are questionable. There is no doubt that more can be said in response, but these points lead us to be sceptical about the prospects of an account of the sense of body ownership in terms of a primitive phenomenal quality.

4.3. Body Schematic Accounts

4.3.1. Body Schema and Action
The accounts so far have been constitutive accounts offered based on a conception of the phenomenology of ownership. A different kind of account comes from consideration of the underlying mechanisms that explain the sense of body ownership. Counterexamples to the account of body ownership in terms of boundedness from cases of somatoparaphrenia suggest that a successful account will need to grapple with various pathologies of body ownership. One way of generating an account is to look at mechanisms impaired in pathological cases, so as to explain what normal functioning requires.

De Vignemont (2007) inaugurated a new class of accounts in terms of the body schema. Impressed by the boundedness theories, her aim is to provide a spatial view that can cope with empirical counterexamples. Thus she needs a spatial representation of the body within which bodily sensations can be localised and a mechanism that can be compromised in illness. What spatial representation of the body could perform this role? She proposes the body schema. "[T]he sense of ownership derives from the localisation of the bodily property within a spatial representation of the body" (2007: 439). "The spatial content of bodily sensations has to be understood relatively to the body schema. According to the spatial hypothesis, the sense of ownership is given by the spatial content. Therefore, the sense of ownership is given by the body schema" (2007: 441).

What is the body schema? Recent work on sensorimotor action in different sensory modalities has drawn on the perception/action model of functional dissociations familiar from the visual system (Jeannerod 1997, Milner and Goodale 2006). In the bodily senses, we find a distinction between body representations for perception as opposed to those for action (Paillard 1999, Dijkerman and de Haan 2007). Body representations for perception are known as the 'body image', whilst body representations for action are known as the 'body schema'. The body image is a representation of one's overall body form that can be manifest in consciousness through perception or imagery. It is an explicit representation of body form, which may include the conscious awareness of current postural configuration. In contrast, the body schema is a dynamic representation of the relative position of body parts that is employed in the control of action and the maintenance of posture.

Notice that de Vignemont begins with answering the mechanism question and draws on this to answer the constitutive question. The phenomenology of body ownership does not play an immediate role. Her choice of the body schema rests on her observation that the sense of body ownership appears to be connected with deficits of action. First, the ownership of prosthetic limbs in amputees appears to depend on their ability to effectively act with the prosthetic limb. When they can effectively act with the prosthetic limb, the limb is thereby represented in their body schema. Since this is also correlated with their coming to have a sense of ownership over the prosthetic limb, representation in the body schema seems to be critical. Second, disorders of ownership are connected with action deficits: patients are paralysed, paraplegic, or have problems with the sense of agency, such as anosognosia for hemiplegia (where patients have a delusion of being able to move a paralysed limb). Since these are action deficits, this strongly suggests that patients have a deficit of the body schema.

De Vignemont makes two key claims: (1) the mechanism that underlies the sense of body ownership is the body schema and disruptions to the body schema disrupt body ownership; (2) what body ownership consists in is representation in the body schema. Naturally, such an answer to the constitutive question may have phenomenological consequences. But it is unclear what the phenomenological consequences of representation in the body schema is. Is the spatial content of bodily awareness thereby first personal or is it like some boundedness property or is it something else? De Vignemont does not tell us. But this is not her explanatory target. De Vignemont (2007) does not ask this phenomenological question and provides no answer to it. So here we see an example of how distinguishing the different questions about ownership is key to understanding what kind of account we are giving.

De Vignemont presents a good case for body schema representation being a necessary condition on ownership. However, is it sufficient? Here are two challenges. First, there is the case of tool use (as she notes in de Vignemont 2018).

Tools are represented in the body schema when we learn to employ them. Iriki and colleagues showed that when monkeys learn to use a tool, there is an extension of the bimodal receptive fields to the reaching area of the tool (Iriki et al. 1996, Maravita and Iriki 2004). The peripersonal space around the hand expands to cover the extent of the tool. This is taken as showing that the body schema of these monkeys has expanded to include the tool. There is evidence that such results apply to humans too. However, tools are represented as being part of the body schema but we have no sense of ownership over them. We do not have a sense of ownership over the utensils which we cook with, for example, and have no worries inserting them into boiling liquids when cooking. Second, there is the case of apotemnophilia (also known as xenomelia and body identity integrity disorder), where patients wish to amputate a limb that is well functioning. The clinical characterisation of apotemnophilia is still very much disputed (see e.g. Sedda 2011, Sedda and Bottini 2014), but there is evidence that there are apotemnophiliacs who both feel and judge that a certain limb does not belong to them but are still able to use that limb effectively. The first-person reports of disownership in some cases is corroborated by evidence that there is a reduced skin conductance response to threat on the disowned limb below the point at which the apotemnopiliacs wish to amputate their limb (Romano et al. 2015). In this case, as Peacocke (2015) points out, given that the apotemnopiliac can walk with his lower leg, it is represented in his body schema, but he has no sense of ownership over it (Hilti et al. 2013). Therefore, representation in the body schema is not sufficient for body ownership. Let us now consider two attempts to develop body schematic accounts which overcome such worries.

4.3.2. First-Person Content in the Body Schema

By way of contrast, let us consider a view which takes the first-personal aspect of body ownership more seriously. Peacocke (2015) hints at an account of body ownership in terms of first-person representational content for the body schema. Discussing the impact of cases like somatoparaphrenia and apotemnophilia, he writes:

> If...it is supposed to be part of the representational content of the body schema that it also labels various body parts as one's own, such a body schema could then contribute to the explanation of these various pathologies. But it would do so then by taking for granted the notion of ownership by a subject, rather than by offering some kind of reductive explanation of the notion.   (2015: 173)

Peacocke is proposing that we posit irreducible first-person representation at the level of the body schema to explain the sense of body ownership. Peacocke emphasises that body ownership requires first-personal content, as is clear in a recent discussion alluding to the RHI: "Precisely the dramatic phenomenology of

156   THE SENSE OF BODY OWNERSHIP

the rubber hand illusion is that it seems, of a rubber hand that one knows is not one's own, that *that hand is mine*... The content of the illusion involves both ownership and the first person" (2016: 351).

Peacocke's contention is that without the first person as part of a constitutive account we will not be able to explain the first-personal phenomenology of body ownership. He claims that the experience of body ownership is constitutively first personal and this is underpinned by an underlying mechanism which processes first-person content. Peacocke thus goes from the content of the phenomenology to requirements on the constitutive explanation and causal explanation of body ownership.

There are two challenges to Peacocke's view. First, the sense of disownership in pathological cases is consistent with there not being any first-personal representation in the case of normal embodiment. We are not obliged to explain the sense of disownership through claiming that first-personal representation at the body schema is disrupted. Second, ownership labelling is not obviously a function of the body schema. The body schema was posited to account for certain dissociations in sensorimotor action between perception and action. In positing the body schema, the neuroscience of action has not relied on any claim that such body representations have first-personal content which is required for action explanation. Thus it is unclear what grounds we have for first-personal representation at the body schema.

4.3.3. The Defensive Body Schema

De Vignemont has responded to the criticisms above by proposing a new account on which ownership is grounded in the *defensive* body schema (de Vignemont 2018 and Chapter 12, this volume). On the basis of empirical considerations, she distinguishes between an instrumental body schema—body representations for the control of action—and the defensive body schema—body representations that are geared for protection of the body. There is evidence that there are distinctive body representations that are responsive to threats to the body and that this is tied to an affective response. In the most comprehensive canvassing of the cases to date, she (2018) shows that ownership phenomenology co-varies with an affective response. Her account is a generalisation of the widely-used skin conductance measure of body ownership for threat responses and captures the idea of one's body as what one has a distinctive prudential concern for. This is an affective conception of ownership, where body ownership is understood as what one has a protective/defensive affective reaction for. This account simultaneously captures both the spatial and affective aspects of body ownership.

An account of ownership in terms of the defensive body schema answers the causal and constitutive questions, but unlike de Vignemont's earlier view, it also has phenomenological commitments: she assume[s] that the phenomenology of ownership must reflect its grounds, and if the grounds consist in the protective body schema—that is, in the representation of the body that is significant for the organism's needs—then the phenomenology of ownership must simply consist in the feeling of the body *as having special significance.* (Chapter 12, this volume: xx)

Her take on the phenomenology of body ownership is that it is a sense of a body as having a special affective and defensive significance. Her account thus draws on an answer to the mechanism question to answer the constitutive question. And the answer to the constitutive question is such that it has phenomenological consequences. The account also provides an answer for the function of ownership: it is to enable self-defence for survival.[11]

5. Towards an Account of the Sense of Body Ownership: Some Morals

Our discussion above allows us to draw some morals about theorising about the sense of body ownership. We focus on the impact of ownership over the whole body and on the phenomenology of body ownership.

5.1. The Mereological Question

When one describes what ownership over a body is, it has to be ownership over the whole body and not only over body parts. Most accounts have focused on explaining the sense of ownership or disownership of individual body parts. But it is not entirely clear how extant accounts are to be extended to the case of the entire body. There are two aspects to note. First, most accounts, even those explicitly concerned with multimodal aspects of bodily awareness, like de Vignemont's, have focused overwhelmingly on somatosensation and its connection to body ownership. Second, an implicit assumption of extant accounts appears to be that spatial boundedness, sometimes in combination with affective elements, plus a special access to that space, is enough for some sense that this body is mine.

In his review of the multisensory mechanisms of full body ownership, Blanke (2012) identified three key aspects of bodily self-consciousness: (1) body ownership (the experience of owning one's body), (2) self-location (the experience of

---

[11] Our focus in this chapter is on distinguishing different questions about the sense of body ownership inherent in key discussions in the literature rather than critically engaging with these key views. For a critical discussion of de Vignemont's (2018) view, see Wong and Hochstetter (2022).

where one is in space), and (3) the first-person perspective (the apparent visual origin from which I perceive the world). We can illustrate this three-way distinction by considering patients who experience 'autoscopic phenomena', such as out-of-body experiences and heautoscopic experiences (Lopez et al. 2008, Blanke 2012). Patients who have out-of-body experiences exhibit a three-way dissociation from their biological body. They typically experience ownership over an illusory body in external space (defective body ownership), experience themselves to be located above their biological body (defective self-location), and experience themselves as having an altered apparent first-person perspective where they are looking back down on their biological body (defective first-person perspective) (Pfeiffer et al. 2014: 4). In heautoscopic patients, they experience seeing a second body of theirs in external space, which they have a sense of ownership over (defective body ownership), and they sometimes report feeling located in both bodies or switching between the two (defective self-location and defective first-person perspective).

Can extant theories of body ownership be extended to the ownership of the whole body? Initially, we might think it is unproblematic. The boundedness account surely concerns the whole body, as do the accounts in terms of the body schema. However, once it is observed that body ownership and self-location come apart, this would appear to put some pressure on both accounts. The account in terms of boundedness coupled with special access to the bounded space could only work as an account of what makes a body *mine* if I am there within those boundaries. But if ownership and self-location can come apart, this assumption is challenged. If we examine the body schematic accounts, the unity of the full body in ownership is given by the unity of the body schema. But this too trades on the assumption that I am there at the location given and is challenged if ownership and self-location come apart.

A related challenge comes from full body illusions. Philosophical views on body ownership inherently require the first-person perspective. However, ownership can be induced from the third-person perspective as in the out-of-body illusion (Lengenhager et al. 2007, Ehrsson 2007). When I feel my body from the inside or look down at my body, I employ a first-person (or egocentric) perspective. In contrast, when I look at myself in a mirror, I am taking a third-person perspective on my body. In Lenggenhager et al. (2007), subjects experienced ownership over an avatar viewed from a visual third-person perspective after they saw the avatar being stroked while they were stroked at the same location and at the same time (as compared with an asynchronous control condition). This poses a challenge to most existing views as the first-person perspective is taken to be inherent in the structure of ownership. Perceiving one's body through a special private access cannot be perceiving it from a third-person perspective. Nor can a sense of boundedness. So all spatial views (e.g. Martin, Bermúdez, and Wu) face a challenge. So far the only view which can accommodate this is the defensive body schema view. But if one has defensive reactions for a body in extrapersonal space then one questions the self-defensive function in that situation. Thus full body illusions poses a challenge to most existing views as the first-person perspective is taken to be inherent in the structure of ownership. These are hurdles that need to be overcome in future accounts and we welcome more philosophical work that directly reflects on full body ownership.

5.2. The Phenomenological Question

In order to characterise the sense of body ownership, we need to have some grip on its phenomenology. One thing we can learn from the discussion above is that the explanatory target of theorising about the sense of body ownership is not yet clear. There is a dispute about whether the first-personal element in the sense of body ownership—that the body feels to be *mine*—is something that is best understood to be an aspect of judgements of ownership or already present in the experience of ownership. It is clear that judgements of ownership have first-person content, but this does not unequivocally establish that the bodily experiences in virtue of which one makes these judgements of ownership have first-person content (see also Wu, Chapter 6, this volume). This raises several issues.

If the target of phenomenological explanation is not unequivocally first-personal experiences of body ownership, what is the target and what are the necessary components? Our discussion of the views above suggests that there are two aspects at least: the first being some spatial aspect and the second being some affective aspect, as suggested by reflection on somatoparaphrenia and its connection to defensive behaviour. How do these aspects contribute to the phenomenology of ownership and how do they relate to self-ascriptions (judgements of ownership)?

There are several ways to proceed here. One is to provide a characterisation of what it's like to feel a body as mine based on introspection and everyday experience. The problem with this method is that even basic forms of bodily awareness are recessive, and it is hard to attend to aspects like the sense of body ownership. A second way is to consider what is lost in the cases of pathologies, trying to use that to infer what is present in the case of healthy individuals. Though this can provide some insight, the problem is that there is no straightforward way to infer what is present in healthy individuals from what is present in pathology. Another method is to exploit the RHI paradigm and use it to pin down some kind of phenomenology of body ownership.

One question is whether the RHI is enough to demonstrate that ownership experiences are first personal, as Peacocke and de Vignemont suggest (see Wu, Chapter 6, this volume, for dissent). Does the RHI show that there is a belief-independent experience of body ownership which is first personal? In subjects who experience the RHI, they report that the rubber hand feels to belong to them even though they know that it is not a part of their body. So while the experience of the RHI also plausibly involves a proprioceptive component (as indicated by the proprioceptive drift measure) and an affective component (as indicated by the threat measure), the content of the illusion is naturally described as consisting of both ownership and the first person.

If we accept that the content of RHI experiences are first-person experiences of ownership, what does this show about the normal experience of body ownership? First, even if the RHI allows us to study ownership experimentally, it is unclear that the experiences of ownership had in the RHI are relevantly like ordinary experiences of embodiment. Even if one stares at or caresses one's hand, one hardly can approach anything like the experience had in the RHI; and in this case, one knows that it is one's hand. In the RHI, one's experience is perhaps much stronger because there is conflict processing here by the brain resulting in a surprising percept. If that is the case, then we can be sceptical about the move generalising from RHI experiences to ordinary experiences of body ownership.

Second, there is a question whether ownership experiences *must* be first-personal. One way to probe this is to ask whether ownership experiences might be self-specific or self-significant experiences, but fall short of a first-person *sui generis* experience of ownership. There is some evidence that non-human animals may experience ownership of an artificial limb after synchronous stimulation. Graziano and colleagues (Graziano 1999, Graziano et al. 2000) found that neurons in area 5 of the monkey parietal cortex which code for limb position became sensitive to the position of a fake arm in view after synchronous stimulation, but not after asynchronous stimulation. This shows that mechanisms for the possibility of inducing ownership are present without demonstrating ownership over the fake arm, because no behavioural evidence was provided. In a recent study, the rubber tail illusion was induced in mice (Wada et al. 2016). After synchronous, but not asynchronous, stimulation of the rubber tail, the mice responded to the grasping of the rubber tail as if their own tail had been grasped. In these cases, the induced experience is self-significant but, plausibly, falls short of any first-person content.[12]

6. Conclusion

We began by asking what we are studying when we claim we are studying body ownership. We distinguished five major questions about the sense of body ownership: the Constitutive Question (What is it?), the Phenomenological Question

---

[12] One possible response here is to distinguish different levels of first-person content, as Peacocke (2014) has done, from non-conceptual *de se* content up to explicit first-person judgements. Peacocke (2014) would judge that mice can have non-conceptual first-person content because they navigate on the basis of cognitive maps and have the capacity for egocentric perception and action.

(What is it like?), the Causal Question (What mechanisms underlie it?), the Functional Question (What does it do?), and the Mereological Question (How do the senses of ownership of the whole body and of body parts relate?). Distinguishing the questions allows us to see clearly what accounts can explain. We argue that theorists should distinguish between these different questions and should recognise different explanatory projects demanded of accounts addressing the different questions.

Another key moral is that an adequate account of the sense of body ownership must be empirically adequate. As we saw, despite insights that the spatial theories offered in terms of distinctive aspects of bodily awareness, the spatial theories could not accommodate somatoparaphrenia. One move that the spatial theorists can make in response is to claim that they only mean to account for the sense of body ownership in everyday experience.[13] However, the question is how to investigate the normal case without the tools of the pathological cases and the RHI. This is not easy. What is clear is that the three anchor points—located bodily sensation, pathologies of body ownership, and the experimental induction of ownership—have to be dealt with and the relation between the different cases addressed. In reflecting on the phenomenology of the sense of body ownership, the experience of ownership in normal embodiment may be much thinner than some of the accounts suggest. It appears to be recessive except for cases where there is conflict or error. A major issue here again is how to relate the treatment of the normal case with that of pathologies and experimental scenarios. Another aspect suggested by our discussion is that we should distinguish different facets of the sense of body ownership (e.g. spatial vs. affective). Instead of treating a single aspect as driving a complete account of the sense of body ownership, we might instead integrate different aspects in a pluralistic account which allows multiple factors to contribute to the sense of body ownership flexibly. Together with future work investigating the impact of empirical studies of full body ownership, we suggest that moving in this more pluralist direction may help us to have a better grasp on what it means to have a sense of ownership of our bodies.*

References

Bermúdez, J.L. (1998). *The Paradox of Self-Consciousness*. Cambridge, MA: MIT Press.

---

[13] De Vignemont (2018) has complained that this would make these accounts unfalsifiable. But this is mistaken, since their account of the normal case could still be wrong.

* We are grateful to Stephen Butterfill, Michael Martin, and Wayne Wu for numerous discussions; and to Manolo Martinez, Jean Moritz Müller, Keith Wilson, and especially Chiara Brozzo, Marie Guillot, Manuel Garcia-Carpintero, and Gregor Hochstetter for their feedback. This project was made possible through the support of grants from the Volkswagen Foundation and the John Templeton Foundation. The opinions expressed in this publication are those of the authors and do not necessarily reflect the views of the John Templeton Foundation.

Bermúdez, J.L. (2005). The phenomenology of bodily awareness. In *Phenomenology and Philosophy of Mind*, edited by D.W. Smith and A.L. Thomasson. New York: Oxford University Press.

Bermúdez, J.L. (2011). Bodily awareness and self-consciousness. In *Oxford Handbook of the Self*, edited by S. Gallagher, 157–179. Oxford: Oxford University Press.

Bermúdez, J.L. (2015). Bodily ownership, bodily awareness and knowledge without observation. *Analysis*, 75(1), 37–45.

Bermúdez, J.L. (2017). Ownership and the space of the body. In *The Subject's Matter: Self-Consciousness and the Body*, edited by F. de Vignemont and A. Alsmith. Cambridge, MA: MIT Press.

Bermúdez, J.L. (2019). Bodily ownership, psychological ownership, and psychopathology. *Review of Philosophy and Psychology*, 10(2), 263–280.

Bermúdez, J.L., Marcel, A., and Eilan, N. (1995). *The Body and the Self*. Cambridge, MA: MIT Press.

Billon, A. (2017). Basic self-awareness: lessons from the real world. *European Journal of Philosophy*, 25(3), 732–763.

Billon, A. (2017). Mineness first: Three challenges to recent theories of bodily self-awareness. In *The Subject's Matter: Self-Consciousness and the Body*, edited by de Vignemont, F., and Alsmith, A.J. Cambridge, MA: MIT Press.

Blanke, O. (2012). Multisensory brain mechanisms of bodily self-consciousness. *Nature Reviews Neuroscience*, 13(8), 556.

Bottini, G., Bisiach, E., Sterzi, R., and Vallar, G. (2001). Feeling touches in someone else's hand. *Neuroreport*, 13(2), 249–252.

Burge, T. (2010). *The Objectivity of Perception*. Oxford: Oxford University Press.

Cassam, Q. (1997). *Self and World*. Oxford: Calderon Press

Cole, J. (1992). *Pride and the Daily Marathon*. London: Duckworth.

Cole, J., & Paillard, J. (1995). Living without touch and peripheral information about body position and movement: Studies with deafferented subjects. In *The Body and the Self*, edited by J. Bermúdez, A. Marcel, and N. Eilan. Cambridge, MA: MIT Press.

Damasio, A. (1999). *The Feeling of What Happens: Body and Emotion in the Making of Consciousness*. New York: Harcourt Brace.

Davies, M., Coltheart, M., Langdon, R., and Breen, N. (2001). Monothematic delusions: Towards a two-factor account. *Philosophy, Psychiatry, & Psychology*, 8(2), 133–158.

de Vignemont, F. (2007). Habeas corpus: The sense of ownership of one's own body. *Mind and Language*, 22(4), 427–49.

de Vignemont, F. (2013). The mark of bodily ownership. *Analysis*, 73, 643–51.

de Vignemont, F. (2018). *Mind the Body*. Oxford: Oxford University Press.

de Vignemont, F., and Alsmith, A. (2017). *The Subject's Matter: Self-Consciousness and the Body*. Cambridge, MA: MIT Press.

Dijkerman, H.C., and De Haan, E.H. (2007). Somatosensory processing subserving perception and action: Dissociations, interactions, and integration. *Behavioral and Brain Sciences*, 30(2), 224–230.

Dokic, J. (2003). The sense of ownership: An analogy between sensation and action. In *Agency and Self-Awareness*, edited by J. Roessler and N. Eilan. Oxford: Oxford University Press.

Ehrsson, H.H. (2007). The experimental induction of out-of-body experiences. *Science*, 317(5841), 1048.

Ehrsson, H.H. (2012). The concept of body ownership and its relation to multisensory integration. In *The New Handbook of Multisensory Processes*, edited by B.E. Stein. Cambridge, MA: MIT Press.

Ehrsson, H.H., Weich, K., Weiskopf, N., Dolan, R.J., and Passingham, R.E. (2007). Threatening a rubber hand that you feel is yours elicits a cortical anxiety response. *Proceedings of the National Academy of Sciences of the United States of America*, 104, 9828–33.

Evans, G. (1982). *The Varieties of Reference*. Oxford: Oxford University Press.

Frith, C. (2005). The self in action: Lessons from delusions of control. *Consciousness and Cognition*, 14(4), 752–70.

Gallagher, S. (2005). *How the Body Shapes the Mind*. New York: Oxford University Press.

Graziano, M.S. (1999). Where is my arm? The relative role of vision and proprioception in the neuronal representation of limb position. *Proceedings of the National Academy of Sciences*, 96(18), 10418–21.

Graziano, M.S., Cooke, D.F., and Taylor, C.S. (2000). Coding the location of the arm by sight. *Science*, 290(5497), 1782–6.

Guillot, M. (2017). I, me, mine: On a confusion concerning the subjective character of experience. *Review of Philosophy and Psychology*, 8(1), 23–53.

Hilti, L.M., Hänggi, J., Vitacco, D.A., Kraemer, B., Palla, A., Luechinger, R., and Brugger, P. (2013). The desire for healthy limb amputation: structural brain correlates and clinical features of xenomelia. *Brain*, 136(1), 318–29.

Iriki, A., Tanaka, M., & Iwamura, Y. (1996). Coding of modified body schema during tool use by macaque postcentral neurones. *Neuroreport*, 7(14), 2325–30.

James, W. (1890). *The Principles of Psychology*. New York: Dover.

Jeannerod, M. (1997). *The Cognitive Neuroscience of Action*. Oxford: Blackwell.

Langdon, R., and Coltheart, M. (2000). The cognitive neuropsychology of delusions. *Mind and Language*, 15, 183–216.

Lenggenhager, B., Tadi, T., Metzinger, T., and Blanke, O. (2007). Video ergo sum: Manipulating bodily self-consciousness. *Science*, 317(5841), 1096–9.

Lopez, C., Halje, P., and Blanke, O. (2008). Body ownership and embodiment: vestibular and multisensory mechanisms. *Neurophysiologie Clinique / Clinical Neurophysiology*, 38(3), 149–61.

Maravita, A., and Iriki, A. (2004). Tools for the body (schema). *Trends in Cognitive Sciences*, 8(2), 79–86.

Martin, M.G.F. (1992). Sight and touch. In *The Content of Experience*, edited by T. Crane. Cambridge: Cambridge University Press, 199–201.

Martin, M.G.F. (1993). Sense modalities and spatial properties. In *Spatial Representations*, edited by N. Eilan, R. McCarty, and B. Brewer. Oxford: Oxford University Press.

Martin, M.G.F. (1995). Bodily awareness: A sense of ownership. In *The Body and the Self*, edited by J.L. Bermúdez, T. Marcel, and N. Eilan. Cambridge, MA: MIT Press.

McDowell, J. (1994). The content of perceptual experience. *Philosophical Quarterly*, 44(175), 190–205

Milner, D., and Goodale, M. (2006). *The Visual Brain in Action*. Oxford: Oxford University Press.

Orbán, K. (2018). A view from no where: The zero perspective view of bodily awareness. *Teorema: Revista Internacional de Filosofía*, 37(3), 39–64.

O'Shaughnessy, B. (1980). *The Will*. 2 vols. Cambridge: Cambridge University Press.

Paillard, J. (1999). Body schema and body image—a double dissociation. In *Motor Control, Today and Tomorrow*, edited by J.P. Scholz, Sofia: Academic Publishing House, 197–214.

Peacocke, C. (2014). *The Mirror of the World: Subjects, Consciousness, and Self-Consciousness*. Oxford: Oxford University Press.

Peacocke, C. (2015). Perception and the first person. In *The Oxford Handbook of the Philosophy of Perception*, edited by M. Matthen. Oxford: Oxford University Press.

Peacocke, C. (2016). The nature and role of first and second person content. *Analysis Reviews*, 76 (3): 345–54.

Pfeiffer, C., Serino, A., and Blanke, O. (2014). The vestibular system: A spatial reference for bodily self-consciousness. *Frontiers in Integrative Neuroscience*, 8, 31.

Roessler, J., and Eilan, N. (2003). *Agency and Self-Awareness*. Oxford: Oxford University Press.

Rohde, M., Di Luca, M., and Ernst, M. O. (2011). The rubber hand illusion: feeling of ownership and proprioceptive drift do not go hand in hand. *PloS one*, 6(6), e21659.

Romano, D., Sedda, A., Brugger, P., and Bottini, G. (2015). Body ownership: When feeling and knowing diverge. *Consciousness and Cognition*, 34, 140–8.

Sedda, A. (2011). Body integrity identity disorder: From a psychological to a neuro-logical syndrome. *Neuropsychology Review*, 21(4), 334–6.

Sedda, A., & Bottini, G. (2014). Apotemnophilia, body integrity identity disorder or xenomelia? Psychiatric and neurologic etiologies face each other. *Neuropsychiatric Disease and Treatment*, 10, 1255.

Shoemaker, S. (1981). Some varieties of functionalism. *Philosophical Topics*, 12(1), 93–119.

Tsakiris, M. (2010). My body in the brain: a neurocognitive model of body-ownership. *Neuropsychologia*, 48(3), 703–712.

Vallar, G., and Ronchi, R. (2009). Somatoparaphrenia: A body delusion. A review of the neuropsychological literature. *Experimental Brain Research*, 192(3), 533–51.

Wada, M., Takano, K., Ora, H., Ide, M., and Kansaku, K. (2016). The rubber tail illusion as evidence of body ownership in mice. *Journal of Neuroscience*, 36(43), 11133–7.

Wong, H.Y. (2014). Personal and sub-personal: Overcoming explanatory apartheid. In *Communicative Action*, edited by T.-W. Hung. Singapore: Springer.

Wong, H.Y. (2018). Embodied agency. *Philosophy and Phenomenological Research*, 97(3), 584–612.

Wong, H.Y., and Hochstetter, G. (2022). Review of *Mind the Body: An Exploration of Bodily Self-Awareness*, by Frédérique de Vignemont, *Mind*, 131, 347–357.

PART II
PUTTING SELF-EXPERIENCE TO WORK

8
The Three Circles of Consciousness

Uriah Kriegel

1. Introduction

A widespread assumption in current philosophy of mind is that a conscious state's phenomenal properties vary with its representational contents. In this chapter, I present (rather dogmatically) an alternative picture that recognizes two kinds of phenomenal properties that do not vary concomitantly with content. First, it admits phenomenal properties that vary rather with *attitude*: what it is like for me to *see* rain is phenomenally different from what it is like for me to *remember* (indistinguishable) rain, which is different again from what it is like for me to *visualize* (indistinguishable) rain—where these differences cannot be traced back to variations in content. Secondly, there is a kind of phenomenal property that varies neither with content nor with attitude but is altogether invariant across all conscious states: a substantive phenomenal commonality among what it is like for me to see, remember, and visualize rain, cats, or dogs. This substantive commonality, I will suggest, is the *for-me-ness* component of what it is like for me to have any of these experiences. I will close by discussing the interrelations among these three concentric layers of phenomenality: content-based, attitude-based, and for-me-ness.

2. Content-Based Phenomenality

It is commonly thought that there is a tight connection between a conscious state's phenomenal character and its representational content. By 'phenomenal character,' I mean what it is like for the subject to be in the relevant state; by 'representation content,' I mean what the state represents. Given an understanding of phenomenal character and representational content, we may understand the notions of a 'phenomenal property' and 'content property' as follows. Suppose C is a conscious state with properties $P_1,..., P_n$. Call a property P_i a 'phenomenal property' of C if the fact that C instantiates P_i contributes constitutively to what it is like for the subject to be in C, in the sense that the following counterfactual obtains: if C had not instantiated P_i, C's phenomenal character would *ipso facto* be

---

Uriah Kriegel, *The Three Circles of Consciousness* In: *Self-Experience: Essays on Inner Awareness.*
Edited by: Manuel García-Carpintero and Marie Guillot, Oxford University Press. © Uriah Kriegel 2023.
DOI: 10.1093/oso/9780198805397.003.0008

different. (I include the 'ipso facto' requirement to exclude cases where change in some property would *merely causally* entrain changes in phenomenal character.) Call a property P_i a 'content property' of C if the fact that C instantiates P_i contributes constitutively to what C represents, in the sense that if C had not instantiated P_i, C's representational content would *ipso facto* be different. (I am using 'represents' non-factively here: when you hallucinate a lemon, what your hallucination represents is a lemon, not *nothing*.)

The philosophy of mind of the past quarter-century has been intensely interested in potential dependence or grounding relations between phenomenal and content properties. Suppose C represents purple (a purple surface or volume, say), and there is a purplish way it is like for its subject to be in C. Then C has a content property P_c (the property of representing purple) and also a phenomenal property P_p (the property of there being a purplish way it is like for the subject to be in C). The facts that C has P_c and that it has P_p have seemed to many to have something to do with each other. Although some have argued that the two could come apart (e.g., Peacocke 1983, Block 1996), most philosophers have tended to think that they cannot: a conscious state instantiates P_c if and only if it instantiates P_p. But this kind of biconditional raises a certain Euthyphro question: does C have P_c because it has P_p (does it represent purple because there is a purplish way it is like to be in it), or does it have P_p because it has P_c (there is a purplish way it is like to be in it because it represents purple)? Thinking about this Euthyphro question in terms of metaphysical dependence, we can distinguish four *prima facie* approaches to it:

(1) *Content first*: C's having P_p (the phenomenal property) asymmetrically depends upon C's having P_c (the content property).
(2) *Phenomenality first*: C's having P_c asymmetrically depends upon C's having P_p.
(3) *No priority*: C's having P_p and its having P_c are mutually dependent.
(4) *Independence*: Neither C's having P_p nor C's having P_c is dependent on the other.

The first position is associated with so-called representationalism or intentionalism (Dretske 1995, Byrne 2001). The second is associated with the 'phenomenal intentionality view' (Horgan and Tienson 2002, Loar 2003). The third can come in several varieties, but one prominent option is an 'identity view' (Chalmers 2004, Pautz 2010), whereby P_c and P_p are ultimately one and the same property, differently described. The fourth position corresponds to what Horgan and Tienson (2002) call 'separatism,' the view that P_c and P_p have nothing to do with each other, metaphysically speaking. A separatist would typically deny the necessary correlation between phenomenal and content properties, but she can also accept the correlation and insist that it does not reflect any metaphysical dependence.

As a purely sociological observation, it should be noted that separatism, once a widespread *assumption* among philosophers of mind, has become a minority position over the past quarter-century. Most debates in the area have concentrated on which of the other three positions is most plausible: representationalism, phenomenal intentionality, or the no-priority view.

This picture of the logical geography requires some refinement, however. For philosophers of both representationalist and phenomenalintentionality persuasions have often sounded an identity-theoretic note. Michael Tye, a leading representationalist, writes: 'Phenomenal character (or what it is like) is *one and the same as* a certain sort of intentional content' (Tye 1995: 137; my italics). Terry Horgan, a leading phenomenal intentionality theorist, is inclined toward the identification of P_c and P_p (personal communication). Yet Tye and Horgan do not seem to have a 'loud agreement', being simply confused about the fact that they actually agree with one another. So how should we make sense of their disagreement?

I think the answer is that disagreement is, in the first instance, on something like *epistemic* rather than metaphysical priority. The representationalist holds that content properties are epistemically more basic: we understand a phenomenal property by reductively explaining it in terms of some content property, which in turn we understand in broadly information-theoretic terms, hence without appeal to phenomenal notions. The phenomenal intentionalist proposes the opposite direction of epistemic priority: we understand the content property in terms of the phenomenal property, and grasp the nature of the latter through direct introspective acquaintance, hence without recourse to representation idiom. A third position is that the single property we have here can be understood neither first under its phenomenal guise nor first under its content guise; on the contrary, upon reflection we realize that the two descriptions must co-refer, as we are unable to grasp the phenomenal property otherwise than as intentional or the intentional property otherwise than as phenomenal.

To summarize, representationalism can be understood as the disjunction of (a) the claim that phenomenal properties are metaphysically grounded in content properties and (b) the claim that phenomenal properties are identical with content properties but the phenomenal description, or conception, of those properties is epistemically derivative upon their content description/conception. The phenomenal intentionality view is a similar metaphysical-priority-or-epistemic-priority disjunctive thesis. And the no-priority view denies both metaphysical and epistemic priority.

Regardless of which line one takes on the question of priority, many philosophers of mind hold that phenomenal properties covary with content properties. More specifically:

Covariance: For any conscious state C and phenomenal property P_p, there is a content property P_c, such that C instantiates P_p if and only if C instantiates P_c.

172　THE THREE CIRCLES OF CONSCIOUSNESS

As we have seen, even the separatist can accept *Covariance*, though most likely she will not.

3. Attitude-Based Phenomenality

Opponents of *Covariance* have often attempted to adduce instances of sensory qualia that, they claim, go beyond conscious state's content. Peacocke (1983) argued that a subject can have a visual experience of two equally sized trees, one of which is farther away from the other, such that (i) the experience represents the two trees as equally sized but (ii) the sensory quale associated with each tree is different (one 'takes up' more of the subject's 'visual field' than the other). Block (1996) argued that when we rub our eyes long enough, we have 'phosphene experiences' that (i) do not represent anything but (ii) involve an unmistakable sensory quality of glowing blobs in our visual field.

For reasons I do not want to go into here, I do not believe that alleged counter-examples of this kind work. All the same, I contend, there are plenty of exceptions to *Covariance*, exceptions which have something in common. These exceptions are, however, of a very different kind.

To appreciate the relevant kind of case, I want to start with a seemingly unrelated distinction between three kinds of belief report. Compare:

(B1)　S_1 believes that there are ghosts.
(B2)　S_2 believes that ghosts exist.
(B3)　S_3 believes in ghosts.

The mental states ostensibly reported by B1–B3 are clearly related: they are all in the business of doxastically committing the subject to the existence of ghosts. But if we take the reports' grammatical structures at face value, they report mental states with subtly but importantly different intentional structures. There are live debates on just how we should understand B1, but here I want to focus on B2 and B3. Note that the specification of *what is believed* in report B2 includes the word 'exist,' suggesting that existence shows up in the *content* of S_2's belief. In contrast, in B3 the specification of what is believed is one word long—it is exhausted by 'ghosts'—and involves no existential term. So as long as we take at face value the reports' grammatical structure, it would seem that S_2's belief commits S_2 to the existence of ghosts in virtue of its content, whereas S_3's does not. At the same time, S_3's belief clearly does commit S_3 to the existence of ghosts (indeed, that is *all* believing in ghosts does!). It follows that this existence-commitment is not part of the content of S_3's mental state. Rather, it would seem to be an aspect of the very attitude of *believing in*: to believe *in* something is to doxastically commit to its existence. One way to put this is to say that while S_2's belief represents ghosts as existing, S_3's belief represents-as-existing ghosts. Here the existential term is used as a modification of the verb 'represents,' suggesting that existence-commitment a *mode* or *way* of representing rather than part of *what* is represented. Another way to say this is that existence-commitment is a *content property* of S_2's belief but an *attitudinal property* of S_3's belief.

Now, we may certainly refuse to take the grammars of B1–B3 at face value, and so deny that existence-commitment is ever an attitudinal property of our beliefs. Still, the contrast between B2 and B3 is useful in bringing out two different intentional structures that conscious states might potentially exhibit. When a conscious state C commits to the F-ness of x, it may be either because C represents x as F (where x's being F is *what* C represents), or because C represents-as-F x (where *what* C represents is only x, and as-F is *how* C represents x).

With this in the background, I may state my main claim in this section as follows: quite a few of the phenomenal properties of our conscious states are attitudinal rather than content properties, properties these have not in virtue of *what* they represent, but in virtue of *how* they represent. More specifically:

Contrarian: For some conscious state C and phenomenal property P_p, there is no content property P_c, such that C instantiates P_p if and only if C instantiates P_c.

I will now, rather dogmatically, go over a series of phenomenal properties that I take to be attitudinal, hence to outstrip content properties. I adopt the dogmatic stance not because I think the claims I make are somehow *obvious*, but because space is limited and I have argued for these claims more fully elsewhere. The exercise in this chapter is to *pull together* the results of those disparate arguments in order to articulate a certain picture of the phenomenal realm.

Consider first a pair of subjects S_4 and S_5, such that (i) S_4 sees my dog, (ii) S_5 visualizes my dog, and (iii) due to extraordinary circumstances, the details, vivacity, and determinacy of S_4's seeing are identical to those of S_5's visualizing. On my view, there is still a difference in the overall phenomenology of S_4's and S_5's experiences. (Nobody in such circumstances would be confused as to whether s/he is perceiving or imagining!) I want to say that the difference between these overall phenomenal characters has to do with the *realness* of that which is represented: perception involves a subtle feeling of realness that attaches to the object, whereas imagination does not, and may even involve a subtle feeling of *unreality*. And yet, I want to claim, *what* is perceived or imagined is strictly the same: my dog. If so, the realness-related difference must be grounded in the *manners* in which the two experiences represent my dog: while S_4's experience represents-as-real my dog, S_5's does not (and perhaps even represents-as-unreal my dog). This is a difference in the experiences' *attitudinal* properties: S_4 does not *see* my dog's

174   THE THREE CIRCLES OF CONSCIOUSNESS

realness, and S_5 does not *visualize* my dog's unreality; they see/visualize only my dog. (True to my dogmatic stance, I have not provided here any *argument* for these claims. For actual arguments, see Kriegel 2015a: ch. 6)

A similar contrast attends, in my opinion, perception and episodic memory. Suppose S_6 sees the rain falling, while S_7 episodically remembers a qualitatively indistinguishable rain (or remembers *seeing* that rain).[1] Moreover, suppose the circumstances are sufficiently odd that the vivacity/determinacy of the two experiences matches. There are various differences between these two experiences, including differences in functional role. But in addition, I contend, there is a certain *phenomenal* difference, one that seems to concern *felt temporal orientation*: in remembering the rain, we experience it as past, but in seeing the rain, we experience it as (in the) present. It is because of this felt temporal orientation that each of us would immediately know whether s/he is busy seeing or remembering rain. Nonetheless, I contend, still dogmatically, the content of the two experiences is strictly the same: a (type-)identical rain is represented. The felt temporal orientation must therefore be 'attitudinally encoded' in these experiences, so to speak. We might say that while S_7's experience represents-as-past the rain, S_6's represents-as-present the rain. (Again, I have offered no *argument* for any of this. For such an argument, see Kriegel 2015b.)

It has sometimes been claimed, against representationalists, that different *perceptual modalities* can represent the same features, but in different *ways* (Block 1996, Lopes 2000). For example, we can see, hear, and smell spatial locations; the resulting visual, auditory, and olfactory experiences differ phenomenally despite representing the same location. This might be construed as a claim about differences in phenomenal attitudinal properties. There have been responses from representationalists on this score, essentially claiming that there are environmental features we can only see and others we can only hear, and that these modality-specific features ensure that the experiences' respective representational contents are in fact different (Dretske 2000, Byrne 2001). Thus, for any location L, there is also the-look-of-L and the-sound-of-L, and it is these kinds of entity (rather than L itself) that the relevant visual and auditory experiences represent. Accordingly, here I do not wish to assume that the properties of being visual, being auditory, and so on are phenomenal attitudinal properties; but nor do I wish to assume the opposite. What I would like to insist on is that in other domains, it is hard to deny that parallel modality-specific phenomenal properties exist.

Consider for example the phenomenology of emotional experience, such as S_8's fear of a snake. It has often been claimed that in fearing a snake, we are experiencing the snake as somehow dangerous to us. If S_8 did not experience the snake as

---

[1] I take no stand here on whether such episodic memory's content is given by the rain, by the past seeing of the rain, or by *both* (see Fernández 2006). Nonetheless, for simplicity I will discuss the matter as though the object of the episodic memory is some external rain.

dangerous, her experience would not properly count as a fear. At the same time, S_8 does not fear *that the snake is dangerous*; no, she simply fears the snake. (Nor does she fear *the snake's dangerousness*, since what she fears is a concrete thing, not an abstract entity.) Plausibly, then, the danger-commitment is 'attitudinally encoded': S_8's experience does not represent the snake as dangerous but rather represents-as-dangerous the snake. If so, the phenomenal difference between fearing a dog and loving him is an attitudinal rather than content difference: in both experiences a dog is what the experience represents; the difference is in the *manner* in which the experience represents what it does. Crucially, in this area the move of positing such intentional objects as the-dangerousness-of-the-dog and the loveliness-of-the-dog is implausible. For what we emote about seems to be manifestly the dog himself: it is the dog who bears his teeth and barks at us, not his dangerousness; it is not the dangerousness-of-the-dog that threatens to bite us, but the dog itself. (Still dogmatic, I refer the reader to Kriegel 2017b for an argument to this effect.)

Moods have often been specially problematic for representationalists. For they appear to be somehow completely undirected, that is, to have *no* representational content. In an attempt to defend a representationalist treatment, it has been suggested that although moods are not directed at anything in particular, they nonetheless have a *generalized* directedness. What this means is that they represent properties of the world as a whole: depression represents the world as dull, anxiety represents the world as threatening, and so on (Crane 1998, Seager 1999). This account manages to assign a representational content to moods, but it has struck many as counterintuitive, insofar as moods seem typically to arise not due to the unfortunate detecting or tracking of such global properties, but from within the subject's psyche, so to speak (Kind 2013). One way to reconcile the intentional character of moods and their endogenous character might be by going attitudinalist. We might hold, for instance, that depression represents-as-dull the world, anxiety represents-as-threatening the world, and so on. Here all that is 'tracked' or 'detected' is the world; the element of dullness or threateningness is 'contributed' by the subject's internal state. (A case for this attitudinal account of mood is in Kriegel 2019.)

Consider next desire, wish, craving, and other phenomena of the will. When S_9 desires (wishes for, craves) chocolate, there is a sense in which the chocolate appears good to her—she *experiences* the chocolate as good, or as good *for her* (not necessarily in a moral sense!). Such 'conative states' are goodness-committal (Stampe 1987) in roughly the same sense fear is danger-committal and belief-in is existence-committal. This is the traditional guise-of-the-good thesis (Tenenbaum 2007). Moreover, this goodness-commitment is part of the *phenomenal character* of conative states: the desire *feels* like it casts chocolate in a positive light. On my view, however, this goodness-commitment is attitudinally encoded: what S_9 desires is not that the chocolate *be good*, nor the chocolate's goodness; no, she simply desires the chocolate. It is what she desires that she hopes to eat, and what she hopes to eat is the chocolate, not its goodness. We might say that the desire casts chocolate in a positive light rather than casts light on a positive chocolate. That is: S_9's state does not represent chocolate as good but rather represents-as-good chocolate. (For the argument, see Kriegel 2017a.)

There is a tradition that takes belief, judgment, and all other intellectual activities to lack proprietary phenomenal character. Recently, however, proponents of so-called cognitive phenomenology have claimed that at least some cognitive states, such as making the judgment that I own a private jet, have a properly intellectual phenomenology irreducible to the phenomenology of whatever accompanying imagery I might experience (Bayne and Montague 2011). One of the main arguments for this draws on the immediacy of our knowledge of such cognitive states (Goldman 1993). It is a notable fact, however, that I can know immediately not only whether I judge *that I own a private jet* or *that the weather is nice*, but also whether I *judge* that I have a private jet or *desire* that I have a private jet (Pitt 2004). The latter two present themselves differently to introspection. What is the difference? One natural suggestion is: while the desire represents-as-good my having a private jet, the judgment represents-as-true (or perhaps represents-as-*obtaining*) my having a private jet. Desire that *p* and judgment that *p* represent *the same thing*, the same state of affairs (*p*), but represent it in different *ways*: *sub specie boni* in one case, *sub specie veri* in the other.

There are, in my opinion, many other, increasingly more subtle phenomenal attitudinal properties in our mental life. In particular, different *types* of cognitive state (judging, accepting, supposing, etc.), different *types* of conative state (desiring, craving, wishing), different types of emotional state (fear, anger, indignation), different types of mood (depression, anxiety, elation) and perhaps different types of perceptual state (visual, auditory, and so on) are distinguished by their specific species of attitudinal properties. But the above array covers some of the most robust and most generic ones: representing-as-true, representing-as-good, representing-as-real/unreal, representing-as-dangerous, representing-as-threatening, and so on. We have here an entire domain of phenomenal properties that goes beyond the content properties of conscious states. In other words, we have here a whole slew of counterexamples to *Covariance*.

If all these counterexamples are sitting right beneath our noses, how could they be missed so easily? I speculate that this has to do with a combination of two factors: (i) the prominence of the 'transparency of experience' thesis (Harman 1990) in contemporary philosophy of mind and (ii) the blindness of the transparency observation to the difference between representing *x* as F and representing-as-F *x*. I close this section with some elaborations on this speculation.

Although the transparency claim is very influential, there is no standard way to formulate it. Here are three significantly different formulations:

(T1)   When we introspect our phenomenal states, we are only aware of the environmental features these states represent.

(T2)   When we introspect our phenomenal states, we are only aware of these states' representational contents.

(T3)   When we introspect our phenomenal states, we are only aware of these states' representational properties.

Representationalists of phenomenal-externalist bent (Dretske 1996, Lycan 2001) have tended to focus on T1, though sometimes the more modest T2 is leaned upon. Phenomenal intentionality proponents have sometimes stressed a variation on T2 (Horgan and Tienson 2002, Kriegel 2007) that we might formulate as follows: when we introspect our phenomenal states, we are always aware of them *qua* contentful states. Now, under certain assumptions, T3 might certainly seem equivalent to T2; but once we recognize attitudinal properties of the form *representing-as-F*, the equivalence disappears. For in a sense such properties are representational as well: they concern ways of *representing* an object, after all. They are not purely vehicular properties that can survive the destruction of the representation. Take away the fear's representation of a snake and you take away its representation-as-dangerous of the snake. So the property of representing-as-dangerous is in a very real sense a representational property—though not a property a state has in virtue of its representational *content*.

And yet, attitude-based phenomenal properties are very different from content-based ones. For phenomenal states do not *inherit* these properties from the character of the represented environmental features. On the contrary, the environmental features are experienced in a certain light in virtue of the way the states do their representing: the chocolate is experienced in a positive light because the stance we take toward it is that of desire rather than (say) fear. If we rather feared the chocolate, our experience would cast it in a dangerous rather than positive light. In this respect, attitudinal-representational properties are deeply different from content-representational properties. But because they are nonetheless representational properties, properties that do not get instantiated independently of the representing of things, when we introspect our phenomenal states we do not encounter anything beyond those states' representings. Introspection itself cannot tell apart—at least not very easily—whether an introspected experience represents x as F or represents-as-F x. For example, while introspection can tell us that our fear of a snake involves both a snaky phenomenology and a danger phenomenology, and indeed that the two are connected, it cannot tell us whether the fear represents the snake as dangerous or

178 THE THREE CIRCLES OF CONSCIOUSNESS

represents-as-dangerous the snake. That is, it cannot tell us whether the relevant representational property is a content property or an attitudinal property. Or at least, it cannot tell us this with the kind of ease and confidence that those who wield the transparency observation tend to expect. In other words, we can *confidently* assert T3, but not T2, let alone T1.[2]

Perhaps a suitably trained introspection *could* (help) instruct us on such matters. But in any case, nothing in the literature on transparency addresses the envisaged kind of subtle introspective exercise. On the contrary, that literature takes the introspective deliverance it focuses on as *obvious*, requiring no patient dwelling and examining. My claim is that all that is delivered therein is the much more coarse-grained truth that nothing we encounter in introspection goes beyond the representational. That the properties encountered in introspection are content properties rather than attitudinal-representational properties is something nobody has ever shown. So while there is an important introspective insight at the heart of the transparency claim, such theses as T1 and T2 are not simple articulations of what introspection delivers, but layer questionable philosophical interpretation on top of what is strictly delivered by introspection.[3]

4. For-Me-Ness

Phenomenal characters can vary, I have argued, not only in content-based ways but also in attitude-based ways. There is a difference between what it is like for me to see red and what it is like for me to see blue, but there is also a difference between what it is like for me to see red and what it is like for me to *imagine* red. Presumably, however, there is also something that remains invariant across all phenomenal characters—a certain commonality of phenomenal characters that marks them as a natural group of phenomena and distinguishes them from other phenomena. There is something *in common* between what it is like for me to see red, what it is like for me to see blue, and what it is like for me to imagine red. The commonality, we may say, is there being something it is like for me.

In this 'something it is like for me,' the element designated by 'something' appears to involve a kind of merely *formal* commonality—'something' functions as a variable that simply ranges over the myriad different ways it could be like for

---

[2] Mindful that I have not offered here any arguments for the attitudinal treatment of the phenomenal properties I claimed above were attitudinal, I hasten to add that the arguments I provide elsewhere (in the above-cited works) are *not* simple introspective assertions. Part of the reason is precisely that I doubt introspection can tell apart representing x as F and representing-as-F x.

[3] This philosophical interpretation is founded on suspect theoretical principles, namely, that the representational character of a mental state is exhausted by its representational content, perhaps even the character of the represented environmental features. These principles embody a blindspot in contemporary philosophy of mind: the routine disregard or unawareness of attitudinal properties of the form *representing-as-F*.

me to be in some conscious state. But there is also another element, or aspect, of 'something it is like for me,' the one designated by 'for me.' Call that element the *for-me-ness* of conscious states. This for-me-ness, I contend, is *not* a merely formal commonality of phenomenal characters. It is a *substantive* commonality, something that is common to all phenomenal characters but which we can also isolate in thought and contemplate 'on its own.' While the bluish way it is like for me to see blue is different from the reddish way it is like for me to see red, the element of *for-me-ness* in these two ways-it-is-like-for-me is strictly identical, and not only in the sense that we can define a genus, or determinable, of which both bluishness and reddishness are species, or determinates, and which *qua* genus or determinable remains invariant. Rather, there is a very specific, very determinate aspect of bluish-for-me-ness and reddish-for-me-ness that is common to the two, namely, for-me-ness as such. Moreover, I want to say, for-me-ness is not just a (substantive) *commonality* among all conscious states, but is also a *peculiarity* of theirs: nonconscious mental states occur *in* me, but are not *for* me in the relevant sense. As a substantive commonality that is also peculiar to its conscious states, for-me-ness is on this view effectively 'the mark of the conscious.'

How exactly should we characterize for-me-ness as such? The issue is vexed and entire volumes can and should be dedicated to it. My thought here is that introducing for-me-ness as the substantive commonality among all phenomenal characters might be the least committal way to home in on it; we can later debate the exact profile of this substantive commonality.

Introducing for-me-ness as the substantive commonality among all phenomenal characters, hence among all conscious states, brings in two dimensions. On the one hand, for-me-ness should be thought of as just a commonality across phenomenal properties, in that it is not some detachable, self-standing quale that can occur on its own (Zahavi 2014). There is no phenomenal character exhausted by the presence of for-me-ness. For-me-ness is always the for-me-ness *of* some concrete felt content (and/or attitude). It is not a quale in its own right, but a standing dimension of any and every specific quale—a *sine qua non* for all qualia. (I use 'qualia' here to denote phenomenal characters, or perhaps components of such; I do not use it in a way that implies a non-representational status.) On the other hand, although for-me-ness is just a commonality among phenomenal characters, and cannot constitute a phenomenal character all by itself, it does have a substantive nature, one that makes a specific *contribution* to (every) phenomenal character. This distinctive contribution can be isolated in thought, as a kind of subjective significance whereby all the subject's experiences are present to her. Every experience is *experienced* by the subject, and is so in a way that goes beyond the mere grammatical appropriateness of the cognate accusative: we do not experience our experiences *just* in the sense in which we smile our smiles and dance our dances, but in a fuller, more substantive sense that captures the for-me-ness of experiences.

180 THE THREE CIRCLES OF CONSCIOUSNESS

Note well: in saying this, I do not mean to imply that the subject must be somehow aware of *herself*, or of some 'me,' in having her experiences. Rather, she may be aware just of the experiences, and it is this awareness that makes these experiences *for her*. If we use the label 'mineness' to designate the more robust phenomenon of awareness of oneself in addition to one's experiences, we could put the point by saying that for-me-ness need not amount to mineness. On my view it is only the thinner phenomenon of for-me-ness that constitutes the mark of the conscious, the substantive commonality among (and peculiarity of) all conscious states.[4]

As a mere commonality and yet a substantive one, for-me-ness serves a double function as both (i) a component among others in a conscious state's overall phenomenal character and (ii) a precondition for the existence of all other phenomenal components (*as* phenomenal components). Compare the keystone of a thirteen-stone masonry arch. On the one hand, it is a stone among others composing the arch, as intrinsically 'beefy' as the other twelve. On the other hand, if we remove it the whole arch collapses, and to that extent it is a precondition for there being any other arch-component. (If the arch collapses, the individual stones do not disappear, but they are no longer arch-components. By the same token, if a conscious representation of a red surface loses its for-me-ness, the representation of the red surface need not disappear—it may become a subpersonal representation—but it is no longer a *phenomenal* property.[5])

All this is of course highly controversial. Many philosophers have denied the very existence of for-me-ness (Dretske 1993, Schear 2009). But such philosophers owe us an alternative account of the substantive commonality among conscious states, or an argument to the effect that there is no substantive commonality among conscious states. In that respect, for-me-ness is not just phenomenologically compelling, but also does a certain explanatory work, insofar as it accounts for the apparent substantive commonality across experiences.

A representationalist might suggest that the substantive commonality among all conscious states is precisely their *contentfulness*. But in fact most representationalists accept that nonconscious states are often contentful as well (tacit beliefs, repressed desires, and subpersonal perceptual representations are some examples). Citing *phenomenal contentfulness* as the ultimate substantive commonality only

[4] My convictions in this area are very weak, but my inclination is to think that for-me-ness does amount to mineness in a normal human adult, but may not in nonhuman animals, children, and certain pathologies (Kriegel 2009: ch. 5).

[5] The analogy may be imperfect, inasmuch as it is mostly the keystone's relational properties that confer on it its special status, so that it is substitutable for almost any stone used in making up the arch; whereas for-me-ness could not swap roles with the property of representing a red surface for the status of enabling all other phenomenality. Still, in both cases there is a single constituent of a structure that is also essential for the status of a number of other items as further constituents of that structure.

raises the question of what makes an instance of contentfulness phenomenal. (My answer: its for-me-ness!) Some representationalists have cited a special kind of *functional role* as common to all conscious representations and distinguishing them from nonconscious ones (Tye 1995). But a commonality of functional role is not a *phenomenal* commonality, if only because a state's functional role is a *dispositional* property, whereas phenomenality is an *occurrent, categorical* property.[6]

Introducing the phenomenon of for-me-ness as the substantive commonality among all conscious experiences is useful in resisting certain undue theoretical expectations. In particular, I have in mind the potential expectation that we should be able to use something like 'phenomenal contrast' (Siegel 2007) to bring for-me-ness into sharper relief. The contrast method has become so pervasive in current philosophy of consciousness that some might expect a contrast argument for for-me-ness. But the expectation is unfulfillable in the case of any phenomenal feature necessarily present in *every* conscious state (see McClelland, this volume). For the contrast method attempts to isolate phenomenal features by juxtaposing experiences in which they are present and ones in which they are absent (or else experiences where there is variation in the determinates of the same phenomenal determinable); whereas it is in the very nature of for-me-ness to be invariant across, and yet present in, each and every conscious experience.

My point is that the contrast method is *blind in principle* to any absolutely ubiquitous and invariant feature of experience, hence to any property constitutive of the very possibility of having a conscious experience. It is simply ill suited for making manifest any such feature. Consider the following case. Sometimes, we only notice that the refrigerator has been humming when it *stops* humming. But the fact that we only *notice* it then does not mean we did not *experience* it while it was humming. Arguably, when the refrigerator stops humming there is an immediate change in our overall phenomenology—which suggests that the humming was part of our overall phenomenology before it stopped. Now, we can imagine a world—call it 'Fridge World'—where people are born with a tiny irremovable object in the back of their necks, which is too small to detect with the naked eye but which hums audibly throughout their lives. Arguably, it is impossible for these people to use the phenomenal contrast method to bring into sharper relief the pervasive presence of this humming quality in their experience. Yet if the hum *were* to stop, there *would* be a change in their overall phenomenology, indeed a *noticeable* change (though how exactly they would conceptualize the change is an open question). This suggests that the hum is phenomenally real but 'invisible' to the contrast method.

---

[6] There are probably other antecedently reasonable candidates for the substantive commonality among conscious states, but for-me-ness offers one clear such candidate, and the one I am adopting here, admittedly with little argument. For more argument, see Kriegel 2009.

182   THE THREE CIRCLES OF CONSCIOUSNESS

There are important differences between the hum in Fridge World and for-me-ness in the actual world. For one thing, for-me-ness, as understood here, is not only ubiquitous in conscious experience, but is *necessarily so*. Accordingly, the corresponding counterfactual is more complicated for it: if for-me-ness were extinguished, one would not simply have a different kind of experience, one would stop experiencing altogether (one would turn into a zombie). In both the hum quale and for-me-ness, though, the absolute universality of the relevant dimension of experience means that it cannot be made manifest using the contrast method. Something more circuitous is needed if we are to fix on the relevant phenomenon. The present suggestion is simply to try to grasp that which (i) remains invariant across all conscious experiences but (ii) can be thought (though cannot occur) in isolation from any specific type of conscious experience. This is just trying to grasp the substantive commonality among all phenomenal characters.

◆◈◆

Elsewhere, I have argued that for-me-ness is also compatible with the transparency of experience (Kriegel 2009: ch. 5). It might be thought that a version of the transparency thesis would undermine the notion that for-me-ness is phenomenally real. Consider the following relatively weak version of transparency:

(T4)   When we introspect our phenomenal states, we are only aware of these states' first-order representational properties.

T4 is weaker than T1 and T2, inasmuch as it makes a claim about representational properties rather than representational contents or represented environmental features. At the same time, it is stronger than T3, insofar as it requires our introspected phenomenal properties to be not just representational properties but *first-order* representational properties. This is intended to rule out higher-order and self-representational properties, such as a state's property of representing itself to represent red. Arguably, the proponents of transparency do not have such higher-order and self-representational properties in mind when they assert transparency. Thus T4 captures a relatively modest version of transparency. Yet it appears to threaten the phenomenological reality of for-me-ness, since the latter does not seem to be a first-order representational property.[7]

On the plausible assumption that for-me-ness is not a first-order representational property, its phenomenal reality is indeed incompatible with the thesis that all phenomenal properties are first-order representational properties. But I would

---

[7] On the view I have defended, for example, it is rather constituted by a self-representational property of conscious states (Kriegel 2009: ch. 4). It is also possible to hold that it is a non-representational property altogether, a kind of 'intrinsic glow' inhering in conscious states. Either view is incompatible with the notion that all phenomenal properties are first-order representational properties.

argue that that the way T4 motivates the thesis that all phenomenal properties are first-order representational properties involves two inferential steps, and both are problematic. The first step involves the following assumption: if when we introspect our phenomenal states, we are only aware of their first-order representational properties, then plausibly, all the phenomenal properties our conscious states actually instantiate when we introspect them are first-order representational properties. (In other words, phenomenal properties do not remain in-principle-hidden from introspection while we introspect.) The second step makes another assumption: if all the phenomenal properties our conscious states instantiate when we introspect them are first-order representational properties, then plausibly, all the phenomenal properties our conscious states instantiate *at any time* are first-order representational properties. (That is, there are no phenomenal properties that show up *only* when we do not introspect.) The point I want to make in the remainder of this section is that the proponent of for-me-ness need not deny T4 itself; she can instead deny one or both of these assumptions.

There are certainly examples of the second assumption failing—cases where a conscious state instantiates a certain phenomenal property so long as it is not introspected, but where the introspecting of that state destroys the relevant phenomenal property. Brentano (1874: 29–30) offered as an example the quality of intense anger. It is in the nature of a certain kind of intense anger—rage, or fury—to be *consuming*. The subject who is not fully consumed by her anger, who maintains a certain emotional distance from it and clear-headedness with respect to it, is not an enraged or infuriated subject. But the very act of introspecting one's anger means that one is no longer consumed by it. In a way, one becomes a partly angry person and partly introspecting person, and has thereby taken some distance from the anger. One is no longer *identified* with one's anger. To that extent, the peculiar phenomenology of rage or fury is a phenomenology we cannot undergo when we introspect—the introspecting of our experience *destroys* its furious, consuming quality. This shows that even if all the phenomenal properties our conscious states instantiate when we introspect them are of a certain type T, there may still be phenomenal properties our conscious states instantiate *when not introspected* which are not of that type.[8]

There may also be cases where a conscious state's phenomenal property is not introspectible, but not because it is destroyed by the introspecting of that state. It persists through the introspecting and yet evades introspective detection. This may seem initially strange, but it falls out of a certain conception of the relationship between for-me-ness and introspection (Kriegel 2009: ch. 5). I cannot *argue* here for the relevant conception, but I can *summarize* it. On this view, most

---

[8] It might be asked how we know of phenomenal properties that disappear under introspection. The answer is that, according to Brentano, there is a kind of non-introspective inner awareness that accompanies all our conscious states. This is also my view; I go into it momentarily.

184 THE THREE CIRCLES OF CONSCIOUSNESS

conscious states 'live' in our stream of consciousness unintrospected, and for those, their for-me-ness consists in a certain (i) inbuilt (ii) peripheral awareness of their occurrence. The awareness is 'inbuilt' in the following sense: in order to have the relevant awareness of one's current conscious state, one need not be in any numerically distinct mental state; rather, it is in virtue of being in that very conscious state that one is aware of its occurrence. And the awareness is 'peripheral' in that it does not occupy the focus of one's attention, but is more akin to peripheral vision, say, or to fringe tactile awareness of the soles of one's shoes.[9] However, it is part of the view that once a subject introspects, what happens is that the same old inbuilt awareness of one's conscious state ceases to be peripheral and becomes focal. Thus to introspect is not to enter a new and distinct mental state, but rather to have one's inbuilt awareness become attentive and central. The inbuilt awareness is a ubiquitous dimension of our conscious life, but while it remains peripheral during most of our conscious life, it becomes focal when we introspect. And just as, in this picture, the for-me-ness of a non-introspected conscious state *consists in* the subject's inbuilt *peripheral* awareness of that state, the for-me-ness of an *introspected* conscious state consists in the subject's inbuilt *focal* awareness of that state.

If we accept this picture of the relationship between for-me-ness and introspection, it is only to be expected that whenever we introspect our conscious state, the for-me-ness is not one of the things introspection reveals to us. For the for-me-ness of an introspected state is the introspecting itself, the revealing to us of *the rest* of the state's phenomenal character (namely, its content-based and attitude-based phenomenal properties). So it turns out that there *is* at least one phenomenal property that remains in principle hidden from introspection while we introspect: introspection does not reveal the introspecting, yet the introspecting does contribute to the overall way it is like for the introspector. (There is a felt difference between seeing a blue sky and introspecting seeing a blue sky!) The contribution the introspecting makes does not have to do with any of the phenomenal elements given in one's introspective awareness, but is the felt givenness itself.

5. Conclusion: Concentric Circles of Phenomenality?

In summary, in addition to content-based phenomenal properties, there are two other types of phenomenal property: attitude-based ones and for-me-ness. Both

---

[9] One *can*, of course, turn one's attention to the periphery of one's visual field, or to one's tactile sensation of the soles of one's shoes. But in the normal go of things, although these are aspects of our overall conscious experience, they remain outside the focus of conscious attention—they 'inhabit' the background or fringe of consciousness.

of these constitute a certain blindspot for the transparency thesis, though for different reasons.

If we accept the views presented in §§3–4, there are at least two substantive commonalities among (i) an episodic memory of a brown dog, (ii) an episodic memory of a white dog, (iii) an episodic memory of a purple butterfly, and (iv) an episodic memory of the sound of a distant bagpipe. One thing common to (i)–(iv) is the for-me-ness they all involve. Another is the attitudinal phenomenal property of representing-as-past characteristic of episodic memory. I now want to compare three models of the latter's role in the composition of what it is like to undergo (i)–(iv). I call them the 'salad model,' the 'tree model,' and the 'circles model.' Each will cast in a different light the interrelations among content-based phenomenal properties, attitude-based phenomenal properties, and for-me-ness.

The salad model. On this model, what it is like for me to episodically remember a brown dog is fixed by the combination of three separate experiential 'ingredients': brown-dog phenomenology, episodic-remembering phenomenology, and for-me-ness. The phenomenal character of remembering a brown dog is simply the 'sum' of the phenomenal contributions made by each of these. But each is a 'detachable' ingredient that could recombine with other phenomenal ingredients to form different experiences. For example, the (content-based) brown-dog phenomenology could combine with (the attitude-based) imaginative phenomenology and with for-me-ness to compose what it is like for me to imagine a brown dog; the (attitude-based) episodic-memory phenomenology could combine with (the content-based) purple-butterfly phenomenology and with for-me-ness to compose what it is like for me to episodically remember a purple butterfly; and so on.

The salad model is perhaps the most straightforward, least theoretically involved model of the composition of phenomenal character. However, there are facts it fails to explain. Most notably, it does not explain why no content-based phenomenal property can constitute the phenomenal character of some experience all by itself—why, that is, a content-based phenomenal property must interlock with *some* attitude-based phenomenal property (and for-me-ness) to generate phenomenal character. This fact becomes a brute basic fact about the phenomenal domain. The salad model also does not explain the special status of for-me-ness as a substantive commonality among *all* phenomenal characters. If a phenomenal character is just a free combination of various ingredients, why does one ingredient show up in every known combo?

The tree model. The second model has the potential to illuminate the features left unexplained by the first model. Here what it is like for me to episodically remember a brown dog is not understood as a composite of three detachable ingredients, but as a *species* of a certain genus, namely, what it is like for me to episodically remember *something*. Another species of the same genus is what it is like for me to episodically remember a purple butterfly and yet another is what it

186   THE THREE CIRCLES OF CONSCIOUSNESS

is like for me to episodically remember a bagpipe sound. All these different species have a substantive commonality among them, namely, the attitude-based phenomenal property of representing-as-past. The genus, what it is like for me to episodically remember (something, anything), is itself a species of an even higher genus, namely, what it is like for me to have an experience (any experience). Other species of this higher genus include what it is like for me to perceive something, what it is like for me to imagine something, and so on. Here the substantive commonality among all the species is for-me-ness, which serves as the *summum genus* of the phenomenal realm. Thus we obtain an elegant picture of the relationship between content-based phenomenal properties, attitude-based phenomenal properties, and for-me-ness. There is a kind of taxonomic tree of conscious experiences in which we can identify four main sections. (1) Atop the tree is the *summum genus* Conscious Experience, whose mark is for-me-ness; (2) below it are species such as Episodic-Memory Experience, Imaginative Experience, and Emotional Experience; (3) below those are subspecies such as Episodic Memory of Brown Dog, Episodic Memory of Purple Butterfly, and so on; (4) at the bottom of the tree is the enormous variety of *maximally determinate* types of experience, such as token episodic memories of some particular brown dog of particular shape and color. For-me-ness is then understood as the substantive commonality unifying the highest genus; attitude-based phenomenal properties constitute the substantive commonalities unifying the second-layer species; while content-based phenomenal properties provide the substantive commonalities that unify the third-layer subspecies.

The tree model is doubtless more elegant than the salad model in the structure it imposes on the phenomenal realm. It also manages to explain what the salad model did not, namely, (i) that content-based phenomenal properties cannot be instantiated without some attitude-based phenomenal properties being instantiated and (ii) that no phenomenal property can be instantiated in the absence of for-me-ness. The explanation is simply that there are genus-species relations among these dimensions of phenomenality, and the relevant patterns of co-instantiation are characteristic of the genus-species relation: just as the property of being a cat cannot be instantiated without the property of being a mammal being instantiated, which in turn cannot be instantiated without the property of animality being instantiated, so content-based phenomenal properties cannot be instantiated without some attitude-based phenomenal properties being instantiated, and the latter cannot be instantiated without for-me-ness being instantiated.

At the same time, there is also a fairly simple and fundamental fact about the phenomenal realm that the tree model fails to explain, namely, that while one can episodically remember a brown dog, one can also visually perceive a brown dog, as well as visually *imagine* a brown dog—and there is a substantive phenomenal commonality among those. The natural explanation of this commonality is that there is a content-based phenomenal 'ingredient' that reappears in each of them—a certain brown-dog phenomenology. This explanation is natural within the salad model, but is unavailable on the tree model. If what it is like to visually imagine a brown dog is just a subspecies of one phenomenal species, while what it is like to episodically remember a brown dog is a subspecies of a completely different phenomenal species, there is no reason to *expect* any similarities between them. In zoology, it is considered a curious fact requiring *special explanation* that wings have evolved on four different occasions: in birds, bats, pterosaurs, and some insects. The reason it is considered a curious fact in need of special explanation is that since bats are mammals and pterosaurs are reptiles, wings appear to constitute a commonality among species that belong to different genera.[10] It would be an odder fact in need of special explanation that content-based phenomenal properties reappear *routinely* in species of many independent phenomenal genera.

In fact, what prevents us from constructing a tree in which the attitude-level is represented as a species of the content-level, rather than the other way round? Thus, what it is like to episodically remember a brown dog, what it is like to visually imagine a brown dog, and what it is like to visually perceive a brown dog could be seen as three subspecies of brown-dog experience. Treating attitudinal properties as 'higher' (more generic) than content properties would appear arbitrary. The only reason we are *tempted* to subordinate the content-level to the attitude-level, rather than the other way round, seems to do with cardinality: there are simply many more content-based phenomenal properties than attitude-based ones.[11] Since there are also many more species than genera, we are *inclined*, once we have chosen the genus-species model, to see content-based phenomenal properties as species of attitude-based ones. However, it remains that the content-based and attitude-based phenomenal properties can combine in crosscutting ways fairly freely—something the tree model does not capture.

The circles model. The salad and tree models' shortcomings had to do with failure to capture certain apparent patterns of co-instantiation among our three types of phenomenal property. We may summarize those patterns in six principles:

(P1) A content-based phenomenal property cannot be instantiated without some attitude-based phenomenal property being instantiated (and vice versa!).

---

[10] I am using 'species' and 'genus' as metaphysical terms here, not zoological ones. (In zoology, these terms are not used as relative terms, so that x could be a species relative to y but a genus relative to z; rather, they are used to designate specific 'layers' in the tree-like taxonomy of the animal kingdom.)

[11] If we are diligent enough, in half an hour we can comprehensively enumerate the attitude-based phenomenal properties characteristic of normal adult human conscious experience; at least, we can enumerate all attitude-based phenomenal properties such experience uncontroversially exhibits, and then all those it *might* exhibit (pending certain controversies, such as that surrounding cognitive phenomenology). In contrast, enumerating the content-based phenomenal properties normal adult human conscious experience exhibits would be an extremely tedious long-term (indeed perhaps interminable) task.

(P2)   Neither content-based nor attitude-based phenomenal properties can be instantiated without for-me-ness being instantiated.

(P3)   Some conscious states vary in their content-based phenomenal properties while remaining invariant in their attitude-based phenomenal properties.

(P4)   Some conscious states vary in their attitude-based phenomenal properties while remaining invariant in their content-based phenomenal properties.

(P5)   In the set of all conscious states, one finds variation in both content- and attitude-based phenomenal properties, but for-me-ness as such remains invariant.

(P6)   There are considerably more content-based phenomenal properties than attitude-based phenomenal properties (and only one for-me-ness property).

Already P1 and P2 count against the salad model, where for-me-ness, for instance, was seen as a self-standing detachable quale that simply happened to attach to every other known quale. For-me-ness is certainly not such a self-standing quale, but rather an invariant dimension across all phenomenal characters. P4 counts heavily against the tree model, meanwhile, despite the blunting force of P6. The genus-species relation is simply ill suited to capture the structure of the phenomenal realm given that substantive commonalities run across the content-level and attitude-level alike.

What I propose under the fancy name 'circles model' is forsooth just an acceptance of P1–P6, *plus an image*. The image is of three (gapless) concentric circles, with content-based phenomenal properties at the outskirts, attitude-based phenomenal properties in the middle, and for-me-ness as the nucleus (Figure 8.1). The image is not supposed to visually represent all the relationships laid out in P1–P6. But it is supposed to be compatible with them, and to avoid the problematic features of the salad and tree images. In using *circles* rather than tree-branches, it makes sense of the notion that different content-based properties can combine with different attitude-based ones, rather than being 'accessible' only to one attitude-level property. In using *continuous* circles, it avoids the image of detachable qualia that can in principle occur on their own (thus respecting the notion that content phenomenality, attitudinal phenomenality, and for-me-ness are but three dimensions of a phenomenal character—dimensions which can be separated in thought but cannot occur separately). The core of the three-circle model is really just the insistence that all six principles are true of the structure of the phenomenal realm.[12]

---

[12] Work on this chapter was supported by the French National Research Agency's grants ANR-11-0001-02 PSL* and ANR-10-LABX-0087, as well as by grant 675415 of the European Union's Horizon 2020 Research and Innovation program. For comments on a previous draft, I am grateful to two anonymous reviewers for OUP. I have also greatly benefited from a discussion of the chapter at NYU and would like to thank the audience there, in particular David Chalmers, Kevin Lande, Andrew Lee, Hedda Mørch, Gabe Rabin, David Rosenthal, and Jonathan Simon.

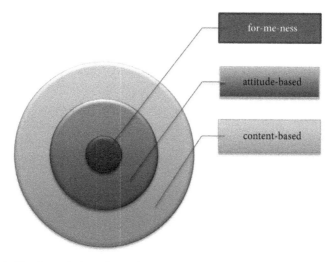

Figure 8.1 The three circles of consciousness

References

Bayne, T. and M. Montague. 2011. *Cognitive Phenomenology*. Oxford: Oxford University Press.

Block, N.J. 1996. 'Mental Paint and Mental Latex.' *Philosophical Issues* 7: 19–50.

Brentano, F. 1874. *Psychology from Empirical Standpoint*. Edited by O. Kraus. Translated by A.C. Rancurello, D.B. Terrell, and L.L. McAlister. London: Routledge and Kegan Paul, 1973.

Byrne, A. 2001. 'Intentionalism Defended.' *Philosophical Review* 110: 199–240.

Chalmers, D.J. 2004. 'The Representational Character of Experience.' In B. Leiter (ed.), *The Future of Philosophy*. Oxford and New York: Oxford University Press.

Crane, T. 1998. 'Intentionality as the Mark of the Mental.' In A. O'Hear (ed.), *Contemporary Issues in Philosophy of Mind*. Cambridge: Cambridge University Press.

Dretske, F.I. 1993. 'Conscious Experience.' *Mind* 102: 263–283.

Dretske, F.I. 1995. *Naturalizing the Mind*. Cambridge, MA: MIT Press.

Dretske, F.I. 2000. 'Reply to Lopes.' *Philosophy and Phenomenological Research* 60: 455–459.

Fernández, J. 2006. 'The Intentionality of Memory.' *Australasian Journal of Philosophy* 84: 39–57.

Goldman, A.I. 1993. 'The Psychology of Folk Psychology.' *Behavioral and Brain Sciences* 16: 15–28.

Harman, G. 1990. 'The Intrinsic Quality of Experience.' *Philosophical Perspectives* 4: 31–52.

Horgan, T. and J. Tienson 2002. 'The Intentionality of Phenomenology and the Phenomenology of Intentionality.' In D.J. Chalmers (ed.), *Philosophy of Mind:*

Classical and Contemporary Readings. Oxford and New York: Oxford University Press.

Kind, A. 2013. 'The Case against Representationalism about Moods.' In U. Kriegel (ed.), *Current Controversies in Philosophy of Mind.* London: Routledge.

Kriegel, U. 2007. 'Intentional Inexistence and Phenomenal Intentionality.' *Philosophical Perspectives* 21: 307–340.

Kriegel, U. 2009. *Subjective Consciousness: A Self-Representational Theory.* Oxford: Oxford University Press.

Kriegel, U. 2015a. *The Varieties of Consciousness.* Oxford and New York: Oxford University Press.

Kriegel, U. 2015b. 'Experiencing the Present.' *Analysis* 75: 407–413.

Kriegel U. 2017a. 'Brentano's Evaluative-Attitudinal Account of Will and Emotion.' *Revue Philosophique* 142: 529–548.

Kriegel, U. 2017b. 'Reductive Representationalism and Attitudinal Representation.' *Midwest Studies in Philosophy* 41: 41–59.

Kriegel, U. 2019. 'The Intentional Structure of Mood.' *Philosophers' Imprint* 19(49): 1–19.

Loar, B. 2003. 'Phenomenal Intentionality as the Basis for Mental Content.' In M. Hahn and B. Ramberg (eds.), *Reflections and Replies: Essays on the Philosophy of Tyler Burge.* Cambridge MA: MIT Press.

Lopes, D.M.M. 2000. 'What Is It Like to See with Your Ears? The Representational Theory of Mind.' *Philosophical and Phenomenological Research* 60: 439–453.

Lycan, W.G. 2001. 'The Case for Phenomenal Externalism.' *Philosophical Perspectives* 15: 17–35.

Pautz, A. 2010. 'Consciousness: A Simple Approach.' In R. Koons and G. Bealer (eds.), *The Waning of Materialism.* Oxford and New York: Oxford University Press.

Peacocke, C. 1983. *Sense and Content.* Oxford: Oxford University Press.

Pitt, D. 2004. 'The Phenomenology of Cognition; or *What Is It Like to Think that P?*' *Philosophy and Phenomenological Research* 69: 1–36.

Schear, J. 2009. 'Experience and Self-consciousness.' *Philosophical Studies* 144: 95–105.

Seager, W. 1999. *Theories of Consciousness.* London: Routledge.

Siegel, S. 2007. 'How Can We Discover the Contents of Experience?' *Southern Journal of Philosophy* (supplement) 45: 127–142.

Stampe, D. 1987. 'The Authority of Desire.' *Philosophical Review* 96: 335–381.

Tenenbaum, S. 2007. *Appearances of the Good.* Cambridge: Cambridge University Press.

Tye, M. 1995. *Ten Problems of Consciousness.* Cambridge MA: MIT Press.

Zahavi, D. 2014. *Self and Other.* Oxford: Oxford University Press.

9

Experiencing Subjects and So-Called Mine-Ness

Martine Nida-Rümelin

1. Introduction

In recent discussions of consciousness it is common to say that experiences have, in addition to their so-called qualitative character, a further interesting and intriguing feature, so-called subjective character (for-me-ness or mine-ness). Philosophers who talk in this way have important and fundamental 'phenomena' in mind which deserve the closest attention. However, as I will argue in this chapter, the terminology thus introduced is inadequate to what it attempts to refer to and it risks leading to conceptual and theoretical confusion.

The claim that experiences have subjective character can be understood as expressing the metaphysical fact that there is someone undergoing the experience *for whom* it is like something to undergo the experience. As we will see, this metaphysical interpretation of what it is for experiences to have subjective character (in the following [subjective character]$_1$) does not trivialize subjective character, as some authors seem to suggest, nor does is detach issues about subjective character from phenomenology.[1]

---

[1] A metaphysical interpretation of 'subjective character' somewhat similar to [subjective character]$_1$ has been mentioned by various authors (compare, for instance, Howell & Thompson, 2017, section 4.2., p. 103, Zahavi & Kriegel, 2017, section entitled 'Introduction', Guillot, 2017, p. 27). They characterize that interpretation as follows: for an experience to have subjective character (in that supposedly trivial sense) is for it to be had by a subject. These authors consider that reading to be 'deflationary'. They think that subjective character in that sense would be detached from phenomenology. This common attitude toward such a metaphysical reading of subjective character is at least misleading and based, in my view, on two related mistakes. First, it is implicitly taken for granted that there is a sense of 'belongingness' or 'being had by someone' such that experiences as well as organs (such as the liver) belong to or are had by someone in that common sense. However, having an experience—contrary to having a liver—essentially involves that it is like something for the subject concerned to have it. There is no other, no phenomenology-neutral manner, so to speak, for an experience to belong to a subject. Therefore, or so I would argue, the distinction some authors draw between an experience being *in* a subject and an experience being *for* a subject does not make sense. To have an experience just is to instantiate experiential properties and to instantiate experiential properties involves (given the metaphysical nature of experiential properties) that it is like something for the subject to have them. Second, these authors appear to implicitly assume that the metaphysical issue about what it is for an experience to belong to a subject and phenomenological issues concerning pre-reflective self-awareness are separate theoretical issues which one may treat independently. I disagree. One cannot

---

Martine Nida-Rümelin, *Experiencing Subjects and So-Called Mine-Ness* In: *Self-Experience: Essays on Inner Awareness.*
Edited by: Manuel García-Carpintero and Marie Guillot, Oxford University Press. © Martine Nida-Rümelin 2023.
DOI: 10.1093/oso/9780198805397.003.0009

The claim that experiences have subjective character sometimes expresses something quite different namely the following idea: a subject undergoing an experience is thereby aware of undergoing the experience where this awareness does not require any reflection or conceptualization. I will use the term "[subjective character]$_2$," when this second interpretation is meant. I will argue that [subjective character]$_1$ and [subjective character]$_2$ are conceptually distinct and yet necessarily co-extensive.[2]

There is a further interesting feature of experience philosophers often have in mind when they use the term "subjective character" or related expressions. Undergoing an experience typically involves—or so one may argue—that the subject concerned is aware of itself in a phenomenally manifest manner; the subject is aware of being the one undergoing the experience as one may put the point. The kind of self-awareness at issue does not require any conceptualization of oneself or of the experiential properties one has but it is, arguably, a pre-condition of acquiring such concepts. One may therefore label that kind of self-awareness pre-conceptual. Furthermore, the kind of self-awareness here at issue requires no reflection. So one may call that particular simple and basic kind of self-awareness "pre-reflective self-awareness." I will use the term "[subjective character]$_3$," for pre-reflective self-awareness in the sense alluded to.[3]

The term "subjective character" and even more frequently the term "mine-ness" is often used to refer to a different phenomenon, namely to something we may call 'the appearance of belongingness to me'. One may explain the appearance at issue pointing out that it may lack in certain well-known pathological cases such as the phenomenon of so-called thought insertion. I will mention that fourth interpretation only to put it aside. As I will argue, it has little to do with [subjective character]$_1$, [subjective character]$_2$, and [subjective character]$_3$, which are in the focus of the present chapter.[4]

---

expect to be able to develop a satisfying account of pre-reflective self-awareness (of what it is to be *aware* of oneself as the subject of the experience one undergoes) without reflecting upon what it *is* to be the subject of that experience since the latter is precisely what one is aware of in the former.

[2] My term "[subjective character]$_2$," is closely related to Guillot' s understanding of "for-me-ness" (see Guillot, 2017, section 2.2). However, she introduces "for-me-ness" as an awareness which has the experience as object. I find this way of talking at least misleading. [Subjective character]$_2$ is, on my understanding, an awareness the subject has of having a certain experiential property. Furthermore, a methodological difference between her approach and mine should be noted. In her paper (2017) Guillot introduces conceptual distinctions thereby aiming at a clarification in the terminology used by philosophers working in the field. My aim is different. I try to identify different real phenomena philosophers appear to have in mind when they use the relevant term. I am not mainly interested in conceptual or terminological distinctions which help interpreting the ongoing discussion but rather in identifying different (potential) *referents* of the term "subjective character." I am mainly interested in developing a clear understanding of those (potential) referents.

[3] Guillot (2017) reserves the term "me-ness" for [subjective character]$_3$.

[4] Guillot (2017) refers to such appearances of belongingness to oneself using the term "mine-ness." (See, however, the last paragraph of section 9 and the associated footnote 24, for an important difference in her understanding of mine-ness and my view about appearances of belongingness to oneself.)

It is quite common in the recent literature to use the terms "subjective character," "for-me-ness," or "mine-ness" in a manner which systematically conflates at least the first three and sometimes even all four phenomena mentioned. The conflation is not harmless at all. It is, in my view, a serious obstacle to theoretical progress with respect to the nature of consciousness and its relation to self-awareness. One purpose of this chapter is thus to criticize a by now widely used terminology and to uncover the ambiguities in reference it involves. In doing so I will also sketch an alternative which not only proposes a different terminology but thereby also suggests a different approach to the nature of consciousness.

A more technical point is worth mentioning before I start. Subjective character or mine-ness is commonly introduced as a feature or property of experiences. This rather new piece of terminology is part of a more general conceptual framework which is widespread in contemporary philosophy of mind and can be labeled *the experience property framework*. Within the experience property framework the problematic properties associated to phenomenal consciousness concerning what it is like to undergo a given type of experience are introduced as *properties of experiences* which are often called either qualia or phenomenal properties. It is thus common not to mention the experiencing individual involved in those events *for whom* it is like something to undergo the experience. However, a closer look reveals that all talk of such qualia or phenomenal properties *of experiences* implicitly presupposes that we have a clear enough understanding of the corresponding properties *of experiencing subjects*. For instance, visual experiences of a certain phenomenal kind are supposed to have some quale (phenomenal property) in common. But what is it that they have in common? Visual experiences of blueness, obviously, have in common that the experiencing subject concerned is visually presented with blueness.[5] I do not see that there is any *other* way to understand the commonality of visual experiences falling into the class of so-called 'blue experiences'. The supposed common 'quale' of blue experiences thus conceptually reduces to a common property of subjects involved in so-called blue experiences.

I am going to assume that *all* one may express talking about supposed properties of experiences (all one can say within *the experience property framework*) can be reduced, if it makes any sense at all, to something one may express talking about experiencing subjects and their properties, to something expressible within

---

[5] In my view, experiential properties such as being presented with blueness are monadic and not relational properties of experiencing subjects. However, I cannot discuss that tricky issue here and it will play no role in what follows. I understand "being presented with blueness" as a predicate used to attribute an experiential property. I do not presuppose that the subject is presented with an instantiated property when presented with blueness. The term "being visually presented with the color blue" would be an equally adequate terminological choice. I argue in my paper (Nida-Rümelin 2018a) that colors are not instantiated but for present purposes, I will not presuppose that claim. Note that "blueness" as used in the above locution does not refer to a property of experiences.

the subject property framework, as one may call it.[6] This is the starting point of the present discussion. I will propose translations of sentences attributing qualitative character and subjective character or mine-ness to experiences into sentences talking about subjects and their properties. This procedure leads to insights and clarifications about the phenomena philosophers intend to refer to when they talk about mine-ness (or subjective character). Before I can start developing the strategy just sketched, a few remarks about the relation between experiences, experiencers, and experiential properties are necessary in order to provide the conceptual background of what will follow.

2. Experiences, Experiential Properties, and Experiencing Subjects

Experiences are events that consist in the instantiation of experiential properties by experiencing subjects. This is how one may state in a natural manner the relation between those particular individuals that are capable of being conscious (experiencing subjects), the particular properties one might call experiential properties (more about them will be said in a moment), and the subclass of events commonly referred to using the term "experience."

A central task in philosophy of mind is to clarify the nature of experiences. One can formulate the question as follows: what distinguishes experiences from other events? What is their common characteristic feature? Let us suppose, as just stated, that experiences just are *instantiations of experiential properties by experiencing beings*. Then it seems clear that there are two more fundamental questions to be clarified: What distinguishes experiencing subjects from other individuals? What distinguishes experiential properties from other properties? If the proposed simple and natural view about the relation between experiences, experiencing subjects and experiential properties is accepted, then the following must be admitted as well: understanding the nature of experiences requires and in fact consists in understanding the nature of experiencing subjects and the nature of their experiential properties.

Let us start with experiential properties. What is it for a property to be an experiential property in the relevant sense? As I understand the term 'experience' here, experiences are phenomenally conscious: it is like something for the subject concerned to be involved in them. Now, given the above explanation, to be involved in an experience is, simply, to instantiate the *corresponding experiential*

---

[6] To establish this claim is the central purpose of my paper (Nida-Rümelin 2018b). I there introduce the subject property framework under the label "framework of experiential properties." An anonymous referee of the present chapter suggested the simpler and more telling term which I am happy to adopt from now on.

property. For instance, to be involved (or to have) a blue experience is to be visually presented with blueness. For every phenomenal type of experiences there is an associated or corresponding experiential property (or rather, there are such corresponding properties) in the following obvious sense: for an event to belong to that phenomenal type just is to consist in the instantiation of those properties. So we need not talk about phenomenal types of experiences at all. We can directly talk about the corresponding experiential properties of experiencing subjects which are conceptually and ontologically more fundamental.

If we understand experiences as phenomenally conscious and as related to experiential properties in the obvious way explained above, then it is clear how experiential properties must be characterized. It is like something for the experiencing subject concerned to have them. They even at least partially *consist* in what it is like for the subject concerned to have them. We thus arrive at the following definition:

Definition 1: A property P is an experiential property if and only if there is some characteristic way it is like for any subject having P to have property P and having P partially consists in what it is like to have P.

It is perhaps important to note that definition 1 is not to be understood as a reductive definition. Reductive definitions explain a term to be introduced by reducing it to already understood terminology which is—in the relevant context— taken to be less problematic. Definition 1 does not in that sense reduce the term "experiential properties" to the "what-it-is-like"-locution. Rather it only serves to hint at what experiential properties have in common. Such a 'hint' can only be successful if the reader has typical examples in mind and takes the definition as a tool for 'picking out' their relevant commonality which in turn must be grasped on the basis of examples.[7]

3. Qualitative Character and [Subjective Character]₁

In recent years a number of philosophers, most prominently perhaps Joe Levine, Terry Horgan, and Uriah Kriegel, have suggested making a distinction between qualitative character and subjective character (or subjectivity). The following passages are examples of how the distinction is usually introduced:

---

[7] If what I say here is right, then using the 'it-is-like-something'-locution in such contexts just serves to formulate what one may call an 'ostensive' definition. If so, then one will make no progress with respect to one's understanding of experiential properties by sophisticated examinations of the grammar of such locutions. Such research (as one may find it, for instance, in Stoljar 2016) may be of interest in its own right but it will not help us make progress with respect to issues about consciousness. For a proposal on the issue of how the term "experiential properties" should be taken to be introduced compare section 3 in my comment on the 'Frankish' version of illusionism in Nida-Rümelin (2016c).

Citation 1

Now there are two features of conscious sensory states that require theoretical elucidation: "qualitative character" and "subjectivity."...In the case at hand, seeing a ripe tomato, there is both a distinctive qualitative character to be reckoned with and also the fact that the state is conscious—"for the subject," in a way that unconscious states are not. (Levine, J. 2006, section 2, §2)

Citation 2

To a first approximation, the experience's bluish qualitative character is what makes it the experience it is, but it's for-me-ness is what makes it an experience at all. A better, if initially less clear, approximation is this: my experience is the experience it is because it is bluish-for-me, and is an experience at all because it is somehow-for-me (or qualitatively-for-me). Thus qualitative character is what varies among conscious experiences, while subjective character is what is common to them. (Kriegel 2011, §2)

Citation 3

Not only *is* the experience bluish, but I am also *aware* of its being bluish. Its *being* bluish constitutes its qualitative character, while my *awareness* of it constitutes its subjective character. (Kriegel 2005, pp. 23, 24)

Citations 1 and 2 introduce 'subjective character' as the experience's being like something *for* the subject concerned. Citation 3 introduces 'subjective character' as the subject's *awareness* of the qualitative character of the experience. Can one equate the fact that *an experience is like something for the subject* with the supposed fact that *the subject is aware of the qualitative character of the experience*? If so, why? I will argue that subjective character in the sense of citations 1 and 2 on the one hand and subjective character in the sense of citation 3 on the other do in fact coincide but that this is not obviously so. It is the result of a substantial assumption which will be defended below.

As illustrated by the above citations, philosophers sometimes attribute qualitative and subjective character to what they call mental states and sometimes to experiences (commonly understood as events). For the purposes of this chapter the difference, if there is a difference, does not matter. My analyses will be formulated with respect to attributions of such features to experiences but they could be formulated in exactly the same manner with respect to the attribution of features to mental states.

Putting the difference just mentioned aside, all three citations—and in fact the totality of the relevant contemporary discussion—is formulated within *the experience property framework*. Since experiences are nothing but instantiations of experiential properties by experiencing beings, everything that can be said within the experience property framework must be translatable, if it makes any sense at all, into the subject property framework. Let us see what happens,

QUALITATIVE CHARACTER AND [SUBJECTIVE CHARACTER]$_1$ 197

therefore, when we translate talk of qualitative character and subjective character into the subject property framework. The target sentences to be translated are (S1), (S2), and (S3) below.

(S1)   Experience E has qualitative character.
(S2)   Experience E has the specific qualitative character Q.
(S3)   Experience E has subjective character.

Let me start with a presupposition that I will take for granted and which naturally leads to the definitions below.

Presupposition PS
For every experience E there are certain uniquely determined properties P_E and a time interval T_E such that the experience is an event consisting in the instantiation of those properties P_E in a certain pattern over T_E by one single experiencing subject S_E.

The properties P_E for a given experience E mentioned in the above presupposition will be called 'the properties associated with E' in what follows and the subject S_E instantiating those properties will be called 'the subject involved in E' or 'the subject concerned'. These locutions can be introduced in a general manner by the following definitions.

Definition 2:
P_E are the properties associated with the event E happening in the time interval T_E if and only if E consists in the instantiation of the properties P_E within T_E.

Definition 3:
If E is an experience with the associated properties P_E then S_E is the individual involved in E if and only if E consists in the instantiation of P_E by S_E.

Let us now ask: How should one translate S1 into the language of experiential properties (that is into the subject property framework)? In other words: what is it for an experience to have qualitative character expressed in a way which reduces talk about supposed properties of experiences to talk about experiential properties? Intuitively the answer is quite obvious: that an experience E has qualitative character means, quite simply, that it is like something for the subject concerned to have the associated experiential properties P_E. This proposal is convincing without any explicit argument but it might be helpful to explicate how the result can be derived from two unproblematic premises.

Premise 1
For an experience E to have qualitative character is for it to fulfill the following condition: it is like something for the subject concerned to be involved in E.

Premise 2

For an experience E to be such that it is like something for the subject concerned to undergo E is for it to fulfill the following condition: it is like something for the subject S_E to have the associated properties P_E.

Premise 3 (motivated by the definition of experiential properties)

For given properties to be such that it is like something for any subject having them to have them is for them to be at least in part experiential.

With these premises, we arrive at the desired result:

Result R1

For an experience E to have *qualitative* character is for it to fulfill the following condition: some of the properties P_E associated with E are experiential properties.

In other words: S1 must be translated into the subject property framework by

S1*:   Some of the properties P_E associated with E are experiential properties.[8]

The equivalence in R1 should be read as explaining what it *is* for an experience to have qualitative character: the right hand side says—within the subject property framework—what it is the left hand side should be taken to express.

Given this proposal it is clear how S2 must be translated into the subject property framework. As just stated, for an experience to have *some* qualitative character or other is for it to be an instantiation of *some experiential properties or other*. Accordingly, for an experience to have some *specific* qualitative character is for it to be the instantiation of *specific* experiential properties. For instance, blue experiences have specific qualitative character only in the sense that they all are instantiations of *being presented with blueness*. To be an instantiation of *that* specific experiential property is what it is for an experience to have the 'quality' or quale (or phenomenal property) often also called 'blueishness'.[9] In general: To say of an experience that it has a specific quality Q (or phenomenal property P) only appears to be an attribution of a qualitative property to an event (an experience). In reality it is a way to talk, rather indirectly, about the property all experiencing subjects share who are involved in an experience of the relevant kind.

For every supposed 'quality' Q attributed to an experience by a sentence of the general schema S2 we should thus be able to find experiential properties P_Q such

---

[8]   To attribute qualitative character to an experience is misleading in many ways as I argue in Nida-Rümelin 2018b and 2016. According to the translation just proposed such talk can be abandoned without any loss. Once the adequacy of the translation is recognized, it is clear that all philosophical puzzles about qualitative character really are puzzles about experiential properties, since for an experience to have qualitative character is nothing but to be an instantiation of experiential properties.

[9]   Blueishness in that specific philosophical sense where it is a supposed property of experiences must not be conflated with blueness in the usual everyday sense where it is a quality given in experience, something the subject is presented with.

QUALITATIVE CHARACTER AND [SUBJECTIVE CHARACTER]₁ 199

that for an experience E to have the supposed quality is for E to be an instantiation of those experiential properties. If no such properties can be found, then no sense can be given to the relevant sentence. So if P_Q are the experiential properties that correspond in the way just explained to the supposed quality Q then the sentence S2, if it makes any sense at all, can be replaced by the following sentence:

S2*:   Experience E is an instantiation of the experiential properties P_Q.[10]

Let us now turn to the question central to the present chapter. How must S3— the attribution of *subjective* character to experiences—be understood and translated into the subject property framework? My claim will be this: on a first reading of 'subjective character'—the one invited by citations 1 and 2 (and by many other passages one may find in the literature)—sentence S3 must be translated by exactly the same sentence as S1! In other words: what is said by attributing *subjective* character in that first sense now under consideration to experiences is nothing more and nothing less than attributing *qualitative* character to experiences.[11]

In what follows I will distinguish different readings of "subjective character" by indexes. The first reading of subjective character now to be considered will be labeled by "[subjective character]₁." My argument for the claim that S1 and S3 express the same fact proceeds as follows: S3 will be translated into the subject property framework using a few premises that should be uncontroversial. It turns out (quite trivially) that the resulting translation is the same as the one arrived at for S1. I assume that we get an adequate and clearer understanding of the original sentences by translating them into the subject property framework. Therefore, if two different sentences taken from the experience property framework must be translated by the same sentences belonging to the subject property framework, then the original different sentences—in so far as they make sense at all—have the same content.

Here are the premises leading to the announced conclusion:

---

[10] To call the proposals just made suggestions for *translations* is perhaps slightly misleading. If I am right that talk of qualitative character of experiences is inadequate and the proposed translation is not, then there must be a difference in meaning. Nonetheless S1* and S2* are translations in this sense: they purport to capture what the original sentences are *meant* to express and what in that sense they *do* express even though (if I am right) in a problematic and misleading manner.

[11] According to Kriegel (2009, chapter 2), specific qualitative characters and subjective character are in the relation of determinates to determinable: "bluish-for-me-ness, reddish-for-me-ness, trumpet-ish-for-me-ness, and so on are all phenomenal characters that are determinates of the determinable something-for-me-ness (or plain for-me-ness for short)." The present analysis supports and explains that claim in a simple manner. For an event to have *subjective* character is for it to have some qualitative character or other, and this, in turn, just *is to be the instantiation of some experiential properties or other*. To have *specific qualitative character is to be the instantiation of specific experiential properties.* This is why specific qualitative characters are determinates of the determinable subjective character in the present sense.

Premise 1'
For an experience E to have *subjective character* is for it to fulfill the following condition: it is *like something* for the subject concerned to be involved in E.

Premise 2'
For an experience E to be such that it is like something for the subject concerned to undergo E is for it to fulfill the following condition: it is like something for the subject S_E to have the associated properties P_E.

Premise 3' (motivated by the definition of experiential properties)
It is like something *for* the subject concerned to have given properties if and only if those properties are at least in part experiential.

With these premises we arrive at

Result R2
What it is for an experience E to have *subjective* character can be expressed in the following way: some of the properties P_E associated with E are experiential properties.

and we must conclude that S3 has to be translated into S1*. So, on a closer look, to attribute [subjective character]$_1$ to an experience is to say of it that it is the instantiation of some experiential properties and to attribute qualitative character to an experience is to say just the same. This result may seem puzzling. One may think that an important distinction got lost. I will answer this worry in a moment. But let me first briefly comment on the argument just given.

Premises 2' and 3' are distinct from premises 2 and 3 only by the emphasis on "for." This makes no difference for their plausibility. They should therefore be just as uncontroversial as premises 2 and 3.

The crucial step is premise 1'. One might think that introducing premise 1' makes the argument which follows superfluous since the explication given by premise 1 of qualitative character and the one given by premise 1' of subjective character are distinct, again, only by the emphasis put on "like something" in the first explication and "for" in the second. Therefore, the objection goes, the result is already assumed in these two first premises of the parallel arguments.

But this is not quite so. The friend of the distinction of qualitative character and [subjective character]$_1$ is likely to think that the different emphases are successful in pointing to different features of experiences. This is, however, a cognitive illusion. The rest of the two parallel arguments leading to the same translation for S1 and S3 and involving the premises 2/2' and 3/3' are required in order to show that this is in fact an illusion. The two parallel arguments are designed to render clearly visible that no two distinct features of experiences can be successfully introduced by such different emphases.

4. Qualitativeness and Subjectivity (in the Sense of [Subjective Character]$_1$) in the Nature of Experiential Properties

We are now left, or so it may appear, with a puzzle. It seems obvious that philosophers making the distinction between qualitative character and [subjective character]$_1$ are not just talking nonsense. They seem to be talking about a genuine distinction. Pointing to the qualitativeness of experience on the one hand and pointing to the subjectivity of experience in the sense of being *for* someone on the other they clearly seem to attract attention to distinguishable and distinct phenomena. Yet, according to the above argument, there is no distinction to be found in the content of sentences attributing qualitative character on the one hand and [subjective character]$_1$ on the other. What should we make of this? Does one have to take a decision? Does on have to either reject the argument given in section 3 or reject the idea that there is a genuine distinction to be made here between qualitativeness and subjectivity (in the sense of [subjective character]$_1$)?

The answer to these questions should be: no. There is no real conflict. One may accept the argument given and yet concede that there is a genuine and important distinction to be made 'in the neighborhood'. To conclude that there is no such genuine distinction would be to over-interpret the result obtained. What should be concluded is rather this: the distinction at issue must be localized in a different place. There are *no distinct features of experiences* corresponding to "qualitative character" and "[subjective character]$_1$" to be found. However, experiential properties are astonishing properties: they are *qualitative properties* in a sense to be clarified and they are *subjective properties* in a sense to be clarified as well. This is the place where we should search and where we can find the real basis for making the distinction between qualitativeness in the relevant sense and subjectivity (in the sense of [subjective character]$_1$): the basis for making the distinction lies in the very nature of experiential properties.

In what sense is it adequate to say that experiential properties are qualitative? This question is quite easy to answer. It is constitutive for every experiential property P that there is some characteristic way it is like to have P. A subject has a given experiential property P in virtue of some detail concerning the way it is like for the subject concerned to live the moment in which it has P. This is the intuitively clear sense in which experiential properties are qualitative.

But in what sense are experiential properties subjective? This is closely related to their being qualitative in the sense just mentioned. Experiential properties can only be instantiated by experiencing beings. Why? They are qualitative in the sense that having them partially determines what it is like for the experiencing subject concerned to live through the moment in which it has that property. Experiential properties thus determine *someone's* overall phenomenological state. So, there cannot be any instantiation of any experiential property without an experiencing subject having that property for whom there is something it is like to have it. This is, in a nutshell, what it *is* for them to be subjective.

We can now give a simple and clear reformulation of ideas found in citation 2. Qualitative character is, says Kriegel, what varies among experiences. This can be read as a claim about properties of experiences which supposedly vary from one type of experience to the other. But we should not misunderstand the claim as talking about properties of experiences at all or rather only in a sense in which it can be restated as a claim about properties of experiencing subjects. According to the present analysis what Kriegel asserts here (or what makes true what he has in mind) is this: types of experiences are different from one another in virtue of the fact that their members are instantiations of *different* experiential properties. These properties are different in virtue of differences with respect to what it is like to have them for the subject concerned. In that sense qualitativeness is what varies among experiences. Subjective character is, says Kriegel, what all experiences have in common. What do they have in common? They have in common that they can only be instantiated by an experiencing subject for whom it is like something to have them. Here too, one might be tempted to read the claim as stating that all experiences share a specific property in common. In a broad sense of 'property' there is nothing to be said against this but the 'property' in question is simply this: experiences are instantiations of properties by specific kinds of individuals (experiencing subjects) such that it is like something at all for those individuals to have the properties at issue. Being an instantiation of properties by an *experiencing subject for whom it is like something to have the instantiated properties* is thus the common feature of all experiences.

Did we thus arrive at a different translation of what it is for an experience to have qualitative character and of what it is for an experience to have [subjective character]$_1$ after all? It might seem so. The above remarks might be summarized as follows: an experience has qualitative character means that among the associated properties are properties that are qualitative in the relevant sense explained above. And for an experience to have subjective character means that among the associated properties are subjective properties in the relevant sense explained above. So don't we now have a different interpretation of S1 and S3 contrary to the result of the preceding section? No. All and only experiential properties are qualitative in the relevant sense. Furthermore, all and only experiential properties are subjective in the relevant sense. Furthermore, this is no coincidence: properties that are qualitative in that sense are necessarily subjective in the relevant sense and vice versa. So the result of section 3 is not undermined: even though we can find both qualitativeness *and* subjectivity (in the sense of [subjective character]$_1$) in the nature of experiential properties, for an experience to have qualitative character and for an experience to have subjective character is one and the same: it is to be an instantiation of experiential properties.

5. Awareness of One's Own Experience ([Subjective Character]$_2$)

As illustrated by citation 3 above, subjective character is often introduced in a different way: as the subject's *awareness* of the experience it undergoes (or of that experience's qualitative character). I will use "[subjective character]$_2$" for this second understanding of subjective character. [Subjective character]$_1$ and [subjective character]$_2$ are conceptually distinct. To say of an experience that it is an instantiation of experiential properties and to say of an experience that the subject involved is aware of undergoing the experience are conceptually distinct assertions. Given my analysis of [subjective character]$_1$ I therefore seem to be committed to attribute conceptual confusion to those philosophers who fail to distinguish [subjective character]$_1$ and [subjective character]$_2$. Since the failure of doing so is common in contemporary philosophy this may well be used as an objection against my proposal.

But, luckily, the situation is different in an interesting way. There is a confusion going on here, I would indeed insist, however the failure to distinguish between [subjective character]$_1$ and [subjective character]$_2$ is, on a deeper level, more a virtue than a vice. I will argue that, assuming a specific claim about the nature of experiential properties that I will defend and that I take to be adequate, there is no difference between [subjective character]$_1$ and [subjective character]$_2$ with respect to the phenomena they refer to. This is what I will argue next. As a result, one then may say that the apparent confusion really manifests an adequate understanding of the phenomena under consideration.

Let us now see, as a first step, how "awareness of an experience" translates in the here proposed framework. If one understands experiences as instantiations of (experiential) properties then awareness of one's own experience E must be awareness of having the associated properties P_E.[12] For instance, to be aware of one's blue experience is to be aware of being visually presented with blueness. This translation has a welcome side-effect: What may appear to be an imprecise going

---

[12] I would like to cite an important and interesting objection raised by an anonymous referee at this point: "A worry here is that the gerundive clause has an implicit 'PRO' subject (cf. Higginbotham 2003): its default reading is 'awareness of **one** having the associated properties PE'. This makes it sound like [subjective character]$_2$ is, after all, substantively different from [subjective character]$_1$, since it appears to involve not just an awareness of the relevant experiential properties being instantiated (as in [subjective character]$_1$), but, in addition, an awareness of **oneself** as what instantiates those properties." The worry would merit a longer reply which I cannot give here. Briefly stated my view is this. Awareness of having an experiential property in the sense of [subjective character]$_2$ is not neutral with respect to who has the relevant property. It would be inadequate to describe it as an awareness of an instantiation of such an experiential property without adding that one is thereby aware of having it oneself. It is surely not an awareness of 'someone having that property' in a way which leaves it open as to who it is. Therefore, I chose the gerundive clause available in English on purpose; I find it particularly adequate. I deny, however, that such 'non-neutrality' of that awareness with respect to who has the relevant property by itself already implies that the subject it aware, *in a phenomenally manifest manner,* of herself as the subject of that experience. Some details relevant to this issue are developed in Nida-Rümelin (2017, sections 6, 7, and 8).

back and forth between "awareness of one's experience" and "awareness of the phenomenal character of one's experience" (see citation 2) then turns out to be perfectly acceptable and not imprecise at all in those cases where the associated properties are all experiential. To be aware of one's experience is to be aware of having the associated properties; to be aware of the phenomenal character of the experience is to be aware of the associated experiential properties (compare the translation of S2 into S2* in section 3). So there is no real difference between the two formulations if the properties associated with an experience E coincide with the associated *experiential* properties. For simplicity I will assume in what follows that for an experience E to have [subjective character]$_2$ means this: the subject S_E involved is aware of the associated experiential properties which may or may not be the totality of the associated properties P_E.

So for an experience to have [subjective character]$_1$ is for it to be the instantiation of properties some of which are experiential. For an experience to have [subjective character]$_2$ is for it to be such that the subject involved is aware of having the associated experiential properties. Now suppose for the moment that there is no difference—*in the special case of experiential properties*—between having a given property P and being aware of having it. Then for an experience to have [subjective character]$_1$ trivially implies that it has [subjective character]$_2$. This is so since, under the above supposition, if an experience is the instantiation of experiential properties (it has [subjective character]$_1$), then the subject is also aware of having all those properties (that the subject has them *is* for it to be aware of having them), so the experience also has [subjective character]$_2$ and trivially so. Now let us suppose (to see the opposite direction), that an experience has [subjective character]$_2$. Then there are experiential properties the subject is aware of having in undergoing the experience (where having them and being aware of having them is even one and the same thing) and so, again, trivially, the experience has [subjective character]$_1$. It follows that there is no real difference between having [subjective character]$_1$ and having [subjective character]$_2$. It is thus quite adequate to what subjective character in the two senses really amounts to if a philosopher uses the two terms in an interchangeable manner. However, the justification for doing so is not visible at the surface. The justification here described relies on a substantial assumption about the nature of experiential properties: having an experiential property and being aware of having it is (in a specific sense of awareness) one and the same thing. In the next section, I will try to motivate and to defend that assumption.

6. Primitive Awareness

There are many senses that can be given to the locution "being aware of having a given experiential property." "John is aware of being presented with blueness" might be interpreted as stating that John has a concept of what it is to be presented with blueness and conceptualizes his own color experience using that concept. Obviously the claim in question (having a given experiential property *is* being aware of having it) is false if awareness is understood in this way. "John is aware of being presented with blueness" might mean that John is attending to this specific aspect of his present state. Awareness of having an experiential property is obviously not identical to having that property if we understand 'awareness' in that sense. If the claim is true on some reading at all, then a very special sense must be given to 'awareness' in that context. It must be a basic kind of awareness which does not require conceptualization or the direction of attention. It cannot be any kind of cognitive achievement since it is something that 'comes for free' with experiencing itself.

Can we find a clear and understandable notion of awareness such that having an experiential property and being aware of having it is one and the same thing? I think we can. To defend this view I will proceed in two steps. First, I will argue that there is a sense of awareness of having an experiential property such that having an experiential property necessarily implies being aware of having it. Second, I will argue that there is even identity between having an experiential property and being aware of having it.[13]

In order to develop an understanding of the relevant kind of awareness we must come back to the nature of experiential properties. To have an experiential property partially consists in what it is like to have it for someone who has it. To introduce the kind of awareness here at issue one may start as follows. In having an experiential property the subject is in an immediate manner aware of the way it is like for her to have that property. But having that property at least partially consists in what it is like for someone to have it. Therefore, by being aware of the way it is like for you to have the property you are aware of having the property.

To clarify this reasoning let me explicitly state the premises of the argument just sketched:

---

[13] A number if philosophers may be interpreted as endorsing the claim that there is a sense of awareness such that having an experiential property necessarily involves being aware of having it. Famously, Brentano holds such a view in his distinction between the primary object of e.g. an auditory experience which is the heard tone and the secondary object of that same experience which is the hearing of the tone (Brentano 1874, vol. 1, book 2). This basic idea is taken up in Kriegel's self-representational theory of consciousness (see Kriegel 2009). A similar idea (about phenomenally conscious experience) is central as well in the motivation for so-called higher order theories of consciousness (see for different versions David Rosenthal 2002 and William Lycan 2004). The claim is sometimes combined with the view that the particular awareness of having the experience is included in the experience itself and yet does not involve the experience being an object of the experience or an object for the experiencing subject. Such one-level and 'non-objectual' views are defended in Dan Zahavi (1999, chapter 2), Zahavi (2006) and in Brie Gertler (2012).—The view here proposed is more radical since it does not just state a necessary link between having an experiential property and being aware of having it, but rather claims the identity of those properties.

206 EXPERIENCING SUBJECTS AND SO-CALLED MINE-NESS

Premise 1 (immediate awareness of what it is like-ness):
Whenever a subject has a given experiential property P, the subject is aware of the way it is like for it to have property P in virtue of having property P.[14]

Premise 2 (nature of experiential properties):
For every experiential property P, having P partially consists in the way it is like for the subject concerned to have property P.

Premise 3 (awareness of having a property by awareness of what constitutes having it):
If having a property P partially consists in what it is like to have it, then awareness of what it is like to have it (in virtue of having it) is awareness of having P.[15]

Consequence:
Whenever a subject has a given experiential property P, the subject is aware of having P.

This argument provides two things at once. For those who acknowledge the intuitive appeal of premise 1, it provides a reason for accepting that *there is* a kind of awareness of having an experiential property P which is necessarily implied by having P. At the same time it provides an understanding of the nature of the kind of awareness which I would like to call primitive awareness. *Primitive awareness of having an experiential property P is awareness of what it is like to have P while having P and in virtue of having P.*

What remains to be shown is, however, the *identity* of having a given experiential property P and primitive awareness of having P. So far we have only been able to argue that primitive awareness of having P is necessarily implied by having P. But the aim is to justify the suggestion that there is no difference between having P and being primitively aware of having P.

To be precise, this further claim can only be justified for specific experiential properties which I would like to call *pure experiential properties.* According to definition 1, having a given experiential property at least *partially* consists in what it is like to have it. This allows us to say that acting in a particular way is an experiential property: there is something it is like to act and to be acting partially

---

[14] Premise 1 is weaker than one might perhaps think on a first reading. In the intended sense of the premise, the attributor of the relevant awareness uses the expression "the way it is like for it [the subject]" to refer to 'the object' of that awareness. Therefore, no phenomenally manifest self-awareness (in the sense of [subjective character]₃) is implied by that attribution.

[15] An anonymous referee took the following example to undermine premise 3: "Water consists in H_2O, yet awareness of the presence of water is not awareness of the presence of H_2O (nor the other way round)." Premise 3, however, does not imply the contrary claim. Premise 3 is not meant to be justified as a special case of the following general principle: If X consists in Y, then any awareness of Y is an awareness of X. Rather, premise 3 is more modest. It only talks about the special case we are concerned with—the case of properties such that the kind of awareness at issue in the second part of the premise (awareness of what it is like to have them while having them) is possible with respect to them. Note that premise 3 does not even have the logical form of the general principle invoked.

consists in what it is like to act (or so one can plausibly argue). But to be acting involves much more; it only *partially* consists in the way it is like for the agent to act. Contrary to this example *pure* experiential properties are such that having them fully (and not only partially) consists in what it is like to have them. Only few expressions in natural language are used to attribute pure experiential properties. But it is easy to introduce technical terms for such properties such as "to be phenomenally presented with blueness."

As I would like to argue now, in the case of pure experiential properties there is no difference between having the property and being primitively aware of having it. In the following argument I will use the notion of someone's overall state and of what-it-is-like aspects of someone's overall states. The overall state of a person as I understand it just is the instantiation of the totality of the properties the person has at the moment at issue. And the what-it-is-like aspects are nothing but the instantiation of pure experiential properties. Therefore, talk of states and what-it-is-like aspects could be eliminated from the theoretical language we need in order to talk about consciousness. However, in the present context it can nonetheless be useful, I believe, to use those notions in order to express the relevant intuition.

The totality of what it is like for a given subject to be in its present state is, in general, rich and complex. It is characterized by a variety of different aspects. For instance, there are the aspects concerning the 'what it is like' of auditory experience (you hear the sharp voices of birds and the wind in the leaves of the trees around you) and there are the what-it-is-like aspects of thought and of bodily movement as well. You need not attend to any of those aspects for them to be there, in a clear and understandable sense, for you. For them to be there for you is for them to be aspects of the overall what-it-is-likeness of your overall state. In other words: For them to be there for you is for them to be part of what it is like to be you at that particular moment. These aspects are directly there for you even if you do not attend to them and even if you have no thought about them; they are constitutive, as we may say, of what it is like to be you at that moment.

One may put it in this way: we are always primitively aware of the totality of the what-it-is-likeness of our present state and by being primitively aware of that totality we are aware of each aspect of that totality. To be primitively aware of an aspect of that totality should not be thought of as involving any kind of conscious singling out of that aspect. The aspect is there for the subject as part of a complex totality and this is the way in which the subject concerned is primitively aware of each particular aspect. Any kind of singling out would be a further step.

For instance, you may be phenomenally presented with pure blue at a given moment and your being so presented with blue is an aspect of the totality of what it is like to be you at that moment. You are primitively aware of that aspect even if, lost in thought, you do not attend to the color or your being presented with it and of course, you need not have formed any concept of 'pure blue' in order to be able to be phenomenally presented with pure blue; nor do you have to think about the color you are presented with in order to be in a state with that particular aspect.—A lot of what I just said is of course controversial and explicitly rejected by those who defend some higher order theory of consciousness.[16] I would like to ask the reader who disagrees to try to see the intuitive attractiveness of the picture just given and to just have a look at what adopting the picture leads us to when we theorize about consciousness.

The picture naturally leads to the claim here aimed at: in the case of pure experiential properties, there is no difference between having them and being aware of having them (if the awareness at issue is understood in the sense of primitive awareness). We are primitively aware of every what-it-is-like aspect of our overall state. That primitive awareness just is, in fact it consists in, that particular 'what-it-is-like-aspect' being there for the subject concerned, where the relevant 'being there for the subject concerned' just *is* for that aspect to be part of the total 'what-it-is-likeness' of the subject's overall state at the moment at issue. For an aspect to be part of the total 'what-it-is-likeness' of a subject's overall state just means that, at the moment at issue, the subject instantiates a specific pure experiential property—the experiential property the attribution of which is rendered true by being in a state with that particular aspect.

Is it adequate to call the reasoning just presented an argument? I'm not sure. If an argument always leads from less problematic premises, by deductive reasoning, to a conclusion one initially thought to be more problematic, then the reasoning sketched is not an argument. The purpose of the reasoning presented is not to convince by deducing a problematic conclusion from less problematic premises. Rather its purpose is to make a certain understanding of experiential properties and awareness of them intuitively accessible and to thereby render the conclusion aimed at clearer in a way which makes it easier to see its intuitive attractiveness.[17] With these remarks in mind the reader might find the following summary helpful.

Premise 1:   To be primitively aware of being in an overall state with aspect A just is to be in an overall state with aspect A.

Premise 2:   For every pure experiential property P, there is an aspect A_p such that having property P is to be in an overall state with aspect A_p.

C1:   To be primitively aware of having a given pure experiential property P is to be primitively aware of being in an overall state with aspect A_p. (from premise 1 and premise 2)

---

[16] A version of higher order theories of consciousness is famously defended in David Rosenthal (2002). See for forceful criticism Siewert (2013).

[17] The methodological background assumptions about the role of intuitions in philosophical practice here at work are very similar to those elaborated in Chudnoff (2017).

C2: To be primitively aware of having a given pure experiential property P is to be in an overall state with aspect A_p. (from C1 and premise 1)

C3: To be primitively aware of having a given pure experiential property P just is to have that property P. (from C2 and premise 2).

Premise 2 will be quite uncontroversial if one finds the talk of aspects of overall states clear enough. The crucial insight I would like to defend here is expressed in premise 1. One may object that premise 1 is (under the presupposition of premise 2) just a different way to express the result (C3) the argument is supposed to show. Does this mean that the argument is begging the question against the opponent who wishes to deny C3? I think that it does and this is why the above 'argument', as mentioned earlier, is not intended to convince by starting from premises the opponent might find less objectionable than the conclusion. The reasoning summarized above may, however, nonetheless serve its intended purpose which is to explicate an intuition. The intuition, I believe, is implicitly shared by many and it manifests, or so I would like to claim, an adequate understanding of phenomenal consciousness.[18]

7. Experiencing Subjects

The notion of an experiencing subject is deeply incorporated in the way we experience the world and in the way we think about other human and non-human animals that we take to be conscious. We have an intuitive and, in a sense, clear understanding of the difference between a mere thing, without any 'inner life' or 'perspective' and an individual, an elephant, for example, for whom it is like something to live through its individual existence. We have a substantial positive understanding of the difference between an experiencing subject and a complex information processing thing without 'the light of consciousness'. All these claims can be seen to be true by reflection upon one's own perception, emotion, and thought.

Yet, experiencing subjects are theoretically puzzling. How can we give an account of the relevant difference between experiencing subjects and other individuals? It seems difficult to do more than use metaphors and examples. The notion of an experiencing subject is arguably fundamental in the sense that no conceptual reduction to other terms can be plausibly proposed. Experiencing subjects arguably have a special ontological status in many ways. For instance, there are reasons to claim that their identity over time does not allow for conceptual or

---

[18] For an interesting defense of the view that question-begging arguments are not necessarily useless, see McKeon (2017).

ontological analyses, that their individuality is non-descriptive and that they are 'simple' in the sense of not having parts.[19]

Upon reflection conscious subjects may appear to have an ontological nature which does not allow for their integration into the standard contemporary scientific world view. In this situation philosophers may hope to get rid of the problems surrounding the puzzling nature of experiencing subjects by developing a philosophical view about consciousness which leaves the experiencing subject out of the picture. It may therefore appear attractive to many to use a theoretical vocabulary which does not contain the notion of conscious beings (experiencing subjects) and so does not make reference at all (or so it may seem) to the individuals involved in experiences.

The following diagnosis is likely to be correct: the widespread adoption of the experience property framework in contemporary philosophy of mind is in part motivated in the way just described. In particular, talking of qualitative character or subjective character of experiences may appear to have the following theoretical advantage: one can theorize about problems surrounding consciousness without ever addressing ontological issues about the nature of experiencing subjects. This may appear to be an advantage since the issues just alluded to concerning the nature of those *for whom* it is like something to undergo an experience may well appear rather mysterious and it may seem hopeless to find an answer to the questions these issues raise.

In fact, however, the experience property framework only *apparently* provides a theoretical language which makes no mention of the subject having experiential properties. For an experience to have qualitative character just *is* for it to be such that it is like something *for the subject concerned* to undergo the experience; and exactly the same must be said about [subjective character]$_1$ and [subjective character]$_2$. As argued earlier, for an experience to have subjective character in the two senses and for it to have qualitative character is for it to be an event which is the instantiation of experiential properties. Experiential properties are instantiated by *experiencing subjects*. It follows that the philosopher who uses the experience property framework—far from avoiding reference to experiencing subjects—really constantly refers to experiencing subjects but does so in a hidden manner which can be easily overlooked. If the argument here provided for a reductive explication of qualitative and subjective character in the two senses discussed so far in terms of experiencing beings and their experiential properties is correct, then the experience property framework does not allow leaving the experiencing subject out of the picture. Experiencing beings are 'in the picture', so to speak,

---

[19] There is no room here to further comment on these claims. I would like to invite those readers who are doubtful about them to take some time to reflect upon the relevant items of his or her conscious life in order to see if there is reason to agree. I hope most readers will come to a positive conclusion. For arguments in favor of some of them, see Nida-Rümelin (2012a and (2012b).

since they are unavoidably referred to and thought about even if only implicitly. Obviously, it would be preferable to make such reference explicit and to explicitly introduce the notion of experiencing individuals into one's theoretical language. This is precisely what the proponent of the subject property framework suggests.

8. Subjective Character—Phenomenological or Ontological?

The specific qualitative character of an experience consists in the experience's being an instantiation of specific experiential properties. Those experiential properties characterize what it is like for the person concerned to have the experience. Let us call such facts about a given token experience *specific phenomenological facts*. To attribute specific qualitative character (for instance so-called blueishness) to a given token experience is to express a specific phenomenological fact. Phenomenal kinds of experiences are characterized by the experiential properties associated with members of that kind. For instance, it is constitutive of being a member of the kind 'blue experience' that the experience is an instantiation of the experiential property of being phenomenally presented with blue. Let us call such facts *general phenomenological facts*.

General phenomenological facts concern types of experiences. They may be contingent facts about such types or non-contingent facts (true in virtue of the nature of such types as in the example just given). Arguably, to know that blue experiences are by their nature instantiations of being presented with blue is to know what it *is* to have a blue experience, it is to know what is essential to blue experiences. Claims about what is essential to blue experiences are ontological claims about a type of experiences (or so I will use the term here) and since they concern a type they are general ontological claims; the facts expressed by them, if true, may be called *general ontological facts*.

General ontological facts are sometimes quite trivial as in the example just given but they may not be trivial at all and sometimes difficult to conceptualize in an adequate manner. Potential examples are these: arguably it is essential to actions that the acting subject experiences itself as originating what happens; arguably it is essential to perception that the perceiving subject experiences the objects perceived as belonging to an independently existing objective reality.

Sometimes claims are made about the ontological nature of specific events as well. For instance, one may say of the event of a stone falling to the surface of a planet that it is a physical event thereby expressing the fact that it belongs to a certain ontological type of events. If such claims are true, then they express *specific ontological facts*. A last terminological proposal: as the example of blue experiences illustrates, general ontological facts are, in certain cases, non-contingent general phenomenological facts. This is so if the nature of the event is characterized in part by what it is like to be involved in it. In that case the instantiation of specific experiential properties is essential to being a member of that kind. Let us call such facts *general ontological facts concerning phenomenology*.

What kind of fact is the one expressed saying that experiences (in general) have [subjective character]$_1$ or [subjective character]$_2$? The following candidates must be considered. It could be (a) a contingent general phenomenological fact or (b) an ontological fact concerning phenomenology or (c) an ontological fact which does not concern phenomenology. Given the analyses proposed we must simply ask the following question: to which of these categories belongs the fact that experiences are the instantiation of experiential properties?

We can surely exclude possibility (a) by stipulation: experiences are not just contingently an instantiation of experiential properties. By the term "experiences" we intend to refer to those events which are the instantiation of such properties. It is, therefore, constitutive for membership in that kind that an event is an instantiation of experiential properties. The remaining possibilities are (b) and (c). The crucial question is this: is it a fact concerning phenomenology that experiences have [subjective character]$_1$ and [subjective character]$_2$?

The answer should be negative. The fact that experiences have subjective character in one of the two senses is an ontological fact. It *does not* concern phenomenology in the following sense: *the claim that experiences have subjective character is not made true by some common feature of the way it is like to have an experience.* It is not made true by a specific experiential property (or several of them) which are without exception and necessarily so instantiated in all experiences.

To have subjective character in the two senses so far discussed just is to be an event which is an instantiation of *some experiential property or other.* To say this must clearly be distinguished from the claim that there are specific experiential properties instantiated in every experience and that those are constitutive of having an experience. No such claim is made when we say that it is essential to experiences (that is: constitutive for being an experience) that experiential properties are instantiated. There is no specific way it is like to have an experience which constitutes its subjective character in any of the two senses. That a specific experience has [subjective character]$_1$ or [subjective character]$_2$ is not a phenomenological fact about it; it is an *ontological* fact about it. To say of an experience that it has subjective character in one of the two senses so far discussed is thus to express a specific ontological fact which *does not* concern phenomenology.

It is therefore a mistake to search for the special 'phenomenal feel' of [subjective character]$_1$ or [subjective character]$_2$. It is like something *for* the subject concerned to have the experience and the subject is primitively aware of having the associated experiential properties; the experience is, in other words, an instantiation of experiential properties. To say this is *not* to attribute a *common* 'phenomenal feature' to all experiences; it is rather to specify that the event at issue falls into the category of those that are instantiations of experiential properties by experiencing beings; it is to specify its ontological nature.

The point just made is perhaps hard to grasp. I therefore would like to put it once again but in a slightly different manner. To have subjective character in the relevant (ontological) sense presently under consideration just is to be an instantiation of very special properties, experiential properties. However, there are *no specific experiential properties* such that having subjective character consists in being an instantiation of *those* specific experiential properties. Phenomenological facts, by contrast, are constituted by the instantiation of some subclass of all experiential properties.

Some will find it difficult, however, to fully abandon the idea that the phenomenon at issue when theorists talk about 'subjective character' is phenomenological in nature. The tendency to think that subjective character is a phenomenal feature of experience may have two sources: first, one may confuse subjective character in the sense here at issue with what one might call 'the appearance of belongingness to me'. Second, one might confuse subjective character in the two senses discussed so far with a deep and in fact *phenomenal* feature of experience, which one may call "pre-reflective self-awareness."

9. The Appearance of Belongingness to Me

"Mine-ness" is often used synonymously to "subjective character" as illustrated in the passages cited above. On the other hand, the term "mine-ness" is sometimes used in order to describe a particular *phenomenal feature* of 'apparent belongingness-to-me' which lacks in certain pathological cases described in the literature.[20] Perhaps the most prominent example is the use of the term "mine-ness" in the context of discussions of so-called "thought insertion." As it is well known, it is part of certain pathological conditions that people have experiences they describe as the occurrence of thoughts that *do not appear to be their own* or as *apparently belonging to someone else*. These cognitive experiences are often described in the literature as lacking so-called mine-ness.[21] Another related example is the use of the term "mine-ness" in the literature about agency. Famously there are patients whose corpus callosum has been cut by surgeons in order to avoid epileptic attacks taking over the whole brain who report that their limbs 'act' in a way which is not 'their own act' (for instance, the arm 'attacks' the person's partner while the subject at issue has no intention to do so).[22] Here too the 'action' is sometimes described by philosophers as lacking 'mine-ness'.

---

[20] For more on that phenomenal feature compare the contributions by Richard Dub, Jordi Fernandez, Alexandre Billon, and Frédérique de Vignemont to the present volume.

[21] Examples of uses of "mine-ness" in this sense in a discussion of thought insertion can be found, for instance, in Pedrini (2016).

[22] For a brief overview of empirical data concerning such patients, compare Uddin (2011).

In both cases cited above the subject at issue experiences the relevant events (the thoughts popping up in his or her mind in the first case, apparently intentional bodily movements in the second) as, in some sense *alien*, as not belonging to him or her. In the case of thought insertion different interpretations of the way in which the thoughts are experienced as alien can and have been proposed: they may appear alien in virtue of their content (their content does not fit or does not appear to fit into the person's personality, values, and/or convictions) and they may appear alien in virtue of the way they appear to be generated (for instance they are beyond voluntary control as if someone else were forcing them upon the person concerned and/or they lack the appearance of being brought about by oneself in the way normal thoughts, at least according to some authors, appear to be).[23] In the case of bodily movements which are not experienced by the person concerned as her own actions it might be the fact that the person has no intention to move in the way her body does or even the fact that she does not experience the movement as actively brought about by herself or both which the subjects concerned have in mind when they describe those movements as alien, as not being 'their own' or as 'not being done by them'.

For present purposes we need not speculate about what might be an adequate description of the phenomenology of such pathological experience. There is nothing wrong or problematic with the use of the term mine-ness in such contexts. There is, after all, an intuitively understandable sense (or rather various such senses) of "mine-ness" in which it is obviously quite adequate to say that what lacks in such cases is a certain phenomenal feature of 'mine-ness' in the sense of 'belonging to me'. And it is an interesting project to search for descriptions of what lacks in such pathological cases and is present in the normal case. Nothing can be said against calling those phenomenal features mine-ness except for the danger of conceptual confusion given the fact that the term "mine-ness" is also used in a very different sense: in a sense in which mine-ness is nothing more and nothing less than subjective character in the two senses so far discussed. In these two senses, for an event to have subjective character simply amounts to being an event which consists in the instantiation of experiential properties.

It will be obvious by now why it would be a bad and fundamental mistake to confuse mine-ness in the relevant sense of subjective character with mine-ness in the sense of apparent belongingness to me. Mine-ness in the first sense is an essential feature of experience; it cannot and it does not lack in the cases at issue. The person experiencing something that he or she describes in the way characteristic to so-called thought insertion does have a cognitive experience: he or she is presented with a content which pops up in her mind; he or she thereby instantiates

---

[23] Compare for a discussion of different accounts, Gallagher (2015).

an experiential property. Furthermore, the person is, in some sense to be specified, under the impression that the thought does not belong to her (mine-ness in the relevant phenomenal sense is lacking). But this too is, of course, to instantiate experiential properties.

Experiences that are properly described as cases of so-called thought insertion are, obviously, instantiations of experiential properties. It follows, according to the analysis proposed, that they have [subjective character]$_1$ and [subjective character]$_2$. Analogous comments apply to the case of 'actions' that are experienced by the subject as belonging to someone else. The fact that an experience of thought insertion or of 'alien action' has [subjective character]$_1$ and [subjective character]$_2$ is an ontological fact about those token experiences and no phenomenal fact about them as argued before. It is not a phenomenal fact about them since the commonality so stated of such experiences does *not* consist in the instantiation of some *specific* experiential properties. One can be misled into thinking that [subjective character]$_1$ and [subjective character]$_2$ are phenomenal features of experiences if one does not clearly distinguish them from appearances of belongingness-to-me which clearly *are* phenomenal features in the sense here suggested: they are instantiations of *specific* experiential properties by experiencing subjects.

Experiences of 'belongingness to me' of the various kinds discussed in the literature are, without any doubt, of great philosophical interest. However, the attention they receive in recent literature is sometimes based on a further potential error which is, in my view, quite fundamental. Contrary to what many appear to be inclined to think, experiences of 'belongingness to me' do *not* have the content "I am the subject of that experience" or "This experience is mine." They should not be described as experiences of 'me being the one who undergoes' the experience at issue. The point is central, so I should elaborate and argue for what I just said.

Let us keep in mind that reference to such experiences is secured by pointing out that they *lack* in certain pathological cases. What exactly is lacking in such cases is, as mentioned, a matter of dispute but there is agreement among philosophers discussing such cases that the people concerned lack the feeling that the experience at issue is in some way (to be specified differently for each of the various kinds of cases) *psychologically related* to themselves. One may think here again of the example of an 'inserted thought' with a content which appears to the person concerned to be totally unrelated to the personality she takes herself to be. Now, it is one thing to be the one for whom it is like something to have a given thought and quite another to have a thought which fits into one's personality. The parallel claim applies, I claim, to all relations between the subject and the relevant experiences which do not appear to obtain (or which appear not to obtain) in the relevant pathological cases. To be the one for whom it is like something to have the thought *is* to be the subject of the thought. We have no reason to suppose that in the pathological cases at issue, the subject is under the impression that she is not the one for whom it is like something to have the 'inserted' thought. Nor do we have reason to suppose that some awareness of being the one for whom it is like something to have the thought is normally present but absent in her. She reports about how it is for her to have the inserted thought. It is plausible to assume that she is, *in that sense*, acutely aware of being the subject of the thought—of it being like something *for her* to have the thought.[24]

Philosophers who struggle to develop a satisfying theoretical understanding of consciousness are intrigued by subjectivity, by the sense in which experiences are 'for' the subject concerned. Interest in subjectivity in that sense is what motivates much of the recent work in so-called mine-ness or subjective character. My point is this: one cannot expect to make progress on the issue of subjectivity in that fundamental sense by studying cases falling into the class here called "experiences of belongingness to me." An experience E belongs to a subject S just in case it is like something for S to undergo E; in that case S is the subject involved in E. Some philosophers are interested in experiences of 'belongingness to me' because they believe that in such experiences we are aware in a phenomenally manifest manner of being the subject of the experience. If this is a philosopher's motivation for studying such cases then her interest is misplaced. As just argued, such experiences are *not* experiences of being the subject of the experience. If we are looking for a phenomenally manifest awareness experiencers have of being the subject of an experience they undergo then we must look in a different place. Such an awareness is surely present in the kind of self-awareness discussed in the next section.

Philosophical discussions about subjective character in recent literature are united by an interest in subjectivity in the sense in which consciousness involves or is characterized by subjectivity. I would like to propose to reserve the term for phenomena that are in fact (and not only by error taken to be) closely related in a systematic manner with subjectivity. If one agrees to do so, then one must exclude mine-ness in the sense of experiences of 'belongingness to me' from being a fourth phenomenon "subjective character" can be taken to refer to. This is why I resist introducing a technical term "[subjective character]$_4$," for experiences of 'belongingness to me'.

---

[24] The following citation taken from Guillot (2017, p. 31) seems to show (see, in particular the last sentence) that Marie Guillot commits the error here targeted. "While, on the first prominent way of discussing subjective character (as for-me-ness), it corresponds to the fact that the subject is aware of her experience (in a special way), on the third interpretation, it corresponds to the subject's awareness of that very fact. As part of the experience being given to a subject, this subject is somehow aware of the experience being her own." The "third interpretation" in Guillot's terminology is the experience of 'belongingness-to-me'. It is characterized in her paper as the kind of 'mine-ness' which lacks in the relevant pathological cases.

10. Pre-Reflective Self-Awareness

Some philosophers in the philosophical tradition and a number of contemporary philosophers as well endorse or appear to endorse the idea that consciousness involves some form of not conceptualized self-awareness which does not require any reflection and yet is the basis of reflective self-consciousness.[25] To refer to the phenomenon one sometimes uses the term "pre-reflective self-consciousness" which I find telling and adequate to what I intend to refer to. Quite often no clear distinction is made between "self-awareness" in the sense of being aware of one's experience (the kind of awareness here called primitive awareness and used in the analysis proposed of [subjective character]$_2$) and self-awareness in the present sense which involves that the awareness at issue is an awareness the subject having the experience has of itself. The distinction is however important to avoid confusion. It is one thing to be (primitively) aware of being presented with blueness, for instance, and quite another to be aware *in a phenomenally manifest manner* of oneself, of the one who is now having the blue experience.[26] Primitive awareness and pre-reflective self-awareness should not be conflated. To make that conceptual distinction does not, however, exclude that primitive awareness of having a given experiential property often or perhaps even always (or perhaps even necessarily) involves or includes pre-reflective self-awareness.

To get a clear intuitive grip on the thesis that such pre-reflective self-awareness is involved in primitive awareness of one's own experiential properties it is perhaps best to consider cases of experiential properties which are such that having them is to be phenomenally presented with some 'object' in a sense of 'object' which does not imply its existence. Even in cases in which the 'object' does not exist (one may think as an example of after images) the experience has what one may call the structure of *basic intentionality*: something (an 'object') is present or presented to a subject. The idea at issue may be put with respect to such cases as follows: the experiencing subject is aware of being the subject in that structure of basic intentionality. The subject is, in other words, aware of being the one who is the individual to whom something is present in a phenomenally manifest way. Consider the following example: you are lying in the grass with your eyes closed and you 'see' moving 'clouds' of various colors. You are primitively aware of 'seeing' those 'clouds'. Your primitive awareness of 'seeing' them is nothing over and above having the experiential property at issue (as argued before). You are aware of 'seeing' the 'clouds' in the simple sense that you are aware of what it is

---

[25] Compare for historical roots of this idea, the Introduction to the present volume.

[26] One may object that being aware of having an experience involves being aware of oneself just like any awareness of an instantiation of a property involves being aware of the object instantiating it. I agree that there is a sense in which primitive awareness involves awareness of oneself but I deny that it implies being aware of oneself in a phenomenally manifest manner *as* the subject undergoing the experience. I see that this point needs further clarification but I cannot start doing this here.

like to be you now and your 'seeing' the 'clouds' is an aspect of what it is like to be you now. The following is the crucial claim: In being aware of that aspect you are aware of yourself as the one for whom it is like something to 'see' those 'clouds' right now. You are, without any direction of your attention upon yourself aware of yourself as the subject to whom those 'clouds' are presented. This is the idea I would like to propose and I believe a number of philosophers have in mind when they say that consciously experiencing involves that the subject is pre-reflectively aware of itself.

Pre-reflective self-awareness in the sense just hinted at raises a number of interrelated and difficult issues to be elaborated and to be clarified. For instance, pre-reflective self-awareness involves awareness *of* oneself, and yet, as many have pointed out, the subject is not given to itself, in pre-reflective self-awareness, as an object among others.[27] It is notoriously difficult to explain what that means. A metaphorical way of putting the point I find helpful is to say that the subject does not show up as an item in its own stream of consciousness when it is, in the relevant way, pre-reflectively aware of itself. Another difficult issue concerns the sense in which the subject is aware of itself *as the subject of the experience* it is presently undergoing. How can such a claim be true, if the subject is not supposed to apply any concept of itself (any "I-concept") or any general concept of experiencing subjects in that awareness?[28] Related to the latter issue, the question arises to what extent one can successfully reflect on the phenomenology of pre-reflective self-awareness without reflecting on ontological issues concerning the essential nature of experiencing subjects. In my view, in that particular realm, phenomenology and ontology must complement and inform each other. It is difficult to see how one can defend the idea that subjects are aware of themselves *as experiencing subjects* without taking a stance on what it takes to be an experiencing subject.[29]

If the thesis of pre-reflective self-awareness is true, then it concerns a kind of self-awareness which is *phenomenally manifest*. Plausibly, it is present in *all* mature human experience.[30] Perhaps it is even present in *all* experience (if experience is

---

[27] Sartre (1943) may be taken to have this claim in mind when he writes: "toute conscience positionnelle d'objet est en même temps conscience non-positionnelle d'elle-même" (p. 19). However, since he attributes self-consciousness to consciousness ("conscience") and not explicitly to the subject, he might as well think of what I call [subjective character]$_2$. For a discussion and historical information about the claim that the subject is aware of itself without being an object of that awareness compare Zahavi (1999), section 3.

[28] For some steps toward an explication, compare the last sections of Nida-Rümelin (2017).

[29] For more on the relation between phenomenological issues concerning self-awareness and ontological issues about the nature of experiencing subjects, compare Nida-Rümelin (2017) and the work in preparation mentioned in footnote *.

[30] As far as I understand the phenomenological descriptions of experiences involved in so-called de-personalization no counterexamples against the claim just made occur in that condition. The described experience of 'detachment' from one's own thoughts, feelings, or actions does not at all exclude that one is nonetheless aware in a phenomenally manifest manner of being the subject of these thoughts, feelings, and actions. Presumably to be in such a condition is so alien precisely because

understood as the instantiation of experiential properties). Perhaps we must assume that the very first experience in the simplest animal capable of experiencing already involves pre-reflective self-awareness. In any case, if pre-reflective self-awareness is indeed present in all mature human experience then it is impossible to attract attention to that aspect by contrasting experiences which have the aspect with experiences lacking it. This fact makes it unfortunately more difficult to achieve shared reference among philosophers reflecting on these issues.[31]

We now have a second error theory at hand for the mistake mentioned before which consists in assuming that subjective character (in the two coinciding senses analyzed) is a *phenomenal* feature of experiences while in fact it is an *ontological* feature (which does not even concern phenomenology). This mistake can be explained by a failure to clearly distinguish between subjective character (in the two senses commented above) and pre-reflective self-awareness.

11. About the Relation between the Three Interpretations of Subjective Character Proposed

Three different interpretations of what it is for an experience to have subjective character have been proposed and discussed in detail:

Interpretation 1: For an experience to have [subjective character]$_1$ just is for it to be an event consisting in the instantiation of experiential properties.

Interpretation 2: For an experience to have [subjective character]$_2$ is for it to be such that the subject involved is primitively aware of having the associated experiential properties.

Interpretation 3: For an experience to have [subjective character]$_3$ is for it to be such that the subject involved is pre-reflectively self-aware.

Conceptually there is a clear difference between these three understandings. A philosopher going back and forth between them without noticing would seem to be guilty of conceptual confusion. Upon a deeper analysis, however, it turns out (as argued in section 3) that there is no difference between having a given experiential property and being primitively aware of having it. So it is the very same fact which renders attributions of [subjective character]$_1$ and attributions of

---

while one feels 'detached' from what one experiences and from what one does, one is nonetheless aware of being the one who is involved in these events as the subject for whom there is something it is like to experience or act. For discussions of de-personalization compare the contributions by Billon, Howell, and McClelland to the present volume.

[31] For discussions of whether the method of contrast is applicable in the present case, compare McClelland's contribution to this volume, section 5.

[subjective character]$_2$ true. Still, the conceptual distinction should not be abandoned or considered to be superfluous. It is a substantial and interesting fact about the nature of experiential properties that having them coincides with being primitively aware of having them.

For an experience to have [subjective character]$_3$, by contrast, is a different fact. It is not the same, or so the discussion presented suggests, as the fact which renders attributions of [subjective character]$_1$ and [subjective character]$_2$ correct. Contrary to the latter two senses of having subjective character, for an experience to have [subjective character]$_3$ is for it to come along with a certain phenomenal aspect: the subject is aware of itself in a *phenomenally manifest manner*. To say that an experience has [subjective character]$_3$ is to make a statement about what it is like to undergo the experience. To say of an event that it has [subjective character]$_1$ or [subjective character]$_2$ is to say of it that it belongs to the ontological category of experiences.

The difference just pointed out is compatible with the speculation that there is a necessary connection between experiencing and being pre-reflectively aware of oneself. Perhaps even the most simple experience a subject undergoes comes along, necessarily, with the subject being pre-reflectively aware of itself. I do not believe that this is so but I will leave the issue to a different occasion.

12. Conclusion: Subjects of Experience and Subjective Character

A central result of the analysis proposed is that one can account for so-called subjective character only by making explicit reference to experiencing subjects. To have [subjective character]$_1$ is to be an event consisting in the instantiation of experiential properties. Experiential properties are such that having them is like something *for the subject involved*. Therefore, no explanation and no theoretical account of subjective character in the first sense can be given without engaging in theorizing about what it is to be an experiencing subject. To have [subjective character]$_2$ is to be an event in which the subject involved is primitively aware of having the associated experiential properties. Being primitively aware of having certain properties is, according to the account proposed, just having experiential properties and so the argument just given re-applies. But even if this identification is rejected it is clear that only experiencing subjects can be primitively aware of having certain properties and that, therefore, understanding [subjective character]$_2$ in a theoretically satisfying manner will require, again, that one gets clear about what it is to be an experiencing subject. Similar remarks apply to [subjective character]$_3$. To have [subjective character]$_3$ is to be an event such that the subject involved is pre-reflectively aware of itself. An account of the nature of experiencing subjects is potentially relevant in two places. First, only an experiencing subject can be pre-reflectively aware of itself. Second, according to what precedes, in pre-reflective self-awareness the subject is aware of itself *as* an experiencing subject. Therefore, an account of what it is to be an experiencing subject is required in order to understand the nature of the one who has that kind of self-awareness and in order to understand the content of that special and fundamental kind of self-awareness.[32]

References

Brentano, Franz (1874), "Psychologie vom empirischen Standpunkte». Leipzig, Duncker & Humblot.

Chudnoff, Eliah (2017), "The reality of the intuitive," *Inquiry* 60: 1–17.

Gallagher, Shaun (2015), "Relations between agency and ownership in the case of schizophrenic thought insertion and delusions of control," *Review of Philosophy and Psychology* 6 (4): 865–879.

Gertler, Brie (2012), "Conscious states as objects of awareness: On Uriah Kriegel, subjective consciousness. A self-representational theory," *Philosophical Studies* 159: 447–455.

Guillot, Marie (2017), "I, me, mine: On a confusion concerning the subjective character of Experiences," *Review of Philosophical Psychology* 8: 23–53.

Higginbotham, James (2003), "Remembering, imagining, and the first person," in A. Barber (ed.), *Epistemology of Language,* Oxford: Oxford UP, 496–533.

Howell, Robert J. & Thompson, Brad (2017), "Phenomenally mine: In search of the subjective character of consciousness," *Review of Philosophy and Psychology* 8: 103

Kriegel, Uriah (2005), "Naturalizing subjective character," *Philosophy and Phenomenological Research* 71 (1): 23–57.

Kriegel, Uriah (2009), *Subjective Consciousness: A Self-Representational Theory,* Oxford University Press.

Kriegel, Uriah (2011), "Self-representationalism and the explanatory gap," in J. Liu & J. Perry (eds.), *Consciousness and the Self,* Cambridge University Press.

Levine, Joe (2006), "Conscious awareness and representation," in Kenneth Williford & Uriah Kriegel, eds., *Self-representational Approaches to Consciousness,* MIT Press: 173–198.

---

[32] A lot of the material presented in the present chapter evolved in discussions in the context of the project "Phenomenal Consciousness and Self-awareness" funded by the Swiss National Science Foundation (project number: 100011_166320). I am grateful to the FNS for its generous support. I would like to thank Julien Bugnon, Donnchadh O'Conaill, and Jacob Naito for many insightful discussions in the context of that project. They helped me a lot to get clearer about issues related to the material here presented. I am grateful to the editors of this volume and a further anonymous referee whose numerous critical comments helped me to correct a number of mistakes and to enhance the quality of this contribution.

Lycan, William (2004), "The superiority of Hop to HOT" in Rocco, Gennaro (ed.), *Consciousness: An antology*, John Benjamins: 93–114.

McKeon, Mathew W. (2017), "Statements of inference and begging the question," *Synthese* 194 (6), 119–143.

Nida-Rümelin, Martine (2012a), "An argument from transtemporal identity for subject body dualism," in George Bealer & Robert Koons, *The Waning of Materialism*, Oxford University Press: 191–211.

Nida-Rümelin, Martine (2012b), "The non-descriptive nature of conscious individuals," in Georg Gasser & Matthias Stefan, eds., *Personal Identity. Complex or Simple?* Cambridge University Press: 157–176.

Nida-Rümelin, Martine (2018b), "The experience property framework: A misleading paradigm," *Synthese* 195 (8):3361–3387.

Nida-Rümelin, Martine (2016), "The illusion of illusionism: Comment on Keith Frankish 'Illusionism as a theory of consciousness," *The Journal of Consciousness Studies*, 23 (11–12):160–171.

Nida-Rümelin, Martine (2017), "Self-awareness," *Review of Philosophy and Psychology* 8 (1): 55–82.

Nida-Rümelin, Martine (2018a), "Colors and Shapes", in Fabian Dorsch & Fiona Macpherson (eds), *Phenomenal Presence*, Oxford University Press: 77–104.

Pedrini, Patrizia (2016), "Rescuing the 'loss of agency' account of thought insertion," *Philosophy, Psychiatry, and Psychology* 22 (3): 221–233.

Rosenthal, David (2002), "Explaining consciousness," in D. Chalmrs, ed., *Philosophy of Mind: Classical and Contemporary Readings*," Oxford University Press, 109–131.

Sartre, Jean-Paul (1943), "L'être et le néant. Essaie d'ontologie phénoménologique." Paris, Gallimard

Siewert, Charles (2013), "Phenomenality and self-consciousness," in Uriah Kriegel, ed., *Phenomenal Intentionality*, Oxford Universty Press: 235–259.

Stoljar, Daniel (2016), "The semantics of what it is like," *Mind* 125 (500): 1161–1198.

Uddin, Lucina Q. (2011), "Brain connectivity and the self: The case of cerebral disconnection," *Consciousness and Cognition* 20 (1): 94–98.

Zahavi, D. (1999), *Self-Awareness and Alterity: A Phenomenological Investigation*, Northwestern University Press.

Zahavi, Dan (2006), "Two Takes on One-Level Theories of Consciousness," *Psyche* 12 (2): 1–9.

Zahavi, Dan & Kriegel, Uriah (2017), "For-me-ness: What it is and what it is not," in D. Dahlstrom, A. Elpidorou, & W. Hopp, eds., *Philosophy of Mind and Phenomenology*, Routledge: 36–53.

10

The Phenomenal Concept of Self and First-Person Epistemology

Marie Guillot

1. Introduction

In experiencing the world, we also often experience ourselves doing so. When the cat brushes my leg, part of what is phenomenally given, beside the warm, silky sensation, is that it's *me* getting the privilege of it. Let us call "self-experience" this phenomenal awareness of oneself, *as oneself*. What follows assumes that at least *some* experiences of the world come with self-experience. For reasons of space, I won't defend this assumption at length (although I will provide in Section 3.3 a brief argument supporting its plausibility);[1] the claims below are to be understood as conditionals based on this hypothesis.

The aim of this essay is to explore the significance of self-experience for the concept of self and the epistemology of the thoughts that include it, or *I-thoughts*. By "the concept of self," I mean the concept that each subject uses to think about herself *as herself* (Castañeda 1966), as she may manifest by using first-person expressions.

I-thoughts are widely believed to be protected against error in a special way, but there is disagreement on which way that is. The most discussed feature is "immunity to error through misidentification" or IEM (Shoemaker 1968). However, in her important 2003 article on the issue, Annalisa Coliva shows that IEM is regularly conflated with two other properties, which she calls respectively the impossibility of "a split between speaker's reference and semantic reference" (hereafter "No-Split"), and the "Real Guarantee." Coliva argues that IEM and No-Split characterize only *some* I-thoughts. What does attach to *all* I-thought, and helps define it, is the "Real Guarantee."

Coliva's compelling essay leaves open some further questions, which this chapter tries to answer:[2] (i) what is the connection between the three epistemic

---

[1] For a defence, see Zahavi and Kriegel (2015), Guillot (2017), and the chapters in the second part of this volume.

[2] Coliva (2017) addresses some of these questions in a different way; but there are potential points of convergence with this chapter. As the below will make clear, I agree with her passing suggestion

---

Marie Guillot, *The Phenomenal Concept of Self and First-Person Epistemology* In: *Self-Experience: Essays on Inner Awareness*. Edited by: Manuel García-Carpintero and Marie Guillot, Oxford University Press. © Marie Guillot 2023. DOI: 10.1093/oso/9780198805397.003.0010

properties? (ii) Why are they so often conflated? (iii) What explains each of them in the first place?

Section 2 introduces Coliva's three epistemic properties. Section 3 points out that they are observed not just in I-thoughts, but also in thoughts containing phenomenal concepts, like "red" or "painful." My central claim is that this is more than an analogy. I-thoughts are epistemologically special for the same reason that phenomenally-grounded judgements are: because the self-concept, too, is a phenomenal concept, of a special kind. This hypothesis explains (Section 4) why each of Coliva's three properties arises in connection with I-thoughts, and with the frequency that they do. It also entails that there is a common source for all three properties, accounting for the widespread conflation. Finally, it provides a unified account of first-person epistemology—heeding Coliva's lesson that its three facets need disentangling, while uncovering their deeper connection.

2. Three Epistemological Properties of I-Thoughts

Many authors believe that, when using the first-person pronoun "I" or the underlying self-concept, one possesses a sure-fire guarantee against error. However, the exact nature of that guarantee has proven elusive.

2.1. Immunity to Error through Misidentification

The most discussed candidate is IEM (Shoemaker 1968). IEM protects a judgement of the form "*a* is F" against the following type of error through misidentification (EM):

EM [T]hat a statement "*a* is φ" is subject to error through misidentification relative to the term "*a*" means that the following is possible: the speaker knows *some particular thing* to be φ, but makes the mistake of asserting "*a* is φ" because, and only because, he mistakenly thinks that the thing he knows to be φ is what "*a*" refers to. (Shoemaker 1968: 557, my emphasis)

Some I-thoughts are immune to this type of mistake when formed on certain grounds. Suppose that I judge, based on inner perception, that I am hungry. Assuming that I'm right in judging (on this basis) that *someone* is hungry, I must also be right in judging (on the same basis) that *I* am hungry.

(2017: 241) that "there are non-conceptual yet first-personal representations, which ground our possession of the first-person concept."

IEM$_{de\ se}$ One way I can't be wrong in judging "I am F" based on grounds G is by knowing that property F is instantiated, where the bearer of F is a person s who is distinct from me.

But not all I-thoughts are IEM. Suppose I read in the newspaper that Marie Guillot has won the lottery, and judge, based on those grounds: "I am the lottery winner." Unfortunately, the winner is a homonym. This is a case of EM: my grounds (the newspaper) do give me knowledge that *someone* won the lottery; but I am mistaken in thinking that *I* have that property.

Here is the standard reconstruction of the general case of EM$_{de\ se}$. An erroneous judgement that "I am F" is justified[3] by an inference of this form:

Predicative premise	a is F[4] ("Marie Guillot won the lottery")
Identification premise	**I am a**("I am Marie Guillot")
Conclusion	I am F ("I won the lottery")

An error through misidentification arises here because the identification premise is *false*: I am right that the person named "Marie Guillot" in the newspaper won the lottery (*predicative premise*), but wrong that *I* am that person (*identification premise*).

IEM is not a sure-fire guarantee characterizing the self-concept as such, since some I-judgements are vulnerable to EM. According to Coliva (2003), the reason why many think otherwise is that they are confusing IEM with either of two other properties. The first one is the (alleged) impossibility of a "split between speaker's reference and semantic reference" in the case of "I," or what I will call for brevity's sake "No-Split."

2.2. The (Im)possibility of a Split between Speaker's and Semantic Reference

An early appearance of No-Split, Coliva argues, can be found in the second part of G. E. M. Anscombe's famous claim that "The object an 'I'-user means by it must exist so long as he is using 'I', *nor can he take the wrong object to be the object he means by 'I'*" (1975: 145–6; my emphasis). Leaving aside the details of Coliva's exegesis, I propose to define "No-Split" as follows:

---

[3] In the sense that the subject could appeal to the inference in question if asked about her reasons to judge as she does. This does not entail that she has to go through the inference, consciously or unconsciously, to form the judgement.

[4] To simplify, I am ignoring the distinction made by Pryor (1999) between this form of EM, and what he calls "which-object" EM, a variant where the predicative premise has an existential form.

226 THE PHENOMENAL CONCEPT OF SELF

No-Split   Let *o* be an occurrence of a term or concept *a*. The intended reference of *o* necessarily coincides with the semantic reference of *o*.

No-Split is a guarantee against splits in reference of the kind made familiar by Donnellan (1966) and Kripke (1977) for definite descriptions in their referential uses (e.g. "Smith's murderer"), and ordinary proper names. Here is an example of the latter kind. Suppose I only know Daniel Dennett from blurry photos. At a conference, I observe in the distance a man with a white beard and an extraordinary shirt. I wrongly take him to be Daniel Dennett (it is, in fact, Saul Kripke). I say, "Dennett is wearing an extraordinary shirt." Now *Kripke* is arguably the person I have a primary intention to refer to here, given that the point of my remark is to single out the wearer of that special shirt. Hence, not all uses of "Dennett" are guaranteed to speaker-refer to their actual semantic referent.

According to Anscombe (as Coliva reads her), this kind of split is excluded with "I," whether in language or in thought, because, she believes, one cannot take someone else to be oneself, as one would have to do if one were to use "I" to speaker-refer (or "thinker-refer") to another (Coliva 2003: 426).

Coliva has two comments on this. First, it is a mistake to identify No-Split with IEM.[5] I would put it like this: No-Split attaches to some acts of *reference* ("*a*"), while IEM attaches to some acts of *predication* ("*a* is F"). Confusing them[6] thus obscures a requirement on the shape a representation must have if the question of IEM is to be raised meaningfully about it. In the case of I-thoughts, it is to conflate a property of *self-reference* (No-Split) with a property of *self-ascription* (IEM).

Coliva's second point is that in any case, it is false that No-Split characterizes all uses of the word 'I' or the self-concept. While this may be contingently rare, the possibility exists of wrongly taking someone else to be me, and using "I" to speaker-refer or thinker-refer to that person.

To show this, Coliva uses an example from Rovane (1987: 153–4), which I will tweak a bit. Suppose Jane is visiting an art museum with her friends John and Rose. Jane, who is admiring an ancient mirror from a distance, glimpses in the mirror the silhouette of Rose, whom she takes to be herself, and an awful painting behind the silhouette. John exclaims: "There isn't a single ugly painting in this room!" Jane replies, based on what she sees in the mirror: "Actually, there is an awful painting behind *me*."

---

[5]   Coliva diagnoses this confusion in Rovane (1987: 153–4) and Christofidou (1995: 227). I would add McGinn (1983: 45, 49 and footnote 11). These are merely representative examples of a widespread conflation.

[6]   It is unclear whether Anscombe herself does, since she uses her own label, *immunity to mistaken identification*; this leaves some room for questioning whether she took herself to refer to the same phenomenon as Shoemaker's IEM.

Here, there is a sense in which Jane's use of "I" speaker-refers to Rose. Suppose John points out the mistake to Jane. She might then say, "Well, *what I meant* is that there is an awful painting behind *Rose*." This makes clear that Jane's primary referential intention in using "I" was directed towards the person in the mirror, namely Rose, whom Jane mistakenly took to be herself. The upshot is that No-Split doesn't cover all uses of "I" in language (or of the self-concept in thought).[7]

What then, is the sure-fire guarantee against error (if any) that attaches to all uses of "I," if not IEM, or No-Split? Coliva believes there is one, which she calls the "Real Guarantee."

2.3. The Real Guarantee

To isolate the relevant property, Coliva (2003: 427 sq.) contrasts cases of splits involving "I" with cases of splits involving other singular expressions, like proper names and definite descriptions.

When a referential split occurs, what typically happens is the following: the subject *doesn't know* which person is the semantic referent of the name "*a*"; that is, she is unable to answer the question "which person is *a*?." That may be because she isn't acquainted with that person, or lacks sufficiently individuating descriptive information about them. This ignorance explains why the speaker may take another person distinct from the semantic referent of "*a*" to be the referent of that expression.

However, in the case of "I," even when there is a referential split, the presumption that *the subject knows which person she is* is never defeated. Where the referring term *a* is "I," the subject can always answer the question, "Which person is *a*?" (Coliva 2003: 428.) In other words, ignorance of the identity of the semantic reference of "I" cannot be appealed to in order to explain the split when it affects "I," as opposed to what happens with other splitting expressions. Rather, in the painting example, it is Jane's ignorance of the identity of the *other* person involved, the person visually presented to her in the mirror (Rose), that leads her to mistakenly identify that person as herself, and explains the split. That is, although one may use "I" to attempt reference to another person because one does not know who *that person* is, and one wrongly takes them to be identical to oneself, one is never under any misapprehension about *one's own*

---

[7] Intuitions may differ as to whether the "me" in "There is a tasteless painting behind me" can really be intended to refer to someone who happens to be distinct from the subject. If one agrees that it can, then the painting scenario is a counter-example to No-Split. If one disagrees, it is, instead, an example of EM with respect to the first-person. If the former (referential split), then *I believe something true of someone else*. If the latter (EM), *then I believe something false of myself*.

228 THE PHENOMENAL CONCEPT OF SELF

identity in doing so (Coliva 2003: 428). Another way of putting this (which ventures beyond Coliva's own analysis) is to say that in the case of "I," splits occur by virtue of *over-identification* (wrongly extending one's self-conception to include another person), rather than the simple *misidentification* involved in the Dennett example.

The sure-fire guarantee that all comprehending uses of the word "I" or the self-concept enjoy is thus neither IEM nor No-Split, but what Coliva calls "the Real Guarantee":

The Real Guarantee (at the level of thought):   The possession of the first-person concept guarantees that the subject knows which person that concept is a concept of. (Coliva 2003: 429)

2.4. Taking Stock

Coliva (2003) contributes a useful three-way distinction to first-person epistemology. The article leaves open some further questions, however. First, why is the conflation so pervasive, including in authors writing after a consensus on the nature of IEM crystallized around Shoemaker's definition? Second, why does each of the three epistemic properties arise in connection with I-thoughts, and why are they distributed as they are, with the Real Guarantee attaching to all I-thoughts, but IEM and No-Split only attaching to a subset of them?

The rest of this chapter proposes some answers. In my view, the reason for the confusion comes from the fact that all three properties derive in various ways from a common source in the nature of the I-concept. Namely, they arise because the I-concept is a kind of *phenomenal concept*.

What I will not do here is to compare the view with other imaginable explanations of the confusion. To keep the discussion focused, I will also leave aside the independent justifications for the phenomenal-concept view, possible objections and alternatives, which I discuss in other places (Guillot 2016 and ms). Support for the view will instead be provided, here, by its explanatory virtues: it explains each of Coliva's three epistemic properties, their distribution across I-thoughts, and the fact that they are commonly conflated.

3. The Phenomenal-Concept Model of the Self-Concept

One motivation for the phenomenal-concept view of the self-concept is that thoughts composed of phenomenal concepts and I-thoughts exhibit similar epistemic profiles.

3.1. Phenomenal Concepts

Phenomenal concepts[8] are experience-dependent concepts. By an experience, I mean, following Gertler (2012),[9] a particular type of event: an instantiation of a particular phenomenal property F, for instance pain, in a subject at a time. I will also sometimes speak of an experience, however, to refer to an experience-*type* (a category of instantiations of the same phenomenal property F); or even as shorthand for F itself. While there is much controversy as to the exact nature and mode of reference of phenomenal concepts,[10] one point of agreement is that a subject cannot acquire a phenomenal concept C unless she has instantiated the relevant phenomenal property F.

A particularly clear case is that of *pure* phenomenal concepts. By this I mean those concepts we use to reflect on and classify our experiences themselves, based on what it is like to have them. Take the concept of having "pins and needles" in one's legs. When a child who has never had this experience asks what the concept means, it is characteristically difficult to enlighten her. She must wait until she first gets pins and needles in her own limbs to acquire the relevant phenomenal concept. She might then have an *aha* moment as she reflects on the curious new experience—"So *this* is what it is to have pins and needles!" But until then, the best she can do to think of the experience is to use a descriptive concept as a proxy—something like "what people feel when they say they have pins and needles."

Now a certain kind of empiricist might retort that *all* concepts are ultimately experience-dependent in the sense that their acquisition requires having had experiences of some sort. This is controversial; but even on such a supposition, phenomenal concepts would still stand out. On acquiring a phenomenal concept C, we acquire the capacity to apply it on the mere basis of having the experience on which its acquisition is dependent, without the mediation of any (subjectively accessible) inference.[11] Once a subject possesses, say, the phenomenal concept of nausea, it is sufficient that she instantiates the phenomenal property to be able to apply the concept directly, based on attending to the experience. As Shea (2014: 556) puts it, "exercises of a phenomenal concept [...] show up at the personal level as *immediate*—the move from having the phenomenal experience to applying the phenomenal concept does not seem to be mediated by any intervening mental process" (my emphasis). This is unlike what happens with concepts such as that of *a prime number*, for example, or that of *a native of Birmingham*,

---

[8] See e.g. Chalmers (2003), Nida-Rümelin (2007), Alter and Walter (2007).
[9] See also Nida-Rümelin, this volume.   [10] See Papineau (2007) for a survey.
[11] This formulation is neutral as to whether phenomenal concepts must *always* be applied in this way. Perhaps we can sometimes apply correctly the phenomenal concept "grief," say, without currently feeling grief or even simulating it. In Guillot (ms), I discuss the implications of various options on this issue in relation with the self-concept.

concepts whose application to a given object typically require various checks or calculations, beyond the mere attention to how things look.

Finally, a *pure* phenomenal concept, in addition to being dependent on exposure to a certain phenomenal property F for its acquisition, and for the capacity to apply the concept non-inferentially, also has F (or one of its instantiations) as its referent. The subjective impression of boredom itself, or a particular episode of being bored, is what the pure phenomenal concept of boredom refers to.

Combining those three features, I will use the minimal definition of Shea (2014) for (what I call) pure phenomenal concepts, adapting it slightly:[12]

[Pure] Phenomenal Concept   A person X's concept C is a [pure] phenomenal concept iff$_{df}$

(i) acquiring C requires X to instantiate or to have instantiated phenomenal property F;

(ii) on acquiring C, X has the disposition to apply C [...] non-inferentially in virtue of instantiating the phenomenal property F;

(iii) C refers to F [or particular instantiations of F]. (Shea 2014: 556)

Removing condition (iii) gives the definition of a phenomenal concept more generally (more about the distinction shortly):

Phenomenal Concept   A person X's concept C is a phenomenal concept iff$_{df}$

(i) acquiring C requires X to instantiate or to have instantiated phenomenal property F;

(ii) on acquiring C, X has the disposition to apply C non-inferentially in virtue of instantiating the phenomenal property F.

I call property F in the above definitions the *phenomenal basis* of a phenomenal concept:

Phenomenal Basis   The phenomenal basis of a phenomenal concept C is the phenomenal property F on which C is dependent (in the ways specified in the definitions above).

The phenomenal basis F of a given phenomenal concept C is the piece of phenomenology that contributes to individuating it: the sensation of nausea for the

---

[12] Shea uses the expression "phenomenal concepts" to refer to what I call "pure phenomenal concepts" here. The difference is purely terminological. My preference for using the expression "phenomenal concepts" as I do is that conditions (i) and (ii) below capture a robust, and epistemically very significant, sense of experience-dependence.

concept "nauseated," for instance. Condition (i) says that this phenomenal basis is a necessary basis for acquiring the concept. Condition (ii) says that is also a sufficient basis for applying it. Condition (iii), restricted to pure phenomenal concepts, says that the phenomenal basis is also the referent of the concept.

3.2. Three Epistemological Properties of Phenomenal Thoughts

Phenomenal judgements, namely judgements composed of phenomenal concepts, display forms of resistance to error that are close counterparts to those Coliva distinguishes in the case of I-thoughts.

Let us start with the Real Guarantee. Intuitively, possessing the phenomenal concept of pins and needles guarantees that the subject knows which aspect of reality that concept is a concept of: it is *this* phenomenal property, this strange bodily sensation. This is plausibly a consequence of the fact that phenomenal concepts are based on acquaintance. The acquisition of the phenomenal concept of pins and needles, as we have seen, requires the subject to *have* (or to have had) the experience of pins and needles, F, to which it refers; which is just another way to say that she must have been acquainted with F.

Chalmers (2003) proposes that the phenomenal quality itself can directly enter the content of a phenomenal judgement that contains the corresponding phenomenal concept:

> The clearest cases of direct phenomenal concepts arise when a subject attends to the quality of an experience, and forms a concept wholly based on the attention to the quality, "taking up" the quality into the concept.   (Chalmers 2003: 235)

One possible way to understand this claim is to say that a pure phenomenal concept (what Chalmers calls a "direct phenomenal concept") canonically refers by "sampling" the phenomenal property it is a concept of, in something like the way that a sample of a certain shade of blue in a paint manufacturer's catalogue can refer to that very shade of blue. On this view, to refer to the sensation of pins and needles under the corresponding phenomenal concept is to refer to it by *exemplification*. In a typical use of a phenomenal concept, the referent itself is present *in* the representation, as a sample experience.[13] This direct presence of the referent rules out any doubt as to its identity for the subject who grasps the representation.

This view of the mode of reference of phenomenal concepts is not uncontroversial. However, whether or not typical *uses* of a phenomenal concept select their

---

[13] The "quotational" model of Papineau (2007) has the same consequence.

referents in the way just sketched, the more basic fact that the *possession* of the concept is based on acquaintance suffices to entail the Real Guarantee. To be acquainted with something is surely a way to know it—indeed, a particularly secure way to know it (Russell 1910). This is not to say that being acquainted with something reveals everything about its nature (Duncan 2015). But it is a way for that thing to be *present* to us, which rules out ignorance as to which one of the various things in the world it is. So a subject's possession of a phenomenal concept C guarantees that she knows which phenomenal property F it is a concept of.

Let us turn to No-Split. I'll call "native" an application of a pure phenomenal concept that is grounded only on an occurrent experience (whether full-blown or imaginatively re-created), to refer to that very (type of) experience. At least in those cases, it is very difficult to imagine how the semantic referent could diverge from the intended referent. They are one and the same thing, presented in the same way at the same time. Suppose I am looking at colour samples and asking myself which one I prefer. When I finally decide, "This one," there seems to be no room for the phenomenal concept of a colour sensation generated there and then to latch on to something else than the colour experience I am presently focusing on: the experience serves as its own label.

But it seems possible to apply phenomenal concepts in more complex ways, however, which opens the door to referential splits. Suppose my friend Rose suddenly starts looking bored, eyes glazing over, and she loses track of the group conversation we're in. I judge, "her boredom is making her drift off." In fact, what she feels isn't boredom, but annoyance at something someone said. Arguably, I intended my tokening of the phenomenal concept of boredom to refer to the phenomenal quality of her current emotion, the one that caused her to drift off (as it happens, the feeling of annoyance). But the semantic referent of the concept is a different phenomenal quality, the one I instantiated when I acquired the concept "boredom."[14] Perhaps what opens the door to the split, here, is that the application of the concept is partly grounded on third-person perceptual information. So, while native uses of phenomenal concepts are covered by No-Split, not all of their extended uses are.

What about IEM? When a phenomenal judgement is formed purely on the basis of an occurrent experience, and when phenomenal concepts are used in both the subject and predicate positions—as in "this headache is painful," or "this feeling of nostalgia is pleasant"—it seems impossible that one should judge correctly, on that basis, that something or other has the property in question, while being wrong about what has it. After all, the judgement is merely articulating various aspects of the total phenomenal quality of one's present experience.

---

[14] I thank an anonymous reviewer for suggesting third-person illustrations for referential splits and EM.

If, however, the judgement doesn't apply to my own occurrent experiences, or if only one of the subject or the predicate is a phenomenal concept, then EM seems possible. Suppose I overhear small children playing in the next room, then one of them crying. Based on the sound, I judge "Olivia is upset." In fact, Anna is the one who is feeling upset, and crying. Here, my perception (of the sound of distress) grounds my knowledge that a phenomenal property (feeling upset) is instantiated by someone, but a different ground (the memory of what Olivia sounds like) makes me misjudge who that someone is. In this judgement, only the predicate (being upset) is expressed with a phenomenal concept;[15] the subject (Olivia) isn't.

It thus appears that the epistemological properties found in connection with I-judgements are also found in connection with phenomenal judgements, and with a similar distribution. As in I-thoughts, the phenomenal counterpart to the Real Guarantee attaches to all occurrences of a given phenomenal concept. No-Split and IEM, on the other hand, may only be associated with some of its occurrences.

3.3. Self-Experience

My guiding intuition is that this is more than an analogy. First-person epistemology, I suggest, has the same source as the epistemology of phenomenal judgements; it comes from the fact that the self-concept, too, is a phenomenal concept.

Phenomenal concepts are experience-dependent concepts. But notice that there is an experience that comes with being a subject: self-experience. Levine (2001) and Kriegel (2009) observe that when we experience the world, we generally experience ourselves, too. When I stroke the cat, there is a certain *qualitative character* to my experience: a way, silky and warm, that it is like to feel the cat. But the experience also has a *subjective character*: there is a way that I am phenomenally aware of myself, as myself, in being aware of the cat.

Whether this subjective character is present in every experience is a matter of dispute (see McClelland and Billon, this volume). The notion of subjective character is also interpreted in different ways by various authors, which has introduced some confusion in the debate, as I argue in Guillot (2017).[16] To clarify, I will use instead the expression "self-experience."[17] I will assume that at least

---

[15] Note that even if the concept "being upset" isn't used in the native way here, it still counts as a pure phenomenal concept in the sense captured by conditions (i)–(iii) in Section 3.1.

[16] See also Howell and Thompson (2017) and Salje and Geddes, this volume.

[17] In Guillot (2017), I distinguished between what I called "for-me-ness," "me-ness," and "mineness." My use of "self-experience," here, coincides with "me-ness." My thanks to Lucy O'Brien for suggesting this helpful term. A case might be made that "mineness" would also be a suitable phenomenal basis for the concept of self, but see Guillot (2017, section 5.2), for an objection. "For-me-ness" could be a phenomenal basis for a generic phenomenal concept of experience, if such exists.

234   THE PHENOMENAL CONCEPT OF SELF

some experiences of the world come with self-experience, by which I mean a phenomenal way that I am presented with myself *as myself*.[18] This is not just a phenomenal awareness of what *happens to be* myself. To illustrate, consider the case of somatoparaphrenia (Vallar and Ronchi 2009, de Vignemont 2013). Sufferers have an altered awareness of one of their limbs, for instance a hand or an arm. The limb comes to be felt as alien, and no longer as "me." For example, a patient with somatoparaphrenia quoted in Maravita (2008:102), also quoted in de Vignemont (2013), asked his doctor: "Once home could I ask my wife, from time to time, to remove this left arm and put it in the cupboard for a few hours in order to have some relief from pain?." As this report makes clear, the patient can still have sensations (such as pain) in the alien limb; so the issue is not an absence of phenomenology altogether. He has experiences of what is in fact (a part of) himself; these experiences, however, are not self-experiences. This is because the patient's experience of his alien arm lacks a certain "way it is like" that attaches to his experience of his "good" arm.

I don't mean this example to suggest that self-experience is limited to (normal) inner bodily awareness. Some phenomenal properties are cross-modal. It might be argued that roundness, for instance, is a phenomenal character that can be shared by visual and tactile experiences alike. Painfulness, and affective phenomenology more generally, also appear to be cross-modal; perceiving one's body from the inside can be painful, but so can be remembering a misfortune. I will assume that self-experience is the same across all the modalities in which one can be self-aware: by feeling one's body from the inside, but also by having intentions, perceiving objects in the outer world, or being in any other kind of conscious mental state.

This claim of cross-modality is controversial,[19] and so is the more basic claim that such a thing as self-experience exists at all.[20] This is not the place for reviewing this debate. I will therefore put my main claim in a conditional form: *if* there is such a thing as self-experience, *then* it is available as a phenomenal basis for a distinctive phenomenal concept; and this concept is our ordinary self-concept.

Let me, however, try to give a measure of initial plausibility to the antecedent of that conditional. In Guillot (2017: 45–6), I offer an argument from justification to the effect that all normal experiences, at least, come with self-experience. Here is the argument in condensed form. Ordinary experiences, such as a tactile experience of the cat's soft fur, give me an *immediate justification* to make certain

---

[18] I am neutral, here, as to whether this is a *sui generis* dimension of our phenomenology, or one that is reducible to other aspects of it.

[19] See Billon, this volume, for a defence.

[20] See Part I of this volume for sceptical considerations. Replies include Zahavi and Kriegel (2015), as well as Billon, this volume.

judgements (Soldati 2012).[21] One is the judgement that the cat has soft fur. That this judgement is immediately justified by the experience means, as Soldati understands it, that the experience gives me "a kind of warrant that does not depend on, for instance, any further inferentially acquired justification." The tactile experience, in other words, is a self-standing[22] reason for me to judge that the cat's fur is soft: it is not itself dependent on any further reason. If I am asked why I judge as I do, the experience is all the evidence I need (and am generally able) to cite. Now, note that the experience of the cat's soft fur also gives me immediate justification, in this sense, to form other judgements:[23] among others, that an experience is occurring; that it is an experience of mine; and, most relevant for my purposes, that *I, myself*, am present. Having *any* (normal) experience is enough on its own to justify my judging that I am present. And if asked for my *reason* to judge this, it is hard to see what else I could invoke than the experience itself. So the relevant epistemic warrant backing the judgement that *I* am present is likely to be something *in* the experience: something about its phenomenal character.[24] This gives some plausibility to the claim that we typically have *experiential* access to ourselves; or, in my terminology here, that a normal experience includes self-experience.

But *if* this self-experience exists, then it is available as a potential phenomenal basis for forming a phenomenal concept in its own right. The obvious candidate is the self-concept. The next section considers how this might go.

3.4. The Self-Concept as a Phenomenal Concept

Based on the supposition that there is such a thing as self-experience, my first claim is that it is the phenomenal basis of a particular phenomenal concept: the self-concept.[25] I can think of the phenomenal impression of the sour by experiencing the phenomenal quality of sourness; in the same way, I can think of myself, under the self-concept, by experiencing what it is like to be me.

---

[21] See also Pryor (2013). The notion of immediate justification has been challenged (see e.g. Comesaña's 2013 reply to Pryor). It would take me too far to engage with this debate here; the role of this paragraph is only to indicate that the case for self-experience is at least *arguable*, sufficiently so to use it as a *hypothesis*. Thanks to Manuel García-Carpintero for pressing me on this.

[22] This doesn't mean that the reason in question is *infallible*. The point is that the experience is what alone justifies the judgement, to the extent, large or small, that it is indeed justified.

[23] I am not suggesting that Soldati himself would endorse the argument I build on his notion of immediate justification.

[24] This could be challenged. For reasons of space, I won't repeat the defence of this specific claim in Guillot (2017: 45–6). Remember that the argument in this paragraph is not meant to be decisive, as my claims based on self-experience are merely hypothetical.

[25] In Guillot (2016), I explore the possibility of applying the phenomenal-concept model to the self-concept with a different phenomenal basis: namely, the generic type of cognitive phenomenology that attaches to thoughts. For reasons that it would take too much space to discuss here, however, the pathological case of thought-insertion now inclines me towards the present variant.

236   THE PHENOMENAL CONCEPT OF SELF

The suitability of the phenomenal-concept model to the self-concept might not seem immediately obvious. Perhaps this is because the discussion of phenomenal concepts has largely been dominated by examples of *pure* phenomenal concepts, such as the concepts of reddishness and pain. These concepts refer to experiences (or the phenomenal properties they manifest). But the self-concept refers to something of a different metaphysical kind: a subject, namely *me*.

However, not all phenomenal concepts (as I defined them above) refer to experiences. We can use our experiences to think about those experiences them-selves, but we can also use them to think about objects we are presented with through the experiences. One example is their causal origin (Papineau 2007). This is what we do with a kind of phenomenal concept Papineau (2007) calls "perceptual concepts," and Gertler (2012) "perceptual demonstratives"; I will call them *phenomenal-causal concepts*. Those concepts can be concepts of kinds, or kind-members, or individuals; what they have in common is that they are con-cepts of empirical objects classified on the basis of the phenomenal impressions they cause in us.

An example of a phenomenal-causal concept referring to a kind or kind-members is our naïve concept of a palm-tree. On seeing a palm-tree for the first time, I took in a new phenomenal "template" (Papineau's term): the characteristic look of a palm-tree, with the elegant arc of the trunk and the crenelated leaves crowning the top. This complex phenomenal profile, when I re-encounter, remember or re-imagine it, will enable me to refer to the *genus* "palm-tree," or to individual palm-trees, which are the causal origin of that experience.

An example of a phenomenal-causal concept referring to an individual is the concept I formed as I kept catching a glimpse of a particular celebrity on the front page of magazines (it turned out later she is called Kim Kardashian, although I didn't need to know that, or to have any other biographical information, to form my concept of her). There is a distinctive way that she looks: glossy black hair, amber eyes, etc. Without knowing anything specific about her beyond this—I am vaguely aware that she is famous, but wouldn't be able to say on what account—I am able to use this particular phenomenal profile, this "look of her," to refer spe-cifically to *her*, the individual who is the causal origin of that experience.

Both my palm-tree concept and my Kim Kardashian concept are phenomenal concepts in the sense captured by conditions (i)–(ii) in Section 3.1. Each is dependent on a particular phenomenal basis. A particular (visual) experience was necessary to acquire the concepts. Once acquired, they enable me to refer to their objects on the mere basis of having the experience again, without any per-ceived gap between attending to the experience and applying the concept. In addition, the reference-rule which individuates each of those concepts has to be spelled out in terms of its phenomenal basis: the referent, as Gertler puts it, is whatever (appropriately) caused the current instantiation of the relevant phenomenology (Gertler 2012: 104). And that reference is "direct," in the sense that it is causally-determined rather than descriptively-determined; relational, rather than satisfactional (Bach 1987).

Now, phenomenal-causal concepts have presumably evolved to enable us to track stable natural objects, such as natural kinds and individuals. It is reasonable to further suppose, then, that concepts of this kind have the *function* to refer to the kind of entity that regularly causes the relevant phenomenal character; i.e. to palm-trees in the case of the concept of a palm-tree.

Because there happens to be a reliable connection between the presence of certain individuals, or of members of a certain natural kind, and the occurrence in perceivers of a certain kind of impression, phenomenal appearances (and hence the phenomenal-causal concepts that are grounded in those appearances) are a good tool for tracking those stable natural objects. But most of those concepts can occasionally fail to perform this function: sometimes what causes a palm-tree-like impression is not a palm-tree (but a fake tree on a film set, say). As we will see in Section 4, there may be metaphysical reasons why the same cannot be said of the self-concept, and this will have consequences for the understanding of first-person epistemology.

Before moving to this next step, however, let me specify a bit the conditional claim towards which this section builds. Supposing self-experience exists, the self-concept is a phenomenal concept having self-experience as its phenomenal basis. Self-experience is typically part of what I grasp when I grasp the self-concept. To the extent that the self-concept refers to an individual rather than to the experience itself, it has similarities with my phenomenal concept for Kim Kardashian (as well as important disanalogies, discussed in Section 4). The proposal is that once I have acquired the self-concept on the basis of attending to my self-experience, I can apply it, on the mere basis of having this experience, to refer to a specific individual; namely the individual (me) who *is the subject of*[26] the self-experience used on this occasion to activate the concept.

It is important to note that this differs from a descriptive view of the self-concept. The relation "being the subject of *this*" (where "*this*" captures a self-experience) doesn't have to be represented; it its only exploited to determine a referent. Similarly, my concept of Kim Kardashian is not descriptive. What little descriptive information I have about her is not individuating. I refer, when using it, to *whatever individual appropriately caused this* (where "this" captures an

---

[26] I won't discuss whether being the subject of an experience is reducible to being its proximate causal origin. What matters is that the subject of experience is one of the things I am presented with by virtue of having the experience. If there is nothing more to being the subject of an experience than being a certain kind of causal origin for it, then the self-concept is a kind of phenomenal-causal concept. Otherwise, it is a different sort of phenomenal concept for an individual, which also satisfies the experience-dependence conditions (i) and (ii) in Section 3.1.

238   THE PHENOMENAL CONCEPT OF SELF

instantiation of the "look of her"), but the italicized description needn't be part of what I grasp in so doing, any more than it generally is when I think of the person pictured in a photograph (Evans 1982).

There is a second point to stress about the formulation above. Once I have acquired the self-concept on the basis of attending to my self-experience, I can apply it to myself on the mere basis of having this experience. The claim here is merely dispositional: saying that possessing this phenomenal self-concept *enables* me to self-refer with it on the mere basis of having a self-experience doesn't mean that I *always* have to base my self-references on occurrent self-experiences. Here I remain neutral with respect to this stronger claim, whose implications are discussed in Guillot (ms).

Let me now move to the way I think the view can explain the three properties Coliva distinguishes in her discussion of first-person epistemology, and help understand why they are so often conflated.

4. A Unified Account for IEM, No-Split, and the Real Guarantee

4.1. Explaining the Real Guarantee

The view gives a simple explanation of why the self-concept enjoys the Real Guarantee. One cannot acquire the self-concept construed as a phenomenal concept without having had self-experience. Which means that I cannot possess the self-concept without grasping *what it's like to be me*. This amounts to saying that I cannot have the self-concept without knowing which person I am.

To explain: self-experience is a way I am phenomenally presented with myself, as myself. In order to possess the self-concept, a subject must have had self-experience. So, a subject's possession of the self-concept guarantees that she has been phenomenally presented with herself, as herself. But being presented with something leaves no doubt as to which of the various things in the world it is.[27] Another way to phrase the point is that being presented with an object puts one in a position to think singular thoughts about that object; thoughts whose content will be about *it*, specifically. In being presented with something, one doesn't necessarily get to know anything sustantive about its nature; but one does have a way to latch onto it and to single it out among other things. Possessing the self-concept, then, guarantees that the subject knows which of the individuals in the world it is a concept of.

---

[27] The stronger (and more controversial) claim by Duncan (2015) and others that we are not just presented with ourselves through phenomenology, but directly *acquainted* with ourselves, would provide an even simpler explanation. See Section 3.3 for a possible defense of that claim.

4.2. Explaining No-Split: I

The phenomenal-concept view also explains why splits between semantic and intended reference are possible, but comparatively rare, in the case of I-judgements.

Note that splits are excluded when only one way of thinking of the referent is active in the act of referring, and when this way of thinking of the referent coincides with the mere grasp of the reference-rule associated with the representation: that is, the grasp of the condition an object has to satisfy to count as the referent (Peacocke 2008). In short, No-Split obtains when the object to which the referring term or concept is applied is only thought about, at least tacitly, as whatever satisfies the reference-rule.

A good example is the word (or underlying concept) "this," when applied to a perceptually salient object, like the cup in front of me: no split between semantic and intended reference seems possible in such cases, because "this" semantically refers to whatever object I am perceptually focused on, and I use "this" precisely to speaker- (or thinker-)refer to the focus of my perceptual attention.[28]

When more than one way of thinking of the object is active, however, there is a risk of a split between semantic and intended reference. Splits happen in circumstances where a referring term or concept is being applied to an object that is singled out *both* by grasping the reference-rule and *via* another epistemic route.

Let me illustrate this contrast with a familiar example from Donnellan (1966): the utterance "John's murderer must be insane." Donnellan distinguishes two cases: (a) that in which I use the description "John's murderer" *descriptively*, while looking at the body of his victim on the crime scene; (b) that in which I use the same description *referentially*, while looking at the suspect in the courtroom.

In the first case (a), I am not thinking of "John's murderer" in any other way than as the person who murdered John. The description "John's murderer" determines its semantic reference satisfactionally, as whatever object satisfies a descriptive condition encoded by the referring expression; and I also intend to use the description to speaker-refer to whoever satisfies the description. There is thus only one epistemic route to the referent. Hence, the description is immune to referential split.

By contrast, when I exclaim "John's murderer must be insane" while looking at the suspect in the courtroom, the description "John's murderer" still determines its semantic reference satisfactionally; but I intend to use that description to designate a man I am being visually presented with. As there are now *two* distinct routes to the referent, a descriptive one and a perceptual one, there is a

---

[28] The Spiro Agnew painting case in Kaplan (1989) does not count as a counter-example, because it isn't a case where "this" is applied to a perceptually salient object.

240 THE PHENOMENAL CONCEPT OF SELF

risk of their failing to converge on the same object, hence a risk of mismatch between speaker (demonstrative) reference and semantic (descriptive) reference (as in the case where the suspect I see in the courtroom is not, in fact, the murderer).

Now let us return to the case of phenomenal concepts. Just by virtue of having the concept "pins and needles," you already know which aspect of reality the referent is; in fact, having been acquainted with the referent is a necessary condition for having the concept at all. Possessing the concept enables you to apply it on the mere basis of experiencing the relevant quality (that particular sensation); whether or not all uses of the concept are of that kind, that is at least the *typical* way such a concept is applied. In that typical case, there is *no need* to have an independent epistemic route to the referent to be able to pick out the aspect of reality one intends to apply the concept to. The same condition that is necessary for possessing the concept of pins and needles, and for grasping in general terms what counts as falling under that concept—namely, *being acquainted with that sensation*—is also sufficient for picking out in particular contexts those aspects of reality that the concept applies to.

This contrasts with, among others, descriptive concepts and names. In those two cases, mastering the referring device does not entail that you are acquainted with the referent, or that you know what object the referent is in reality. In the typical case, when a descriptive concept is applied to an individual object encountered in reality (like the suspect in the trial for John's murder), you have in mind both the description and a perceptual presentation, giving at best defeasible evidence that the object is what satisfies the description. Similarly with names: using a name *a* to pick out correctly the thing that is *a* in reality takes more than just knowing the reference-rule for *a*, namely that it applies to whatever was baptised with the name *a*. It also takes knowing which object that is.

Thus, when one uses phenomenal concepts, splits can happen in cases where more than one epistemic route to the referent is active; but that is not the default case because there is *no need* for it. This correctly predicts that No-Split doesn't cover the self-concept across all its occurrences (as Coliva observes), but that splits are contingently rare. In most cases, when I deploy the self-concept, I apply it to something that is singled out in reality on the same basis of self-experience that also grounds my competence with the concept. Splits occur in connexion with the self-concept only in more complex cases where more than one epistemic route to the purported referent is active. This is precisely what happens in the painting example, where the self-concept is applied to something that is picked out in reality through a third-person visual presentation, a route that is distinct from the self-experience that determines the semantic referent of the concept and grounds its acquisition, as well as its typical uses.

4.3. Explaining No-Split: II

There is a deeper sense in which the self-concept is resistant to referential splits, however. I argued in Section 3 that the self-concept works in something like the way a phenomenal-causal concept works. But there is a particular type of referential split that ordinary phenomenal-causal concepts are vulnerable to, and that is ruled out by the self-concept. Here is an example involving the phenomenal-causal concept of a panda. I am taking a child on a visit to the zoo. Something that looks to me like a panda is playing with a ball. In fact, it is a human being in a panda costume. I draw the child's attention and point: "Look, a panda!." Intuitively, something has gone wrong.

The semantic reference of a particular *occurrence* of the phenomenal-causal concept panda is whatever causes the panda-like impression on that occasion. But presumably, the concept as a *type* also has the *function* to track pandas, in referring to the kind of things that look panda-like. And in referring to whatever is causing a panda-like impression, one does, usually, refer to a panda. However, a token of the concept might occasionally refer to something different—a human being wearing a panda costume, in the zoo example. In that case, we might say that a referential split of a kind has occurred. The agent, in mastering the concept, grasps that tracking pandas is what it is for; so part of her intention at the zoo is to refer to a thing of the kind in question. On that occasion, however, this intended reference fails to coincide with the semantic reference of her use of the panda-concept, which is an object of a different kind.

This, however, is one way the self-concept differs from phenomenal-causal concepts. Split scenarios of the kind just described can't occur in connection with the self-concept. I speculate that this has to do with the metaphysics of the entity referred to by the self-concept. Experiencing the phenomenal profile of a panda isn't always to be presented with a panda. But having a self-experience is always to be presented with *me*. Pandas themselves are not *defined* as what causes panda-like impressions. On the other hand, I find it plausible that being phenomenally aware of myself as myself, as I am in self-experience, contributes to defining what and who *I* am. Subjects are things that are aware of themselves as themselves; and being this particular subject is being what is aware of this subject as myself.

Behind these intuitions is a metaphysical assumption I find compelling: if I have self-experience, then it is an essential property of mine, and it is key to individuating me. A prominent strand in the philosophy of personal identity, illustrated by Locke and Shoemaker among others, assumes that "a human person would go where his or her mind goes" (Johnston 2010: 47). Dainton (2005) makes the intuition a bit more precise, by noting that the sort of psychological continuity that matters is *phenomenal* continuity:

242 THE PHENOMENAL CONCEPT OF SELF

[C]ould your stream of consciousness continue on but fail to take you with it? [...] Whatever else we might be, we are not the kind of being that can cease to exist whilst our consciousness continues on. (2005: 1–2)

Relatedly,

an account of our existence and persistence conditions that is rooted in purely phenomenal unity and continuity—the sorts of unity and continuity found in our streams of consciousness—will be more compelling, more believable, than any account that is not. (2005: 2)

If we accept the existence of self-experience, the intuition, I think, can be specified further. Could the flow of self-experience continue on but fail to take me with it? Whatever else I might be, I would add, I am not the kind of being that can cease to exist whilst my self-experience continues on.[29]

If one is prepared to go along with this supposition, a first consequence is a point of nomenclature. If self-experience is an essential property of mine, there is a sense in which to be acquainted with it is to be acquainted with me. The self-concept thus has features in common with both pure phenomenal concepts and phenomenal-causal concepts. As the latter can, it refers to an individual, on the model of direct causal reference operative for my Kim Kardashian concept. As with the former, however, it leaves no gap between being acquainted with the concept's phenomenal basis (self-experience) and being acquainted with its referent (myself).

A second consequence is that the self-concept is immune to the type of split scenario sketched above. There is accord between the reference-rule for the self-concept and the individuation-conditions for the entity that the concept refers to. On the semantic side, a typical token of the concept exploits an occurrent self-experience to refer to whatever is the subject of it. On the metaphysical side, I am individuated as whatever is the subject of self-experience. This predicts that the self-concept is protected from empty reference, as it is indeed. This also blocks the specific way in which phenomenal-causal concepts are vulnerable to occasional referential splits. Pandas are not defined as the sources of panda-like impressions; other things, like puppets and decoys and people wearing panda costumes, can give off panda-like impressions; and pandas can also give impressions that are not panda-like. So I may use my phenomenal-causal panda concept in an occasion in which it will refer to something that, unbeknownst to me, isn't a panda (for instance a person wearing a panda costume), or in which there will be nothing at all to be referred to (as when a panda-like impression is just an

---

[29] Dainton, who is sceptical about self-experience as I define it, would not endorse this.

illusion). But no similar split can arise in connection with the self-concept. Since I, the subject, am metaphysically individuated as what has self-experience, and as this is just what constitutes the concept's semantic reference, it is not the case that I could, along similar lines, mis-refer or make a failed attempt to refer when I deploy the self-concept, at least when its use is based only on its phenomenal basis. Whatever appears to me via the subjective character of my experiences is me, because that is just what a self is.

In short: the semantic reference of an occurrence of the phenomenal concept of a panda is whatever causes the panda-like impression. But the concept as a type also has the function to track pandas, in referring to what causes panda-like impressions. However, a given token of the concept can fail to perform that function, causing a form of referential split. By contrast, the semantic reference of an occurrence of the phenomenal concept of self is whatever has the self-experience on which that occurrence of the concept depends. But the concept as a type also has the function to track *me*, in referring to the subject of self-experience. And as long as the concept is applied on the sole basis of self-experience, it never fails to perform that function.[30]

4.4. Explaining IEM

Let us turn, finally, to IEM. In Section 2.2 above, $IEM_{de\,se}$ is defined as the property that attaches to an occurrent first-person judgement of the form "I am F" based on grounds G if the following holds:

$IEM_{de\,se}$: one way I can't be wrong is by knowing (based on G) that property F is instantiated, where the bearer of F is a person s that is distinct from me.

IEM and "Identification-Freedom"

I will assume here that something like what is known as the "Simple Account" of IEM[31] is correct. Some authors, following the ideas of Evans (1982), further elaborated by Wright (2012), hold that IEM judgements are so immune because of their underlying justificational architecture. The inference on which they are grounded, by contrast with the type of inference behind EM (see Section 2), doesn't involve a separate identification premise. This makes it *a fortiori* impossible that the identification premise should be false; which leaves no room for a mistaken identification. The absence of an identification premise, in turn, reflects

---

[30] Not all readers will accept the metaphysical assumption on which this account turns. But of those, some will accept the self-experience assumption, which is sufficient for the more generic account of No-Split in Section 3.2.

[31] See e.g. Wright (2012) and García-Carpintero (2018) for detailed analyses of the account.

244 THE PHENOMENAL CONCEPT OF SELF

the fact that IEM judgements are based on a type of epistemic source that simultaneously yields information about the instantiation of a property, and about the *locus* of that instantiation. I know directly that *a* is F, without having to judge antecedently that *b* is F and that *a* is *b*. The key of this now-standard account of IEM is the *unity of the grounds* for tokening each of the two components (the subject component *a* and the predicative component F) of the judgement that *a* is F.

Experience is one epistemic source that offers the required sort of unity of grounds. It yields some experiential content (e.g. the presence of hunger or pain) together with the information that *I* am the experiencer. $\text{IEM}_{de\,se}$, for this reason, is found only (with some very limited exceptions) in connection with self-attributions of experiential properties, based on experience.

The Two Sides of Experience as a Source of Identification-Freedom

The picture I propose correctly predicts that when it comes to I-judgements, IEM occurs almost only[32] when those judgements are grounded in experience; and it explains why the unity of grounds is satisfied in this case.

Following Levine (2001) and Kriegel (2009), I have been assuming that there are two dimensions in the phenomenal character of normal experiences: (i) a *qualitative character*, such as hunger; and (ii) a *subjective character*. Having a certain experience, for instance as of hunger, is thus in itself sufficient grounds for doing two things:

- Tokening the phenomenal concept of hunger (based on the qualitative character of the experience);
- Tokening the phenomenal concept of self (based on the subjective character of the very same experience).

So, to judge "I am hungry," there is no need for an error-vulnerable transition via a judgement of identity based on separate grounds. Hence, there is no room for error through misidentification.

This account is in line with the "Simple Account," according to which the source of IEM is the absence of an identification premise. But it goes one step further, in explaining *why*, in the core class of I-judgements enjoying $\text{IEM}_{de\,se}$ (i.e. I-judgements grounded in experience), no such identification premise is needed. That is because an ordinary experience, on its own, provides a sufficient basis for

---

[32] Not all I-judgements enjoying $\text{IEM}_{de\,se}$ are experiential self-attributions. A very small class of non-experiential I-judgements also enjoy it. The judgement "I am saying this," for instance, is IEM, whether it is based on experience or on mere reflection on the descriptive content of the concepts involved. But this is in some ways a limiting case. My claim here is just that experience is the most important (and probably also the most interesting) source of $\text{IEM}_{de\,se}$ for reasons having to do with the phenomenal nature of the self-concept.

tokening the concepts involved on both the subject-side and the predicate-side of an I-judgement formed directly on the basis of this experience, thus also providing the required unity of epistemic grounds.[33]

The account also makes the correct predictions as regards the distribution of IEM across I-thoughts. As noted in Section 2, not all I-thoughts are IEM: "I am hungry," judged on the basis of experience, is IEM; but "I am the lottery winner," judged on the basis of testimony, is not. This is exactly what the phenomenal-concept view would lead us to expect. On this account, only those I-judgements where the predicate, as well as the subject, is a phenomenal concept, and where both concepts are activated on the sole basis of a single occurrent experience (here, hunger), are IEM.

Could this account of $IEM_{de\,se}$ be generalized to other cases of IEM? I suspect that it might, at least for some of the other kinds of indexical judgements, such as temporal and simple demonstrative judgements, which may also plausibly be phenomenally-grounded. This, however, is left for further work. It might be that *some* types of judgements exhibiting IEM, on the other hand, will turn out not to fit well with the phenomenal-concept account. If Wright (2012) is right that some mathematical judgements are IEM, for instance, then this is likely to be a case that is out of the reach of my account. But we should bear in mind that the two key components of the Simple Account of IEM, namely the unity of epistemic grounds and the resulting identification-freedom, are very abstract and high-level properties. They might come to be instantiated in different ways and for different reasons in different cases, which would leave room for a degree of pluralism in accounting for IEM in different domains. My proposal here is merely that in the case of $IEM_{de\,se}$, the required unity of grounds and identification-freedom have a phenomenal origin. Thus, even if the account I offer should form only a part of a general theory of IEM, it does provide an explanation, both complete and germane to the standard account, in the limited case at hand.

5. Conclusion

To conclude, let me rehearse my five main claims, all conditional on the hypothesis that there is such a thing as self-experience as I defined it.

First, the self-concept is a phenomenal concept of a special kind, with common features both with pure phenomenal concepts and with phenomenal-causal concepts, and it is based on self-experience.

This explains all three of the epistemological properties distinguished by Coliva.

---

[33] For a much more detailed account of $IEM_{de\,se}$ which also appeals to the special justification given by a phenomenal state to both the predicate and subject side of first-person experiential judgements, see García-Carpintero (2018).

246 THE PHENOMENAL CONCEPT OF SELF

It explains the Real Guarantee, and why this guarantee applies to every tokening of the self-concept. This is because possessing the self-concept requires that you have the specific experience of what it's like to be you; you thus can't have the concept without knowing which person you are.

It explains No-Split, and correctly predicts that splits between the intended reference and the semantic reference of the self-concept are possible, but atypical. This is because intended reference with the self-concept is, by default, directly based on an occurrent self-experience, through which one is presented with oneself. But this is also how the semantic referent is fixed. This means that intended and semantic reference don't take distinct epistemic routes, which could fail to converge on the same object.

It explains $IEM_{de\ se}$, and correctly predicts that not all self-attributions, but all basic experiential self-attributions, are IEM. This is because in my normal experiences, the total phenomenal character I am aware of has two components: a qualitative character, and a subjective character, or self-experience. Each justifies the application of a dedicated phenomenal concept: respectively, the concept of a quality like hunger, and the self-concept. The same basis—this single experience—is thus sufficient for grounding the tokening of the concepts corresponding to the predicate and subject components of a judgement of the form "I am F." But not all judgements of the form "I am F" are based solely on an experience. So while basic experiential I-judgements are IEM, not all I-judgements are.

Finally, and as a consequence of the previous four claims: all three of the epistemological properties observed in connection with I-thoughts derive from the same source; namely, the fact that the self-concept is a phenomenal concept. This common source makes it more intelligible why the conflation of the three properties is widespread, and in particular why some writers, as Coliva is right to point out, take IEM to be a property of self-reference.

Understanding the self-concept as a phenomenal concept thus provides an explanation of all three epistemic properties, and makes the correct predictions as to their frequency: all acts of self-reference under the self-concept enjoy the Real Guarantee, many but not all are immune to a split between intended and semantic reference, and many but not all I-judgements are IEM. It also makes intelligible a long-standing confusion in the debate on first-person epistemology. These explanatory virtues of the phenomenal-concept model of the self-concept give some additional plausibility to the claim that there is self-experience.

Acknowledgements

Financial support was provided by the DGI, Spanish Government, research project FFI2016-80588-R, a Juan de la Cierva fellowship (Spanish Government), n°JCI-2012-13921, and the Marie Skłodowska Curie project PHENOSELF,

FP7-IEF-622127. This work benefited from discussion of related ideas with many colleagues, including Uriah Kriegel, Rory Madden, Lucy O'Brien, and Peter Pagin, as well as audiences in Paris and Barcelona. I am very grateful to Julien Bugnon, Santiago Echeverri, Manuel García-Carpintero, and two anonymous reviewers for extremely helpful comments.

References

Alter, T. and S. Walter (eds.) (2007). *Phenomenal Concepts and Phenomenal Knowledge: New Essays on Consciousness and Physicalism*. Oxford: Oxford University Press.

Anscombe, Gertrude E. M. (1975). "The first person." In S. D. Guttenplan (ed.),*Mind and Language*, 45–65. Oxford: Clarendon Press.

Bach, K. (1987). *Thought and Reference*. Oxford: Oxford University Press.

Castañeda, Hector-Neri. (1966). "'He': A study in the logic of self-consciousness." *Ratio (Misc.)* 8 (December): 130–157.

Chalmers, David. (2003). "The content and epistemology of phenomenal belief." In Q. Smith and A. Jokic (eds.), *Consciousness: New Philosophical Perspectives*. Oxford: Oxford University Press.

Christofidou, A. (1995). "The first person: The demand for identification-free self-reference," *The Journal of Philosophy* 92: 223–234.

Coliva, A. (2017). "Stopping points: 'I', immunity and the real guarantee," *Inquiry* 60 (3): 233–252.

Coliva, A. (2003). "The first person: Error through misidentification, the split between speaker's and semantic reference and the real guarantee." In *Journal of Philosophy* 100: 416–431

Comesaña, J. (2013). "There is no immediate justification." In M. Steup, J. Turri, and E. Sosa (eds.), *Contemporary Debates in Epistemology*, 2nd edition. Oxford: Wiley-Blackwell.

Dainton, B. (2005). "The self and the phenomenal." In G. Strawson (ed.), *The Self? Ratio* (special issue). Oxford: Wiley-Blackwell.

de Vignemont, F. (2013). "The mark of bodily ownership." *Analysis* 73 (4): 643–651.

Duncan, M. (2015). "We are acquainted with ourselves." *Philosophical Studies* 172 (9): 2531–2549.

Donnellan, K. S. (1966). "*Reference* and Definite Descriptions." *The Philosophical Review* 75 (3): 281–304.

Evans, G. (1982). *The Varieties of Reference*, posthumous edition by J. McDowell. Oxford: Clarendon Press.

García-Carpintero, M. (2018). "*De se* thoughts and immunity to error through misidentification." *Synthese* 195: 3311–3333.

Gertler, Brie. (2012). "Renewed acquaintance." In Declan Smithies and Daniel Stoljar (eds.), *Introspection and Consciousness*, 89–123. Oxford: Oxford University Press.

Guillot, M. (ms). "What kind of phenomenal concept might the concept 'self' be?"

Guillot, M. (2017). "*I me mine*: On a confusion concerning the subjective character of experience." *Review of Philosophy and Psychology* 8: 23–53.

Guillot, M. (2016). "Thinking of oneself as the thinker: The concept of self and the phenomenology of intellection," *Philosophical Explorations* 19 (2): 138–160.

Howell, R. J. & Thompson, B. (2017). "Phenomenally mine: In search of the subjective character of consciousness." *Review of Philosophy and Psychology* 8: 103–127.

Johnston, M. (2010). *Surviving Death*. Princeton, NJ: Princeton University Press.

Kaplan, D. (1989). "Demonstratives." In J. Almog, J. Perry, and H. Wettstein (eds.), *Themes from Kaplan*, 481–563. Oxford: Oxford University Press.

Kriegel, Uriah (2009). *Subjective Consciousness: A Self-Representational Theory*. Oxford: Oxford University Press.

Kripke, S. (1977). "Speaker's reference and semantic reference." *Midwest Studies in Philosophy* 2: 255–276.

Levine, J. (2001). *Purple Haze: The Puzzle of Consciousness*. Oxford: Oxford University Press.

Maravita, A. (2008). "Spatial disorders." In S. F. Cappa, J. Abutalebi, J. F. Demonet, P. C. Fletcher, and P. Garrard (eds.), *Cognitive Neurology: A Clinical Textbook*, 89–118. New York: Oxford University Press.

McGinn, C. (1983). *The Subjective View: Secondary Qualities and Indexical Thoughts*. Oxford: Clarendon Press.

Nida-Rümelin, M. (2007). "Grasping phenomenal properties." In T. Alter and S. Walter (eds.), *Phenomenal Concepts and Phenomenal Knowledge: New Essays on Consciousness and Physicalism*. Oxford: Oxford University Press.

Papineau, David. (2007). "Phenomenal and perceptual concepts." In T. Alter and S. Walter (eds.), *Phenomenal Concepts and Phenomenal Knowledge: New Essays on Consciousness and Physicalism*. Oxford: Oxford University Press.

Peacocke, C. (2008). *Truly Understood*. Oxford: Oxford University Press.

Pryor, J. (2013). "There is immediate justification." In M. Steup, J. Turri, and E. Sosa (eds.), *Contemporary Debates in Epistemology*, 2nd Edition. Oxford: Wiley-Blackwell.

Pryor, J. (1999). "Immunity to error through misidentification." *Philosophical Topics* 26 (1/2): 271–304.

Rovane, C. (1987). "The epistemology of first person reference." *The Journal of Philosophy* 84: 147–167.

Russell, B. (1910). "Knowledge by acquaintance and knowledge by description." *Proceedings of the Aristotelian Society* 11: 108–128.

Shea, N. (2014). "Using phenomenal concepts to explain away the intuition of contingency." *Philosophical Psychology* 27 (4): 553–570.

Shoemaker, Sydney (1968). "Self-reference and self-awareness." *Journal of Philosophy* 65 (19): 555–567.

Soldati, G. (2012). "Direct realism and immediate justification." *Proceedings of the Aristotelian Society* 112: 29–44.

Vallar, G. & Ronchi, R. (2009). "Somatoparaphrenia: A body delusion. A review of the neuropsychological literature." *Experimental Brain Research* 192 (3): 533–551.

Wright, C. (2012). "Reflections on François Recanati's 'Immunity to error through misidentification: What it is and where it comes from'." In Simon Prosser and Francois Recanati (eds.), *Immunity to Error through Misidentification: New Essays*, 247–280. Cambridge: Cambridge University Press.

Zahavi, D. and U. Kriegel (2015). "For-me-ness: What it is and what it is not." In D. O. Dahlstrom, A. Elpidorou, and W. Hopp (eds.), *Philosophy of Mind and Phenomenology: Conceptual and Empirical Approaches*. London: Routledge.

11

The Bounded Body

On the Sense of Bodily Ownership and the Experience of Space

Carlota Serrahima

1. The Sense of Bodily Ownership: Defining Desiderata

If I now close my eyes and pay attention to my body, I would say my legs are crossed and my hands are resting on the keyboard in front of me. I would also report, if asked to, some mild, intermittent twinges in the right side of my lower back. I would thus be reporting some of my current bodily experiences.

Upon scrutiny, it is clear that by entertaining judgments such as "I can feel that my legs are crossed" I am taking myself to be the subject of a mental state, but also the subject of the body to which I am ascribing certain properties. Evidence of this are the two first-person pronouns in the statement mentioned. Indeed, eyes closed, not only do I realize that it is me who feels some legs being crossed, or an aching back, but also that these crossed legs and aching back are mine. This chapter revolves around the latter fact: bodily sensations[1] are mental states typically suitable to be reported in judgments that are *de se* in that subjects endowed with a conceptual system or language typically express them by qualifying the felt body with a first-person indexical. I do not simply report feeling *a* back when in pain; I also report feeling that the painful back is *mine*.

Let us call the judgments in which bodily sensations are reported "judgments of somatosensation." And let us grant that, when one sincerely asserts judgments of somatosensation that are first-personal in this sense, one expresses awareness of the body one feels to be one's own. The notion of a *sense of bodily ownership* (SBO) captures this fact:

---

[1] Bodily sensations include proprioception (experiences of bodily movement and posture), sensations related to balance, touch, feelings of bodily temperature, pain, and interoception. I will use "somatosensation" and its derivatives, as well as "bodily experiences," to refer generally to all bodily sensations.

Carlota Serrahima, *The Bounded Body: On the Sense of Bodily Ownership and the Experience of Space* In: *Self-Experience: Essays on Inner Awareness*. Edited by: Manuel García-Carpintero and Marie Guillot, Oxford University Press.
© Carlota Serrahima 2023. DOI: 10.1093/oso/9780198805397.003.0011

THE SENSE OF BODILY OWNERSHIP: DEFINING DESIDERATA 251

[SBO]: For one to have a sense of bodily ownership is for one to be aware of the body one feels in bodily sensations as being one's own.[2]

At this point, a question emerges that provides the backbone of the debate in which this essay takes part: what is the specific character of this awareness? One could defend that subjects are aware of the body they feel in bodily sensations as being their own only if they *judge* that that body is their own (Alsmith, 2015). This would seem to assume that the SBO consists, maybe only partly but crucially, of judgments involving a relative of the I-concept. This view is thus compatible with the idea that bodily experiences themselves involve no specific component that stands for the first-person figuring in judgment—hence being, so to speak, selfless. Let us label accounts along these lines *Cognitive Accounts*.[3] Cognitive Accounts are compatible with there being some phenomenology specifically attached to the SBO, perhaps cognitive phenomenology. However, while such phenomenology could then be said to be part of what the SBO consists of, it would not be part of the epistemic basis for judgments of ownership, but rather some byproduct of them.

However, the foregoing question can plausibly be answered in the opposite sense. One can defend that there are *experiences* of bodily ownership that are independent of cognitive acts of bodily self-attribution (Alsmith, 2015, 883). Let us call the accounts within this trend *Phenomenal Accounts*. According to Phenomenal Accounts, there is some component of bodily sensations themselves that stands for the first person that eventually figures in judgment. On these views, the SBO consists of a certain aspect of what it is like to undergo bodily sensations, and therefore the epistemic basis for judgments of somatosensation that are *de se* in the way indicated will involve a genuinely first-person element.

Given the phenomenal richness of bodily experiences, this element could be specified in several ways. As the discussion has been set, it seems natural to say that bodily experiences are mental states that convey something to the experiencing subject. In particular, by undergoing them, subjects are typically aware of the state and condition of a body: in this minimal sense, bodily experiences are mental states with content. This content can be spelled out at least in terms of properties or qualities (position, painfulness, and the like) that seemingly qualify the body or some of its parts. On these grounds, this content is generally said to have both a qualitative and a spatial dimension.[4]

---

[2] I am using "awareness" non-factively in [SBO]. For instance, the SBO is present in cases in which one takes a felt, inexistent body (part) to be one's own, as is usually the case for phantom limbs.

[3] The labels "Cognitive" and "Phenomenal" for the accounts sketched are due to Alsmith (2015).

[4] Ordinarily, we might say of *sensations*, rather than of the *properties* they convey, that they are localized. This might reveal something about the nature of these properties (see e.g. Brewer, 1995). But I must leave this discussion aside. Here I will talk interchangeably about bodily sensations and

252   THE BOUNDED BODY

Phenomenal Accounts divide according to the role they assign to these dimensions in accounting for the SBO. For one thing, a distinction has been traced between *deflationary* and *inflationary* views (Bermúdez, 2011; Bermúdez, 2015). Deflationism defends that the component of bodily sensations that constitutes the SBO is not "a positive quality over and above the felt quality of sensation and the location" (Martin, 1995, 270). The sense that the felt body is one's own is then spelled out in terms of how space is represented in bodily experiences (Martin, 1995; de Vignemont, 2007;[5] Bermúdez, 2018); or of the kind of qualities one feels as instantiated when undergoing them (Dokic, 2003). This trend crucially distances itself from inflationism. Bodily sensations—inflationism would maintain—do involve a dedicated mineness *quale*, irreducible to any of their other aspects (Billon, 2017). From this perspective, the awareness involved in bodily experiences that the felt body is one's own consists of this specific *quale*. Somewhere between these two strands, some authors enrich the phenomenology of bodily experiences and specify the SBO in terms of their affective character (de Vignemont, 2018; this volume; Bradley, 2021); or of an intrinsic, pre-reflective self-consciousness involved in all such components (Gallagher, 2017).

This chapter pursues two aims. On the one hand, it critically assesses a kind of deflationist approach. In particular, I engage with two related proposals that analyse the SBO in terms of the spatial content of bodily sensations by spelling it out as a sense of boundedness. The first was put forward by Mike Martin (especially Martin, 1995; but also Martin, 1992 and Martin, 1993); the second by Frédérique de Vignemont (2007), allegedly in continuity with the former. The discussion of these views is built around what will be defined as basic desiderata for any account of the SBO. It is indeed surprising how little attention has been devoted to specifically stating what an account of this phenomenon has to explain. Offering a proposal in this respect is thus the second aim of this chapter. In what follows I put forward its core components.

Surely, the outline of views just presented is to be framed within the context of acknowledging that there is such a thing as being aware of the body one feels as being one's own. On this assumption, we wonder about the nature of this awareness. Any proper answer to this question will arguably imply a picture of bodily sensations, namely a specification of what their content is and what it is like to undergo them. The foregoing debate-framing already suggests a basic desideratum that we should impose on this picture: it must offer, or allow for, an explanation of the first-personal character of all judgments aimed at reporting bodily sensations that are *de se* in the sense indicated. Our inquiry thus pursues the following *Judgment Formation Goal*:

---

bodily properties as localized, not meaning to entail that the former *qua* mental states are physically located, nor experienced as such.

[5] De Vignemont's view has evolved very significantly from 2007 (see in particular de Vignemont, 2018). In this chapter I will address her 2007 view as representative of a spatial account with the aim of shedding light on what seem to me compelling reasons to go beyond it.

[*Judgment Formation Goal*]:   any account of the SBO must explain the fact that we self-attribute the felt body for all judgments of somatosensation in which we do so.[6]

With this first aim in view, the second desideratum that, I contend, all accounts of the SBO must meet relies on a central feature of the relation between bodily sensations and judgments of somatosensation. This feature illuminates a contrast between bodily sensations and external perception, when it comes to the types of judgments we ordinarily conceive of them as possibly yielding. To illustrate this, recall that Ernst Mach (1914) once got on an omnibus and had a visual perception of what seemed to him a shabby pedagogue at the other end. He then realized that he was actually looking in a mirror, subsequently thinking "I am a shabby pedagogue!". After the revelation, but not before, he was aware that the body he visually perceived was his own.

Surprising as revelations of this kind are in ordinary life, they seem in order. More generally put, several of our experiences beyond bodily sensations involve bodies as part of their content—for instance, visual experiences. Yet, this being the case, it does not seem especially problematic for a visual experience to occur in which a body is represented but is not taken by the perceiver to be her own.[7] This happens ordinarily when we perceive the bodies of others, and situations in which the relevant experience does indeed represent our own body, such as Mach's, are also relatively common.

The case seems remarkably different for bodily sensations. In fact, in the philosophical literature on bodily awareness it has been pointed out that, whenever bodily experiences occur, they necessarily come with their subject's awareness that the body experienced is her own (e.g. O'Shaughnessy, 2008; Martin, 1995; Dokic, 2003). This points in the direction of claiming something for which we now have empirical evidence to be impossible, or at least inconceivable. After lesions in their right parietal lobe, somatoparaphrenic patients have delusional beliefs about the contralesional side of their bodies according to which this side, or parts of it, do not belong to them (Vallar and Ronchi, 2009; Invernizzi et al., 2013). Some such patients, however, are able to feel sensations in their "disowned" limbs. These patients undergo bodily experiences that have a body as their content, but they are not aware of the body they feel as their own. These cases argue

---

[6] This goal should be acceptable by so-called *de se* skeptics, for whom strictly speaking bodily self-attributions are not grounded on anything in the content of bodily experiences (Cappelen and Dever, 2013; Magidor, 2015). Likewise, cognitivists in the abovementioned divide should also be committed to it. Notice that the goal allows a refinement of that divide: the difference between Phenomenal and Cognitive Accounts mainly lies in that the former pick up a specific aspect of the phenomenology of bodily experiences to stand for the SBO, thus not focusing only on facts about the relevant cognitive acts. However, we now see that Cognitive Accounts should also be able to specify the grounds for the relevant judgments.

[7] An exception to this might be the awareness of bodily location based on the position of the apex of the visual field. This is not problematic for my point. At most it suggests, plausibly, that awareness of bodily location on the mentioned grounds involves complications similar to the ones discussed in the SBO debate.

254   THE BOUNDED BODY

strongly for a nuanced formulation of the previous observation: there is a *seemingly necessary* link between the occurrence of bodily sensations and the involvement of the first person in the content position in the experiencing subject's reports of them.

It might be said that even this formulation is too concessive. After all, once somatoparaphrenia has become common knowledge in the literature, there is a sense of seeming in which it is no longer true that it *seems* to us that this necessary link exists.[8] I contend that there is still a sense in which this intuition of necessity is relevant, despite the challenge from somatoparaphrenia. In fact, it seems to lie at the heart of the specific philosophical interest that the SBO raises. Notice that another context in which a similar tension arises is the discussion on the relation between being phenomenally conscious and self-attributing the states of which one is conscious in this way. The apparent compellingness of this connection, undoubtedly lying behind its philosophical import, also informs the work on the phenomenon of thought-insertion, which arguably challenges it.[9] In parallel, bodily sensations are relevant to discussions on self-consciousness in a way that other mental states are not. Maybe on the grounds of what is normally the case, bodily sensations, unlike exteroceptive perception in general, seem to us to be about ourselves in a specially compelling way.[10]

This prescribes a second objective for theories about the SBO. On the assumption that we want them to fulfil the *Judgment Formation Goal*, it is crucial that they also account for what arguably is a central feature of the relation between bodily experiences and judgments of somatosensation: whatever it is about bodily experiences that explains the awareness that they are about *me*, it will need to be sufficiently distinctive of them *vis à vis* external perception. Straightforwardly put, we are pursuing the following *Intuitive Goal*.

[*Intuitive Goal*]:   any account of the SBO must specify the SBO in terms that explain the seemingly necessary link that bodily experiences, but not exteroceptive experiences, have with the awareness of the experienced body as one's own.

That somatoparaphrenia, as well as other empirical cases, imposes constraints on views on the SBO is acknowledged in our third and last goal, which demands of any such view that it be extensionally adequate:

---

[8] I am thankful to an anonymous referee for pressing me on this point.

[9] See, e.g., Frith (1992); Campbell (2002); Gallagher (2015). As a matter of fact, this is the other theoretical context in which the expression "sense of ownership" has been successful.

[10] Some illusions of ownership such as the rubber hand illusion (Botvinik and Cohen, 1998), in which the self-attribution might be found compelling in the way indicated, are usually described as exteroceptively induced. Arguably, the success of the rubber hand illusion depends also on proprioceptive feedback, as well as on matters of perspective. In any case, I am appealing here to a general intuition of contrast between external perception and bodily experiences that may have exceptions in both directions.

[*Empirical Goal*]: any account of the SBO must leave room for the specific, sometimes abnormal relations between bodily sensations and the awareness of the felt body as one's own we seem to have evidence for in some pathological and experimental cases.

The views dealt with in this chapter will be assessed in the light of the *Judgment Formation* and *Intuitive* goals. From the next section on, I aim to present a set of points, mainly of a conceptual kind, to the effect that the analysis of the spatial content of bodily sensations in terms of what I shall call the *Boundedness Thesis* fails to meet these goals. This will invite, in the concluding section, a reflection on the close connection between these two objectives.

2. The Bounded Body

The focus of this section will be what I shall call the *Boundedness Thesis*:

Boundedness Thesis (BT): the SBO consists of the fact that, when having bodily sensations, the body is felt as having certain boundaries.[11]

In line with the idea that bodily experiences involve awareness of bodily space, in that they involve being aware of qualities instantiated somewhere in the body, BT points to the relation that seems to hold between experiencing qualities as instantiated in a body and singling out this body in the experience. Let us assume that, in sensory experiences, the latter means tracing, or being able to trace, the limits of the relevant body with respect to other physical objects or to its surroundings. BT says that the SBO consists of this awareness of the bodily boundaries.

In this section I address two views that embody the defence of BT under two different versions. The first focuses on the following phenomenological datum: it is the localization of felt bodily properties that entails a sense of the boundaries of the body. Each of the points in space where the properties are felt to be located contribute to the delineation of a figure, and such figure is that of the body for which one has a sense of ownership. Crucially, as BT proposes, we have this sense in virtue of being aware of the delineation. Here is a specific formulation of this thesis:

---

[11] Bermúdez (2018, 211–214) presents a similar notion of *Boundedness* ("Bodily events are experienced within the experienced body (a circumscribed body-shaped volume whose boundaries define the limits of the self")) as a feature of bodily experiences. Yet, he argues for the need to supplement it with *Connectedness* ("The spatial location of a bodily event is experienced relative to the disposition of the body as a whole") for both to jointly ground the SBO. Since in this chapter I argue against the sufficiency of the first item, I do not engage with Bermúdez's (2018) view.

BT-First version: The SBO consists of the awareness of the body as bounded. This awareness is entailed by the experienced location of the qualities felt in bodily sensations.

The second view also acknowledges the phenomenological point that feeling bodily properties as located involves a sense of the boundaries of the body. Yet, it indicates that the phenomenally conscious location is ultimately explained by the subject's possession of a representation of the body: one has a map of one's own body and, when having bodily sensations, pinpoints different spots in it. This allegedly makes the boundaries of the represented body, namely one's own, phenomenally salient: by being felt as located, sensations convey a sense of the limits of what the map represents. Straightforwardly put, in terms of BT:

BT-Second version: The SBO consists of the awareness of the body as bounded. This awareness is entailed by the experienced location of the qualities felt in bodily sensations. These qualities are experienced as located in virtue of the subject's possession of a representation of her own body.

BT-Second version adds to *BT-First version* the appeal to a body representation. As a Phenomenal Account in the spirit of BT, it assumes that the sense of boundedness involved in bodily sensations stands for the first-person figuring in proprioceptive judgments. Yet, it claims that the relevant body representation will carry out further explanatory work by accounting for the fact that bodily properties can be felt as localized, and in particular as localized within what is felt as one's own body. Without further ado, I shall now address each of these views in turn.

2.1. On the Felt Bodily Boundaries

In order to spell out *BT-First version* we need to start by substantiating the idea that the experience of, for example, a prick in the toe or a tickle in the nape of the neck entails awareness of the body as bounded. Mike Martin[12] develops this point thoroughly. A natural way to present it is to start from the description of the peculiarities of the phenomenology of haptic touch, and then eventually to notice that its core feature—the awareness of boundaries—shows up in all bodily experiences, at least to some degree. This is how I shall proceed.

---

[12] I read Martin's view as aimed at the explanatory project described in section 1, and so seem to do de Vignemont (2007, 2013) and Gallagher (2017). It seems to me that there is textual evidence supporting this reading—see, e.g., Martin (1995, 269 and 273), and compare Bermúdez's (2011, 163) formulation of deflationism with Martin (1995, 270). For a different interpretation, however, see Bermúdez (2018).

In haptic perception, one perceives objects through touch by directly exploring them in an active and controlled way. Haptic touch typically unfolds over time and involves a range of bodily movements, the experience finally comprising cutaneous stimulation along with motor feedback (Fulkerson, 2014, 6). Feeling the irregularities of the edge of a table by caressing it with the fingertips, for instance, is a case of haptic touch. Even if haptic experiences are mainly object-directed, in that one engages in them to perceive the properties of objects other than the body, their content is typically said to be dual: it involves awareness both of external objects and of the body. When touching the surface of my worktable, not only do I feel the roughness of the wood but also I am aware of a certain pressure on my fingers.

The nature of the relation between exteroceptive perception and bodily awareness in touch is not uncontroversial.[13] We can however leave this discussion aside and notice, in what seems a neutral enough claim, that the tactually accessed properties we are aware of in haptic experiences will be attributed, in judgments about these experiences, to two different entities: the touched object—the *rough table*—and the body—fingers *being depressed* against the table. Reporting the experience in one way or the other involves an attentional shift: either one attends to the object, as seems more natural in exploratory touch, or one makes an attentional effort and focuses on the body felt while touching.[14] Pursuing this attentional effort, a description of the phenomenology of bodily awareness in haptic touch will surely include the following: "[o]ne measures the properties of objects in the world around one *against one's body*" (Martin, 1992, 203, my emphasis). Haptic perception crucially involves the experience of contact between body and objects: the bodily awareness involved in it is the awareness of the limits of the body in correlation with the pressure of objects against them. In this sense, touch is a clear case of a bodily experience in which the awareness of bodily boundaries is phenomenally salient. Feeling pressure *on* the fingertips in exploring the surface of the table implies becoming aware of their silhouette.

This invites a reflection on the role of a notion of sense field in touch in contrast with the function that the sense field has in sight. As Martin puts it, "[n]ormal visual experience is essentially experience of objects as they fall within the visual field; tactual experience is essentially experience of objects as they press from the outside onto the limits of a felt sensory field" (1992, 210). While the sense field in sight is the visually perceived area within which objects are distributed, the objects of touch appear in virtue of our awareness of certain bodily regions that, exactly matching the shape of perceived objects, actually constitute the field. To the extent that the sensory field is identified with the dimension of

---

[13] See Fulkerson (2014), ch. 4, for a careful review of different views in this respect.

[14] In Martin's (1992) analysis, exteroceptive awareness in touch is a result of attending to bodily awareness in a certain way. For comments on Martin's view, see Scott (2001) and Fulkerson (2014). See also Husserl (1989) and Katz (1989) for related claims about the role of attention in unfolding the duality of touch.

258   THE BOUNDED BODY

bodily awareness of the experience, the perception of objects involved in it will properly be described as that of something that falls outside of the field.

Indeed, notice that tactile experience typically involves awareness that the touched object *is not* the body. More generally, "the cutaneous sense field is only a tactual field containing objects of touch in as much as it is embedded within a *space* which extends beyond any such field" (1992, 209, my emphasis). Touch *qua* bodily sensation involves the awareness of bodily boundaries, which in turn equates to the awareness of such boundaries standing out against a wider space. This turns out to be, on Martin's account, a common feature of all bodily sensations.

It is rather straightforward to see how these considerations generalize to other bodily sensations. Consider the situation in which you raise your hands above your head and are kinaesthetically aware of their relative position (1995, 271; 1993, 212). You feel your hands by having kinaesthetic sensations from them, which means that they seem to extend to at least the point in space where you feel sensation (1993, 210). This awareness thus consists of an awareness of how the hands are placed within a space that goes beyond that in which you actually feel them—since it implies feeling the hands as outlined. By appealing to the awareness of boundaries, the idea of the dual content posited for tactile experiences is generalized *mutatis mutandis*. Arguably, to the extent that all somatosensorily perceived qualities are grasped as located somewhere in the body, they count as signalling the points to which the body extends, namely where its limits are and where the space in which it is inscribed begins. An acute prick in the toe indicates a particular point beyond which there might be a thorn; a tickle in the nape of the neck conveys a sense of there being an immediately contiguous area in which the air is moving in an unusual way.

Up to this point we have clarified part of *BT-First version* by spelling out the claim that experiencing the body through localized bodily sensations entails an awareness of it as bounded. Let us assume that this description of the experience of bodily space is accurate. I shall now discuss the central claim of this version of BT, namely that the SBO *consists of* the awareness of the body as bounded.

The view under consideration states, more specifically, that "wherever a sensation feels to be located, *one's body appears* to extend to at least that point in space" (1993, 210, my emphasis). The boundaries are the limit between what one feels as the own body and what is felt as other. When, exploring my worktable, I switch the focus of attention from the texture of the wood to the pressure on the fingers, what I am actually doing is switching attention from what is going on beyond one of my boundaries to what goes on beneath it (1995, 270). This is how *BT-First Version* is finally defined: the experienced location of the qualities felt in bodily sensations entails an awareness of boundaries that is awareness of *my* body as bounded.

The view certainly conveys a descriptive analysis of the bodily experience of space, appealing to a notion of sense field that involves awareness of properties within it and of objects outside of it. In close connection with this, it specifies the Cartesian intuition that I am not present in my body as a sailor in a ship (Descartes, 1996, 81): contrary to how the sailor presumably experiences the properties of the ship she is in, the spatial distribution of somatosensorily felt properties is such that they fall within what I feel as *my own* space. However, the claim that we experience certain qualified regions of space will not be particularly explanatory unless it is further substantiated in a way that, conceptually, is sufficiently independent from the very notion of ownership. The notion of a boundary the relevance of which stems from the fact that it appears as the limit between what is felt as one's own and what is felt as other seems unsatisfactory in this respect. For, we could still ask: on what grounds does the subject take the body on one of the sides of the boundary—the body Being Depressed in the worktable example—to be her own in the relevant sense, while taking the object on the other side—instantiating Roughness—not to be hers? Why should either side of the perceived boundary have the special import it has?[15]

It might be replied that this misses the point about what deflationary views are supposed to be. The SBO *just is* the sense that one's own body extends up to certain boundaries: "for me to feel as if some part of my body occupies a region of space...is for it to seem to me as if that region falls within one of the boundaries of my body" (Martin, 1995, 270). This certainly deflates the SBO, and the demand for conceptual independence—the reply goes—is misplaced.

As far as I see, the reply itself involves a misunderstanding regarding what is essential to deflationism. Insofar as we are dealing with Phenomenal Accounts, the phenomenological analysis of sensations must be sufficient to explain why, given a bodily sensation, we typically use a first-person pronoun to qualify its content; and deflationism is supposed to do so without appealing to a specific mineness component. In particular, in the view at stake it must be the representation of space, independently described, which explains its manifesting itself first-personally in judgment. The fact that we experience properties on what is felt as *our own* side of a boundary does not meet the independence constraint.

The way to defend *BT-First version* would be to show that the bare description of bodily sensations in terms of properties that delimit boundaries can do the expected grounding work. This is what I want to question in what follows. I contend that this description does not make it intelligible why we tend to report the relevant experiences in first-personal terms. This is clear if we observe that the notion of a sense of boundedness is plausibly involved as well in episodes of visual

---

[15] Considerations along the lines that bodily sensations only involve the body that is *in fact* our own—which play a crucial role in Martin's definition of them as genuinely perceptual—are tangential to this question, which addresses specifically the phenomenal grounds for the salience of the felt body. I will elaborate on this a bit more in the next section. Pointing out, alternatively, that the relevant side of the boundary is felt in a special way, e.g. "from the inside," just stresses the need to search for something qualitatively distinctive of this experiential mode, beyond its spatial content.

260 THE BOUNDED BODY

perception whose contents we do not self-attribute. Besides, what indeed seems to be a crucial difference between the two types of experiences won't be accounted for just by appealing to boundedness.

According to *BT-First version*, what is most special about bodily sensations with respect to visual perception has to do with the notion of a sense field. We are aware of the objects of touch, for instance, as something we do not feel in the same way as we feel the body. On this view, this is so because of our awareness of the boundary of the field. But upon further scrutiny, vision and bodily sensations may not be so radically distinct in this particular respect. Husserl noted that, in visual experience, at every moment we are aware that the world extends beyond what is actually falling within our visual field at that moment (1983, §27).[16] An anticipation of subsequent perceptions seems to be built into the content of each particular perception: the visual field is experienced as related to other regions of space of which we are aware in a different way, and to which we might or might not eventually turn our attention—such as, for example, the region behind our bodies. Hence, it doesn't seem far-fetched to claim that objects with properties are distributed within the visual field to fill it up to its boundaries, which delimit it with respect to other non-actually-perceived regions of space. This questions the sufficiency of such a description of spatial experience to explain what it is that makes us typically judge that the body in bodily sensations constitutes *our own* region of space, in opposition to what occurs with the space and objects falling within the visual field.

There is, however, a compelling disanalogy between the sense fields of sight and bodily sensation. In the visual case, "I can let my attention wander away from the writing table which was just now seen and noticed...to all the Objects I directly 'know of' as being there and here in the surroundings of which there is also consciousness" (Husserl, 1983, 51–52). While in vision I am aware of an environment standing beyond the currently perceived visual field which is in principle visually accessible as a function of my bodily movement and shifts of attention, in bodily sensations "the sense of falling within a boundary may be no more than the sense that the location in question is within a space that seems to extend into regions that one *could not* currently be aware of *in this way*" (Martin, 1995, 271, my emphasis). One might want to insist that the distinctive aspect of bodily sensations is that a contrast between what the subject is somatosensorily aware of and what she could not be aware of in this specific way is part of their content. In contrast, visual perception involves awareness of the fact that one could be aware of what stands on the other side of the boundary in the same way as one is aware of what falls within the visual field.[17] The peculiar nature of the

---

[16] Dokic (2003, 326) also appeals to this idea through Merleau-Ponty to discuss Martin's view. However, his point is different from the one I make here.

[17] Interestingly, for Husserl this is correlated with the subject's kinaesthetic awareness, which indicates her possibilities for action (1997, section IV; 1989, section I, ch. 3). The Gibsonian notion of

subject's awareness of one of the sides of the boundary in contrast with the other could then ground the SBO.

This line of argument is promising. But at this point we need to evaluate how much work the notion of boundedness would be doing in such a view. The proposal would appeal to *ways of being aware* of regions of space: maybe to correlations between regions and types of properties we are aware of as instantiated in them; or between regions and the types of cognitive faculties by which we are aware they can be grasped. But even if these regions would be demarcated by perceived boundaries, such boundedness would seem subsidiary in the context of an explanation of the fact that some regions, or the bodies in them, are taken to be *ours*.

In sum, my point in this section is that *BT-First version* fails at meeting, on the one hand, the *Intuitive Goal*: there doesn't *seem* to be a necessary link between having visual experiences and self-attributing their contents, even if arguably a sense of boundedness is part of their phenomenology. Hence, *BT-First version*'s specification of the SBO doesn't pick up a distinctive enough element of bodily experiences *vis à vis* exteroception to account for the compelling involvement of the first person in the former. On the other hand, by the same token, the view falls short of the *Judgment Formation Goal*. The notion of a sense of boundedness doesn't suffice to explain why bodily sensations are expressed first-personally, since a sense of boundedness is generally involved in visual experiences which do not yield judgments in which we self-attribute visual contents.[18]

Notice, however, that none of the points made in this section question the prospects of deflationist accounts in general; nor do they in principle rule out the possibility that a more sophisticated account of spatial representation in bodily sensations can meet the goals satisfactorily. Informed by empirical evidence that disputes the adequacy of a view based only on the phenomenology of bodily sensations, *BT-Second version* adds a further element to the picture. Let us now move on to evaluating whether it offsets the shortages of the view examined.

2.2. The Role of the Body Schema

De Vignemont (2007, 436) points out that Martin "reduces the sense of ownership to the sense of the boundaries of one's own body" but he "does not go into detail about the delineation of the boundaries of one's own body." She then proceeds to investigate "the nature of the spatial representation of the body that underlies

---

affordance also stresses this point. On the connections between the Husserlian and the Gibsonian analyses of visual perception, see Zahavi (2002).

[18] A consequence of *BT-First version* is that, necessarily, if a subject has a located sensation she will feel the body part where it is located as her own. Somatoparaphrenia constitutes a powerful counterargument to this (de Vignemont, 2013). Hence, it is also doubtful that *BT-First version* meets the *Empirical Goal*.

the sense of ownership," submitting an account that intends to supplement Martin's in the pursuit of a common aim. I take de Vignemont (2007) to defend *BT-Second version*:

BT-Second version: The SBO consists of the awareness of the body as bounded. This awareness is entailed by the experienced location of the qualities felt in bodily sensations. These qualities are experienced as located in virtue of the subject's possession of a representation of her own body.

On this view, the SBO still consists of a sense of boundedness identical to a sense of one's own boundaries. I just discussed the limitations of an appeal to this brute phenomenological fact alone as a deflationist strategy on how self-attribution of the felt body is possible. *BT-Second version* offers a further explanatory tool: what ultimately grounds the subject's awareness of the felt boundaries as her own is that the properties felt in bodily sensations are pinpointed within a representation of what is in fact the subject's own body. The relevant representation thus explains why the awareness of boundaries that follows from the location of sensation involves a phenomenology of ownership. On the face of it, the resulting "feeling of ownership" would seem to allow the view to meet the *Judgment Formation Goal*. Besides, since it is typical and exclusive of bodily experiences that they gain their spatial content by reference to the relevant body representation, the *Intuitive Goal* would also be met.

My aim in this section is to question that the appeal to body representations as it stands in *BT-Second version* grants that bodily experiences involve a phenomenology of ownership—and so, in particular, a sense of *our own boundaries*. I thus question that this supplemented version of BT can satisfactorily account for the SBO.

It is generally accepted in debates on bodily awareness that embodied subjects deal with different representations of their bodies—representations cashed out here minimally as mental resources that track the state of the body and encode it: the content of bodily experiences relies on representations of the body that are multimodal, resulting from the integration of visual, proprioceptive, and vestibular information (de Vignemont, 2014). In de Vignemont (2007), the type of body representation proposed as relevant for this discussion is the body schema, a sensorimotor map of the body based on information that can be constantly updated on the basis of afferent and efferent processes, including the posture and relative position of body parts, the size and strength of the limbs, or the degree of freedom of the joints.[19] From a functional point of view, the body schema enables

---

[19] For reviews of the numerous terminological and conceptual confusions involved in this notion, in particular its conflation with the notion of body image, see Tiemersma (1989) and Gallagher (2005, ch. 1).

and constrains movement and the maintenance of posture, being the kind of representation involved in the control of action. The relevance of the body schema in the discussion on the SBO is inferred from empirical evidence showing correlations between variations in ownership rating and functions typically associated with this body map. Bodily sensations, among other sensory inputs, are essential for the emergence of the schema, although they subsequently become weaker or disappear in the constitution of a bodily representation that is most of the time unconscious.

In my view, there is a threat to the general strategy of resorting to bodily representations for Phenomenal Accounts. By positing representations as grounds of the SBO, the difficulty of explaining how bodily experiences yield *de se* judgments carries over to the representations. In other words, if we posit a bodily map as a tool to explain how I manage to locate bodily properties within what I am aware of as my body, then it seems that the relevant map would have to be a representation of my body *as mine*, at the risk of the relevant sensations just being felt to delimit *a* body:[20] I might have a very detailed map of my body, but having "a sense" that the body represented in it is mine is a different and crucial issue. Yet, it is not obvious what it means for a map to (unconsciously) represent a body as one's own—beyond the fact that the relevant body representation elicits the behaviour typically taken to show that one recognizes a certain body as one's own—such as making assertions in which one uses "my" to talk about the felt body—or the phenomenally conscious mental states that would cause this behaviour.

This strategy ultimately leaves us with a sort of explanatory gap between an unconscious representation and the phenomenology of ownership allegedly involved in those states whose content is to be spelled out by reference to it. This gap doesn't seem to be bridged by appealing to the fact that the relevant representation just represents the one and only object that counts as our own body. Dokic (2003) traces a useful distinction between the sense of ownership and what he calls the "fact of ownership." The fact of ownership is that any property (veridically) perceived somatosensorily is a property of one's own body. Using the terms that occupy us here, the fact is that any property (veridically) perceived somatosensorily is felt to be at a location that falls within a map that *actually* represents one's own body.

Indeed, it is the case that, at least in normal circumstances, the body that we feel somatosensorily is our own. This fact grants the following: *if* there is anything like a phenomenology of ownership attached to the contents of experiences at all, then it makes sense that it is attached to the contents of bodily experiences, since in normal circumstances this awareness of the felt body as one's own will be veridical. A similar line of thought is this: if there is anything like a phenomenology

---

[20] Peacocke (2015) makes a connected point, focusing on the idea that this representation would assume, rather than explain, ownership.

264   THE BOUNDED BODY

of mental state ownership at all, then it makes sense that we have it with respect to those mental states we access phenomenally, since, as it turns out, we typically only have access to our own mental states this way.

Yet, what is at stake here is precisely the defence that there is such a phenomenology. One might doubt that the fact that I notice my own mental states, but not those of others, phenomenally, fully explains, or indeed entails, that I feel them phenomenally *as my own*.[21] In the same way, one might doubt that the fact of ownership fully explains, or indeed entails, that there is a phenomenology of ownership for the body felt in bodily sensations—in particular, that we feel its boundaries *as our own*. The gap I am pointing to arises precisely because we are dealing with a Phenomenal Account: that the boundaries made salient by the location of bodily sensations be those of the subject's actual body is not equivalent to them *being felt* as such, and it is not clear why an (unconscious) bodily representation should contribute to an explanation of why the latter is the case, or indeed entail that it is. And importantly, as previously argued, the plain location of sensations within certain boundaries falls short of accounting for the SBO.[22]

Admittedly, de Vignemont (2007, 443) indicates a solution to this difficulty. She suggests that the first-personal component of the body schema is *gained* by the fact that it is the map of the body with which we act: we feel as our own the one and only body with which we can act directly, and the body schema is the representation tracking this body.

This paves the way for a suggestive account of the SBO in which agency plays a crucial role. *BT-Second* version might have to be specified thus: ultimately, a bodily sensation involves what we feel as our own body if it presents the relevant properties as located within (the map of) the body that we can use directly for action. On this view, the sense of boundedness *qua* phenomenology of ownership would then be grounded on the phenomenology of agency. As far as I can see, this is tantamount to acknowledging the limitations of the notion of boundedness as grounds for the SBO. In fact, the considerations in this section suggest that a straightforwardly agentive view might actually be preferable: for, how independent can the self-attribution of the body with which one acts be of the fact that one perceives this body via the bodily sensations involved in one's engagement in action?[23] The agentive view that follows naturally is one in which bodily sensations,

---

[21] And indeed many doubt this. See, e.g., the chapters by Salje and Geddes, McClelland, Howell, and Soldati in this volume.

[22] This elaborates what I stated in footnote 15.

[23] This does not need to entail that bodily sensations are necessary for *any* subject to possess a body representation that plays the functional role typically associated with the body schema. Patients with deafferentation, for example, compensate their proprioceptive deficits with visual tracking of the body (Cole and Paillard, 1995). This suggests that the various sensory modalities typically involved in building the relevant body representation can compensate each other in cases of deficit. In fact deafferentation has been interpreted as a pathology in which motor deficits are compensated by mechanisms closer to the body image than the body schema (e.g. Gallagher and Cole, 1995; Wong, 2009).

provided with a spatial content, delimit the body with which we can act directly; and this, in turn, gives rise to a specific bodily map attached to action, as well as to a sense of bodily ownership. Interesting as it sounds, the view departs from—in fact, it would seem to deny—the claim that a sense of boundedness be sufficient as grounds for the SBO.[24]

To sum up, *BT-Second version* intended to overcome the shortages of *BT-First version* by appealing to a bodily representation. Given our *Intuitive Goal*, the appeal to the body schema seemed initially appealing. I have argued, however, that it is not clear how the relevant representation qualifies as a representation of my body as my own, or in general as one that provides bodily sensations with a phenomenology of ownership. Besides, a natural attempt to specify the view in agentive terms seems to depart from the notion of boundedness. All in all, the appeal to bodily representations in the framework of BT does not represent much of a step forward for explaining why bodily sensations are typically expressed first-personally—that is, in the direction of meeting the *Judgment Formation Goal*.

3. Conclusion

In this chapter, I have focused on two particular Phenomenal Accounts that ground the SBO on the notion of a sense of boundedness. Other views within this trend have been offered after these, some by their very proponents (de Vignemont, 2018; this volume), and some going beyond related notions of boundedness (Bermúdez, 2018). But I take the reflections in this chapter to have relevant programmatic upshots.

On the one hand, meeting the *Intuitive Goal* involves meeting the *Judgment Formation Goal*. The *Intuitive Goal* simply calls our attention to the fact that whatever it is that explains *de se* judgments of somatosensation should be involved in bodily sensations in a way that makes sense of the apparent compellingness of their first-personal expression.

On the other hand, and importantly, meeting the *Judgment Formation Goal* will have a direct bearing on the *Intuitive Goal*. The former asks to specify the trait that explains why we self-attribute the felt body in judgments of somatosensation. A proper account of the SBO will arguably be one in which the selected trait be generally and typically involved in bodily experiences—since it is part of what we are assuming that these experiences generally and typically yield judgments of this sort. In other words, it will immediately be one capable of meeting the *Intuitive Goal*.

---

[24] I am thankful to one of the referees for helping me shape these remarks on agency.

Hence it makes sense, as a strategy to show the limitations of a view regarding the *Judgment Formation Goal*, to stress that it specifies the SBO in terms of an element involved in other experiences that do not yield first-person judgments. While showing that the selected trait is not sufficient to explain that we form these judgments, this just amounts to pointing out a view's limitations regarding the *Intuitive Goal*. This is the strategy I followed in assessing *BT-First version*.

Finally, the fact that the body schema, appealed to as specifically involved in bodily sensations, fails to accomplish the grounding task in *BT-Second Version* reveals something essential. The specificity of a given trait doesn't straightforwardly make it a good candidate to ground the SBO. We undergo many experiences that involve type-specific traits and yet do not yield judgments that are *de se* in the sense relevant here. It seems there must be something about the selected specific trait that makes it suitably first-personal. This, I think, is the major difficulty for Phenomenal Accounts of a deflationist sort: what is it that makes a phenomenal component "suitably first-personal"? This worry is also what might make the inflationary notion of a specific mineness *quale* appear as an ultimately useful and simple explanatory tool (de Vignemont, 2013, 650): the first person might just have the status of a primitive. In any case, the phenomenal richness of bodily experiences suggests a long way to go before we can renounce the idea that a notion of ourselves as ourselves is intrinsic to them.

Acknowledgments

This chapter arose from a talk at the conference *The Sense of Mineness*, organized by the editors of this volume under the auspices of LOGOS in Barcelona in March 2015. I am grateful to the participants at this conference, and to the members of the LOGOS Reading Groups on the *de se*, for fruitful discussions on these issues. Special thanks are due to Frédérique de Vignemont, Marta Jorba, Daniel Morgan, Francesc Perenya, and Dan Zahavi for very helpful comments on earlier versions of this chapter, as well as to Manuel García-Carpintero, Marie Guillot, and an anonymous referee. I have had more illuminating discussions with Michele Palmira on the details of this chapter than I can recall. Thanks also to Michael Maudsley for the linguistic revision.

References

Alsmith, A.J.T. (2015). Mental Activity & the Sense of Ownership. *Review of Philosophy and Psychology*, 6, 4, 881–896.

Bermúdez, J.L. (2011). Bodily Awareness and Self-Consciousness. In: S. Gallagher, ed., *The Oxford Handbook of the Self*. New York: Oxford University Press, 157–179.

Bermúdez, J.L. (2015). Bodily Ownership, Bodily Awareness and Knowledge without Observation. *Analysis*, 75, 1, 37–45.

Bermúdez, J.L. (2018). Ownership and the Space of the Body. In: J.L. Bermúdez, *The Bodily Self. Selected Essays*. Cambridge, MA: MIT Press.

Billon, A. (2017). Mineness First: Three Challenges to the Recent Theories of the Sense of Bodily Ownership. In: A. Alsmith and F. de Vignemont (eds.), *The Subject's Matter: Self-Consciousness and the Body*. Cambridge, MA: MIT Press.

Botvinik, M. and Cohen, J. (1998). Rubber Hands 'Feel' Touch that Eyes See. *Nature*, 391, 756.

Bradley, A. (2021). The Feeling of Bodily Ownership. *Philosophy and Phenomenological Research*, 102, 2, 359–379.

Brewer, B. (1995). Bodily Awareness and the Self. In: J.L. Bermúdez, T. Marcel, and N. Eilan, eds., *The Body and the Self*. Cambridge, MA: MIT Press, 291–310.

Campbell, J. (2002). The Ownership of Thoughts. *Philosophy, Psychiatry, & Psychology*, 9, 1, 35–39.

Cappelen, H. and Dever, J. (2013). *The Inessential Indexical: On the Philosophical Insignificance of Perspective and the First Person*. Oxford: Oxford University Press.

Cole, J. and Paillard, J. (1995). Living without Touch and Peripheral Information about Body Position and Movement: Studies with Deafferented Subjects. In: J.L. Bermúdez, T. Marcel, and N. Eilan, eds., *The Body and the Self*. Cambridge, MA: MIT Press, 245–266.

de Vignemont, F. (2007). Habeas Corpus: The Sense of Ownership of One's Own Body. *Mind & Language*, 22, 4, 427–449.

de Vignemont, F. (2013). The Mark of Bodily Ownership. *Analysis*, 73, 4, 643–651.

de Vignemont, F. (2014). A Multimodal Conception of Bodily Awareness. *Mind*, 123, 492, 989–1020.

de Vignemont, F. (2018). *Mind the Body*. New York: Oxford University Press.

de Vignemont, F. (this volume). The Phenomenology of Bodily Ownership. In: M. García-Carpintero and M. Guillot, eds., *Self-Experience: Essays on Inner Awareness*. Oxford: Oxford University Press.

Descartes, R. (1996). *Meditations on First Philosophy: With Selections from the Objections and Replies*. J. Cottingham, transl. and ed. Cambridge: Cambridge University Press.

Dokic, J. (2003). The Sense of Ownership: An Analogy between Sensation and Action. In: J. Roessler and N. Eilan, eds., *Agency and Self-Awareness: Issues in Philosophy and Psychology*. New York: Oxford University Press, 320–344.

Frith, C. D. (1992). *The Cognitive Neuropsychology of Schizophrenia*. Hove: Erlbaum.

Fulkerson, M. (2014). *The First Sense: A Philosophical Study of Human Touch*. Cambridge, MA: MIT Press.

Gallagher, S. (2005). *How the Body Shapes the Mind*. New York: Oxford University Press.

Gallagher, S. (2015). Relations between Agency and Ownership in the case of Schizophrenic Thought Insertion. *Review of Philosophy and Psychology*, 6, 4, 865–879.

Gallagher, S. (2017). Enhancing the Deflationary Account of the Sense of Ownership. In F. de Vignemont and A.J.T. Alsmith, eds., *The Subject's Matter: Self-Consciousness and the Body*. Cambridge, MA: MIT Press.

Gallagher, S. and Cole, J. (1995). Body Schema and Body Image in a Deafferented Subject. *Journal of Mind & Behaviour*, 12, 360–390.

Husserl, E. (1983). *Ideas Pertaining to a Pure Phenomenology and to a Phenomenological Philosophy: First Book*. F. Kersten, transl. Dordrecht: Kluwer Academic Publishers.

Husserl, E. (1989). *Ideas Pertaining to a Pure Phenomenology and to a Phenomenological Philosophy. Second Book*. R. Rojcewicz and A. Schuwer, transl. Dordrecht: Kluwer Academic Publishers.

Husserl, E. (1997). *Thing and Space: Lectures of 1907*. R. Rojcewicz, transl. Dordrecht: Kluwer Academic Publishers.

Invernizzi, P., Gandola, M., Romano, D., Zapparoli, L., Bottini, G., and Paulesu, E. (2013). What is Mine? Behavioral and Anatomical Dissociations between Somatoparaphrenia and Anosognosia for Hemiplegia. *Behavioural Neurology*, 26, 139–150.

Katz, D. (1989). *The World of Touch*. L.E. Krueger, transl. and ed. New Jersey: Lawrence Erlbaum Associates, Publishers.

Mach, E. (1914). *The Analysis of Sensations, and the Relation of the Physical to the Psychical*. London: The Open Court Publishing Company.

Magidor, O. (2015). The Myth of the De Se. *Philosophical Perspectives*, 29, 1, 249–283.

Martin, M.G.F. (1992). Sight and Touch. In: T. Crane, ed., *The Content of Experience*. Cambridge: Cambridge University Press, 199–201.

Martin, M.G.F. (1993). Sense Modalities and Spatial Properties. In: N. Eilan, R. McCarty and B. Brewer, eds., *Spatial Representations*. Cambridge, MA: Basil Blackwell Ltd., 206–218.

Martin, M.G.F. (1995). Bodily Awareness: A Sense of Ownership. In: J.L. Bermúdez, T. Marcel, and N. Eilan, eds., *The Body and the Self*. Cambridge, MA: MIT Press, 268–289.

O'Shaughnessy, B. (2008). *The Will: A Dual Aspect Theory*, 2 vols. Cambridge: Cambridge University Press.

Peacocke, C. (2015). Perception and the First Person. In M. Mathen, ed., *Oxford Handbook of the Philosophy of Perception*. Oxford: Oxford University Press, 168–180.

Scott, M. (2001). Tactual Perception. *Australasian Journal of Philosophy*, 79, 2, 149–160.

Tiemersma, D. (1989). *Body Schema and Body Image: An Interdisciplinary and Philosophical Study*. Amsterdam: Swets & Zeitlinger.

Vallar, G. and Ronchi, R. (2009). Somatoparaphrenia: A Body Delusion. A Review of the Neuropsychological literature. *Experimental Brain Research*, 192, 533–551.

Wong, H.Y. (2009). On the Necessity of Bodily Awareness for Bodily Action. *Psyche*, 15, 1.

Zahavi, D. (2002). First-person Thoughts and Embodied Self-Awareness: Some Reflections on the Relation between Recent Analytical Philosophy and Phenomenology. *Phenomenology and the Cognitive Sciences*, 1, 7–26.

12

The Phenomenology of Bodily Ownership

Frédérique de Vignemont

When I report that I feel my legs crossed, there are two occurrences of the first person. The first occurrence refers to the subject of the proprioceptive experience (*I* feel), and it reveals the subjectivity of the bodily sensation (what it is like *for me* to have my legs crossed). The second occurrence refers to the limbs that feel being crossed (*my* legs), and it reveals what has been called the sense of bodily ownership, for want of a better name (the awareness of the legs that are crossed *as my own*). Whereas it is the former occurrence of the first person that has attracted most attention from philosophers, especially in relation to the epistemic property of immunity to error through misidentification relative to the first person (Shoemaker, 1968), my focus will be on the latter occurrence, and in particular on its experiential dimension. In a nutshell, what is it like to feel one's legs as one's own? But first, does it feel like anything? Bermúdez (2011) has structured the debate between two poles, what he calls inflationary and deflationary conceptions of ownership. However, it is not clear what divides these two conceptions: the existence of a phenomenology of bodily ownership or its nature? Consider, for instance, Bermúdez's own deflationary conception. On the one hand, he denies the existence of "a positive phenomenology" (Bermúdez, 2011, p. 163). On the other hand, he grants, "there is a phenomenology of ownership" (Bermúdez, 2015, p. 38). Hence, what seems to be at stake here is how to characterize the phenomenology of bodily ownership, and not whether there is such a thing. But then the debate is more complex than the apparently simple inflationary/deflationary divide (see Figure 12.1).

In brief, when considering the sense of bodily ownership, one needs to answer at least three questions. First, is there a phenomenology of ownership? Another way to put it is whether it feels the same when one is aware of one's leg as one's own and when one is not. Most conceptions easily grant that it makes a phenomenological difference, and it is only the most extreme version of the deflationary conception that denies it, collapsing into eliminativism. Now if there is a phenomenology of ownership, then one must ask about its nature. Is it an inherent quality of the sensory phenomenology of bodily awareness, such as the location at which one feels sensations, or is it beyond the sensory qualities? And if it is beyond, then what is it? Is the feeling of ownership simply an irreducible feeling

---

Frédérique de Vignemont, *The Phenomenology of Bodily Ownership* In: *Self-Experience: Essays on Inner Awareness.*
Edited by: Manuel García-Carpintero and Marie Guillot, Oxford University Press. © Frédérique de Vignemont 2023.
DOI: 10.1093/oso/9780198805397.003.0012

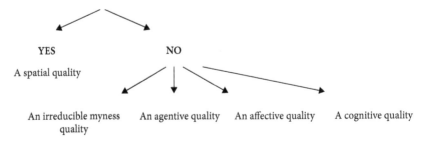

Figure 12.1 A brief overview of the sense of bodily ownership

of myness? Or is it a specific type of agentive feelings, which is grounded in the control that one exerts over one's body? Or is it a specific type of affective feeling, which is grounded in the special significance of one's body for survival? Or is it a cognitive feeling, or possibly even a metacognitive one?

Here I will defend the view that there is a phenomenology of bodily ownership, but deny that it should be conceived of in sensory terms. This does not entail, however, that one needs to posit feelings of myness. After considering several reductionist attempts, I will defend what I call the Bodyguard hypothesis, which spells out the phenomenology of bodily ownership in affective terms.

1. Beyond the Feeling of Myness

The notion of myness (or mineness) has recently attracted a lot of attention in the literature on consciousness. When it comes to bodily awareness, the point is not only that one feels as one's own the bodily sensations that one experiences but also that one feels as one's own the body itself that one experiences. The notion of feeling of myness is then often taken as a kind of primitive and its nature is rarely, if ever, characterized. In a representationalist framework, one may suggest that an experience consists in a feeling of myness if and only if its content explicitly includes the relation of ownership (e.g. as of being my own). The feeling of myness may then seem attractive because of its explanatory role for the first-personal character of the sense of bodily ownership. In brief, a feeling of myness seems to be a legitimate justificatory ground for judgements with a content of the type 'the body is mine'.

However, Bermúdez denies this legitimacy. He bases his argument on Anscombe's theory of knowledge without observation. Anscombe (1962) claims that we have sensations of bodily posture but they are not separately describable from the knowledge that we have of our posture, and their content is too general to be used as reliable indicators of our bodily position. Hence, she argues, knowledge of bodily posture cannot derive from bodily sensations. Bermúdez (2011, 2015) applies Anscombe's analysis to the sense of ownership. He claims that sensations that can be used as epistemic basis must meet two criteria. On the one hand, they must be independent: they cannot simply duplicate the content of the judgement because, Bermúdez (2015) claims, one cannot justify an assertion by simply repeating it. On the other hand, they must be "focused": their content must provide information that is precise and specific. If they are too vague, they fail to justify the specific judgement that one makes. He then concludes that the feeling of myness fails to meet these two criteria. "It is highly implausible that there is a determinate quale of ownership that can be identified, described and considered independently of the myness that it is supposed to be communicating" (Bermúdez, 2015, p. 39). Consequently, feelings of myness cannot ground bodily self-ascription. He then concludes that there are no feelings of ownership. "There are facts about the phenomenology of bodily awareness (about position sense, movement sense, and interoception) and there are judgments of ownership, but there is no additional feeling of ownership" (Bermúdez, 2011, p. 167).

This conclusion, however, seems too hasty, and this is so for several reasons. The first difficulty finds its origin in Anscombe's argument itself and in her epistemology. Why do contents have to be separately describable to ground judgements? And how to characterize such contents? The distinction between the sensations that can be separately describable and those that cannot is indeed problematic. In particular, the whole argument rests on the assumption that one cannot describe the sense of ownership without referring to the fact that this is one's own body. But why is it so? Bermúdez gives no argument but simply states that there cannot be independent descriptions. He further adds that ownership is "a phenomenological given" (2015, p. 44) and that it is impossible to ground it in further nonconceptual content. But again this seems to be simply begging the question.

The second problem that Bermúdez faces concerns the conclusion that he draws. He does not simply deny that feelings of myness can play an epistemic role; he goes further and makes a metaphysical claim: there are no feelings of myness. On his view indeed, their lack of epistemic role sheds doubt on their very existence: if they played no epistemic role, then why would one have such feelings? However, this epistemic objection is not fatal. Anscombe herself does not deny the existence of sensations of "pressure here, a tension there, a tingle in the other place" (Anscombe, 1962, p. 72), which accompany position and which can play a *causal* role for bodily self-knowledge. Likewise one may suggest that feelings of myness could play a causal role too.

272 THE PHENOMENOLOGY OF BODILY OWNERSHIP

Finally, not only does Bermúdez deny the existence of myness feelings, but also of ownership feelings in general. For him, I assume, they are one and the same thing but do they really have to be? One may indeed propose a reading to the notion of feeling of ownership different from the one given by Bermúdez. On this interpretation, the feeling of ownership is simply a qualitative experience *in virtue of which* we experience our bodies as our own, but it does not have to be a qualitative experience *about* ownership. This more liberal interpretation does not fall under Anscombe's objection: if ownership feelings do not have a myness content, then they can be separately describable, and thus they can ground bodily self-ascriptive judgements. Consequently, if we follow Bermúdez's line of thought, they can exist. This does not show that they do exist but at least we have removed one objection against them.

The question now is: are there other fundamental objections? Not really. More precisely, the general strategy for those who deny ownership feelings has been only critical, questioning arguments in favour of these feelings instead of providing arguments that these feelings do not, or cannot, exist (see Wu, this volume). Here I shall focus only on one example of this kind of strategy. One of the main arguments in favour of ownership feelings is what has been called the argument from cognitive impenetrability: there is a feeling of x if it seems to one that x while one correctly judges that there is no x (Harcourt, 2008). This type of dissociation is well illustrated by classic perceptual illusions, such as the Müller-Lyer illusion: one can have a visual experience of the two lines as being different, while having the belief that they are of the same size. If we can show that one can feel a hand as being one's own while believing that this is not one's own, then we have good evidence that there are belief-independent feelings of ownership. This dissociation is exactly what happens in the Rubber Hand Illusion (hereafter RHI). In the classic set-up, one sits with one's arm hidden behind a screen, while fixating on a rubber hand presented in one's bodily alignment; the rubber hand is then stroked in either synchrony or asynchrony with one's hand (Botvinick and Cohen, 1998). The illusion, which occurs only in the synchronous condition, includes the following components (see Table 12.1).

The RHI reveals clear dissociation between what it seems to the subject and what the subject believes (participants are well aware that this is a mere rubber hand that they see). The content of their experience is simply at odds with the content of their judgements (e.g. "It feels like my hand but I do not believe that it is my hand"). The fact that there is such an illusion does not show that there is a feeling of myness, but it supports the hypothesis that there is a feeling of ownership, as I defined it. Interestingly, the argument from cognitive impenetrability has also been used to reject cognitive theories of emotions. There is indeed a well-known phenomenon of emotional recalcitrance: when you suffer from vertigo, you can know that there is no danger of falling and still feel afraid of falling. It has been argued that one could not account for such recalcitrance if emotions consisted in

Table 12.1 The Rubber Hand Illusion

Phenomenological level *(measured by questionnaires)*	Referred sensations	Participants report that they feel tactile sensations as being located, not on their real hand that is stroked, but on the rubber hand.
	Sense of ownership	They report feeling as if the rubber hand belonged to them, were part of their body, or were their hand.
Behavioural level	Proprioceptive drift	They mislocalize the finger that was touched in the direction of the location of the rubber hand.
Physiological level *(measured by their skin conductance response)*	Arousal	When they see the rubber hand threatened, they display an increased affective response.

judgements (for discussion, see Tappolet, 2016). Likewise it seems difficult to account for the RHI if the sense of ownership consisted in judgements only.

Now the argument of cognitive impenetrability has been criticized on the ground that an illusion can be belief-independent without necessarily involving illusory feelings McDowell, 2011); (Alsmith, 2015; Bermúdez, 2015; Mylopoulos, 2015.[1] For instance, one can *suppose* or *imagine* that x while one knows that x is not true. Hence, one might dispute the experiential interpretation of the RHI and propose an alternative one, which is purely cognitive (Alsmith, 2015; Wu, this volume). However, it is not sufficient to claim that one can analyse the RHI in non-experiential terms, one has also to show that the cognitive analysis fares better than the experiential one. So far it is not clear that one has succeeded in doing so (for a detailed discussion, see Vignemont, 2017).

To summarize, although the argument from cognitive impenetrability may not be a sufficient proof for the existence of ownership feelings, it is still a powerful one. From now on, I shall thus assume that bodily ownership is not only something that we know of but that it is also something that we experience. The phenomenology of ownership may remain most of the time thin and evasive, unless in marginal circumstances, but it does exist. The crucial question now is what it consists in. One might discard Bermúdez's objection and maintain that it is an irreducible feeling of myness (Billon, 2017). However, irreducible feelings should always be the last resort. I shall thus inquire whether one can succeed in accounting for the first-personal character of the sense of ownership without appealing to such a

---

[1] It is worth mentioning that those who question the validity of the argument from cognitive impenetrability primarily target *sensory* phenomenology: a person does not need to have a sensory experience of x just because it seems to her that x although she knows that x is false. However, they seem to be willing to accept a non-sensory phenomenology of x, and more particularly of the cognitive type (Alsmith, 2015; Bermúdez, 2015; Mylopoulos, 2015).

notion. But how far can we go in our reductionist approach to the sense of bodily ownership? To answer this question shall be my task in the rest of this chapter.

2. A Spatial Phenomenology

Let us start by considering the main reductionist approach, which reduces the sense of bodily ownership to the spatiality of bodily experiences, a proposal that can be phrased along the following lines:

The sense of bodily ownership consists in the sense of the spatial boundaries of one's body.

This view is well described by Martin (1992, 1993, 1995) for whom the sense of bodily ownership is nothing more than the felt location of bodily sensations. Bodily sensations thus confer a sense of ownership on the body part in which they are felt to occur (Brewer, 1995; Cassam, 1995). However, we shall see that the spatial conception fails to account for the first-personal character of the sense of bodily ownership, leaving open the possibility to feel sensations in a body part that feels as alien.

2.1. The Sense of Bodily Boundaries

when one feels a bodily sensation to have a location there is no issue over whose body it appears to belong to. (Martin, 1992, p. 201)

Martin defends the position that the sense of ownership involves being aware that one's body has limits, that it has spatial boundaries beyond which this is no longer one's body. In a nutshell, there is no individuation of the body that one feels as one's own if there is no discrimination from what is not one's body. This discrimination, however, should not be phrased in terms of self versus non-self to avoid a circular account of ownership. It can be simply phrased in spatial terms, between inside and outside bodily boundaries in which one can experience bodily sensations.

One may reply that one can be aware of the boundaries of the body without being aware of the boundaries of the body *qua* one's own. This is the case, for instance, in visual experiences: I can be visually aware of my body as a bounded object within a larger space when I see it. However, there is a fundamental difference in spatial organization between visual experiences and bodily experiences.

Consider first the case of vision. The boundaries of the body that I see are not co-extensive with my visual field. Many other objects can occupy my visual field, including many other bodies. Therefore, visual awareness of bodily boundaries cannot confer a sense of ownership on the body part that is seen (Brewer, 1995; Martin, 1995; Bain, 2003). By contrast, it seems that when I have a bodily sensation, I do not feel it in one body as opposed to another body; I feel it in my own body only. According to what Martin (1995) calls the sole-object view, in order for an instance of bodily experience to count as an instance of perception, it must be an experience of what is in fact the subject's actual body. Bodily awareness has a unique object, namely, one's own body, and there cannot be veridical bodily experiences that do not fall within the limits of one's own body. There is thus an identity between one's own body and the body in which one locates bodily experiences, and this identity, Martin claims, enables the spatial content of bodily experiences to ground the sense of bodily ownership. Sensations that are felt beyond the actual limits of one's body, as in the case of phantom limbs, are not problematic for Martin's view because the phantom limbs are experienced within the apparent confines of the bodies that the amputees experience as their own. The same can be said of the RHI. One way to interpret the illusion is indeed that one experiences the rubber hand as one's own in virtue of feeling tactile sensations as being located in it. These sensations, on Martin's view, should be conceived as hallucinatory or illusory but they validate the hypothesis that it suffices to feel sensations as being located in a body part or in an object to experience this body part or this object as one's own: "this sense of ownership, in being possessed by all located sensations, cannot be independent of the spatial content of the sensation, the location of the event" (Martin, 1995, p. 277). What would be more problematic for Martin is if one could feel sensations in a limb and yet fail to experience the limb as being one's own. But Martin assumes that this is simply impossible:

> If the sense of ownership is a positive quality over and above the felt quality of the sensation and the location—that there is hurt in an ankle for example—then it should be conceivable that some sensations lack this extra quality while continuing to possess the other features. Just as we conceive of cold as the converse quality of warmth, could we not also conceive of a converse quality of sensation location such that one might feel pain in an ankle not positively felt to belong to one's own body. If O'Shaughnessy is right, we can make no sense of either possibility. (Martin, 1995, p. 270)

However, the problem that we shall now see is that what Martin claims as being unintelligible does actually happen. Consequently, contrary to what he claims, it does not suffice for one to feel sensations in a body part to experience this body part as one's own.

2.2. The Puzzle of Disownership

Experiencing no ownership for our own body might be hard to conceive but we can have a glimpse of what it feels like when we fall asleep on our arm: when we wake up, our arm feels numb and almost as an alien dead object attached to our body. Whereas it suffices for us to change our position to feel the hot tingle of blood rushing back in along with a sense of ownership, there is a variety of what may be called disownership syndromes that can last for days or even weeks (e.g. somatoparaphrenia, depersonalization, xenomelia, deafferentation). Patients suffering from these syndromes report that they no longer experience some of their limbs (quite often the left arm) as being their own and they may even attribute it to another person.

What is even more surprising is the fact that the patients can experience a sense of bodily disownership despite the fact that they still feel sensations in their so-called 'alien' limb. This is the case in xenomelia, but also in the neurological disorder of somatoparaphrenia. Following a lesion of or an epileptic seizure in the right parietal lobe, these patients deny that their limbs belong to them:

> E: Close your eyes and tell me what you feel when I'm touching your hand. P: That's not my hand!! […] It's not mine […] Someone left it there. I don't know who he was […] I don't know who attached it to my body. E: Isn't it a little bit weird to have a foreign hand with you? P: No! My hand is not like this!
>
> (Invernizzi et al., 2012, p. 148)

Somatoparaphrenia is often associated with somatosensory deficits and spatial neglect (Vallar and Ronchi, 2009), but patients with somatoparaphrenia do not systematically feel their 'alien' hand as numb. More specifically, nociceptive perception is preserved in many patients and they can even cry out in pain if the examiner pinches their 'alien' hand (Melzack, 1990). For instance, one patient asked his doctor: "Once home could I ask my wife, from time to time, to remove this left arm and put it in the cupboard for a few hours in order to have some relief from pain?" (Maravita, 2008, p. 102). Touch is more frequently affected, but in some rare cases, it can also be preserved. For instance, Moro et al. (2004) described the case of two patients with somatoparaphrenia, who were able to report with perfect accuracy when they were touched on their 'alien' hand if their 'alien' hand was in their right hemispace. Yet they maintained that the hand on which they felt touch was not their own, but someone else's.

Hence, contrary to Martin's prediction, patients with somatoparaphrenia can report feeling sensations to be located in the hand that they disowned. Bodily experiences lack the first person at one level: patients are aware that they feel bodily sensations, but they are not aware that they feel them in their body. One may then try to save Martin's view by interpreting their denial of ownership as being *irrational*. These patients are indeed delusional and they display a strong feeling of confidence that this is not their own hand: "Feinberg: Suppose I told you this was your hand? Mirna: I wouldn't believe you" (Feinberg et al., 2005, p. 104). One may then suggest that somatoparaphrenic patients do experience their hand as their own, but merely overlook their experience of ownership because of reasoning deficits, thus leading them to have delusions of disownership. The sense of disownership would then be only at the doxastic level, and not at the experiential level (Wu, this volume).

But can reasoning deficits suffice to explain their delusion? According to the two-factor model of delusions, one needs to distinguish between the factors that trigger the initial implausible thought (and thus contribute to explaining the thematic content of a particular delusion), and the factors that explain the uncritical adoption of the implausible thought as a delusional belief (Langdon and Coltheart, 2000). Abnormal rationality can then account for the feeling of confidence in the delusion, but not for the initial delusional belief itself. Instead, the delusion results from sensory or motor impairment leading to abnormal experiences that the patient tries to account for.

In addition, not all patients who describe a sense of bodily disownership have reasoning deficit; some only feel "as if" their limb did not belong to them and are fully aware that it is their own. Consider the case of patients with xenomelia who have an overwhelming desire to be amputated of one of their perfectly healthy limbs: "Inside I feel that my legs don't belong to me, they shouldn't be there [...] I would almost say as if they're not part of me although I feel them, I see them, I know they are" (Corrine in "Complete Obsession," BBC, 17th February 2000). The patient correctly judges the legs as being her own, she only feels *as if* they were not. A cognitive interpretation would have difficulties accounting for her report, for the distress that she experiences because of her sense of disownership, and even more for her urge to have her legs cut off. It would have even more difficulties in accounting for the case of Ian Waterman, which is especially interesting because his situation involves neither brain lesion nor psychiatric disorder. After some very rare acute sensory neuropathy he lost all proprioception and touch below the neck: if he closes his eyes, he does not know where his limbs are. However, he has spared thermal sensations and pain. Still at the beginning of his disease, these sensations did not suffice for him to have a sense of ownership for his deafferented body and he reported feeling alienated from it. However, Ian Waterman did not believe that his body was alien; he only felt *as if* it did not belong to him.

> Ian has described how he would sometimes wake to feel a hand on his face and not know to whom it belongs. Until he realised it was his own, the experience was momentarily terrifying. Since he has normal perception of warmth and

touch in his face, but only of warmth in the hand, it is interesting that he cannot, or does not, use warmth of the hand alone to identify self from non-self.

(Cole, 1995, p. 85)

To recapitulate, Martin's argument in favour of the spatial conception was the following:

- If "the sense of ownership is a positive quality over and above the felt quality of the sensation and the location."
- Then it should be conceivable that "one might feel pain in an ankle not positively felt to belong to one's own body."
- This is inconceivable.
- Hence, there is no sense of ownership over and above bodily sensations.

However, we have seen that although bodily experiences and the sense of ownership normally go together, they can sometimes come apart. Hence, feeling bodily sensations in a body part does not exhaust the phenomenology of bodily ownership.

2.3. Bodily Ownership and Bodily Presence

I have argued that one does not have to accept Martin's gloss of the awareness of bodily boundaries in terms of ownership. So what dimension of bodily awareness, if not ownership, does Martin describe? He claims that by being aware of the locations at which one can feel sensations and those at which one cannot, one becomes aware of the boundaries of one's body but also of a space larger than one's body, a space within which this body is located along with other objects. In this sense, one's body is perceived as being one object among others. I propose that this anchoring in three-dimensional external space corresponds to a *feeling of bodily presence* instead of a feeling of bodily ownership.

The notion of feeling of presence has been originally proposed to characterize the distinctive visual phenomenology associated with actual scenes and objects, which is lacking in visual experiences of depicted scenes and objects (Noë, 2005; Matthen, 2005; Dokic, 2010). Seeing an object as present involves being aware of it as a whole three-dimensional object located in egocentric space, as an object that one can explore from different perspectives and that one can actually grasp, while seeing a picture of the same object only involves being aware of its material surface with certain configurational properties.

In the same way that there is a feeling of presence associated with visual experiences of actual scenes and objects, I suggest that there is a feeling of *bodily presence* normally given by the spatial phenomenology of bodily experiences (for more details, see de Vignemont, 2020). For instance, when something brushes our knee, not only do we feel a tactile sensation, we also become suddenly aware of the presence of our knee as being located in egocentric space, as a body part that we can reach and grasp. This is well illustrated by the experience of phantom limbs. Many amputees indeed experience from the inside the continuous presence of their lost limbs. Because of his feeling of the presence of his amputated leg, a patient thus reported: "every morning I have to learn anew that my leg is enriching a Virginia wheat crop or ornamenting some horrible museum" (Mitchell, 1871, p. 567).

Let us return to the cases that we described. Because of their preserved sensations patients with somatoparaphrenia can feel the "alien" limb as being intrusive, as being always here. A patient, for example, complained: "It was very difficult to begin with...to live with a foot that isn't yours...It's always there, always present..." (Halligan et al., 1995, p. 176). One may then suggest that the feeling of bodily presence is preserved but not their feeling of ownership. There seems to be a priority of presence over ownership: one first needs to feel one's body as being here before feeling it as being one's own. It is therefore possible to experience presence without ownership but not the reverse. The awareness of bodily boundaries, which is at the origin of the feeling of bodily presence, is thus a necessary condition for the sense of ownership but it is not a sufficient one.

What these dissociations reveal is the necessity to distinguish what Peacocke (2014) calls the degree 0 of nonconceptual self-representation, which can be described in terms of "this body," and the degree 1, which involves *de se* content of the type "my body." They further show that it does not suffice to experience the spatial phenomenology of bodily sensations, and thus to have a feeling of presence, for having states with degree 1 content. In other words, the awareness of one's body as one's own does not simply consist in the awareness of one's body as a bounded object. What somatoparaphrenia and the other borderline cases that I described reveal is that we should not confuse spatial awareness and self-awareness, presence and ownership: one can be aware of the boundaries of the body without being aware of the boundaries of the body *qua* one's own (Dokic, 2003; Serrahima, this volume). As Peacocke (2017, p. 292) asks:

> So the question becomes pressing: What more is required to make a nonconceptual content c the first-person nonconceptual content i? This is equivalent to the question: What is it for an organism to be at Degree 1 of self-representation rather than Degree 0? It is also equivalent to the question: What minimally brings a subject into the (referential) content of a mental state?

3. An Agentive Twist

I will now assess whether the spatial conception is more successful in its account of the sense of bodily ownership if it is enriched with agency. The sense of bodily

280 THE PHENOMENOLOGY OF BODILY OWNERSHIP

ownership might indeed borrow, so to speak, its first-personal character from the self-referentiality of agency. The agentive conception may be spelled out in the following terms:

The sense of bodily ownership consists in the sense of the spatial boundaries of one's body as being under direct control.

In line with this agentive conception, I proposed in 2007 that the body that one experiences as one's own is the body represented in one's body schema, which can be defined as a sensorimotor representation of one's body used for planning and guiding action (de Vignemont, 2007). This hypothesis may seem promising insofar as it can successfully account for the sense of disownership in both deafferentation and somatoparaphrenia. As noted earlier, Ian Waterman did not simply lose proprioception and touch. He also lost his ability to control his body. And while unfortunately he did not regain normal bodily sensations, he regained control by exploiting more extensively visual information, and once he did so, he regained his sense of bodily ownership (Gallagher and Cole, 1995). Likewise, in no reported cases can somatoparaphrenic patients control their 'alien' limb. One may then be tempted to explain their sense of disownership as follows:

The patient with somatoparaphrenia is no longer able to move her paralysed limb, which is at odds with her prior experience of her limb. This generates the thought that the limb cannot be hers: it is an alien limb. This initial thought is then accepted uncritically as true (Rahmanovic et al., 2012, p. 43).

In other words, paralysis would alter the body schema, which in turn would lead to a sense of disownership. The agentive conception can thus avoid what appeared as fatal objections to the spatial conception. However, it fails where the spatial conception may be able to succeed, namely, in its account of the RHI. The agentive conception indeed predicts that action planning, which is based on the body schema, should be modified by the incorporation of extraneous body parts. This is the case in some versions of the RHI (e.g. Kammers et al., 2010), but there are other versions in which action planning seems to be impervious to the embodiment of extraneous hands: the motor system does not take the location of the rubber hand as a starting parameter when planning reaching and grasping movements (Kammers et al., 2009). A critic of the agentive conception can use this result to show that the body schema does not ground the sense of bodily ownership. The objection may run as follows: (i) the rubber hand is left out of the body schema that guides the movements; (ii) yet participants report ownership over it; (iii) thus, it is false that one experiences as one's own only body parts that are represented in the body schema.

The RHI thus seems hardly compatible with the agentive conception, unless one refines the notion of body schema. Here it is interesting to note that the movements that are usually tested are goal-directed instrumental movements such as pointing and grasping, but there is a different range of movements that is worth exploring, namely *defensive movements*. Physiological response to threat (as measured by their skin conductance response, or SCR) has indeed become the main implicit measure of the RHI: it has been repeatedly shown that participants react when the rubber hand is threatened, but only when they report it as their own after synchronous stroking, and the strength of their reaction is correlated with their ownership rating in questionnaires (Ehrsson et al., 2007). Their reaction to threat is also present at the motor level. In brief, it has been shown that participants automatically activate significantly more their motor cortex to withdraw their hand when they see the rubber hand threatened if they feel the rubber hand as their own than if they do not (Gonzalez-Franco et al., 2014). This finding suggests that the sense of ownership has a specific agentive mark in the context of self-protection.

What the affective and motor responses to threat highlight is the fact that the body matters for survival. It has a special significance for the organism's evolutionary needs. Because of this significance, there is a specific sensorimotor representation of the body to fix what is to be protected, which I call the *protective body map*. It is well defined by Klein (2015) who posits a similar notion in his account of pain:

> There's a body schema representation which is primarily concerned with protective action: that is, one which maps out parts of our bodies that we should pay special attention to, avoid using, keep from contacting things, and so on. Call this a defensive representation of the body: it shows which parts of the body are in need of which sorts of defense.   (Klein, 2015, p. 94)

One may thus suggest that the protective body map, which is involved in self-defence, has incorporated the rubber hand.[2] One may further propose that it is the causal ground of the sense of bodily ownership.

4. An Affective Phenomenology

We have seen that the agentive conception is too liberal to account for the specific relationship between bodily control and the sense of ownership. However, thanks to the notion of protective body map, one might be able to solve the difficulties that a more general agentive conception faces, while doing justice to the intuition that the sense of bodily ownership is intimately related to action. The protective body map also fits with a spatial conception of bodily ownership, but it does not

---

[2] For further discussion of the agentive conception, see Vignemont (2017).

represent simply spatial boundaries; it represents spatial boundaries that have *affective valence*. I thus defend what may be conceived as an affective conception of the sense of bodily ownership:

The sense of bodily ownership consists in the sense of the spatial boundaries of one's body as having a special significance for the self.

4.1. The Bodyguard Hypothesis

I have shown that it is not any kind of sensorimotor representations that can ground the sense of bodily ownership; only the protective body map can do so thanks to its agentive and affective dimensions. According to what I call the Bodyguard hypothesis, one experiences as one's own any body parts that are represented in the protective body map. Given the suite of cognitive capacities that human beings normally have, the protective body map is thus the causal ground of the sense of bodily ownership.[3]

To make it clear, the Bodyguard hypothesis should not be confused with the following view: the body that one protects is the body that one experiences as one's own.[4] Since one protects many things besides one's body and since one does not always protect one's body, this latter thesis is indeed clearly untenable. But this thesis is not entailed by the Bodyguard hypothesis. First, one should not neglect that protective behaviours can be analysed at many different levels, and only the lowest one is relevant here. Consider the pleasure that some experience in extreme sports, for instance. Even if the mountain biker is ready to risk his life by going downhill on a very steep and dangerous slope, he also pays extreme attention to his immediate environment and he is ready to react in case of obstacles. More generally, the affective conception that I defend does not assume that the protective body map is the only factor that decides which body is to be protected, even at the most primitive level. Like any other behaviour, protective behaviours can result from complex decision-making processes, involving a variety of beliefs, desires, emotions, moral considerations, and so forth.

As we did with the spatial and agentive conceptions, we must now put our new view to the test. We have seen that it can successfully account for the RHI, in which the ownership rating in questionnaires is correlated with the strength of arousal when the rubber hand is under threat. But can it account as well for disownership syndromes? How do patients react when they see their 'alien' body

---

[3] Here I limit the scope of the Bodyguard hypothesis to humans, leaving aside the delicate issue of the sense of bodily ownership in other animals.

[4] Neither is it that the more I protect a body part, the more I feel it as mine. Arguably, all the sensitive parts of the body are included in the protected body schema and they cannot be more or less represented.

part threatened? Interestingly, they do not react.[5] In one study on somatopara-phrenia, patients saw either a Q-tip or a syringe approaching either their right hand, which they felt as their own, or their left hand, which they felt as alien (Romano et al., 2014). The experimenter then measured their SCR. When the syringe approached the right hand, the SCR increased, as expected. But when the syringe approached the left 'alien' hand, there was no modification of the SCR. These findings are consistent with their broad pattern of attitudes. Many patients with somatoparaphrenia, for instance, often try to get rid of their 'alien' limb, by pulling it out of their bed, giving it to the doctor, putting it in the garbage, and so forth: "Yes, please take it away. I don't care about its destiny as it is not mine" (Gandola et al., 2012, p. 1176). They can also display misoplegia (i.e. dislike of one's body) and self-inflicted injuries.

However, one might wonder whether the Bodyguard hypothesis is compatible with the fact that patients with somatoparaphrenia negatively react to the pain that they feel as being located in their 'alien' limb. Since the protective body map no longer includes the limb, one should expect these patients to behave as if they were not concerned but this is not so. As seen earlier, one somatoparaphrenic patient asked to have his 'alien' arm removed and put in a cupboard to stop the pain (Maravita, 2008). But does his reaction truly qualify as protective? It may protect his feelings, but to want one's limbs to be dismantled is clearly not a good way to protect one's body. Arguably, his aversive reaction is disembodied, so to speak: the patients react to their emotional suffering rather than to their physical pain (for a distinction between the two, see Klein, 2015). Consequently, I would speculate that it does not recruit the protective body map.[6]

Now that we have a better grasp of the causal grounds of the sense of bodily ownership, we can hope to have a better understanding of what it feels like to experience one's body as one's own. I will propose that the phenomenology of bodily ownership is best characterized in affective terms. To explore this affective phenomenology, I will take as a starting point a 'familiar' affective feeling, namely, the feeling of familiarity.

4.2. Affective Feelings

I see my students entering the classroom. The phenomenology of my experience includes the visual phenomenology of the colour of their eyes and of the shape of

---

[5] Unfortunately, we have no evidence on that issue with Ian Waterman, although it is described that he withdraws his hand more slowly when injured (Gallagher and Cole, 1995). However, evidence from other patients suffering from disownership syndromes and from illusions of disownership indicates the same lack of affective response to threat (Newport and Gilpin, 2011; Romano et al., 2015).

[6] As far as I know there is no study of pain behaviours in somatoparaphrenia but my prediction is that they would be different for the hand that is felt by the patient as her own and the hand that is felt as alien.

their faces, but it includes something more. When I see them, I am aware that I know them: they look familiar. The feeling of familiarity cannot be reduced to the recognition of the visual features of the face. Instead, it involves autonomic responses, which result in increased arousal in front of familiar faces (Ellis and Lewis, 2001). It can be defined as a specific type of affective phenomenology elicited by the perception of objects and events that have personal significance. The phenomenology of my visual experience is thus dual, both sensory and affective, and the two components can be dissociated (Dokic and Martin, 2015). For instance, it is possible to have preserved sensory phenomenology with no affective phenomenology. This is what happens in Capgras syndrome. Patients with Capgras syndrome can see that a person is visually identical to their spouse, for example, but they do not feel that she is their spouse and they believe that this person must be an impostor. Their sensory phenomenology is thus intact, but they lack the affective responses normally associated with it, as shown by the absence of arousal when they look at familiar faces: visual recognition is preserved, but not autonomic recognition (Ellis et al., 1997). Their delusion of an impostor is only an attempt to explain their 'incomplete' perceptual experiences of their spouse. By contrast, patients with Frégoli delusion have an anomalously heightened affective responsiveness for unknown individuals, and thus believe that they are surrounded by familiar persons in disguise (Langdon et al., 2014).

I do not want to argue that the affective quality of bodily ownership can be reduced to the feeling of familiarity. First, the function of the feeling of familiarity is not to track exclusively our own body: our body feels familiar, but so do many bodies. One may still try to spell out the phenomenology of ownership in terms of a special kind of familiarity feeling, possibly a feeling of 'extreme' familiarity. However, this feeling would still lack the specific motivational force that characterizes the sense of bodily ownership. The affective significance that defines familiarity results from previous encounters with the person but it has no positive or negative valence. Roughly speaking, the enemy that you fight can feel all too familiar. By contrast, the special significance of one's body that is represented by the protective body map results from selective pressure and has a clear positive valence: it motivates one to protect the body that has such a significance. Hence, the feeling of familiarity does not fully capture the phenomenology of bodily ownership. Nonetheless it captures the idea that there can be specific affective feelings that reveal the significance of objects and events for the subject. Familiarity is just not the right type of significance for the sense of bodily ownership. How, then, should one characterize it, if it is not in terms of familiarity?

Here I will appeal to the notion of narcissism. I am not claiming that the sense of bodily ownership should be reduced to self-love (especially since the story of Narcissus ends badly), or to the sentiment of bodily care. The notion of caring is indeed too broad to account for the special relationship that one normally has only with one's own body. One cares about many things, and sometimes even more than one cares about one's own body. For many, for instance, there is little doubt that their children matter more for them than themselves. The notion of bodily care may also seem too cognitively rich and complex. As I described it, the protective body map is a nonconceptual representation that arises from a low-level mechanism that is biologically rooted. It may contribute to the sentiment of bodily care that we experience but it seems likely that many other factors contribute to this sentiment.

The notion of narcissistic feelings is thinner. A feeling is said to be narcissistic if it aims at securing what is best for the organism. This is how Akins (1996) describes the narcissistic function of sensory systems.

> What the organism is worried about, in the best of narcissistic traditions, is its own comfort. The system is not asking, 'What is it like out there?', a question about the objective temperature states of the body's skin. Rather it is doing something—informing the brain about the presence of any relevant thermal events. Relevant, of course, to itself.   (Akins, 1996, p. 349)

According to Akins, narcissistic perception is not about what is perceived, but about the impact of what is perceived for the subject. She grounds her hypothesis on the analysis of thermal sensations, which indicate what is safe or dangerous for the body given its thermal needs. The protective body map can be conceived as another instantiation of narcissistic function. It informs the brain about the potential relevance of the location of the sensation for the organism's needs. For example, if a spider crawls on my hand, I feel its contact within the frame of the body to protect. Thanks to their protective reference frame, bodily experiences are thus not about the body *simpliciter*; they are about this specific body that has a narcissistic significance. In the same way that the significance that characterizes familiarity is phenomenologically accessible, the awareness of the body that has narcissistic significance results in a special affective phenomenology, namely, a narcissistic feeling: one is aware of bodily boundaries as having a special significance for the self. This specific affective phenomenology that is grounded in the protective body map goes over and above the sensory phenomenology of bodily experiences. It cannot be reduced to the sensory recognition of bodily properties, but involves autonomic responses. We can now reinterpret cases of somatoparaphrenia in which patients can still feel bodily sensations located in the body part that feels alien. As in Capgras syndrome, these patients have their sensory phenomenology preserved, while their affective one is missing. By contrast, participants who experience the RHI have their affective phenomenology misguided (directed towards the wrong hand), and should thus be compared to patients suffering from the Fregoli delusion.

286   THE PHENOMENOLOGY OF BODILY OWNERSHIP

Let us now see whether the Bodyguard hypothesis can meet the challenge that any theory of the sense of bodily ownership encounters, namely, to account for its first-personal character (e.g. I feel *my* legs crossed), while avoiding a circular account.

4.3. The First-Personal Character of the Sense of Bodily Ownership

On the face of things, the Bodyguard hypothesis seems to face a dilemma that was pointed out by Peacocke (2015) against my earlier account in terms of body schema (de Vignemont, 2007). If the protective body map represents one's body *qua* one's own, then it presupposes what it is supposed to explain, but if it does not, then one is left with no explanation of the first-personal character of the sense of bodily ownership. I shall consider each horn of the dilemma.

The narcissistic quality expresses the value of the body for the self but it may seem that this specific body is valuable for the self in virtue of being experienced as one's own. If so, the Bodyguard hypothesis faces a version of the classic Euthyphro dilemma. Plato noted that an action is just because it pleases the gods, but the action pleases the gods because it is just. Similarly, it might seem that I experience my body as my own because it has a special significance for me, but for my body to have such significance presupposes that I experience it as mine, or at least that I represent it as mine. Put another way, if the protective body map represents one's body *qua* one's own, then it can account for the first-personal character of the sense of bodily ownership, but it does so "by taking for granted the notion of ownership by a subject, rather than by offering some kind of reductive explanation of the notion" (Peacocke, 2015, p. 174).

However, the Bodyguard hypothesis only assumes that the function of the protective body map is to represent the body that matters for the organism's survival; it does not assume that it represents the body that matters for the organism's survival *qua* one's own, even in a nonconceptual way. This distinction is important if one wants to block the risk of circularity. Consequently, being aware that this is my body presupposes that my body has a special affective significance for me, and for my body to have such significance is for it to be the body to protect for the organism's evolutionary needs. Because biology provides an independent standard to ground the notion of significance that is used by the bodyguard hypothesis, there is no circularity.

The Bodyguard hypothesis can thus reply to the first horn of the dilemma, but it may then seem to fall into the second one: since the protective body map itself has no first-person component, how can it be at the origin of the first-personal dimension of the sense of bodily ownership? To show that the Bodyguard hypothesis has the resources to provide such an account we might want to revisit Akins's notion of narcissism.

According to Akins, the narcissistic question can be phrased as follows: "But how does this all relate to ME?" (Akins, 1996, p. 345). On her view, this question does not only affect the content of my experiences, filtering only what is relevant to me; it also marks the structure, or the format, of my experiences, like a signature: "by asking the narcissistic question, the *form* of the answer is compromised: it always has a self-entered [sic] glow" (p. 345). The notion of self-centred glow calls to mind perspectival experiences. For instance, when I see a tree, I experience the location of the tree in its spatial relation to me and my egocentric experience "there is a tree in front" can ground self-locating beliefs of the type "I am facing a tree." Likewise, when I feel a spider on my hand, I experience the location of the spider in its narcissistic relation to me and my bodily experience "I feel a spider on the body that matters" can ground ownership judgements of the type "I feel a spider on my body" because the function of the protective body map is to track my own body.

To recapitulate, it is a fact of the matter that there is a specific body that one should protect to survive and reproduce and it is the function of the protective body map to reliably covariate with it. The protective body map is normally recruited as a spatial frame of reference for bodily experiences, ascribing a narcissistic value to the body that one experiences. One is then aware of one's body as one's own and one is motivated to protect it (see Figure 12.2). In some rare cases, however, the protective body map malfunctions. Then it can either incorporate extraneous limbs, leading to illusory sense of ownership and heightened affective response, or exclude a part of one's biological body, leading to pathological sense of disownership and diminished affective response.

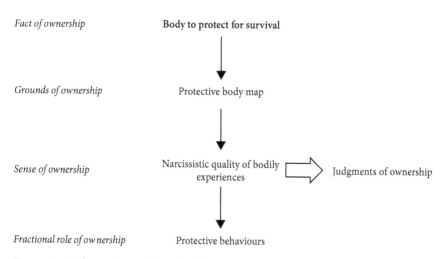

Figure 12.2 The Bodyguard hypothesis

References

Alsmith, A.J.T. (2015). Mental activity & the sense of ownership. *Review of Philosophy and Psychology*, 6, 4, 881–896.

Akins, K. (1996). Of sensory systems and the " aboutness" of mental states. *The Journal of Philosophy*, 93(7), 337–372.

Anscombe, G.E.M. (1962). On sensations of position. *Analysis*, 22(3), 55–58.

Bain, D. (2003), Intentionalism and pain. *Philosophical Quarterly*, 53(213), 502–523.

Bermúdez, J.L. (2011). Bodily awareness and self-consciousness. In S. Gallagher (ed.), *Oxford Handbook of the Self*. Oxford: Oxford University Press.

Bermúdez, J.L. (2015). Bodily ownership, bodily awareness, and knowledge without observation. *Analysis*, 75(1), 37–45.

Billon, A. (2017). Mineness first. In F. de Vignemont and A. Alsmith (eds.), *The Subject's Matter: Self-Consciousness and the Body*. Cambridge, MA: MIT Press.

Botvinick, M. and Cohen, J. (1998). Rubber hands 'feel' touch that eyes see. *Nature*, 391, 756.

Brewer, B. (1995). Bodily awareness and the self. In J.L. Bermúdez, T. Marcel, and N. Eilan (eds.), *The Body and the Self*. Cambridge, MA: MIT Press.

Cassam, Q. (1995). Introspection and bodily self-ascription. In J.L. Bermúdez, T. Marcel, and N. Eilan, (eds), *The Body and the Self*. Cambridge, MA: MIT Press.

Cole, J. (1995). *Pride and a Daily Marathon*. Cambridge, MA: MIT Press.

de Vignemont, F. (2007). Habeas corpus: The sense of ownership of one's own body. *Mind and Language*, 22(4), 427–449.

de Vignemont, F. (2017). *Mind the Body*. Oxford: Oxford University Press.

de Vignemont, F. (2020). Varieties of bodily feelings. In U. Kriegel (ed)., *The Oxford Handbook of Consciousness*. Oxford: Oxford University Press, pp. 82–101.

Dokic, J. (2003). The sense of ownership: An analogy between sensation and action. In J. Roessler and N. Eilan (eds.), *Agency and Self-Awareness: Issues in Philosophy and Psychology*. Oxford: Oxford University Press.

Dokic, J. (2010). Perceptual recognition and the feeling of presence. In B. Nanay (ed.), *Perceiving the World*. New York: Oxford University Press.

Dokic, J. and Martin, J.-R (2015). 'Looks the same but feels different': A metacognitive approach to cognitive penetrability. In A. Raftopoulos and J. Zeimbekis (eds.), *Cognitive Effects on Perception: New Philosophical Perspectives*. Oxford: Oxford University Press.

Ehrsson, H.H., Wiech, K., Weiskopf, N., Dolan, R.J., and Passingham, R.E. (2007). Threatening a rubber hand that you feel is yours elicits a cortical anxiety response. *Proceedings of the National Academy of Sciences of the United States of America*, 104(23), 9828–9833.

Ellis, H.D. and Lewis, M.B. (2001). Capgras delusion: A window on face recognition. *Trends in Cognitive Sciences*, 5(4), 149–156.

Ellis, H.D., Young, A.W., Quayle, A.H., and De Pauw, K.W. (1997). Reduced autonomic responses to faces in Capgras delusion. *Proceedings of the Royal Society of London: Series B: Biological Sciences*, 264(1384), 1085–1092.

Feinberg, T.E., DeLuca, J., Giacino J.T., Roane, D.M., and Solms, M. (2005). Right hemisphere pathology and the self: Delusional misidentification and reduplication. In T.E. Feinberg and J.P. Keenan (eds.), *The Lost Self: Pathologies of the Brain and Identity*. New York: Oxford University Press.

Gallagher, S. and Cole, J. (1995). Body schema and body image in a deafferented subject. *Journal of Mind and Behaviour*, 16, 369–390.

Gandola, M., Invernizzi, P., Sedda, A., Ferrè, E.R., Sterzi, R., Sberna, M.,…and Bottini, G. (2012). An anatomical account of somatoparaphrenia. *Cortex*, 48(9), 1165–1178.

González-Franco, M., Peck, T. C., Rodríguez-Fornells, A., and Slater, M. (2014). A threat to a virtual hand elicits motor cortex activation. *Experimental Brain Research*, 232(3), 875–887.

Halligan, P. W., Marshall, J. C., and Wade, D. T. (1995). Unilateral somatoparaphrenia after right hemisphere stroke: a case description. *Cortex*, 31(1), 173–182.

Harcourt, E. (2008). Wittgenstein and bodily self-knowledge, *Philosophy and Phenomenological Research*, 77(2), 299–333.

Invernizzi, P., Gandola, M., Romano, D., Zapparoli, L., Bottini, G., and Paulesu, E. (2012). What is mine? Behavioral and anatomical dissociations between somatoparaphrenia and anosognosia for hemiplegia. *Behav Neurol.*, 261–2, 139–150.

Kammers, M.P., de Vignemont, F., Verhagen, L., and Dijkerman, H.C. (2009). The rubber hand illusion in action. *Neuropsychologia*, 47, 204–211.

Kammers, M.P., Kootker, J.A., Hogendoorn, H., and Dijkerman, H.C. (2010). How many motoric body representations can we grasp? *Exp Brain Res.*, 202(1), 203–212.

Klein, C. (2015). *When the Body Commands*. Cambridge, MA: The MIT Press.

Langdon, R. and Coltheart, M. (2000). The cognitive neuropsychology of delusions. *Mind and Language*, 15, 183–216.

Langdon, R., Connaughton, E., and Coltheart, M. (2014). The Fregoli delusion: A disorder of person identification and tracking. *Top Cogn Sci.*, 6(4), 615–631. doi: 10.1111/tops.12108. Epub 2014 Sep 13

Maravita, A. (2008). Spatial disorders. In S.F. Cappa, J. Abutalebi, J.F. Demonet, P.C. Fletcher, and P. Garrard (eds.), *Cognitive Neurology: A Clinical Textbook*. New York: Oxford University Press, 89–118.

Martin, M.G.F. (1992). Sight and touch. In T. Crane (ed.), *The Content of Experience*. Cambridge: Cambridge University Press, 199–201.

Martin, M.G.F. (1993). Sense modalities and spatial properties. In N. Eilan, R. McCarty, and B. Brewer (eds.), *Spatial Representations*. Oxford: Oxford University Press.

Martin, M.G.F. (1995). Bodily awareness: A sense of ownership. In J.L. Bermúdez, T. Marcel, and N. Eilan (eds.), *The Body and the Self*. Cambridge, MA: MIT Press.

Matthen, M. P. (2005). *Seeing, Doing, and Knowing: A Philosophical Theory of Sense Perception*. Oxford: Oxford University Press.

McDowell, J. (2011). Anscombe on bodily self-knowledge. In A. Ford, J. Hornsby, and F. Stoutland (eds.), *Essays on Anscombe's Intention*. Cambridge MA: MIT Press.

Melzack, R. (1990). Phantom limbs and the concept of a neuromatrix. *Trends in Neuroscience*, 13(3), 88–92.

Mitchell, S. W. (1871). Phantom limbs. *Lippincott's Magazine of Popular Literature and Science*, 8, 563–569.

Moro, V., Zampini, M., and Aglioti, S.M. (2004). Changes in spatial position of hands modify tactile extinction but not disownership of contralesional hand in two right brain-damaged patients. *Neurocase*, 10–6, 437–443.

Mylopoulos, M. (2015). Agentive awareness is not sensory awareness. *Philosophical Studies*, 172(3), 761–780.

Newport, R. and Gilpin, H.R. (2011). Multisensory disintegration and the disappearing hand trick. *Curr. Biol.*, 21(19), R804–R805.

Noë, A. (2005). Real presence. *Philosophical Topics*, 33, 235–64.

Peacocke, C. (2014). *The Mirror of the World: Subjects, Consciousness, and Self-Consciousness*. Oxford: Oxford University Press.

Peacocke, C. (2015). Perception and the first person. In M. Matthen (ed.), *The Oxford Handbook of the Philosophy of Perception*. Oxford: Oxford University Press.

Peacocke, C. (2017). Philosophical reflections on the first person. In F. de Vignemont and A. Alsmith (eds.), *The Subject's Matter: Self-Consciousness and the Body*. Cambridge, MA: MIT Press.

Rahmanovic, A., Barnier, A. J., Cox, R. E., Langdon, R. A., and Coltheart, M. (2012). "That's not my arm": A hypnotic analogue of somatoparaphrenia. *Cognitive Neuropsychiatry*, 17(1), 36–63.

Romano, D., Gandola, M., Bottini, G., and Maravita, A. (2014). Arousal responses to noxious stimuli in somatoparaphrenia and anosognosia: Clues to body awareness. *Brain*, 137(Pt 4), 1213–1223.

Romano, D., Sedda, A., Brugger, P., and Bottini, G. (2015). Body ownership: When feeling and knowing diverge. *Consciousness and Cognition*, 34, 140–148.

Shoemaker, S. (1968). Self-reference and self-awareness. *The Journal of Philosophy*, 65, 555–567.

Tappolet, C. (2016). *Emotions, Values and Agency*. Oxford: Oxford University Press.

Vallar, G. and Ronchi, R. (2009). Somatoparaphrenia: A body delusion. A review of the neuropsychological literature. *Experimental Brain Research*, 192(3), 533–551.

13

Emotions of Mineness

Richard Dub

1. Introduction

When I raise my arm, it feels to me that I am the one raising my arm. When my arm is raised by someone else, the experience is different. The first motion but not the second is imbued with something like a feeling of intent, often referred to as the sense of agency or the sense of authorship. A related feeling is the sense of bodily ownership. My arm feels different to me than your arm or a prosthesis does. It feels to me that it is mine; it feels within the boundaries of my person.

Each of these feelings constitutes a form of self-awareness. An experience of agency represents an action as mine; an experience of ownership represents a body part as mine. Together, feelings of agency and feelings of ownership are what I will call *feelings of mineness*.[1]

Feelings of mineness are mysterious, having been the subject of many competing claims about their mechanisms, their structure, their function, and their place within a taxonomy of mental phenomena. I propose to investigate a hypothesis about where they fit into such a taxonomy. Might feelings of mineness be *emotions*?

It's an intriguing idea, floated a number of times in passing but never addressed in much detail. In the psychologist Dan Wegner's influential work on the feeling of conscious will (2002), he refers to an "emotion of agency," but he does not defend his word choice and he does not place the experience anywhere within a general theory of the emotions. Other authors have claimed that mineness is closely connected to affectivity, but the exact nature of the relationship is not always made explicit, and rarely do authors so baldly state that feelings of mineness are emotions. I shall state it baldly. Feelings of mineness are emotions, to be slotted alongside anger, fear, envy, and pride.

---

[1] The term 'feelings of mineness' is used in different ways by different authors. I don't intend for my term to refer to the subjective character of all conscious experience, as some do (see Salje and Geddes, and McClelland in this volume for discussion). My intended notion is best clarified by following the theory as it is developed throughout the chapter. Although feelings of authorship and feelings of ownership are regularly discussed together, some readers might find it odd that I classify them as members of a common category. I justify this decision in section 4.

Richard Dub, *Emotions of Mineness* In: *Self-Experience: Essays on Inner Awareness*. Edited by: Manuel García-Carpintero and Marie Guillot, Oxford University Press. © Richard Dub 2023. DOI: 10.1093/oso/9780198805397.003.0013

The defense has three main parts. In section 2, I present an overview of emotion theory, detailing what the intentional structure and functional role of feelings of mineness would have to be like in order for them to be emotions, and arguing that they fit quite well in existing theory. In section 3, I present what I take to be one of the best pieces of evidence for the thesis: the existence of delusions of mineness. Finally, in section 4, I address an outstanding criticism: emotions are typically taken to be necessarily evaluative, intimately linked to value and valence, but feelings of mineness are not obviously evaluative. I offer a number of possible responses by considering the representational structure of feelings of mineness in more detail.

1.1. Evidence for Feelings of Mineness

Before embarking, it is worth motivating the topic by considering the sources of evidence that we have for feelings of mineness. Why do we think that there are feelings of mineness in the first place?

Researchers draw from at least three major sources. The first is subjective phenomenology and personal introspection. Feelings of mineness are not unfamiliar. Moving your arm feels different than having your arm moved; your arm feels different to you than my arm does. Something must be posited in order to explain this difference in subjective experience.

Secondly, experimental manipulations allow us to generate artificially-induced feelings of mineness, such as in the Rubber Hand Illusion (Botvinick and Cohen, 1998). In this illusion, a participant sees a rubber hand being stroked while their own hand, hidden from view, is simultaneously stroked. The participant comes to feel that the rubber hand is their own. This feeling can occur even though the participant judges and knows that the rubber hand is in fact not their own, suggesting a distinction to be made between the feeling of bodily ownership and the judgment of bodily ownership. Illusory feelings of agency can be established through similar manipulations (Wegner, Sparrow, and Winerman, 2004).

Finally, a number of psychopathologies seem to involve aberrant feelings of mineness. A person might feel her arm is not her own. Another might feel he is not in control of his body. In more extreme cases, delusional judgments are formed. A person in the grip of a delusional episode might assert that her mother's arm is attached to her body, or that she is being controlled by evil forces. Consider the following three delusional syndromes that we might call *delusions of alienation*:

Alien Control: the subject claims of his or her actions that they are those of someone else.

Somatoparaphrenia: the subject claims of his or her body part that it is that of someone else.

Thought Insertion: the subject claims of his or her thoughts that they are those of someone else.

In these cases, something that belongs to the delusional individual (in some sense) is repudiated and attributed to an outsider. Explanations of these delusions usually posit a feeling of agency or ownership that has gone awry in some way.

Altogether, the evidence compels inquiry. Feelings of mineness demand further investigation.

2. Emotion Theory

If feelings of mineness are emotions, what must they be like? This question cannot be answered independently of a theory about what emotions are, and every theory is contentious.

Yet, there is consensus on some points. One relatively agreed-upon fact is that emotional processes are *multicomponent phenomena*, made up of various constituent processes (Sander, 2013). Philosophers and affective scientists disagree on the precise component processes that are necessary for a mental event to be an emotion. Some focus on the intentional structure and experiential character of the feeling of an emotion, others on the elicitation conditions, and others on bodily responses and action tendencies. I'll consider these three sorts of component—emotional feeling, emotion elicitation, and emotional response—in turn.

2.1. The Intentional Structure of Emotional Feelings

Emotions are mental episodes. They differ from moods in that they have specific intentional objects. While moods such as grumpiness are generalized and have no particular object, emotions are directed. I can be sad that I've lost a job, happy in my success, or scared of an approaching figure. Different types of emotion take different types of entities as permissible targets. Some emotions take propositions as their objects; others take individuals.

In addition to having intentional objects, emotions have formal objects (Kenny, 1963).[2] The formal object of an emotion is the property that the emotion represents the intentional object as exemplifying. For instance, the formal object of fear is dangerousness. To be scared of a bull is to affectively represent the bull as

---

[2] Psychologists use the terms 'core relational theme' or 'molar appraisal' to designate formal objects.

dangerous. Different emotion types have different formal objects. To be sad about something is to represent it as a loss; to be angry about something is to represent it as obstructive or offensive; to be ashamed about something is to represent it as degrading. Formal objects of emotions are the properties that emotions are designed to track, and they are how emotions portray the world (Deonna and Teroni, 2012). If the intentional object of one's emotion does not exemplify the formal object—if the object of one's fear is not actually dangerous, for instance—then the emotion is *incorrect*: it has gone wrong in some way.

If feelings of mineness are emotions, they have intentional objects and formal objects. What might these be? For now, it will be enough to say that feelings of mineness represent their intentional objects as being *mine* in some way. For instance, a feeling of agency affectively represents a motion or an action as being mine (i.e. being authored by me, being caused by me, or something of that sort); a feeling of bodily ownership represents a body part as being mine (i.e. being part of me, constituting me, or something of that sort). In cases where the intentional object is not actually mine—that is, where I did not cause the action or where the body part is not my own—the feeling is incorrect. It misrepresents the world.

Much of the philosophy of emotions concerns exactly how emotions represent their intentional objects as exemplifying their formal objects. There are three main proposals. Judgment theories of emotion maintain that emotions are judgments: to feel fear is to judge that the object of one's fear is dangerous. Perceptualist theories of emotion maintain that emotions are perceptions: to feel fear is to perceive that the object of one's fear is dangerous. Finally, non-reductionist theories maintain that emotions are *sui generis* mental attitudes: to feel fear is to be in a *sui generis* mental state that represents the object of one's fear as dangerous.

Judgment theories have been historically most popular, but they are beset with problems. One major issue concerns *recalcitrant emotions*: cases where we judge that the object of an emotion does not exemplify its formal object yet we still continue to feel the emotion. I can know that the bull before me is not dangerous yet persist in being afraid of it. A second problem is that judgment theories are overly intellectualized, requiring emoters to deploy demanding conceptual resources. If fear is the judgment that something is dangerous, then anything experiencing fear deploys a concept of dangerousness. There are reasons not to want to attribute concept possession of this sort to cats, mice, or babies.

Put judgment theories to the side. The other two theories are not infected with the same problems. For the perceptualist, to experience a recalcitrant emotion is to undergo a type of illusion (Tappolet, 2012). The bull affectively looks dangerous even though I know it is not dangerous, just as in an optical illusion two lines look different lengths even though I know they are the same length. To escape the charge of being overly conceptually demanding, the perceptualist can hold that dangerousness is non-conceptually represented in perception. I see the bull, and I see it (non-conceptually) as dangerous. Non-reductionist theories do not typically hold that the formal object of an emotion is a part of the content of the emotion at all. Rather, the formal object of an emotion is part of the *attitudinal force* of the emotion (Deonna and Teroni, 2012). An analogy can be made with belief and truth. To believe a proposition is to represent it *as* true, yet doing so does not require representing truth.

Just as emotions such as fear need not conceptually represent dangerousness, feelings of mineness need not conceptually represent mineness or the self. The possibility that feelings of mineness have this sort of intentional structure is often missed, and it is common for theorists to hold that feelings of mineness are purely non-conceptual.[3] However, a distaste for conceptual representation of the self should not lead us to conclude that feelings of mineness are non-conceptual. One of the reasons to think that emotions are conceptual is that their objects can be very conceptually complex and demanding: I can be afraid of a potential fall in the stock market within the year. Something similar appears to be true for feelings of mineness—particularly in pathological cases. A person with schizophrenia might feel that she is causing the sun to move across the sky, that she is causing the car three lanes over to make a right turn, or that she is causing slight deviations in the stock market. It is difficult to see how such a feeling could be had without deploying a concept of the stock market.

These cases can't be explained as non-conceptual feelings accompanied with conceptual judgments, for one might rationally judge that one is not controlling the stock market even while continuing to feel that one is controlling it: an instance of a recalcitrant feeling. To explain why the feeling has the object it does, we will probably need to admit that the feeling itself has conceptual content. An experience of agency over stock market deviations deploys a concept of stock market deviations. Yet this does not imply the deployment of a concept of agency. The lesson here is that feelings of mineness can be conceptual without requiring a concept of the self. On a non-reductionist theory of emotion, feelings of mineness can be representational and conceptual without mineness or the self being represented at all. On a perceptualist theory, the feeling represents selfhood or mineness non-conceptually, but it might yet represent its object conceptually.

Thus, feelings of mineness appear to be adequately and fruitfully analyzed as having the intentional structure of emotions.

2.2. Appraisals and Emotion Elicitation

One of the more important components in a model of emotion is the mechanism of emotion generation. When are emotions elicited? Very low-level stimuli such

---

[3] See for instance, Synofzik et al. (2008).

296 EMOTIONS OF MINENESS

as a loud bang or a noxious smell can generate emotional responses. Yet much of the time, emotions don't map cleanly to simple perceptual stimuli. A word from a colleague can lead to pride in one context but contempt in another.

The reigning theory of emotion which accounts for the huge variety of emotional causes is *appraisal theory*. Pioneered by Arnold (1960) and Lazarus (1968) and developed by Scherer (1984, 2001), appraisal theory is premised on the idea that emotions are elicited and differentiated by a series of *cognitive appraisals* that evaluate the significance of events. When confronted with a possible object of emotional response, our minds automatically and subpersonally ask a pattern of questions about it. Such questions include: Is this relevant to my goals or values? What is the probability that it will be relevant? Does it obstruct or aid my goals or values? Do I have the power to change it or cope with it? The pattern of answers to these "appraisal checks" determines the sort of emotion that is elicited.

While there is convergence on the general assumptions underlying appraisal theory, there continues to be debate on the particulars, including the precise nature and sequence of these appraisal checks, and whether there is a dedicated module or neurological structure that implements appraisal processes.[4] Nonetheless, certain appraisal criteria find their way into most of these models, including goal relevance, coping potential, and novelty. Also included in most models is an *appraisal of agency* (Roseman, 1984, 2001; Smith and Ellsworth, 1985). This appraisal considers whether the self, another agent, or no agent at all is causally responsible for the intentional object under consideration. The appraisal of agency is posited because it is difficult to explain how certain emotions are cognitively distinguished from one without an evaluation of personal involvement. Pride, guilt, and regret seem constitutively linked with perceived self-agency, while envy and contempt are linked to perceived causation by others (Roseman, 2009).

While the appraisal of agency is used in eliciting many different types of emotions, it would obviously be highly relevant to the elicitation conditions of a feeling of agency. Appraisal theories thus appear to have the resources to accommodate feelings of agency being an output of the appraisal process.

The claim that feelings of agency are generated through appraisal processing might seem to be at odds with standard accounts of how the feeling of agency is elicited. According to a popular neurocomputational model of motor action, the feelings of agency that attend to bodily movements are the products of computational mechanisms that generate motor action. This is the comparator model of Frith, Blakemore, and Wolpert (2000). On this model, a mechanism known as the inverse model generates fine-grained motor commands in order to satisfy a goal. A copy of these commands is sent to motor systems to be executed, while a

---

[4] Sander et al. (2003) implicate the amygdala.

second copy, known as the efference copy, is sent to a mechanism known as the forward model, which predicts what the state of the body will be when these commands are executed. Comparisons are made between this prediction and the perception of the bodily state that actually results from the motor action. A feeling of agency results if there is a match (Bayne and Pacherie, 2007; Pacherie, 2008; Wu, this volume).

While this seems like a very different story than one based upon an appraisal of agency, the two do not conflict. Comparisons made by the forward model can be a cause of agentive phenomenology without being a proximate cause. I propose that the information outputted by comparator mechanisms is used as a source of information and evidence about agentive control by downstream appraisal processes. Appraisals depend upon information from many different mental states and processes. The appraisal of agency must be based on information from somewhere, and comparator mechanisms are a rich source of reliable information in making this evaluation. It makes sense that they would be called upon.

It is these appraisal processes that determine agentive phenomenology. This interpretation is preferable to one in which the comparator mechanisms are a proximate cause of feelings of agency. Firstly, as Synofzik et al. (2008) write, "there are many cases where the comparator output is neither a sufficient nor a necessary condition" (p. 226). Mylopoulos (2012) presents a number of cases where the comparator model does not accurately predict agentive phenomenology. If the outputs of the forward model are only one source of information for the appraisal of agency, they can be outweighed by other sources of information that disagree, perhaps by strong beliefs about one's own actions or by self-narratives (Stephens and Graham, 2000).

Secondly, the feeling of agency can be directed toward external events, such as the movement of the sun, as well as internal events that are not motoric, such as one's thought processes. The comparator model is a poor fit for these feelings of agency. If feelings of agency are generated by appraisals, appraisal processes can rely on other sources when information from the comparator is unavailable. Therefore, there can be a unified explanation for the feeling of agency across all such cases without dismissing the contribution that comparator mechanisms make in motoric cases.

A general lesson we can draw is that many cognitive models of feelings of mineness can be reinterpreted as upstream mechanisms which output information that is used by downstream appraisal mechanisms. These appraisal mechanisms generate feelings of mineness.[5]

---

[5] I have said less about feelings of ownership in this section. The appraisals that elicit feelings of ownership are less clear, and this is partly because it is less clear what their formal object is. I return to this question in section 4. For now, it is enough to say that feelings of ownership, if emotions, are elicited by appraisal mechanisms.

2.3. Emotional Response

We've considered the intentional structure of emotions and the causal conditions that give rise to emotions. Let's now turn our attention to the effects that emotions have upon us.

Different sorts of emotion generate different bodily changes. We tense in anger; we jump in surprise; we shrink in fear. Bodily alterations associated with emotion include autonomic changes, hormonal changes, musculoskeletal changes such as changes in posture, reflex behaviors, as well as facial, vocal, and gestural expressions. At least *prima facie*, feelings of mineness appear to be impoverished in their bodily effects of this sort. If feelings of mineness are correlated with dedicated facial expressions, these expressions have gone heretofore unnoticed. We should not hope that any discoveries of this sort will be forthcoming.

To what extent, then, are bodily effects necessary of emotion? A number of influential research traditions place great importance on bodily change. For instance, Ekman (1972) hypothesized that basic emotions are linked to "affect programs," which produce a suite of autonomic responses and emotion-specific expressions. A separate tradition stemming from William James holds that emotions are perceptions of bodily change. Neo-Jamesians such as Damasio (1994) and Prinz (2004) hold guard on this line.

While some basic emotion types might be easily associated with particular patterns of bodily response,[6] many emotion theorists tend to be more profligate in the emotions types that they countenance. Admiration, intellectual interest, and aesthetic appreciation are harder to typify in terms of overt bodily change (Solomon, 1976). Prinz argues that even these sorts of emotion co-occur with subtle bodily alterations such as changes in skin conductance, and he cites evidence that brain areas associated with bodily response are activated during these emotional episodes (2005, p. 13). It is not obvious that feelings of mineness don't generate low-level bodily responses of this sort, and there is some evidence that they in fact do (Moseley et al., 2008). Future research might bear out that feelings of mineness are correlated with bodily reactions no less subtle than those of other emotions.

In any event, making this case is not crucial to determining whether feelings of mineness are emotions. Affect program theories and neo-Jamesian theories propose that emotions are correlated with particular patterns of bodily response, but the quest for such patterns has been replete with problems (Reisenzein, 2000; Russell, 2009). In opposition to affect program and neo-Jamesian theories, competing theories such as component processing models do not make stringent demands upon bodily expression and effect (Sander 2013). When emotional

---

[6] Although this too is contested; see Russell (2009).

responses are not bodily, they are *mental*. Emotions change the structure of our desires, motivations, and intentions (Clore, 1994; Frijda, 2009; Tappolet, 2010). They fix attention (Vuilleumier, 2005). And they affect our beliefs and cognitions.

This last fact leads to what I take to be the most powerful piece of support for the emotional status of feelings of mineness. Pathological feelings of mineness have the capacity to generate *delusions*. This, I will argue, is strong evidence for their affective nature. Although feelings of mineness do not appear to generate particular and dedicated patterns of bodily change, this is not a necessary criterion of emotionhood. Feelings of mineness generate mental changes, impinging upon our cognition in a way that is characteristic of emotional response. I take up this line of argument at more length in the next section.

3. Delusions and Mineness

In order to continue this argument, I must step back and defend a particular model of delusion formation: an affective model of delusion formation. This model was proposed by McLaughlin (2009) and is endorsed and developed by Dub (2017).

Delusions are powerful convictions, typically with bizarre content, that are held despite overwhelming evidence to the contrary. They are a first-rank positive symptom of schizophrenia, and symptomatic of other psychoses and disorders. Most models of delusion are "bottom-up" models, holding that delusions are responses to strange or anomalous feelings (Bayne and Pacherie, 2007). For instance, the Capgas delusion—the delusion that a loved one has been replaced with an imposter—forms in response to a powerful feeling of unfamiliarity.

There are two major strains of thought on how an anomalous feeling leads to the delusional conviction: one-factor theories and two-factor theories.[7] One-factor theories claim that the pathological feeling is enough to account for the generation of the delusion. Two-factor theories claim that there must be a second pathological factor involved: some sort of disorder or bias in reasoning that causes the experience to be taken at face value. After all, given one's background beliefs, it isn't rational to conclude on the basis of a feeling of unfamiliarity that one's spouse has been replaced with an imposter. So, two-factor theorists claim a pathology in reasoning must be posited.

However, two-factor theories have a problem in explaining why this pathology in reasoning doesn't manifest everywhere else. For instance, let's suppose that the pathology in reasoning under consideration is that individuals with delusions don't consider hypotheses that would conflict with their experiences. This theory

---

[7] See Maher (1974) and Davies et al. (2001), respectively.

would predict the Capgras delusion, but it would also predict that these delusional individuals would be suckered by optical illusions. They should say that a person walking across an Ames room—an illusion of perspective that makes figures at one end of a room look much larger than figures at the other end—doesn't just appear to grow in size: they genuinely do grow in size. People with delusions aren't suckered in this way. Two-factor theories have difficulties with the fact that delusions can be *monothematic*—i.e. on a single topic—with reasoning otherwise seemingly unimpaired.

This example makes clear that for either the one-factor theorist or the two-factor theorist, there must exist a certain type of experience with the power to generate delusional convictions. Perceptual experiences don't have this power.

McLaughlin's conclusion is that certain experiences, if powerful enough, are affectively overwhelming. They force themselves upon the subject's judgments in virtue of being affectively "hot." Perceptual experiences don't have this power to overwhelm: phantom limb patients don't form the delusion that they have an invisible arm because their illusory sensory experience is not of an affective sort.

This analysis appears to put delusional experience squarely in the camp of emotional experience, comporting well with the fact that psychosis is correlated with emotional dysfunction (Birchwood, 2003).[8] In fact, even traditional emotions appear to have the capacity to create delusions. Delusional jealousy, erotomania, and depressive delusions all seem to be generated at least in part by feelings of jealousy, love, and despair. More prosaically, we are prone to forming all sorts of irrational convictions on the basis of emotion. Intense road rage can cause us to think that the drivers on the road around us deserve the fruits of our fury and wrath. We don't pathologize this mental state and consider it a delusion, but it is structurally and etiologically similar. As the rage subsides, so do the thoughts of vengeance. Unlike the feelings in everyday emotional experience, the feelings at the root of delusions are pathologically constant and unusually powerful. They don't easily fade.

A further similarity between the thoughts arising out of delusional experience and emotional experience concerns a phenomenon known as 'double-bookkeeping'. This refers to a feature of delusional experience wherein an individual appears to operate from two different belief stores simultaneously (Sass, 1994; Dub, 2017). For instance, a person might say that her food is poisoned while she continues to eat it; a person with schizophrenia might make conflicting assertions, some reflecting his "delusional reality" and others reflecting "consensual reality." This bifurcated worldview can be difficult to understand until one recognizes that recalcitrant emotions double-bookkeep in a similar manner. Under the spell of road rage, I can know full well that the drivers on the road

---

[8] It should be noted that McLaughlin writes in passing that the feelings he is interested in are not emotions (p. 147), yet he doesn't offer a reason for thinking this.

around me are perfectly competent even as I simultaneously assert that they are incompetent fools.[9]

If this account is accurate, then we have good reason to think that the experiences that lead to delusions are emotions. Let us consider what this account implies about feelings of mineness by applying it to *delusions of alienation*.

3.1. Delusions of Agency and Control

In delusions of alien control, a subject claims that he or she is not in control of his or her actions, but is being puppeted around by an alien force. Frith describes individuals with these symptoms as being "no longer aware of the 'sense of effort' or the prior intention that normally accompanies a deliberate act" (1992, p. 114).

How are delusions of alien control to be explained on an affective model of delusions? The model states that an overwhelming experience explains why a delusion is so readily adopted and steadfastly defended. Therefore, a lack of an experience will not do. We must say that the person undergoing alien control has a powerful feeling of their actions *being not theirs*. This is different than the person *not feeling* their actions to be theirs. (Note that the scope of the negation is different.) The latter posits a lack of feeling; the former posits a feeling of lack. Delusional minds are not just minds minus mineness. They're minds minus mineness plus a little something more.

Individuals under delusions of alien control experience feelings of *passivity* or *alienation* from their actions. Just as I use "feelings of mineness" to cover both feelings of agency and feelings of ownership, I'll henceforth use "feelings of alienation" to cover both feelings of passivity and feelings of disownership. Much of what I say about feelings of mineness will also apply to feelings of alienation, *mutatis mutandis*. As argued in section 2.2, the lack of a feeling of agency or the judgment of missing agency might be partly causally responsible for a subsequent feeling of alienation.

Other delusions of disordered agency are founded not upon feelings of passivity, but genuine feelings of agency. In delusions of expanded agency, a person experiences agency over motions that he or she does not in fact have agency over. For instance, Torrey (2013) cites a person with schizophrenia who claimed, "I felt that I had power to determine the weather, which responded to my inner moods, and even to control the movement of the sun in relation to other astronomical bodies" (p. 27). He also describes those who experience control over the minds of others:

---

[9] In light of double-bookkeeping, some authors prefer not to think of delusions as beliefs at all. On a *non-doxasticist* account, delusions are not beliefs (Dub, 2017). Doxasticists prefer to think of delusions as partitioned beliefs. Either theory will do for my purposes.

302 EMOTIONS OF MINENESS

> A relatively common delusion is that a person can control other people's minds. One young woman I saw had spent five years at home because each time she went into the street she believed that her mind compelled other people to turn and look at her. She described the effect of her mind as "like a magnet—they have no choice but to turn and look." (p. 29)

There are multiple ways that a person can have disordered agential phenomenology. They can experience agency where they should not, they can experience passivity where they should not, or they can fail to experience either agency or alienation where they should. Only the first two lead to delusions. Cases of the third type can occur in episodes of depersonalization, in which an individual might claim that their movements feel to them as if they are not their own (Sierra, 2009, p. 146). These individuals don't form a delusion; their complaint is merely a report of their phenomenology.[10] When we attend to our actions, we often find a feeling of agency; those with depersonalization find nothing of the sort, and they describe their experience as of something missing (Billon and Kriegel, 2015).[11]

Many authors write as if a feeling of passivity is not a part of agential phenomenology. They assume there are only two possibilities: an action is imbued with a sense of agency, or it is not. For instance, Bayne and Levy (2006) consider the thesis that "minimal actions" such as pacing a room when deep in thought are not experienced as one's own actions. They respond, "[M]inimal actions sure seem like actions to us! There seems a marked phenomenological difference between feeling one's arm go up in the context of an automatic action and feeling one's arm being raised by a friend" (p. 51). The argument here relies on the assumption that the phenomenological difference can only be explained if the former bears a feeling of authorship that the latter lacks. This ignores an alternate interpretation: the former lacks a feeling that the latter bears. The latter is experienced as not one's own action.

I won't argue for this in detail, but I suspect that many of our automatic actions and perhaps even many of our willed actions lack agential phenomenology. I experience feelings of agency when I attend to my actions or when an action being mine is appraised as relevant, but most of the time I don't experience

---

[10] Blunted affect is a symptom of depersonalization, providing further evidence that feelings of mineness are emotions. A generalized loss of emotion can result in a loss of felt agency.

[11] The Cotard delusion—the delusion that one is dead or does not exist—is usually claimed to be an extreme and delusional form of depersonalization. I reject this interpretation. On my account, the Cotard delusion arises from a powerful feeling, whereas depersonalization consists in a lack of feeling. However, depersonalization and Cotard syndrome are causally linked in that a missing feeling of mineness can bring about feelings of alienation. A potential problem with this interpretation is that individuals with the Cotard delusion explicitly describe their experience as of something missing, not something added. However, the difference between a lack of a feeling and a feeling of a lack is conceptually sophisticated and difficult to phenomenally identify and describe. We should not read too much into particular word choices. Moreover, Cotard patients *do* lack something: regular and expected feelings of mineness. Their reports of a lack in experience are not inaccurate.

actions as either agential or non-agential. (This fits well with an affective interpretation of feelings of mineness. My not being sad about something does not imply that I am happy about it or that I experience any other emotions toward it at all.) Arguments for the ubiquity of agential phenomenology often have the form of Bayne and Levy's argument. These arguments are unsuccessful, as they ignore the contribution to phenomenology made by feelings of passivity.

3.2. Somatoparaphrenia and Delusions of Bodily Ownership

Asomatognosia is a condition characterized by loss of awareness of a part of one's body, typically a paralyzed limb. This unawareness is manifested in patterns of neglect toward the body part or an inability to recognize it. Occasionally, a person with asomatognosia develops a delusion known as somatoparaphrenia, in which the person denies that the body part is their own and claims that it belongs to someone else, such as their mother or a doctor (Feinberg and Venneri, 2014). As in delusions of control, somatoparaphrenia involves a feeling of alienation: a feeling of disownership. The patient feels that the body part is not theirs, and this generates a delusion that the body part is not theirs.

Many authors, such as Romano et al. (2015), write that patients with somatoparaphrenia lack a feeling of ownership. De Vignemont (2011, 2014), on the other hand, is very cognizant of the fact that there is a distinction between a lack of a feeling of ownership and a feeling of disownership, arguing that patients with somatoparaphrenia experience feelings of disownership that are the causal result of disordered feelings of ownership.

Are there cases analogous to delusions of expanded agency? That is, are there cases where a person feels pathologically powerful ownership over external items and then forms a delusion that these items are in fact parts of their body?

If there are, they are difficult to find. One place to look might be in the literature on hoarding. Some people place such value upon whatever possession they fix their attention on that it renders them unable to throw the object away without great discomfort and pain (Steketee and Frost, 2010). These individuals are apt to talk their belongings being "a part of them." Such talk might be merely metaphorical, but certain cases are hard to explain away as poetic. Grisham and Barlow present a hoarder giving an idiosyncratic reason for refusing to throw away used band-aids: "These used band-aids are a part of me because they contain my blood" (2005, p. 48). This is very likely a confabulated and *post hoc* explanation on the part of the hoarder, but it's hard to see why he or she would offer this as a reason unless he or she delusionally judged them to be a part of him or her.

The rarity or possible nonexistence of delusions of expanded bodily ownership suggests that sensory or proprioceptive information is important, if not crucial, to the appraisal process leading to a feeling of bodily ownership. Only body parts

3.3. Thought Insertion

People beset with delusions of thought insertion claim that their thoughts are inserted into their minds by others. A prominent explanation for this delusion appeals to the comparator model of the feeling of agency. Thinking is conceived of as a kind of motor process; a loss of felt agency over one's thoughts is produced in a way analogous to how a loss of felt agency over one's bodily movements is generated (Campbell, 1999).

However, it is increasingly popular to hold that delusions of thought insertion result not from a disordered sense of agency over one's thoughts, but from a disordered sense of ownership (Bortolotti and Broome, 2009; Pickard, 2010; Fernandez, 2010; Martin and Pacherie, 2013). One reason to prefer this interpretation becomes evident when comparing delusions of thought insertion with delusions of influenced thinking or thought control (Bortolotti and Broome, 2009, p. 220). In thought insertion, an individual claims that someone else's thoughts have been placed into her mind; in influenced thinking, an individual claims that someone else is forcing her to think about certain things, but the thoughts are still her own. Ownership is disrupted in the former delusion but not the latter.

Whether a distorted feeling of agency or a distorted feeling of ownership is held responsible, theories of thought insertion are usually hypothesized to involve something missing from the experience of the person suffering from thought insertion delusions. The affective model of delusion formation demands that patients be experiencing a feeling of alienation of some sort: either a feeling of passivity or a feeling of disownership. Zahavi and Kriegel (2015) consider this possibility:

> [T]he difference between thought insertion patients and healthy subjects may pertain not to an element in the experience of the latter missing from that of the former, but on the contrary to a new, additional element in the experience of the former that is absent in the latter. For example, thought insertion patients may simply have a phenomenology of alienation from (some of) their own thoughts that healthy subjects do not experience. (pp. 43–4)

In contrast, obsessive thoughts or everyday unbidden thoughts might be thoughts that are accompanied with a feeling of agency but without either a feeling of ownership or of disownership (Billon, 2013).

Thought insertion is not the only sort of mental insertion. Pickard (2010) points out that other impulses and emotions can be experienced as inserted. On the affective model, these are simply other intentional objects of an emotion of alienation. To feel that an emotion is not one's own is to have a higher-order emotion of alienation about it. Many different mental episodes can be the objects of feelings of mineness or feelings of alienation.

To summarize the chapter thus far: feelings of mineness have the structure of emotions. They are accommodated by appraisal theory. And they have mental effects of emotional experience in that they directly result in judgments, including delusional judgments. Given this evidence, it seems quite plausible that they are emotions.

There is, however, a final outstanding problem with this claim. Feelings of mineness and alienation are not obviously valenced or evaluative. This is often taken to be criterial of emotion. How should one respond to this complaint?

4. Evaluation and Formal Objects

Valence is a key notion in the literature on the emotions, but it is also a contentious notion. Some psychologists define valence in terms of the intrinsic pleasantness or unpleasantness of a feeling. Others hold that valence should be defined in terms of the action tendencies produced by the emotion: positive emotions dispose one to approach, and negative emotions dispose one to avoid. These definitions have fairly striking counterexamples. Anger is a prototypically negative emotion, but anger can feel good and send one into a fight pattern, which is a form of approach.

A better conception has to do with how emotions evaluate the world. Emotions represent their objects as instantiating values. They have value properties as their formal objects. Positive emotions represent their objects as good in some particular sort of way; negative emotions represent their objects as bad in some particular sort of way. Fear has dangerousness as its formal object—it represents its intentional object as dangerous—and being dangerous is a way of being bad (Deonna and Teroni, 2012).

On the face of it, feelings of mineness do not have evaluative formal objects. Arguably, feelings of agency represent their objects as being caused by me or intended by me; feelings of ownership represent their objects as being a part of me or constituting me. These properties seem descriptive, not evaluative. Sometimes it is good that something is caused by me, and sometimes it is bad that something is caused by me, but if one of these is so, it depends upon further facts. Being-caused-by-me is, *prima facie*, not positive in itself nor is it negative in itself.

To determine whether feelings of mineness and alienation are emotions, we need to consider their formal objects in closer detail. At this point, it is necessary to address a potential concern. Why am I lumping feelings of ownership and feelings of authorship together? The two appear to have distinct formal objects. In what sense are they subtypes of a supertype?

My answer is twofold. Firstly, I am open to the possibility that they are distinct emotions with distinct formal objects. Feelings of authorship and feelings of ownership are often discussed together, and both can be analyzed as emotions. By presenting both feelings together, I'm killing two birds with one stone. That said, perhaps it will turn out that one is an emotion and the other is not. I'm open to that empirical possibility.

Secondly, and more controversially, I think it is an open question whether the two feelings really are distinct in type. Feelings of agency and feelings of ownership differ in the sorts of intentional object they take. We feel that we own *things* in the world (such as body parts); we feel that we have agency over *events* in the world (such as actions). Feeling a thing in the world as mine is phenomenologically different than feeling an action in the world as mine, but this difference can be explained at the level of content, not attitude type. Being scared of a barking dog feels different than being scared of your credit card being declined, but this felt difference doesn't imply that two different emotion types are in play.

A standard argument for feelings of ownership and feelings of agency being distinct presumes that it is possible to have a feeling of ownership but lack a feeling of agency (or vice versa) toward one and the same intentional object (Marcel, 2003, pp. 75–6). Gallagher and Zahavi (2007) give a nice example:

> It is possible to experience myself moving and to have a sense of ownership for it, and thus say that it is my movement, but have no sense of agency for the movement, for example in normal reflex or in involuntary movements. If someone is moving my arm, or the doctor is knocking my knee, it is clearly my body that is moving, although I am not the author of that movement.   (p. 160)

When someone moves my arm, I don't feel agency for the movement (and perhaps I feel passivity for the movement). But do I feel ownership for the movement as Zahavi and Gallagher claim? I do not think so. I feel ownership over the *arm*, but the arm is a different intentional object than the movement of the arm.

I feel that the arm is mine. I feel that it is moved: I have tactile and proprioceptive sensations of my arm moving. And in addition to these feelings, I judge the arm is mine and that it is moved. Those facts are enough to account for my being able to say that the movement is mine, and enough to account for what Zahavi and Gallagher take to be "the sense of ownership" for the movement. What would the phenomenological difference be between the case where all the above are held true and I feel ownership over movement, and the case where all the above are held true and I don't feel ownership over the movement? I can't imagine one. I see no phenomenological role that requires us positing an additional feeling of ownership over the movement.[12]

In any event, even if feelings of agency and feelings of authorship take different types of intentional object, this is not enough to establish that they are the same emotion. An important requirement would be that they share the same formal object. So: what are the formal objects of feelings of agency and feelings of ownership? How do they represent their objects?

I take this to be an unsettled question. Rather than stumping for a particular answer, I will offer a menu of four possible answers, each of which I take to be a contender: mineness is an evaluative property; mineness is not evaluative but mineness is not the formal object of the feeling of mineness; feelings of mineness are non-evaluative emotions; feelings of mineness are not emotions but are psychologically similar. I'll consider each in turn.

The first possibility is that mineness is an evaluative property. It is notable that the terms 'authorship' and 'ownership' in ordinary English do not obviously refer to descriptive properties. Owners own houses, cars, intellectual property, and so on. This notion of property ownership depends upon a system of norms and social regulations that assign rights and responsibilities. Similarly, authors author books, plays, pieces of music, and so on. Contributing to the creation of these objects is not enough to be considered an author: works that involve the labor of many individuals make this clear (VerSteeg, 1995). To claim authorhood is to establish a normative title over a work. Perhaps feelings of mineness represent their objects as *my property*, where property is grounded in normative responsibilities that I bear and rights that I am conferred.

This is not enough to establish *being-my-property* as a value in itself. We can get closer to understanding it as a value by considering a precursor of the property in the animal world: *territoriality*. Deirdre Barrett (2010) writes that, beginning in the 1960s, social ethology placed a huge emphasis on the importance of territory, and "[c]oncepts of personal property, ownership of land, and violent defense of these were explained as arising from an 'imperative' or instinct" (p. 110). This "imperative" could have been quite adequately enforced by an emotion, in much the same way that disgust causes us to adhere to an imperative to not consume toxic foods.

Barrett goes on to find it problematic for this thesis that humans have been ancestrally nomadic and non-territorial. She suggests that a territorial impulse could have arisen from a need to defend nightly campsites. This is plausible, but there is a smaller locus of territory worth defense that each of our nomadic ancestors carried from place to place: his or her own body. On the proposal I here offer,

---

[12] In the second edition of their text (2012, p. 179), Gallagher and Zahavi respond to a similar but distinct criticism by de Haan and de Bruin (2010).

308   EMOTIONS OF MINENESS

the imperative to protect property finds its origins in a phylogenetically primitive emotion of bodily protection. To experience a feeling of ownership toward an object is to represent it as *worth defending* or *requiring defense*.[13] We physically protect our bodies because of a powerful affective experience against intruders. This bodily emotion eventually extended to external objects, permitting territorial protection.[14]

It is also plausible that the emotion extended in an orthogonal direction, acquiring the ability to take *events* as intentional objects. Just as we identify with our bodies and protect them, we identify with our actions and trains of thought, and we protect them against interlopers who would stand in the way of their completion. We justify what we do and what we think partly because of an emotional urge to defend them. Herein lies the origin of the feeling of agency.

Feelings of alienation thus represent *inappropriate trespass*. The emotion represents its objects as things we should veer away from because others will find them worth protecting. This explains why subjects with somatoparaphrenia will attempt to throw their unfamiliar limbs out of bed rather than smile with amused befuddlement about having acquired a new arm. Their emotion represents the limb not simply as alien, but as something protected by another and over which they have no claim.[15]

A second possibility is that mineness is a descriptive property, but mineness might not be the formal object of feelings of mineness; the formal object might be *relevant*-mineness. The trick here is to affix an evaluative modifier on a descriptive adjective in order to create an evaluative adjective phrase describing the formal object.

This move is not unmotivated. According to most appraisal theories of emotion, a primary appraisal check determines whether the object under consideration is congruent or incongruent with one's goals, concerns, or values. This relevance detection is taken to be crucial to emotion processing by many psychologists (Sander, 2013, p. 22). Thus, a feeling of ownership does not simply represent, say, a limb as being part of me. It represents that limb as being a part of me and its being so as relevant to my concerns (see also Billon, this volume).

A third possibility is that mineness is a non-evaluative emotion. To take this option is to deny that emotions need be evaluative. Although it is a bromide in

---

[13] This is similar to de Vignemont's Bodyguard hypothesis (this volume).

[14] A referee informs me that the French Ideologists at the turn of the 18th century (such as Tracy in his *Traité d'Idéologie*), inspired by Locke, argued that we could get insights on the legal concept of property by studying the origin of the sense of bodily ownership.

[15] On this view, mineness is positive and alienation is negative. This means that things of mine have *pro tanto* value to me and alien things have *pro tanto* disvalue. These can be outweighed by other evaluative considerations. Danger is negative, but it is sometimes all-things-considered good for me to encounter danger (for example, if I'm being paid to deal with dangerous things, or if they give me a thrill). Also, note that this view does not imply that it is bad to have feelings of alienation, even though feelings of alienation are negative emotions.

the philosophy that emotions are evaluative and have valence, it is strikingly difficult to find an argument to this effect. Because prototypical emotions are evaluative, it seems that philosophers and psychologists have tacitly decided through induction that all emotions are evaluative. Yet there are problem cases. Surprise is standardly taken to be an emotion, but it is difficult to assign a valence; some surprises are good and some are bad. The formal object of surprise appears simply to be novelty, which is a descriptive property. The existence of surprise and the paucity of solid arguments for emotions being evaluative make it tempting to posit non-evaluative emotions.

A final possibility is that feelings of mineness are not emotions, though structurally similar to emotions in other respects. If one rejects an evaluative analysis of the formal object of feelings of mineness and yet is wedded to the idea that emotions must be evaluative, then this will be where one will land. However, taking this tack does not require rejecting the model propounded throughout the rest of this chapter. Feelings of mineness might well be caused by appraisals, generate cognitions and judgments in a way that is nearly unique to the emotions, etc., even though they are barred from entering the pantheon of emotionhood for failure to meet a criterion. Taxonimizing feelings of mineness is less crucial than determining their intentional structure, functional role, and place within a psychological architecture. To say that they are like emotions in all respects but one is progress nonetheless.

5. Conclusion

In these pages, I have defended the thesis that feelings of mineness and feelings of alienation are emotions. Feelings of mineness slide easily into existing emotion theory, having the intentional structure, the elicitation mechanisms, and the cognitive effects of other emotions. And we must understand them as affectively "hot" in order to explain how they are able to generate delusions. We thus have good reasons to postulate that they are emotions. The only worrying difference between feelings of mineness and other emotions is that feelings of mineness are not obviously valenced. I have given an array of responses. Which is correct will be determined by further investigation.

References

Arnold, M. B. (1960), *Emotion and Personality*, Vol. 1: *Psychological Aspects*, Columbia University Press.

Barrett, D. (2010), *Supernormal Stimuli: How Primal Urges Overran Their Evolutionary Purpose*, W. W. Norton.

310 EMOTIONS OF MINENESS

Bayne, T. J. and Levy, N. (2006), The feeling of doing: Deconstructing the phenomenology of agency, in N. Sebanz and W. Prinz, eds, *Disorders of Volition*, MIT Press.

Bayne, T. and Pacherie, E. (2007), Narrators and comparators: The architecture of agentive self-awareness, *Synthese* 159(3), 475–491.

Billon, A. (2013), Does consciousness entail subjectivity? The puzzle of thought insertion. *Philosophical Psychology* 26(2), 291–314.

Billon, A. and Kriegel, U. (2015), Jaspers' dilemma: The psychopathological challenge to subjectivity theories of consciousness, in R. Gennaro, ed., *Disturbed Consciousness*, MIT Press, pp. 29–54.

Birchwood, M. (2003), Pathways to emotional dysfunction in first-episode psychosis, *The British Journal of Psychiatry* 182(5), 373–375.

Bortolotti, L. and Broome, M. (2009), A role for ownership and authorship in the analysis of thought insertion, *Phenomenology and the Cognitive Sciences* 8(2), 205–224.

Botvinick, M. and Cohen, J. (1998), Rubber hands "feel" touch that eyes see, *Nature* 391(6669), 756–756.

Campbell, J. (1999), Schizophrenia, the space of reasons and thinking as a motor process, *The Monist* 82(4), 609–625.

Clore, G. (1994), Why emotions are felt, in *The Nature of Emotion*, Oxford University Press, pp. 103–11.

Damasio, A. (1994), *Descartes' Error: Emotion, Reason and the Human Mind*, Putnam.

Davies, M., Coltheart, M., Langdon, R., and Breen, N. (2001), Monothematic delusions: Toward a two-factor account, *Philosophy, Psychiatry, & Psychology* 8(2–3), 133–158.

de Haan, S. and de Bruin, L. (2010), Reconstructing the minimal self, or how to make sense of agency and ownership, *Phenomenology and the Cognitive Sciences* 9(3), 373–396.

de Vignemont, F. (2011), Embodiment, ownership and disownership, *Consciousness and Cognition* 20(1), 82–93.

de Vignemont, F. (2014), Pain and bodily care: Whose body matters? *Australasian Journal of Philosophy* 93(3), 542–560.

Deonna, J. and Teroni, F. (2012), *The Emotions: A Philosophical Introduction*, Routledge.

Dub, R. (2017), Delusions, acceptances, and cognitive feelings, *Philosophy and Phenomenological Research* 94(1), 27–60.

Ekman, P. (1972), Universals and cultural differences in facial expressions of emotions, in *Nebraska Symposium on Motivation, 1971*, University of Nebraska Press.

Feinberg, T. E. and Venneri, A. (2014), Somatoparaphrenia: Evolving theories and concepts, *Cortex* 61, 74–80.

Fernandez, J. (2010), Thought insertion and self-knowledge, *Mind and Language* 25(1), 66–88.

CONCLUSION 311

Frijda, N. (2009), Action tendencies, in D. Sander and K. R. Scherer, eds, *The Oxford Com-panion to Emotion and the Affective Sciences*, Oxford University Press, pp. 1–2.

Frith, C. D. (1992), *The Cognitive Neuropsychology of Schizophrenia*, The Psychology Press.

Frith, C. D., Blakemore, S.-J., and Wolpert, D. M. (2000), Abnormalities in the awareness and control of action, *Philosophical Transactions of the Royal Society B: Biological Sciences* 355(1404), 1771–1788.

Gallagher, S. and Zahavi, D. (2007), *The Phenomenological Mind: An Introduction to Philosophy of Mind and Cognitive Science*, Routledge.

Gallagher, S. and Zahavi, D. (2012), *The Phenomenological Mind: Second Edition*, Routledge.

Grisham, J. R. and Barlow, D. H. (2005), Compulsive hoarding: Current research and theory, *Journal of Psychopathology and Behavioral Assessment* 27(1), 45–52.

Kenny, A. (1963), *Action, Emotion and Will*, Routledge & Kegan Paul.

Lazarus, R. S. (1968), Emotions and adaptation: Conceptual and empirical relations, in W. J. Arnold, ed., *Nebraska Symposium on Motivation*, Vol. 16, University of Nebraska Press, pp. 175–266.

Maher, B. A. (1974), Delusional thinking and perceptual disorder, *Journal of Individual Psychology* 30(1), 98.

Marcel, A. J. (2003), The sense of agency: Awareness and ownership of action, in J. Roessler and N. Eilan, eds, *Agency and Self-Awareness: Issues in Philosophy and Psychology*, Clarendon Press, pp. 48–93.

Martin, J. and Pacherie, E. (2013), Out of nowhere: Thought insertion, ownership and context-integration, *Consciousness and Cognition* 22(1), 111–122.

McLaughlin, B. P. (2009), Monothematic delusions and existential feelings, in T. Bayne and J. Fernandez, eds, *Delusion and Self-Deception*, Psychology Press, pp. 139–164.

Moseley, G. L., Olthof, N., Venema, A., Don, S., Wijers, M., Gallace, A., and Spence, C. (2008), Psychologically induced cooling of a specific body part caused by the illusory ownership of an artificial counterpart, *Proceedings of the National Academy of Sciences* 105(35), 13169–13173.

Mylopoulos, M. (2012), Evaluating the case for the low-level approach to agentive awareness, *Philosophical Topics* 40(2), 103–127.

Pacherie, E. (2008), The phenomenology of action: A conceptual framework, *Cognition* 107(1), 179–217.

Pickard, H. (2010), Schizophrenia and the epistemology of self-knowledge, *European Journal of Analytic Philosophy* 6(1), 55–74.

Prinz, J. (2004), *Gut Reactions: A Perceptual Theory of Emotion*, Oxford University Press.

Prinz, J. (2005), Are emotions feelings? *Journal of Consciousness Studies* 12(8–10), 9–25.

Reisenzein, R. (2000), Exploring the strength of association between the components of emotion syndromes: The case of surprise, *Cognition and Emotion* 14, 1–38.

Romano, D., Sedda, A., Brugger, P., and Bottini, G. (2015), Body ownership: When feeling and knowing diverge, *Consciousness and Cognition* 34, 140–148.

Roseman, I. J. (1984), Cognitive determinants of emotion: A structural theory, in P. Shaver, ed., *Review of Personality & Social Psychology*, Vol. 5, Sage Publications, Inc., pp. 11–36.

Roseman, I. J. (2001), A model of appraisal in the emotion system: Integrating theory, research, and applications, in K. R. Scherer, A. Schorr, and T. Johnstone, eds, *Appraisal Processes in Emotion: Theory, Methods, Research*, Oxford University Press, pp. 68–91.

Roseman, I. J. (2009), Agency (psychological perspectives), in D. Sander and K. R. Scherer, eds, *The Oxford Companion to Emotion and the Affective Sciences*, Oxford University Press, pp. 19–21.

Russell, J. A. (2009), Emotion, core affect, and psychological construction, *Cognition and Emotion* 23(7), 1259–1283.

Sander, D. (2013), Models of emotion, in J. Armony and P. Vuilleumier, eds, *The Cambridge Handbook of Human Affective Neuroscience*, Cambridge University Press, pp. 1–53.

Sander, D., Grafman, J., and Zalla, T. (2003), The human amygdala: An evolved system for relevance detection, *Reviews in the Neurosciences* 14(4), 303–316.

Sass, L. A. (1994), *The Paradoxes of Delusion: Wittgenstein, Schreber, and the Schizophrenic Mind*, Cornell University Press.

Scherer, K. R. (1984), Emotion as a multicomponent process: A model and some cross-cultural data, *Review of Personality & Social Psychology* 5, 37–63.

Scherer, K. R. (2001), Appraisal considered as a process of multilevel sequential checking, *Appraisal Processes in Emotion: Theory, Methods, Research* 92, 120.

Sierra, M. (2009), *Depersonalization: A New Look at a Neglected Syndrome*, Cambridge University Press.

Smith, C. A. and Ellsworth, P. C. (1985), Patterns of cognitive appraisal in emotion, *Journal of Psychology & Social Psychology* 52, 813–838.

Solomon, R. C. (1976), *The Passions: Emotions and the Meaning of Life*, Doubleday.

Steketee, G. and Frost, R. (2010), *Stuff: Compulsive Hoarding and the Meaning of Things*, Houghton Mifflin Harcourt.

Stephens, G. L. and Graham, G. (2000), *When Self-Consciousness Breaks: Alien Voices and Inserted Thoughts*, MIT Press.

Synofzik, M., Vosgerau, G., and Newen, A. (2008), I move, therefore I am: A new theoretical framework to investigate agency and ownership, *Consciousness and Cognition* 17(2), 411–424.

Tappolet, C. (2010), Emotion, motivation and action: The case of fear, in P. Goldie, ed., *Oxford Handbook of Philosophy of Emotion*, Oxford University Press, pp. 325–345.

Tappolet, C. (2012), Emotions, perceptions, and emotional illusions, in C. Clotilde, ed., *Perceptual Illusions: Philosophical and Psychological Essays*, Palgrave-Macmillan, pp. 207–224.

Torrey, E. F. (2013), *Surviving Schizophrenia, 6th Edition: A Family Manual*, Harper Perennial.

VerSteeg, R. (1995), Defining author for purposes of copyright, *The American University Law Review* 45, 1323.

Vuilleumier, P. (2005), How brains beware: Neural mechanisms of emotional attention, *Trends in Cognitive Science* 9, 585–94.

Wegner, D. M. (2002), *The Illusion of Conscious Will*, MIT Press.

Wegner, D. M., Sparrow, B., and Winerman, L. (2004), Vicarious agency: Experiencing control over the movements of others, *Journal of Personality and Social Psychology* 86(6), 838.

Zahavi, D. and Kriegel, U. (2015), For-me-ness: What it is and what it is not, in D. Dahlstrom, A. Elpidorou, and W. Hopp, eds, *Philosophy of Mind and Phenomenology: Conceptual and Empirical Approaches*, Routledge, pp. 36–53.

14

What Is It Like to Lack Mineness?

Depersonalization as a Probe for the Scope, Nature, and Role of Mineness

Alexandre Billon

1. Introduction

Patients suffering from depersonalization complain of feeling detached from their body, their mental states, and actions, or even from themselves.

In this chapter, I argue that depersonalization consists in the lack of a phenomenal feature that marks my experiences as mine, which is usually called "mineness," and that the study of depersonalization constitutes a neglected yet incomparable probe to assess *empirically* the scope, role, and even the nature of mineness.

Here is how I will proceed. After describing depersonalization (§2) and arguing that it involves a lack of mineness (§3) I will confront a series of objections (§4). I will then spell out what depersonalization can teach us about the scope of mineness (§5), about its role and psychological function (§6), and even about its nature (§7).

2. Depersonalization

Depersonalization consists in a deep modification of the way things seem to a subject, or at least, if we do not want to assume that the subject's reports should be trusted at this stage, in reports of such deep modifications. Here are two characteristic examples:

> I feel some degree of 'out of it' all the time [...] I can sit looking at my foot or my hand and not feel like they are mine. This can happen when I am writing, my hand is just writing, but I'm not telling it to. It almost feels like I have died, but no one has thought to tell me. So, I'm left living in a shell that I don't recognize anymore. (Sierra, 2009, 27)

> It was as if it was not me walking, it was not me talking, as if it was not me living [...] I can look at me, I am somehow bothered by my body, as if it wasn't me, as

---

Alexandre Billon, *What Is It Like to Lack Mineness? Depersonalization as a Probe for the Scope, Nature, and Role of Mineness*
In: *Self-Experience: Essays on Inner Awareness*. Edited by: Manuel García-Carpintero and Marie Guillot, Oxford University Press.
© Alexandre Billon 2023. DOI: 10.1093/oso/9780198805397.003.0014

if I lived on the side of my body, on the side of myself if you want. I don't know how to explain.

>   (Janet and Raymond (1898, 70); translations from the French are mine)

Even though there are some mild or short-lived depersonalization-like episodes, I will focus here on the severe form of the disorder, which is usually distressing and makes the subjects seek medical help—call it "pathological depersonalization." Patients' reports are diverse and, as witnessed by the two examples above, often quite complex. They can, however, be rather precisely clustered.

Dementalization. A first cluster involves reports of feeling as if one's mental states were alienated or missing—call that "dementalization." The mental states in question are often emotions:

I have no interest in what I appear to be feeling. It is someone else who feels mechanically. (Janet, 1908, 515)

But dementalization can also affect bodily sensations such as pain:

It was not a genuine pain, it was a pain that did not reach the soul...It is a pain, if you want, but the surface of my skin is miles away from my brain, and I do not know whether I am suffering. (Janet, 1928, 65)

When a part of my body hurts, I feel so detached from the pain that it feels as if it were somebody else's pain. (Sierra and Berrios, 2000)

It can likewise affect memories or imaginings ("some complain that they have altogether lost the power of imagination" (Sierra, 2009, 25–6)), perceptual states ("My eyes see but the sensation of what I see is completely absent" (Sierra, 2009, 8)) and, more broadly, thoughts ("thoughts running through their brain [which] seem somehow foreign" (Simeon and Abugel, 2006, 26)).

Desomatization. A second cluster involves reports of feeling some bodily parts as alien or missing—call it "desomatization." An item of the Cambridge Depersonalization Scale, the gold standard for assessing depersonalization, thus reads: "Parts of my body feel as if they didn't belong to me" (Sierra and Berrios, 2000, 160).

Deagentivation. A third cluster involves reports of feeling alienated from one's actions—call it "deagentivation"—("It is not me who acts, I see myself acting...I am a puppet...I am myself surprised by the precision of the automaton" (Janet, 1908, 515)).

Death and Inexistence complaints. In the most extreme forms, patients can report feeling dead ("I don't feel alive in any way whatsoever" (Sierra, 2009, 8, 29); "a state of nothingness, no mood at all, as if I were dead" (Simeon and Abugel,

2006, 30)) or even nonexistent ("she feels like she just does not exist" (Simeon and Abugel, 2006, 8); "I doubted of my own existence and at times even disbelieved in it" (Krishaber, 1873a)). Although reports of death and inexistence are arguably connected, they should arguably be distinguished, as some patients seem to mean that they feel like they do not exist, not even in some kind of afterlife. Instead of saying that they feel as if they did not exist, patients can also say that they are not aware of themselves anymore, or that they feel as if they were not themselves *at all*. All such complaints seem, moreover, to be strictly first-personal: what the patient feels lacking or nonexistent is an I. In other words, the patient seems to be well aware that there is something walking and talking when he is, but it seems to him as though this thing that walks and talks is not something that can legitimately be referred to in the first-person singular.[1] This explains why these patients, who question their very existence, can express reluctance to use the first-person pronoun (Billon, 2017b).

Even though there are delusional forms of depersonalization, and even though the distinction between delusional and non-delusional cases might be somehow vague, patients suffering from depersonalization are often *clearly* non-delusional. In line with current conventions, I will restrict the term depersonalization to non-delusional cases.

Depersonalized patients have also been shown to display an intact executive functioning and rationality (Sedman, 1972, see also Guralnik et al., 2000, 2007). Despite their bodily complaints, their sensorimotor and interoceptive abilities have also proven perfectly normal (Cappon and Banks, 1965, Michal et al. 2014; see also Janet, 1928). Depersonalization would affect around 2% of the population.

3. Depersonalization as a Lack of Mineness

How should we understand depersonalization? Is there a simple feature that could account for the whole spectrum of depersonalized patients' complaints? It was early suggested that our experiences all come with a certain phenomenal feature in virtue of which they seem to be ours to us, and that such a feature would be lacking or altered in depersonalized patients. This phenomenal feature was diversely called "the personal mark" (Ribot, 1883), the "feeling of personality" (Janet and Raymond, 1898), the "feeling of the self" ("le sentiment du moi") (Dugas, 1898), the "feeling of oneself" or "coefficient of personality" (Dugas and Moutier, 1911), and even "emesthesis" (from the Greek "ἐμού αἴσθησις": feeling mine, Dugas, 1936). In line with the modern terminology we can call this lacking phenomenal feature "the mark of mineness" or, simply "mineness." The lack of

---

[1] Patients who are also suffering from extreme forms of derealization can however deny that anything exists.

mineness in fact quickly became definitional of depersonalization, and mineness was quickly dubbed "personalization" as witnessed for example by the following remarks of Jaspers:

> Every psychic manifestation, whether perception, bodily sensation, memory, idea, thought or feeling carries *this particular aspect of 'being mine'* of having an 'I' quality, of 'personally belonging', of it being one's own doing. This has been termed *personalisation*. If these psychic manifestations occur with the awareness of not being mine…we term them phenomena of depersonalization.
>
> (Jaspers, 1962, 121)[2]

What reason is there to suppose that depersonalized can be accounted by a lack of mineness? First, some patients seem to complain directly of a lack of a mark of mineness or of something near enough, such as a " clear feeling of 'I' " (Simeon and Abugel, 2006, 25), an "experience of a 'me'" (Simeon and Abugel, 2006, 143–4), a "feeling of myself" (Janet and Raymond, 1898, 73), or an "awareness of myself" (Krishaber (1873a, 171) and Janet (1903, 324)). Second, and more importantly, a lack of mineness can nicely explain the various aspects of depersonalization that we have isolated:

- *Dementalization* would result from mental states lacking their normal mineness and feeling accordingly alien or lacking. A lack of mineness for pains, emotions, and thoughts in general would explain why they are reported as feeling alien or even missing (if I do not feel like a given state is mine, I do not feel like I have it).[3]
- *Deagentivation* would result from and intentions-in-action lacking their normal mineness, making the actions they guide feel alien.
- *Desomatization* would result from bodily sensations lacking their normal mineness, making the bodily part "in" which they occur seem alien or even missing (see de Vignemont (2007, 2014) for a precise account of how an

---

[2] Here Jaspers is implicitly referring to the philosopher Dugas, who coined the term "depersonalization," and to Ribot, an extremely influential French philosopher and psychologist, who would come to be despised as an old-fashioned naturalist with the rise of Bergsonism. When introducing the term "personalization," Dugas and Moutier (1911) quoted the following passage from Ribot, which Jaspers merely rephrased:

> I am not talking about the reflexive awareness of oneself but of a natural and spontaneous feeling of oneself that is ubiquitous among healthy individuals. Each of my conscious states has this double aspect of being thus or thus *and of being mine*: it is not a pain but my pain, the vision of a tree but my vision of a tree. Each has its *personal mark* in virtue of which it appears to me as being proper to me, and without which it appears to me as alien.   (Ribot, 1883:169)

The term "depersonalization" is in fact borrowed from the Swiss writer Amiel, who introduced this neologism in his monumental journal, along with others such as "impersonalization," to describe his own case. From his journal, it is obvious that Amiel could receive the diagnosis of depersonalization.

[3] Given that patients can disavow cognitive states as well this explanation presupposes (or implies) that there is such a thing as cognitive phenomenology.

318 WHAT IS IT LIKE TO LACK MINENESS?

alteration of bodily sensations' mineness can lead to the feeling that some bodily parts are alien).

- *Death and nonexistence complaints* would result from a substantial and global attenuation of mineness. Such attenuation would estrange the patient from all his experiences, leading to the impression that *he* really has no experience and that he is phenomenally dead. It would ultimately even estrange him from himself, leading to the impression that he is not there, he is not himself, or that he does not exist (see Billon (2015, 2017b and below for details).

Of course, neither (i) the direct complaint of lack of "feeling of oneself" nor (ii) dementalization, desomatization, deagentivation and death, or nonexistence complaints, logically entail that depersonalization must be construed as a lack of mineness. The argument is rather abductive here.[4] It is that the best explanation of both (i) and (ii) is a (more or less severe, extended, and intense depending on the severity of depersonalization) lack of mineness. More specifically, dementalization complaints to the effect that some mental states seem alien naturally suggest a lack of mineness. A lack of mineness can also explain other dementalization complaints (to the effect that certain mental states are lacking as opposed to alien) as well as desomatization, deagentivation and death, and nonexistence complaints. And the preference for a unified explanation means that we should explain these other symptoms in terms of a lack of mineness too.

It might be objected that the fact that depersonalized patients complain that things seem to them to be so and so does not mean that it really does. But here again, given that depersonalized patients are non-delusional and (normally) rational, given, moreover, that we have no reason to suspect that they are lying or (even if they confess understandable difficulties in expressing what they feel) that they do not mean what they seem to mean, the best explanation of their complaints that things seem to them to be so and so is that they believe that they seem to them to be so and so.[5] And the best explanation of why they believe that is that things do indeed seem to them to be so and so.[6]

---

[4] I thank Tom McClelland for pressing me on that point.

[5] This is not to say that the patients' speech should always be interpreted literally and taken at face value. Patients' reports have a characteristic "as if" form: depersonalized subjects says that it is *as if* P: as if their body or their thoughts wasn't theirs, as if they were dead or inexistent... The "as if" is usually interpreted as a "mark of mere appearance," by which the patients mean that it seems to them as if P or that they have an experience as of P even though they know that P is false. It might however sometimes be a mark of approximation, indicating that "an experience as of P" only approximately or figuratively captures what they feel (see Radovic and Radovic, 2002). Patients can also explicitly use metaphors, as the patient of Janet (1928, 65) quoted earlier, who said, "the surface of my skin is miles away from my brain." I am grateful to Jan Pieter Maes for pressing me on that point.

[6] Most accounts or descriptions of depersonalization agree on the presence and centrality of these impressions. The ICD-10 for example states that "the individual [suffering from depersonalization] feels that his or her own feelings and/or experiences are detached, distant, not his or her own, lost etc."

We can thus decompose the abductive argument for the "mineness view of depersonalization" in two steps. Call the awareness of one's mental states and bodily parts as one's own, the kind of awareness that is, that underlies our judgments of ownership, the *sense of ownership*. Call the awareness of one's actions as one's own the *sense of agency*, the awareness of oneself as an 'I' (the kind of awareness that underlies our standard use of the first-person) *basic self-awareness* (Gertler, 2010), and the awareness of oneself as alive *life-awareness*. Call *self-awareness*, finally, the cluster of all these forms of awareness.

1. Patients complain of a distorted self-awareness.
2. The best explanation of why patients complain of a distorted self-awareness is that their self-awareness is indeed distorted.
3. The best explanation of this distorted self-awareness is a more or less widespread lack of mineness.[7]

I do not want to suggest that the senses of ownership and agency, or even basic self-awareness are all or nothing matters. In order to account for the diversity of patients' complaints, I believe it is better to assume, on the contrary, that they all come in degrees. The sense of ownership could thus either be merely diminished—the subject failing to be *clearly* aware of this state as his own—or fully absent—the subject failing to be aware of this mental state as his own. Mineness would accordingly come in degrees as well. We can thus account for varying severity of depersonalization not only in terms of the extension of the lack of mineness—does it concern a few or many mental states?—but also in terms of its intensity—is the mark of mineness merely diminished or is it altogether absent from the mental states to which it is lacking?

Before concluding this section, I should add a note on "mineness" and on related notions. In a recent paper, Marie Guillot (2016) has argued that mineness is often conflated with two other notions, which she calls respectively for-me-ness, me-ishness. Mineness, for-me-ness, and me-ishness are all meant to capture what she calls the "subjective character of experience," that is, the fact that the subject should figure in the description of (at least some) experiences. She notices, however, that the subject can play different roles in the description, leading to close but different notions. The subject can indeed appear variously:

- as one of the two relata in the relation of phenomenal awareness to her experiences, i.e. as the one who is appeared to;

---

[7] It should be emphasized that mineness and the sense of ownership are different. The sense of ownership is a form of *awareness*. Mineness is a *feature of experience*. Mineness can naturally explain the sense of ownership, but there are many explanations of the latter that do not appeal to phenomenal features at all, and invoke rationality (cf. e.g. Kant's *Critique of Pure Reason*, B404-6, and Strawson (1963, 97)) or cognitive states more broadly (cf. e.g. Alsmith, 2015).

- as also appearing to herself in being aware of the other relatum (the experience);
- as appearing to herself as the owner of the experience. (Guillot, 2016)

She calls for-me-ness the first way subjective character is talked about, me-ishness the second, and mineness the third. Guillot convinced me that these three notions are indeed different: they could only be equivalent under some substantial "bridging assumptions" or under some much precisified definitions. I tend to believe that the bridging assumptions linking for-me-ness and mineness are true, so that these are in fact the same thing, but I will not suppose that this is the case here.[8] I will, however, freely interpret claims about subjective character or for-me-ness as claims about mineness as well when their authors identify both notions in some places.

4. Answering Objections

I have argued that depersonalization should be explained by a (more or less intense and global) lack of sense of ownership for mental states, which should itself be explained in experiential terms, by a (more or less intense and global) lack of mineness.[9] Now, some influential objections have been addressed to the claim that other, relevantly similar, psychiatric symptoms such as thought insertion—patients complaining of having thoughts in them which are not their own—really involve a lacking sense of ownership, and, *a fortiori*, a lacking mark of mineness.

I would like to show that even if they were cogent in the case of thought insertion, which I very much doubt, none of these objections would in any case generalize to the case of depersonalization.

4.1. The Rationality Objection

The first and perhaps most famous objection against a lacking sense of ownership is perhaps Jaspers'. Jaspers believed that it is impossible to make sense of a subject who is aware of one of his thoughts without being aware that this thought is his

---

[8] I also believe that mineness involves me-ihness. Mineness is a phenomenal feature in virtue of which I am aware of an experience as mine, it is thus a phenomenal feature in virtue of which *I am aware of myself* as the owner of this experience.

[9] Remember that a lack of a sense of ownership for intentions-in-action accounts for the altered sense of agency and that a widespread lack of sense of ownership accounts for the death impression and for the impaired basic self-awareness and the related nonexistence impressions.

own.[10] So instead of taking patients suffering from thought insertion as evidence that the sense of ownership for thoughts can break down, he concluded that these patients are simply unintelligible, in the sense that it is impossible to rationalize their claims. Now, such an objection might have some degree of plausibility in the case of thought insertion, which mostly affect schizophrenic patients.[11] After all, these are delusional patients and it is notoriously hard to make sense of their claims. As we have seen, however, depersonalized patients are not delusional, their reality testing is intact, and there is ample evidence that they are just as rational as anyone, so it seems impossible to claim that they are too irrational to be made sense of. And the best way to make sense of their reports is, I have argued, to suppose that their sense of ownership and their mineness are (more or less globally and intensely) lacking.

4.2. The Agency Objection

Jaspers' rationality against a lacking sense of ownership (and mineness) in thought insertion is not extremely influential today. The following objection has, however, made it to the orthodoxy. It relies on the distinction between the sense of ownership for X and the *sense of agency* or *authorship* for X (the sense of being the agent or the author of X). According to this objection,

(i) we should not deny an intact sense of ownership for the inserted thoughts because patients would implicitly acknowledge such a sense of ownership;
(ii) and we need not do so for we can account for inserted thoughts by supposing that the subject has an intact sense of ownership but lack a sense of agency or authorship for them (Gallagher, 2000; Graham and Stephens, 2000).

Now, I am not convinced by (i) and I also doubt that this is the real motivation of advocates of the orthodox agency view of thought insertion (see Billon, 2013). In any case, it should be clear that (ii) does not generalize to the case of depersonalization. If (ii) cannot immediately be ruled out, in the case of thought insertion, it is because it is at least somehow plausible that our thoughts *normally* come with at least a certain sense of agency or authorship.[12] This allows advocates of the

---

[10] "We are not able to have any clear sight of a [conscious] psychic event without our self-awareness being involved" (Jaspers, 1913/1962: 578). See Billon (2013) and Billon and Kriegel (2015) for more on the interpretation of thought insertion.

[11] Such an objection is echoed in Coliva (2002)'s remarks on immunity to error through misidentification in thought insertion; and in Berrios (1991)'s expressivist theory of delusions.

[12] I say '*somehow* plausible' because unbidden or intrusive thoughts seem not to come with any sense of agency, and they also seem quite common (see Billon, 2013).

agency view to argue that a thought lacking such a sense of agency or authorship would seem (abnormally) alien to its subject. However, depersonalization quite commonly affects other-inflicted pains, but other-inflicted pains do not *normally* come with *any* sense of authorship or agency.[13] It is accordingly impossible to explain the sense of alienation for such pains, of which depersonalized patients complain, in terms of a lacking sense of agency or authorship. Even those who appeal to agency or authorship to deny that thought insertion genuinely involves a lack of sense of ownership should accordingly grant that depersonalization does involve such a lack anyway.

4.3. The Endorsement Objection

Partly in response to the agency view of thought insertion, some have put forward an endorsement view. The latter replaces (ii) by (ii*):

(ii*) we can account for thought insertion by supposing that the subject has an intact sense of ownership but lack a *sense of endorsement* for them (Fernández, 2010).[14]

The sense of endorsement is the sense of being committed to a thought. It is normally witnessed by various dispositions such as our disposition to provide reasons for endorsing the thought content, and to act consistently with the thought being true. Now again, even if thoughts normally came with a sense of endorsement, this would not be true of other-inflicted pains. For sure, there are ways to understand endorsement so that some pains, even if they are other-inflicted, might sometimes count as being endorsed by their subject (see Fernandez's chapter in this volume, who construes an experience as endorsed whenever it is considered fitting, merited, or appropriate). However, this is certainly not the normal case for other-inflicted pains. So there is no way a lacking sense of endorsement might explain the feeling of abnormal alienation that characterizes depersonalized pains. Just like the agency objection and for the very same reason, the endorsement objection thus fails in the case of depersonalization.

---

[13] Various approaches to the mind such as enactivism or Friston's "predictive brain" hypothesis have recently questioned the claim that there is a clear divide between action and other cognitive functions such as perception. I do not believe that they could make us entertain the least doubt with regard to the claim that my other-inflicted pain typically *feel* passive, not my own doing. If my other-inflicted pains typically came with a sense of agency, I would have to confess that I do not understand what "sense of agency" means. I thank an anonymous referee for pressing me on that point.

[14] Fernandez (2010) does not speak of the sense of ownership in our sense (see his fn. 2, p. 68), and even if it is natural, in the context of the debate, to attribute to him the lack of endorsement account summarized by (ii*), strictly speaking, what he says seems consistent with lack of ownership accounts (supposing that endorsement explains ownership) or with what I shall call later lack of ownership* accounts (supposing that endorsement explains ownership*).

4.4. The Ownership* Objection

Finally, one could grant that inserted thoughts really lack a certain sense of ownership, but argue that

- (i') there are two notions of ownership, say ownership* and ownership, and we should not deny that patients have a sense of ownership;
- (ii') we can account for thought insertion in terms of a lacking sense of ownership*.

This strategy has been adopted by Campbell (2004) who construes the sense of ownership* as the combination of the sense of ownership and the sense of agency or authorship, and by Bortolotti and Broome (2009), who construe it as a combination of the sense of ownership and of the sense of endorsement. Whatever the value of such objections against ownership views of thought insertion, they do not generalize to ownership views of depersonalization. They indeed falter on the same problem as the agency and the endorsement objections: an other-inflicted pain does not *normally* come with any sense of ownership*, so its alienation will not be explained by a lacking sense of ownership.

4.5. The Extra Disownership Objection

Wittgenstein's once said that "the existence of [the] feeling of strangeness does not give us a reason for saying that every object which we know well and which does not seem strange gives us a feeling of familiarity" (Wittgenstein, 1953, §596). With Uriah Kriegel, we have suggested elsewhere that thought insertion might be better explained by an extra sense of disownership (explained, itself, by an extra mark of alienness) rather than by a missing sense of ownership (explained itself by a missing mineness) (Billon and Kriegel, 2015). Again, this objection against the ownership view of thought insertion does not generalize to depersonalization. In the latter case, there is good enough evidence that patients *lack* a certain form of awareness and the phenomenal features underlying it, rather than that they *have an extra* awareness grounded on an extra phenomenal feature. It is that patients explicitly complain that a certain feeling or impression that they used to have is now lacking.[15] Here are a few characteristic examples:

> There was literally no more experience of 'me' at all.
>
> (Simeon and Abugel, 2006, 143–4)

---

[15] Interestingly, the great psychologist Pierre Janet coined the term "feeling of incompleteness" ("sentiment d'incomplétude") to designate the core of depersonalization's experience.

They claimed they could think clearly, and properly about everything, but the essential was *lacking* even in their thoughts.   (Sierra, 2009, 8, emphasis mine)

The functions and acts of ordinary life, it is true, still remain to me; but in every one of them there is *something lacking*. That is, the sensation which is proper to them.   (Sierra, 2009, 8)

Of course, patients could be confused or very unreliable phenomenologists. Given that we have no evidence to suppose that this is the case, however, we should by default trust them. Their testimony is evidence that depersonalization involves the lack of a normal sense of ownership and of a normal mark of mineness rather than the extra presence of a sense of disownership and of a mark of alienness.[16]

From now on, I will admit that depersonalization involves a lack of mineness and I will spell out what depersonalization can tell us about the scope, the role, and the nature of mineness.

5. The Scope of Mineness

5.1. Four Views about the Scope of Mineness

We can distinguish four theses about the scope of mineness. *Universalists* claim that all conscious states come with a mark of mineness. Gallagher (2004) and Zahavi (2008) are universalists. Although he more readily speaks of subjective character or for-meness than mineness, there is evidence that Uriah Kriegel is a universalist too (Zahavi and Kriegel, 2016). Kriegel also attributes universalism to Brentano (Billon and Kriegel, 2015).

In reaction to pathological cases, such as schizophrenia or depersonalization, which seem to involve conscious states lacking mineness, some authors have put forward a weaker claim, to the effect that at least *in non-pathological cases*, all conscious mental states come with mineness—call this claim *generalism*. After Ribot (1883), many French clinicians and philosophers espoused generalism. It was the case, in particular of Dugas (1898); Taine (1892); Dugas and Moutier (1911). Today, generalism is endorsed, for example, by Metzinger (2004, 283, 445) and Guillot (2016).

Universalists and generalists belong to a broad Cartesian tradition that sees the self as normally involved in its experiences.[17] At the other end of the spectrum,

---

[16] Despite this evidence, however, two influential psychologists of the early 20th century maintained that depersonalization involves an extra mark of alienness rather than a lacking mark of mineness: Leroy (1901) and Oesterreich (1908).

[17] See Henry (1990, I) and the references therein for an argument to the effect that Descartes indeed understood the self as phenomenally involved in its experiences. See also Billon (2013).

some believe that the self is in general absent from its experiences. Among these "Humean" philosophers, we can distinguish *existentialists*, who claim that in non-pathological cases some (but not all) mental states have a mark of mineness, and the more radical *nihilists*, who believe that no conscious states come with mineness. Lane (2015) is arguably an existentialist: he believes that mineness requires an explicit representation of the subject as the owner of its experience, and that such explicit self-representations are rare. Howell and Thompson (2016) have also recently argued that only those reflecting on experiences have mineness.[18] Finally, Schear (2009) and Dainton (2008, 242–4) have offered abductive arguments for nihilism, to the effect that what the mark of mineness is supposed to explain is in fact better explained without it (see also Salje and Geddes, this volume).[19]

Against their critics, universalists and generalists have put forward a debunking theory, explaining that the subjective character is introspectively elusive precisely because it is universal or general, and that we normally *lack the appropriate contrast cases* to make it salient (cf. e.g. Kriegel, 2009, 51–2) Dugas and Moutier, 1911, 40, and Billon, 2016).[20] In reply to Schear and Dainton's abductive arguments, they have also claimed that mineness really provides the best explanation of the targeted phenomena (Zahavi and Kriegel, 2016).

Now whatever we might think of these replies, the case of depersonalization seems to provide an independent, empirical argument against existentialists and nihilists. Patients' testimonies explicitly suggest that there is a phenomenal feature that usually goes unnoticed and that at least normally (that is in non-pathological cases) marks all our experiences as ours. As explained by Dugas and Moutier (1911:14):

Depersonalization is a disorder that can affect every mental fact, perception, memory, feeling, action, etc. therefore *every mental fact* implies personal consciousness or personalization [i.e. mineness]

Indeed the best explanation of depersonalization involves a lack of mineness for all kinds of conscious mental states. But this explanation could not be true unless all conscious states normally came with mineness. The case of depersonalization

---

[18] McClelland (this volume) also addresses the scope debate and provides further references.

[19] While the explanandum Dainton focuses on is the sense of ownership for our experiences (our awareness for our experiences as our own), the one Schear targets is the ease with which we can come to know or report our experiences. Bermúdez (2015) also puts forward an abductive argument against a mark of mineness for bodily sensations, arguing that our knowledge of our bodily properties and bodily parts as our own is better explained without a mark of mineness.

[20] As noticed by McClelland (this volume) the alleged lack of contrast is dialectically ambivalent: it explains why mineness can be overlooked, but suggests that it is very hard if not impossible to ascertain phenomenologically.

thus disconfirms nihilism and existentialism, and vindicates the theory of error put forward by the Cartesian camp.[21]

5.2. Constraints on Mineness

Zahavi and Kriegel (2016) have argued that nihilists and existentialists often put too many constraints on the way mineness should be if it exists, which would explain why they deny its existence or its generality. I believe this diagnostic is correct. Dainton (2008, 243) for example suggests that mineness should be a single, "particular sensation or feeling," that it should be simple ("a single simple form of experience"), that it should be immutable ("unmodifiable"), and even primitive ("a primitive quality of mineness"). Similarly, Lane (2015) seems to believe that mineness necessarily involves an explicit representation of the subject by himself. All these constraints are misguided. In fact, some influential univer-salists and generalists have explicitly argued:

- that mineness is a feature of experience rather than a discrete experience (see e.g. Zahavi and Kriegel, 2016);
- that it is a non-intentional feature (that is, a feature of the mode rather than the content of our experiences) and that it does not involve, thus, any repre-sentation of oneself (see e.g. Henry (1990));[22]
- that it changes over time (see e.g. Ribot, 1883 and Taine, 1892);
- that it is not primitive (see below).

In fact, when depersonalization was discovered, at the end of the 19th century, most researchers became convinced that it would allow them to develop a reductive account of mineness. Many such accounts were put forward, invoking sensory (Taine, 1892), sensorimotor (Bergson, 1896), interoceptive (Ribot, 1883), or affective capacities (Dugas, 1898).[23, 24]

---

[21] It might seem that the case of depersonalization obviously favours generalism against universal-ism. However, things are not so clear. I have argued elsewhere that some of the patients' testimonies provide at least some evidence that the phenomenality of the "depersonalized mental states" might be just as altered and diminished as their mineness (Billon, 2015). The available evidence is however still rather limited here, and exploring this line of thought further would take me beyond the scope of the present essay.

[22] Notice that claiming that mineness is non-intentional allows one to deny the first premise of McClelland (this volume) "Representational Impediment," to the effect that we need to represent our experiences as our own in order for them to appear to us as our own.

[23] Bergson (1896) provides a sensorimotor theory of what we might call the mark of the present and the mark of the real, but he supposes that the latter accounts for the sense of owning real mental states and limbs which is precisely lacking in depersonalization.

[24] In fact, many of these authors also believed, precisely like Dainton, that a conscious state feels mine when it is co-conscious with other background phenomenal states (this was the case for example of Ribot, who took the relevant background phenomenal states to be mostly interoceptive).

5.3. The Psychological Unity of the Mark of Mineness

Even if I take Dainton to be wrong in suggesting that the mark of mineness should be a single, simple, unchanging experience, I believe that there is a weaker claim that is correct, and that could support a nihilist or an existentialist argument. It is that the mark of mineness should be somehow unified. The mark of mineness being *the phenomenal feature* (singular) grounding our sense of ownership for all our experiences, it cannot exist unless the features grounding our sense of ownership for different experiences at different times have something in common, or, more broadly, are sufficiently unified to constitute a *single* phenomenal feature. I believe, however, that the case of depersonalization provides good reason to believe that the mark of mineness is relevantly unified. As we shall see, the unity of mineness arguably follows from the fact that depersonalization is itself a unified phenomenon, viz. that it is a single psychological entity.

Here is the argument from the unity of depersonalization to the unity of mineness:

1. Depersonalization is a single psychological entity: it is a single syndrome.
2. A single psychological entity should receive a unified psychological explanation. Now, the unified explanation of a psychological entity consisting in a series of disordered psychological function F1...Fn should appeal to *a single psychological factor* F, whose abnormal condition C*, explains the disorders of F1...Fn.
3. But if the abnormal condition C* of F explains the dysfunction of F1...Fn, then its normal condition C should explain their normal functioning.
4. In the case at hand (where the disorders of F1...Fn are dysfunctions of self-awareness and where F is mineness) this implies that the mark of mineness should be a *single psychological* factor.[25]

Apart from the fact that depersonalization can be explained in terms of mineness, for which I have already argued, the only substantial premise in this argument is the first one, to the effect that depersonalization is indeed a unified entity (the other premises follow, I believe, from the definition of a psychological explanation and of a single psychological entity). This premise should not be confused with the claim that depersonalization is a discrete condition that can occur on its own, as opposed to as part of another syndrome, or else with the claim that depersonalization is always a clinically significant condition. It is less controversial than these last two theses, and it is quite an orthodox claim. The only researcher I know who has questioned it is Sacco (2010). He has denied that depersonalization

[25] Jose-Luis Bermudez, who criticizes this argument (see Bermudez, 2017) has helped me sharpen it.

"is unidimensional in nature" on the grounds that (i) it can be induced by different "precipitating causes" (he cites for example epilepsy, drug use, meditation, vertigo, major life stress, self-focus, etc.); (ii) it can have different "affective implications" (some subjects having non-pathological depersonalization-like experiences find them pleasant); (iii) and an influential theory explains it in biological terms (Sierra and Berrios, 1998) while another explains it in cognitive terms (Hunter et al. 2003). However, Sacco focuses on a much wider condition than the one we have considered, wider condition that includes what he calls "normal depersonalization" (short-lived or mild sense of depersonalization-like experiences which do not lead to a significant distress), and he explicitly agrees that pathological depersonalization, on which I have focused here, has much less diverse precipitating causes and affective implications. So even if (i)–(ii) threatened the unity of the condition on which Sacco focuses, it is not clear that it would threaten the unity of depersonalization in the narrower sense used here (viz., pathological depersonalization). Moreover, in the sense in which he uses these terms, "precipitating causes" of X are just *distal* causes of X, and "affective implications" of X are the ways a subject can emotionally appraise X. Accordingly, it is quite dubious that their multiplicity is relevant to the unity of X. Consider for example a burn: it can be "precipitated" by friction, heat, chemicals, and radiation, and it can be extremely distressing or quite indifferent depending on its severity; yet there should be little doubt that it is a single medical entity. In order to show that depersonalization is disunified, Sacco would have to show that its various "precipitating causes" in fact cause different things, things whose nature should be explained differently. Now (iii) might have shown this if the two cited theories of depersonalization were both true and inconsistent with each other. I see no reason, however, to suppose that this is the case. The point of cognitive neuropsychology is precisely to unify neurophysiological and cognitive explanations and one of the leading researchers on depersonalization, Sierra, has in fact contributed to both theories and put forward, along with David, a *neurocognitive* theory of depersonalization (Sierra and David (2011)). Finally, there are positive reasons to think that depersonalization is psychologically unified. The usefulness of the concept of depersonalization in the clinical practice is one. Another one is, for example, the success of the neuropsychological model of depersonalization put forward by Sierra and David (2011).

6. The Role of Mineness

6.1. Epiphenomenal Mineness?

As we have seen, some philosophers have argued against the existence of mineness on the ground that it would not optimally explain the features of our self-knowledge

THE ROLE OF MINENESS   329

that it has been claimed to explain. In particular, while Kriegel and Zahavi have both argued that mineness—or "subjectivity"—provides the best explanation of how easy it is to come to know our experiences when we have them, Schear (2009) has put forward an alternative explanation that dispenses with mineness.

The case of depersonalization suggests that mineness might not ground these features of self-knowledge: despite their lack of mineness or "subjective character," depersonalized patients indeed seem to be capable of becoming aware and knowing their occurrent mental states just as well as we do, and with the very same ease.[26] The case of depersonalization suggests, however, that mineness might explain many other phenomena and that it is not at all epiphenomenal. Depersonalized patients indeed display a series of deficits that might be explained in terms of an alteration of mineness and reveal some of the roles it plays. Here are the most obvious impaired capacities (we have already mentioned the first three):

1. *Sense of ownership for mental states and bodily parts.* They report feeling as if some of their mental states or bodily parts were alien, which suggests their sense of ownership is impaired.
2. *Sense of agency.* They report feeling as if their actions were alien, which suggests that their sense of agency is impaired.
3. *Basic self-awareness.* In extreme cases, they seem reluctant to refer to themselves in the first-person singular (some say they feel like they should use the third-person or the first-person plural instead) which suggests that they are not properly aware of themselves as 'I's, and that their basic self-awareness is impaired.
4. *Self-certainty.* They also seem to resist the *cogito* intuition, being uncertain that they think and exist. A famous patient of Pitres and Régis' for example wondered, "Am I thinking? [...] As nothing proves that I am thinking, I cannot know whether I exist. [...] I hear so I think, so I am. But am I really sure that I think?..." (Hesnard, 1909, 179–82).
5. *Remembering in the first-person.* Even though their memory is objectively normal, they frequently express difficulties remembering things in the first-person, claiming not to feel concerned by or involved by what they imagine (Hesnard, 1909, 87–91, Dugas and Moutier, 1911, III). Sierra (2009, 33–4) presents the problem as follows:

> although the ability to retrieve information seems unaffected, patients frequently complain that memories, particularly of personal events (i.e. episodic memory) seem to have lost any personal meaning: "I can

---

[26] Salje and Geddes (this volume) criticize Gallagher's (2012) claim that mineness would optimally explain Immunity to Error through Misidentification. The fact that depersonalized patients often seem to lack this feature (see Billon, 2016, fn. 23) seems however to vindicate that claim.

remember things, but it seems as if what I remember did not really happen to me" [...] Another common clinical observation is that autobiographic memories in depersonalization are usually remembered from a vantage point outside of the body. That is, the event is visualized as if it had been witnessed from outside, rather than through the person's own eyes.

6. *Imagining in the first-person.* They can express similar difficulties to form mental images (i.e. to imagine perceiving things) and, more broadly, to imagine scenes in the first-person (Deny and Camus, 1905, Dugas and Moutier, 1911, 80–94, Sierra, 2009, 35).[27]

In order to show that mineness plays a decisive role in the explanation of these capacities we need to show that an impairment of mineness explains the alteration of these capacities in depersonalization. To do that, we need both to:

- specify exactly the role mineness is supposed to play in the impaired function;
- and rule out other explanation of the target impairment.

In arguing that patients display an impaired awareness of their mental states, bodily parts, and actions as their own, as well as an impaired awareness of themselves as 'I's, I have outlined such a defence for the sense of ownership, the sense of agency and basic self-awareness. Much more work would be needed for a full-blown defence, however, especially if we are to take seriously all rival accounts of the target phenomena. I have devoted two separate essays to such a full-blown defence in the case of self-certainty and basic self-awareness (Billon, 2015, 2016, 2017b). Here I would just like to show that, provided that it explains the impaired sense of ownership, the lack of mineness can *very simply explain* not only the impaired sense of agency, basic self-awareness, and self-certainty, but also the memorial and imaginative deficits mentioned above (see Figure 14.1).

I have already hinted at how an impaired sense of ownership explains an impaired sense of agency: If my sense of ownership for an intention-in-action is impaired, I will not be properly aware of the action it drives as being mine, that is, my sense of agency for this action will be impaired. I have also suggested a rough, intuitive explanation of the impaired basic self-awareness. The latter can be slightly refined by appeal to the following "reflexive rule," which seems to hold in virtue of the meaning of the first-person (see e.g. Kaplan, 1989, 505, 523–4, Recanati, 2007):

---

[27] I follow Recanati (2007, 193) and many others in taking mental imagery to be a case of first-person imagination. The claim is independently plausible and helps making sense of the patients' complaints.

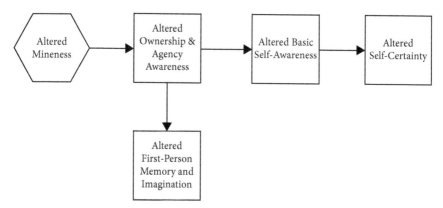

Figure 14.1 An altered mineness can explain the most common symptoms of depersonalization.

- **Reflexive Rule.** An I-thought bears on its owner.[28]

This rule must be mastered by any subject having I-thoughts, and we can assume that any (normally) rational adult also knows that this rule governs I-thoughts (i.e. that I-thoughts must bear on their owner). If a subject's sense of ownership got globally impaired, it would seem to him as if he is not the owner of his thoughts. When he thinks about it, it would seem to him as if this rule cannot apply to him and as if he is not, accordingly, entitled to I-thoughts and to uses of the first-person. The global impairment of this subject's sense of ownership would thus constitute an alteration of the kind of awareness that underlies this subject's use of the first-person, that is, by definition, of his basic self-awareness.[29] Moreover, if a subject does not feel entitled to refer to himself in the first-person he will also feel like "I exist" is not felicitously assertable.[30] He will, in that sense, be in a position to doubt that he exists. So a wide impairment of the sense of ownership, explained by an extended alteration of mineness, can arguably account

---

[28] Perry (1986) has influentially argued that some I-thoughts do not refer to or represent the subject but only "concern" him. We can stipulate that a thought *bears* on a subject if it either refers to him or concerns him, and that even if it does not refer to its subject, a given thought can be considered an I-thought provided that it concerns its subject.

[29] This argument, it should be noted, does not presuppose that basic self-awareness requires knowledge (as opposed to mere mastery) of the reflexive rule: it only presupposes that rational adults typically know the rule. Similarly, it does not presuppose that basic self-awareness is necessarily a high-level explicit self-representations, but only that it underlies, among rational adults, the high-level explicit self-representations in which it gets typically expressed. It is thus consistent with views that construe basic self-awareness as a low-level, pre-reflective, non-representational phenomenon.

[30] Provided that the negation is understood in a metalinguistic way, whereby 'x is not P' means "x is P' it is not felicitously assertable" (see Horn, 1989, ch. VI), "I do not exist" will be felicitously assertable. I have defended elsewhere that this metalinguistic interpretation helps one make sense of the patients' reports (Billon, 2017b, 2016).

both for an impaired basic self-awareness and an impaired capacity to be certain of one's thoughts and existence.

We can similarly explain patients' memorial and imaginative distortions. Memories and imaginings in the first-person are those that get typically expressed by expressions such as "I remember/imagine F-ing" or "I remember/imagine that I F-ed/am F-ing." First-person imaginings and first-person memories have an I-thought for content, and bear, by the reflexive rule, on their very owner.[31] Now, if I lacked a sense of ownership for a memory or an imagining episode E, I would not be properly aware of E as being mine, which means that I would not be properly aware that I am the owner of E. If I reflected on E's content, it would accordingly seem to me that it does not bear on me, and that it is not a memory or an imagining episode that is run from my own point of view (as opposed from no point of view at all or from someone else's point of view).[32] An alteration of subjectivity can thus explain, though an alteration of their sense of ownership for memories and imaginings, the patients' disordered first-person memories and imaginings.

6.2. Towards a Biological Function for Mineness?

Once we have noticed that mineness really plays a significant role in our mind, explaining our sense of ownership and agency, our basic self-awareness, and our capacity to imagine and remember things in the first-person, it is natural to wonder what its biological function might be. Tom McClelland (this volume) challenges the idea that mineness has a biological function at all. Here again, I believe depersonalization can provide new insights on this issue.

It is well known that life-threatening events can precipitate fleeting depersonalization-like experiences (Noyes and Kletti, 1977) and that some traumatic experiences can trigger genuine forms of depersonalization (see e.g. Shorvon, 1946). Now, a lack of the sense of ownership for mental states, and in particular for affective states such as moods, emotions, and algedonic states of pleasure and pain should allow the subject to dissociate from these states and feel less concerned by what they represent. A lack of mineness for affective states could thus make subjects care less about the objects of these affective states.[33] It has been suggested that this might hinder or attenuate the normal response to certain threats, which might be functional in certain circumstances, for example when the threat is not localizable in space, when it is absolutely inescapable, or

---

[31] This does not entail that every I-thought refers to its subject (see fn. 29).

[32] If I reflected on E itself, rather than on its content, it might also seem to me that I am not imagining anything myself. Patients can in fact explicitly report being unable to imagine anything.

[33] I assume that my normal conscious emotions, moods, and algedonic states are partly constituted by experiences and that they seem to be mine to me in virtue of the mineness of these experiences.

THE ROLE OF MINENESS   333

when it requires a "cold blooded" reaction (Sierra and Berrios (1998), Sierra (2009, 152–3).[34] Similarly, being unable to remember or visualize a past traumatic event from the inside, or in the first-person, more broadly, might soften its impact on our psychic life and make it more bearable.[35] A few empirical studies indeed support the idea that memories and imaginative episodes from the inside following trauma might me maladaptive. Kenny and Bryant (2007) have for example assessed the relationship between avoidance (a maladaptive coping response characterized by a tendency to withdraw into oneself, and to fear commitment) following trauma and the vantage point of memories, and found that avoidance was negatively correlated to an external point of view for negative memories but not for neutral ones or positive ones. Shilony and Grossman (1993) have studied, more broadly, the influence of depersonalization-like experiences on coping. They interrogated seventy-five undergrad students who had gone through traumatic experiences and found that those who had suffered from depersonalization-like experiences during the traumatic events suffered from less psychopathology (however, see the discussion of Sierra, 2009, 71–2). These results support Sierra and Berrios (1998)'s adaptive theory of depersonalization to the effect that depersonalization is a "hard-wired defence mechanism."

Now assuming that this theory is correct, the lack of mineness characterizing depersonalization would have a defensive function, allowing one to disavow or alienate his affective states when they are dysfunctional, and to distance oneself from one's harmful traumatic memories. Conversely, a normal mark of mineness would allow one to fully endorse one's affective states, and to avow one's memories. Affective states generally represent their subject as concerned with something. My fear of the dog for example represents me as endangered by the dog. In having one fully endorse his affective states, the mark of mineness of affective states

---

[34] Patients' affective states are not only alienated, they are also, in virtue of their alienation, attenuated. I take it, indeed, that to have an affective state is to *feel oneself* concerned by something. To be afraid of a dog is for example to feel oneself endangered by the dog. And this feeling oneself implies a sense of ownership for the emotions. An emotion totally lacking a sense of ownership is not, accordingly, a genuine emotion and one whose sense of ownership is partially lacking is at best an attenuated emotion. Depersonalized patients thus typically express both attenuated and false emotions:

I only feel anger from the outside, by its physiological reactions.
(Dugas and Moutier, 1911, p. 121)

I am afraid of my thoughts, for my brain, etc. but fundamentally I am not afraid at all. If only I could have a genuine fear.... (Dugas and Moutier, 1911)

I look at my hands that are writing this text. How curious! They are still interested in some things. (Dugas and Moutier, 1911:127)

It was painful and my arm felt like withdrawing, but it was not a genuine pain, it was a pain that did not reach the soul...It is a pain, if you want, but the surface of my skin is miles away from my brain, and I do not know whether I am suffering. (Janet, 1928, 65)

[35] Memories from the inside are those in which I remember being, so to speak, at the centre of the scene. Memories in the first-person are those that get typically expressed in the first-person. Even if the converse might not hold (see Recanati, 2007, XXIX), memories from the inside are all in the first-person.

would allow one to fully identify with the entity concerned by what these affective states represent. It is arguable that except in the exceptional cases described above (in which the threat is not localizable or inescapable, or the affective state too strong) this would be extremely useful. It would be extremely useful in these cases because emotions often correctly represent their subject as concerned by their object, and taking them at face value is often necessary for survival. I suggest, thus, that the role of the mark of mineness is, at least in part, to *feel oneself fully concerned* by what our affective states represent.

7. The Nature of Mineness

The discovery of depersonalization, at the end of the 19th century, led to a renewal of interest in mineness and in the cluster of capacities we have called "self-awareness," including the senses of ownership, the sense of agency, and basic self-awareness. It was generally acknowledged, at that time, that our normal mineness explained our normal self-awareness and that the study of depersonalization would give us insights into the nature of both mineness and self-awareness. When they published their great synthesis on depersonalization, in 1911, Dugas and Moutier already knew enough to rule out most theories of self-awareness, depersonalization, and mineness of their predecessors, and they argued forcefully against almost all of them.

Here, I would like to briefly put forward a challenge, based on depersonalization and inspired by Dugas and Moutier, confronting *psychological theories of mineness*, that is, theories that try to give a reductive account of mineness in psychological terms. This challenge suggests that such reductive theories must fail and that mineness can only be explained in purely neurophysiological (as opposed to "psychological or neuropsychological") terms.

Among psychological theories of mineness, we can distinguish, very roughly, between

- *Sensory theories*, which invoke the five senses to explain mineness.
- *Sensorimotor theories*, which invoke the five senses *and agency*, explaining for example mineness in terms of the capacity to *react* appropriately to certain stimuli.
- *Affective theories*, which invoke the subjects' affects (emotions, moods, and other states, if there are any, which are of the same kind as these)
- *Interoceptive theories*, which invoke the subject's interoception, that is, her perception of her inner organs.
- *Cognitive or executive views*, which invoke the subject's thoughts or executive functions.

These five theories, it should be noted, need not be incompatible with each other: on some "enactive" views of perception, for example, the latter is a matter of action; on Jamesian views of emotions, affectivity hinges centrally on interoception, etc. These five theories have all been defended by at least some protagonists of the debate on depersonalization. Krishaber (1873b) and Taine (1892) have for example defended the sensory view; Deny and Camus (1905) the interoceptive, "cenesthetic" view; Dugas (1898) (but not Dugas and Moutier (1911)) the affective view; and Bergson (1896) the sensorimotor one. Janet (1928) has held a complex executive view, according to which mineness hinges on certain metacognitive abilities. Today, de Vignemont (this volume) arguably endorses the affective view.[36] Kriegel's (2009) self-representational theory of subjectivity, and even Rosenthal's (2005) higher order theory of consciousness, which posit a representation of our conscious mental states to account for their subjectivity, might be considered as other cognitive theory mineness (see Billon and Kriegel, 2015).

Now each of these theories can come in two flavours, an *objective* one and a *subjective* one. Objective theories only appeal to objective psychological capacities, that is capacities that can be measured objectively such as objective sensory capacities (as measured by sensory discrimination tasks), objective sensorimotor abilities (as measured, for example, by the subject's capacity to react appropriately to certain stimuli) objective affective capacities (as measured, for example, by facial expressions), etc. In contrast to these *objective theories* some theories invoke the subjects' experiences—their perceptive experiences, for example, as measured by their verbal reports. We can call them *subjective*.

Now there is good clinical evidence that depersonalized patients' sensory, sensorimotor, and interoceptive capacities are objectively normal (see for example Janet, 1928, 40, 63–4). There is also good clinical evidence that their affective capacities are objectively normal (see Dugas and Moutier, 1911, 121–8, Sierra, 2009, 25–6), that the patients' cognition and executive functions are intact (Dugas and Moutier, 1911, I–VI, but see Janet, 1928). It has, moreover, been shown experimentally that their sensorimotor abilities are normal Cappon and Banks (1965), that their interoceptive abilities are also equally normal (Michal et al., 2014) and that their executive functions are normal (Sedman (1966) could not distinguish patients from controls, Guralnik et al. (2000, 2007) only found a slight difference in certain low-level aspects of spatial attention during tasks involving a perceptual overload). All this suggests that even though their mineness is lacking, most objective psychological capacities of depersonalized patients are normal, and that most objective psychological theories accordingly fail to explain mineness.

---

[36] Gerrans (2017) puts forward a sophisticated affective theory that, he convincingly argues, is immune to the objections developed below against affective theories. Dub (this volume) does not claim that mineness can be explained in affective terms, by emotions, but that it is itself an emotion.

336   WHAT IS IT LIKE TO LACK MINENESS?

It should be acknowledged though, that even if this criticism applies to almost all the objective theories we have reviewed so far, it does not apply to those, such as Rosenthal (2005)'s and Kriegel (2009)'s representational theories—which I consider as objective cognitive theories—that appeal to subtle factors that could not be tested by any of the studies I have mentioned so far.[37]

What about subjective theories? Consider subjective sensory and sensorimotor theories first. It is true that the patients' perceptual experiences and agentive experiences are abnormal. But this abnormality, as we have seen, consists in or is explained by a lack of mineness; so it will not, on pain of circularity, explain why the patients' sensory and agentive experiences lack mineness. It will at best explain why the patient's non-sensory and non-agentive experiences lack mineness. So an explanation of the patient's condition that appeals to distorted sensory or agentive experiences will at best be partial, explaining only the mineness of our non-sensory or non-agentive experiences. Conversely, an explanation of our normal mineness in terms of sensory or agentive experiences will at best be partial and it will not succeed in explaining our normal mineness in general.

This point against subjective sensory and sensorimotor theories of mineness generalizes to theories invoking interoceptive or affective experiences. The patients' interoceptive and affective experiences are indeed abnormal, but their abnormality seems to consist in or to be explained by a lack of mineness. "I only feel anger from the outside, by its physiological reactions" says for example a patient of Dugas and Moutier's (1911, 121). A patient of Janet's similarly explains, after having been pinched: "It was painful and my arm felt like withdrawing, but it was not a genuine pain, it was a pain that did not reach the soul ... It is a pain, if you want, but the surface of my skin is miles away from my brain, and I do not know whether I am suffering" (Janet, 1928, 65). Now if interoceptive and affective experiences are only altered in that they lack mineness, and feel alien, then their abnormality will at best provide a partial explanation of the patient's condition, explaining, maybe, why their non-affective and non-interoceptive states lack mineness, but not, on pain of circularity, why the affective and interoceptive states lack mineness. Conversely, a subjective explanation of our normal mineness in terms of affects or interoception will at least be partial and it will fail to explain our normal mineness in general.

I do not know of any subjective cognitive theory, but it seems that the above argument could generalize as well to such theories, at least if we assume that in case the cognitive phenomenology of depersonalized patients is altered, its alteration consists in or is explained by a lack of mineness for thoughts.

The above argument seems to thwart most psychological theories of mineness we have reviewed here. The first step of the argument shows that most objective

---

[37] The fact that these theories appeal to factors that cannot yet be empirically tested might count as evidence against them though.

theories fail because their explanans is normal in depersonalized patients who lack mineness. The second step shows that subjective theories fail because their explanans themselves consists in or are explained by a lack of mineness. This two-step argument suggests, more broadly, that the following challenge will be hard to meet for *any* psychological theory of mineness invoking the normal character of a factor F as explanans:

- In order to argue that our normal F explains our normal mineness, one must show both that F is abnormal among depersonalized patients and that their abnormal F is not to be explained by a lack of mineness.

This challenge, as we have seen, thwarts all the theories of mineness we have reviewed so far.[38] Importantly, it also bears on other theories. To take one example among others, it also challenges Dainton's (2008, 242–4) *co-conscious background* theory of mineness. According to this theory, I am aware of a conscious state as being mine just in case it is co-conscious with certain background phenomenal states.[39] Now, it is arguable that the patient's alien states might fail to be co-conscious with their background states (see Hesnard, 1909, III). It seems however that the lack of mineness in depersonalization can simultaneously affect *all* conscious states, *including those in the background*. But the alien character of the background itself cannot be explained, it seems, by the co-conscious theory. This suggests that mineness is explanatory prior to co-consciousness and cannot be explained by the latter: it is because a state has mineness that it is co-conscious with the background when the latter has mineness too, not because it is co-conscious with the background that has mineness. This, in turn, suggests that Dainton's co-conscious background theory fails.

8. Conclusion

I have argued that depersonalization involves a more or less global and intense lack of mineness and that its study accordingly constitutes a useful empirical probe for the study of mineness. This probe gives us good reason to believe that mineness is a general, if not universal, feature of our experiences, and that, even if it does not play the epistemic role that has often been attributed to it, it has an important role to play in our mental life explaining our normal self-awareness (sense of ownership for mental states, sense of bodily ownership, sense of agency,

---

[38] In Billon (2017a), I develop this challenge and argue that it threatens many recent theories of mineness and the sense of ownership, suggesting that mineness is psychologically irreducible.

[39] Dainton considers that this theory eliminates minenes rather than reducing it because he imposes, as we have seen, too many constraints on mineness.

338 WHAT IS IT LIKE TO LACK MINENESS?

and basic self-awareness) our normal self-certainty and our normal first-person memories and imaginings. This probe also gives us good reason to think that mineness has a genuine biological function: it is thanks to mineness that we feel properly concerned by what really matters to us. Finally, this probe allows us to reject many psychological theories that have been put forward to explain mineness and suggests that it might be psychologically irreducible.[40]

References

Alsmith, A. (2015). Mental activity & the sense of ownership. *Review of Philosophy and Psychology*, 6(4): 881–896.

Bergson, H. (1896). *Matière et mémoire*, trad. fr. *Œuvres*. Paris: PUF.

Bermúdez, J. L. (2015). Bodily ownership, bodily awareness and knowledge without observation. *Analysis*, 75(1): 37–45.

Bermúdez, J. L. (2017). Bodily ownership, psychological ownership and psychopathology. *Review of Philosophy and Psychology*, 10(2): 263–280.

Berrios, G. (1991). Delusions as "wrong beliefs": A conceptual history. *The British journal of psychiatry: Supplement*, 159(14): 6–13.

Billon, A. (2013). Does consciousness entail subjectivity? The puzzle of thought insertion', *Philosophical Psychology*, 26(2): 291–314.

Billon, A. (2015). Why are we certain that we exist? *Philosophy and Phenomenological Research*, 91: 723–59.

Billon, A. (2016). Making sense of the Cotard syndrome: Insights from the study of depersonalisation, *Mind and Language*, 31: 356–91.

Billon, A. (2017a). Mineness first: Three challenges to recent theories of the sense of bodily ownership, in A. Alsmith and F. de Vignemont (eds) *The Subject's Matter: Self-Consciousness and the Body*. Cambridge, MA: MIT Press.

Billon, Alexandre (2017b). Basic Self-Awareness. *European Journal of Philosophy* 25 (3):732–763.

Billon, A. and Kriegel, U. (2015). Jaspers' dilemma: The psychopathological challenge to subjectivity theories of consciousness', in R. Gennaro (ed.) *Disturbed Consciousness*. Cambridge, MA: MIT Press, 29–54.

Bortolotti, L. and Broome, M. (2009). A role for ownership and authorship in the analysis of thought insertion. *Phenomenology and the Cognitive Sciences*, 8(2): 204–25.

Campbell, J. (2004). The ownership of thoughts. *Philosophy, Psychology, Psychiatry*, 9(1): 35–9.

---

[40] I thank Matt Duncan, Tom McClelland, and Jean Pieter Maes and two anonymous referees for very useful comments.

CONCLUSION 339

Cappon, D. and Banks, R. (1965). Orientational perception, Ii: Body perception in depersonalization. *Archives of General Psychiatry*, 13(4): 375–9.

Coliva, A. (2002). Thought insertion and immunity to error though misidentification. *Philosophy, Psychiatry & Psychology*, 9(1): 27–34.

Dainton, B. (2008). *The Phenomenal Self*. Oxford: Oxford University Press.

Deny, G. and Camus, P. (1905). Sur une forme d'hypochondrie aberrante due à la perte de la conscience du corps. *Revue Neurologique*, 9(461): 15.

Dugas, L. (1898). Un cas de dépersonnalisation. *Revue Philosophique de la France et de l'Étranger*, 45: 500–7.

Dugas, L. (1936). Sur la dépersonnalisation. *Journal de Psychologie Normale et Pathologique*, 34(3–4): 276–82.

Dugas, L. and Moutier, F. (1911). *La dépersonnalisation*. Paris: F. Alcan. Available at http://www.biusante.parisdescartes.fr/histmed/medica/cote?79749

Fernández, J. (2010). Thought insertion and self-knowledge. *Mind & Language*, 25(1):66–88.

Gallagher, S. (2000). Self-reference and schizophrenia: A cognitive model of immunity to error through misidentification. In D. Zahavi (ed.) *Exploring the Self: Philosophical and Psychopathological Perspectives on Self-Experience*. New York: John Benjamins, 203–39.

Gallagher, S. (2004). Neurocognitive models of schizophrenia: A neurophenomenological critique. *Psychopathology*, 37: 8–19.

Gallagher, Shaun (2012). First-person perspective and immunity to error rough misidentification, in S. Miguens and G. Preyer (eds.) *Consciousness and Subjectivity*. Leipzig: Ontos Verlag, 187–214.

Gerrans, Philip (2017). Depersonalization Disorder, Affective Processing and Predictive Coding. *Review of Philosophy and Psychology* 10(2): 401–418.

Gertler, B. (2010). *Self-knowledge*. London: Routledge.

Graham, G. and Stephens, G. L. (2000). *When Self Consciousness Breaks, Alien Voices and Inserted Thoughts*. Oxford: Oxford University Press (MIT Press edition).

Guillot, M. (2016). I Me Mine: on a Confusion Concerning the Subjective Character of Experience. *Review of Philosophy and Psychology* (1): 1–31.

Guralnik, O., Schmeidler, J., and Simeon, D. (2000). Feeling unreal: Cognitive processes in depersonalization. *American Journal of Psychiatry*, 157(1): 103–9.

Guralnik, O., Giesbrecht, T., Knutelska, M., Sirroff, B., and Simeon, D. (2007). Cognitive functioning in depersonalization disorder. *The Journal of Nervous and Mental Disease*, 195(12): 983–8.

Henry, M. (1990). *Phénoménologie matérielle*. Épiméthée. Paris: PUF.

Hesnard, A. (1909). *Les troubles de la personnalité: dans les états d'asthénie psychique: étude de psychologie clinique*. Paris: F. Alcan.

Horn, L. R. (1989). A natural history of negation. University of Chicago Press.

Howell, R. and Thompson, B. (2016). Phenomenally mine: In search of the subjective character of consciousness. *Review of Philosophy and Psychology*, 8(1): 102–127.

Hunter, E. C. M., Phillips, M. L., Chalder, T., Sierra, M., & David, A. S. (2003). Depersonalisation disorder: a cognitive–behavioural conceptualisation. *Behaviour Research and Therapy*, 41(12): 1451–1467.

Jaspers, K. (1913/1962). General Psychopathology. Translated by J. Hoenig and Marian W. Hamilton. Manchester University Press.

Janet, P. (1903). *Les obsessions et la psychasthénie. Analyse des symptômes*, vol. 1. Paris: Félix Alcan.

Janet, P. (1908). Le Sentiment de Dépersonnalisation. Journal de Psychologie normale et pathologique, 5: 514–516.

Janet, P. (1928). *De l'angoisse à l'extase. Les sentiments fondamentaux*, vol. 2. Paris: Alcan. available at http://classiques.uqac.ca/classiques/janet_pierre/angoisse_extase_2/Janet_angoisse_2_1.pdf

Janet, P. and Raymond, F. (1898). Névroses et idées fixes, vol. 2. Paris: Félix Alcan.

Jaspers, K. (1962). *General Psychopathology*. Manchester: Manchester University Press.

Kaplan, D. (1989). Demonstratives. In J. Almog, J. Perry, and H. Wettstein (eds.) *Themes from Kaplan*. Oxford: Oxford University Press, 481–563.

Kenny, L. M. and Bryant, R. A. (2007). Keeping memories at an arm's length: Vantage point of trauma memories. *Behaviour Research and Therapy*, 45(8): 1915–20.

Kriegel, U. (2009). *Subjective Consciousness: A Self-Representational Theory*. Oxford: Oxford University Press.

Krishaber, M. (1873a). *De la névropathie cérébro-cardiaque*. Paris: Masson. Available at http://gallica.bnf.fr/ark:/12148/bpt6k767014

Krishaber, M. (1873b). *De la névropathie cérébro-cardiaque*. Paris: Masson.

Lane, T. (2015). Self, belonging, and conscious experience: A critique of subjectivity theories of consciousness. *Disturbed Consciousness: New Essays on Psychopathology and Theories of Consciousness*. MIT Press, Cambridge, Mass., pp. 103–140 (2015).

Leroy, E.-B. (1901). Sur l'illusion dite dépersonnalisation. *L'Année Psychologique*, 8:519–522.

Metzinger, T. (2004). *Being No One: The Self-Model Theory of Subjectivity*. Cambridge, MA: MIT Press.

Michal, M., Reuchlein, B., Adler, J., Reiner, I., Beutel, M. E., Vögele, C., Schächinger, H., and Schulz, A. (2014). Striking discrepancy of anomalous body experiences with normal interoceptive accuracy in depersonalization-derealization disorder. *PLoS ONE*, 9(2): e89823.

Noyes, R. and Kletti, R. (1977). Depersonalization in response to life-threatening danger. *Comprehensive Psychiatry*, 18(4): 375–84.

Oesterreich, K. (1908). *Die Entfremdung der Wahrnehmungswelt und die Depersonalisation in der Psychasthenie*. Leipzig: Verlag Barth.

Perry, J. (1986). Thought without representation. *Proceedings of the Aristotelian Society, Supplementary Volumes*, 60: 137–51.

Radovic, Filip and Radovic, Susanna (2002). Feelings of unreality: A conceptual and phenomenological analysis of the language of depersonalization. *Philosophy, Psychiatry, and Psychology*, 9(3): 271–9.

Recanati, F. (2007). *Perspectival Thought: A Plea for (Moderate) Relativism*. Oxford: Clarendon Press.

Ribot, T. (1883). *Les maladies de la personnalité*. Paris: F. Alcan.

Rosenthal, D. M. (2005). *Consciousness and Mind*. New York: Oxford University Press.

Sacco, R. G. (2010). The circumplex structure of depersonalization/derealization. *International Journal of Psychological Studies*, 2(2): 26.

Schear, J. K. (2009). Experience and self-consciousness. *Philosophical Studies*, 144(1): 95–105.

Sedman, G. (1966). A phenomenological study of pseudohallucinatios and related experiences. *Acta Psychiatrica Scandinavica*, 42: 35–70.

Sedman, G. (1972). An Investigation of Certain Factors Concerned in the Aetiology of Depersonalization. Acta Psychiatr Scand, 48(3): 191–219.

Shilony, E. and Grossman, F. K. (1993). Depersonalization as a defense mechanism in survivors of trauma. *Journal of Traumatic Stress*, 6(1): 119–28.

Shorvon, H. (1946). The depersonalization syndrome. *Proceedings of the Royal Society of Medicine*, 39(12): 779–91.

Sierra, M. (2009). *Depersonalization: A New Look at a Neglected Syndrome*. Cambridge: Cambridge University Press.

Sierra, M. and David, A. S. (2011). Depersonalization: A selective impairment of self-awareness. *Consciousness and Cognition*, 20(1): 99–108.

Sierra, M. and Berrios, G. E. (1998). Depersonalization: Neurobiological perspectives. *Biological Psychiatry*, 44(9): 898–908.

Sierra, M. and Berrios, G. E. (2000). The Cambridge depersonalisation scale: A new instrument for the measurement of depersonalisation. *Psychiatry Research*, 93(2): 153–64.

Simeon, D. and Abugel, J. (2006). *Feeling Unreal: Depersonalization Disorder and the Loss of the Self*. New York: Oxford University Press.

Strawson, P. F. (1963). *Individuals: An Essay in Descriptive Metaphysics*. London: Routledge.

Taine, H. (1892). Note sur la formation de l'idée de moi, in H. Taine (ed.) *L'intelligence*. Paris: Hachette, 465–74. available at http://www.biusante.parisdescartes.fr/histmed/medica/cote?50417

Vignemont, F. de (2007). Habeas corpus: The sense of ownership of one's own body. *Mind and Language*, 22(4):427–449.

Vignemont, F. de (2014). The mark of bodily ownership. *Analysis*, 73(4):643–651.

Wittgenstein, L. (1953). *Philosophical Investigations*, ed. G. E. M. Anscombe and R. Rhees, trans. G. E. M. Anscombe. Oxford: Blackwell.

Zahavi, D. (2008). *Subjectivity and Selfhood: Investigating the First-Person Perspective.* Cambridge, MA: MIT Press.

Zahavi, D. and Kriegel, U. (2016). *For-Me-Ness: What It Is and What It Is Not.* In D. Dahlstrom, A. Elpidorou & W. Hopp (eds.), *Philosophy of Mind and Phenomenology.* Routledge. pp. 36–53.

15

The Ownership of Memories

Jordi Fernández

1. Introduction

A subject's inner awareness of their phenomenal states has a number of interesting features.[1] Among them, there is a feature that is especially familiar to us. Normally, when a subject is aware of their phenomenal states, the subject takes those states to be their own; the subject attributes those states to themselves. If your inner awareness reveals the occurrence of the thought that it is about to rain, for example, then you will attribute to yourself the thought that it is about to rain; you will take yourself to be the thinker of that thought. It seems uncontroversial that our awareness of our phenomenal states leads to the self-attribution of those states, as opposed to the attribution of those states to others. What is less clear is why this is the case.

A simple explanation which comes to mind rather easily is the following. The reason why a subject attributes the phenomenal states that they experience through inner awareness to themselves is that, when a subject is aware of one of their phenomenal states, the subject is not only aware of the fact that the relevant state is instantiated, but they are also aware of the fact that the state is theirs. We can abbreviate this view by saying that inner awareness of phenomenal states carries with it a 'sense of mineness' or an 'experience of ownership' (Gallagher 2005; Zahavi 2008). This view explains why our awareness of our phenomenal states leads to the self-attribution of those states. For suppose that the view is right and, when a subject is aware of one of their phenomenal states, they are aware of the relevant state as being theirs. It does not seem surprising, then, that the subject attributes the phenomenal state to themselves. After all, on this view, what the subject would be doing by self-attributing the phenomenal state is simply trusting their episode of inner awareness.

---

[1] I will use the term 'phenomenal state' to refer to mental states with phenomenal properties; states for which there is such a thing as what it is like to be in them. I will also assume that there is a phenomenology of agency, and that there is a phenomenology of thought. See (Bayne 2008) for a discussion of the former, and (Bayne and Montague 2011) for a discussion of the latter. Accordingly, I will include actions and thoughts in the category of phenomenal states.

Jordi Fernández, *The Ownership of Memories* In: *Self-Experience: Essays on Inner Awareness.*
Edited by: Manuel García-Carpintero and Marie Guillot, Oxford University Press.
© Jordi Fernández 2023. DOI: 10.1093/oso/9780198805397.003.0015

344   THE OWNERSHIP OF MEMORIES

But is there really, in episodes of inner awareness, an experience of a phenomenal state as the subject's own, over and above the experience of the instantiation of that state? The concern is that perhaps being aware of a phenomenal state, and being aware of it as the subject's own, is one and the same thing.[2] And if there really aren't two different experiences in our awareness of our phenomenal states, but only one, then the sense of mineness turns out to be just a fiction. It seems reasonable, therefore, to demand some reasons for believing in the existence of the sense of mineness as a genuine experience. Relatedly, one would also want to know more about the nature of this experience, since it is not straightforward what qualifies as experiencing a phenomenal state as being one's own. Unless some progress can be made on both of these fronts, it seems that the simple explanation of why inner awareness of phenomenal states leads to the self-attribution of those states sketched above will not get off the ground.

The objective of this chapter is to address both of these issues with regards to the specific case of episodic memories.[3] I will begin by highlighting, in section 2, a phenomenon that gives us a reason for believing in the existence of the sense of mineness in our awareness of our episodic memories. This is the condition of 'disowned memory', wherein a subject claims to have memories that are not theirs. In section 3, I will consider a proposal about the nature of the sense of mineness for episodic memories that is based on a particular diagnosis of disowned memory. According to the 'identification model' of the sense of mineness, the experience of a memory as the subject's own is the feeling of being identical with the witness of the remembered scene. I will argue that, while this model does account for some details in the available reports of disowned memory, it is also in tension with other details in those reports. Accordingly, I will put forward, in section 4, an alternative proposal. According to the 'endorsement model' of the sense of mineness, the experience of a memory as the subject's own is the experience of the memory as matching the past. I will argue that this model squares with the details in the available reports of disowned memory which are in tension with the

---

[2] Interestingly, Georg Lichtenberg takes his disagreement with Descartes on the nature of introspection to be precisely about the issue of whether being aware of a mental state and being aware of a mental state as one's own are one and the same experience or not. Lichtenberg seems to think that Descartes is wrong in assuming that they are identical experiences (1990, 168). The issue of whether being aware of a phenomenal state and being aware of a phenomenal state as one's own are one and the same experience or not hinges on one's criterion for the individuation of properties. For, presumably, experiences are properties of the subject. In what follows, I will assume that property P and property Q are identical if and only if, necessarily, for any object x, x has P if and only if x has Q. On this criterion for the individuation of properties, the question becomes that of whether a subject could be aware of a phenomenal state without being aware of it as their own.

[3] The distinction between episodic and semantic memory is introduced by Endel Tulving in (Tulving 1972), and it has undergone several revisions since then. For our purposes here, it will suffice to characterize episodic memory as the type of memory that we have of events, or states of affairs, which we experienced in the past. By contrast, we can think of semantic memory as the type of memory that we have of events which we have learnt to have taken place in the past, and of states of affairs which we have learnt to have been the case in the past.

identification model, as well as with those which are explained by it. In section 5, I will suggest a template for generalizing the proposed model of the sense of mineness for episodic memories to accommodate other cases of disowned phenomenal states, such as disowned thoughts, disowned impulses, disowned feelings, and disowned actions.

2. Disowned Memory

What considerations can be offered in support of the idea that our awareness of our episodic memories carries with it a sense of mineness? In this section, I will suggest that one such consideration involves a condition wherein a subject reports to have a memory while, at the same time, claiming that the memory in question is not theirs. I will refer to this condition as 'disowned memory'.

Disowned memory is extremely rare. As a matter of fact, the only relatively clear case of disowned memory that is reported in the philosophical and psychological literatures seems to be that of patient R.B., a case investigated in detail by Stanley Klein (2015, 2013, 2012).[4] Shaun Nichols and Stanley Klein have argued that the case of patient R.B. has interesting philosophical implications for the connection between memory and personal identity (Klein and Nichols 2012). Patient R.B. suffers, due to head trauma sustained during a bicycle accident, various cognitive deficits including, it seems, a remarkable memory impairment. Patient R.B. can have, we are told, accurate memories of scenes from his past. And yet, for some of those memories, he also claims that the memories at issue are not his, and that he does not own them.[5] Here are some of the claims which patient R.B. makes, and which Klein and Nichols take to be reports of episodic memories:[6]

Report 1

I was remembering scenes, not facts... I was recalling scenes... that is... I could clearly recall a scene of me at the beach in New London with my family as a child. But the feeling was that the scene was not my memory. As if I was looking at a photo of someone else's vacation. (Klein and Nichols 2012, 686)

---

[4] Does the extreme rarity of the disorder diminish its significance? The appeal to disowned memory will be made to argue that the experience of a memory, and that of a memory as one's own, can come apart in a subject. Since this is arguably sufficient to show that the two experiences are distinct, it does not seem to matter whether, as a matter of fact, only one subject has suffered this disorder or whether, by contrast, this is a relatively common disorder.

[5] In what follows, I will speak of scenes and states of affairs as the intentional objects of episodic memories interchangeably. I will be assuming that scenes are best construed as states of affairs, though nothing in the discussion that follows should hinge on that assumption.

[6] For the sake of brevity, not all of R.B.'s reports cited in the literature are reproduced in this list. Reports 4 and 5, for example, are part of a longer exchange between Klein and patient R.B. in (Klein and Nichols 2012). As far as I can see, however, those reports which are not reproduced here are neutral on whether the correct interpretation of R.B. is that discussed in section 3, or it is the interpretation to be proposed in section 4.

Report 2

Things that were in the present, like my name, I continue to own. Having been to MIT had two different issues. My memories of having been at MIT I did not own. Those scenes of being at MIT were vivid, but they were not mine. But I owned 'the fact that I had a degree from MIT'. That might have simply been a matter of rational acceptance of fact. (Klein and Nichols 2012, 686)

Report 3

I can picture the scene perfectly clearly...studying with my friends in our study lounge. I can 'relive' it in the sense of re-running the experience of being there. But it has the feeling of imagining, [as if] re-running an experience that my parents described from their college days. It did not feel like it was something that really had been a part of my life. Intellectually I suppose I never doubted that it was a part of my life. Perhaps because there was such continuity of memories that fit a pattern that lead up to the present time. But that in itself did not help change the feeling of ownership. (Klein and Nichols 2012, 686)

Report 4

RB: I can see the scene in my head. I'm studying with friends in the lounge at my residence hall. I am able to re-live it. I have a feeling...a sense of being there, at MIT, in the lounge. But it doesn't feel like I own it. It's like I'm imagining, re-living the experience but it was described by someone else. (Klein and Nichols 2012, 687)

Report 5

RB: I can recall memories [from the non-ownership period of his life] at will. I have normal control over remembering facts and scenes from my past. But when I remember scenes from before the injury, they do not feel as if they happened to me—though intellectually I know that they did—they felt as if they happened to someone else. (Klein and Nichols 2012, 687)

Report 6

What happened over the coming months was interesting: every once in a while, I would suddenly think about something in my past and I would 'own' it. That was indeed something 'I' had done and experienced. Over time, one by one I would come to 'own' different memories. Eventually, after perhaps eight months or so, it seemed as if it was all owned. As if once enough individual memories were owned, it was all owned. For example, the MIT memory, the one in the lounge...I now own it. It's clearly part of my life, my past. (Klein 2013, 6)

Report 7

When I remember the scene with my friends, studying, I remember myself walking into the room...and...other things I did and felt...But it feels like something I didn't experience...(something I) was told about by someone else. (Klein 2015, 18)

It seems that R.B. is having a highly unusual experience. R.B. claims, on the one hand, to have certain memories and, on the other hand, not to own those memories. It is hard to know how to make sense of these reports. There seem to be three interpretative approaches to R.B.'s reports that one may take. One may, first of all, attribute to R.B. an awareness of the instantiation of certain memories without the awareness that the memories at issue are R.B.'s own.[7] Call this the 'something-missing' approach. Alternatively, one may see R.B.'s case as a case where there is a phenomenology of alienation that is absent from normal memories. Call this the 'something-extra' approach. And, finally, one may see R.B.'s reports as expressions of episodes of awareness which do not share any phenomenological common core with our awareness of normal memories. Call this the 'something-entirely-different' approach.[8] Which is the most preferable approach?

The something-extra approach explains why R.B. disowns some of his memories. In addition to the phenomenology that we undergo when we are aware of our memories, he has an extra experience of alienation. The difficulty for this approach concerns the question of whether there is something, phenomenologically speaking, that my different episodes of awareness of normal memories have in common. Intuitively, when I am aware of my memory of my first kiss, and when I am aware of my memory of my first bicycle fall, for example, it seems that my two experiences are different in one respect. There is a quasi-sensory painful-ish way it is like for me to be aware of the latter memory, but not of the former one. At the same time, the two experiences seem to have something in common as well. In both cases, I seem to be aware of my memory as my own. Now, this intuition is difficult to capture if we take the something-extra approach towards a case in which a subject disowns some of their memories. For the approach suggests that the awareness of the occurrence of a memory cannot be instantiated without the awareness of the memory as the subject's own. (After all, any case in which the two types of awareness appear to come apart, such as a case of disowned memory, will be treated instead as a case in which the subject has an experience of alienation in addition to the two types of awareness of their memory.) But if the awareness of the occurrence of a memory and the awareness of it as one's own cannot be instantiated without each other, then what reason do we have to consider them different experiences?[9] In the absence of a reason, the something-extra

---

[7] Some of the claims that Klein and Nichols make about R.B. suggest that they are adopting this approach. Thus, they claim that R.B. lacks the feeling that the memories that he experiences 'belong to him' (Klein and Nichols 2012, 684). Likewise, they claim that those memories lack a 'sense of mineness' (Klein and Nichols 2012, 677).

[8] See (Billon and Kriegel 2015) for a defence of the coherence of the something-extra approach, and the coherence of the something-entirely-different approach, in other cases of disowned mental states.

[9] André Billon and Uriah Kriegel motivate the intuition that there is something common in a subject's experience of their various phenomenal states along the lines sketched above in (Billon and Kriegel 2015, 29–30). As far as I understand their view, however, they also think that the awareness of the occurrence of a phenomenal state, and the awareness of it as the subject's own, are necessarily co-instantiated. On the criterion for the individuation of properties that is being assumed here, this turns out not to be a consistent position. (See note 2.)

348 THE OWNERSHIP OF MEMORIES

approach pushes towards the view that, when I am aware of my memory of my first kiss, for example, I am aware of the occurrence of this memory, and my awareness of the memory as my own is nothing over and above that experience. Similarly, when I am aware of my memory of my first bicycle fall, I am aware of the occurrence of this memory, and my awareness of the memory as my own is nothing over and above that experience. Thus, the two episodes of awareness turn out to have no phenomenological element in common, which seems counter-intuitive.

The something-entirely-different approach seems to raise a different type of difficulty. If the phenomenology that R.B. undergoes when he is aware of his memories is nothing like ours, then it is hard to see why R.B.'s reports are so similar to the claims that we ourselves would make if we had normal memories of being at a beach in New London, or of being at the MIT study lounge. It is also hard to see how adopting this approach would help us explain why R.B. disowns some of his memories. Why should we expect that R.B., in virtue of having a phenomenology which radically differs from ours when he is aware of his memories, will disown those memories and not, let us say, claim that he is aware of having certain premonitions? If the phenomenology that R.B. undergoes is radically different from ours, then it does not seem possible to explain, on the one hand, the similarities between his reports and the reports that we would make of normal memories and, on the other hand, the differences between those two sets of reports, by attributing to R.B. such a phenomenology.

It seems, therefore, that the most plausible way of reading R.B.'s reports is by attributing to him an awareness of the instantiation of certain memories without the awareness that those memories are his own, that is, by adopting the something-missing approach. If the something-missing approach is the right approach to take towards R.B.'s reports, then what R.B.'s case seems to show is that the awareness of an episodic memory as being the subject's own is dissociable from the subject's awareness of the occurrence of that memory. And if the two experiences are dissociable, then we should conclude that they are different experiences. Thus, it seems that what the case of patient R.B. ultimately shows is that the sense of mineness is a genuine experience; an experience which, ordinarily, is part of the characteristic phenomenology of our awareness of episodic memories, even though it turns out to be separable from it.

This means that, at least in the case of our awareness of episodic memories, the simple explanation of why inner awareness leads to the self-attribution of phenomenal states seems to be available to us. We can account for the fact that we self-attribute those episodic memories that are revealed to us in inner awareness by appealing to the fact that, in normal circumstances, our awareness of those memories is accompanied by an experience of those memories as being our own. We can appeal to this experience of ownership, or this sense of mineness, because that seems to be precisely the experience which is missing from patient R.B.'s awareness of those memories that he disowns. This, however, does not provide us with a full grasp of what R.B. means when he claims not to own some of his memories. After all, we have left the question of what it takes for a subject to experience a memory as being their own open. Let us therefore turn to this question now.

3. The Identification Model of Memory Ownership

Stanley Klein and Shaun Nichols have put forward a proposal regarding the nature of the sense of mineness for episodic memory. What patient R.B. lacks, they tell us, is 'a sense of numerical personal identity with the past person' (Klein and Nichols 2012, 689). Since the main idea in this proposal concerns R.B.'s identity with a past person, let us abbreviate this view as the 'identification model' of the sense of mineness for episodic memory. Notice that Klein and Nichols's proposal that R.B. lacks the sense of being identical with a person in the past can be understood in at least two ways. On one version of this proposal, what R.B. is trying to express when he claims not to own some of his memories is that he lacks the sense of being identical with the person who had the remembered perceptual experience in the past. Let us call this view the 'experiencer version' of the identification model. On a different version of this proposal, what R.B. is trying to express when he claims not to own some of his memories is that he lacks the sense of being identical with the person who was experienced as being part of the remembered scene.[10] Let us call this view the 'object version' of the identification model. What are the virtues and shortcomings of each version of this model?

Both versions of the identification model square with a number of details in R.B.'s reports. In report 1, for example, R.B. claims to have felt that the remembered scene was 'not his memory'. And, in report 2, R.B. claims to have experienced that the remembered scenes were 'not his'. We can make sense of these claims if the experiencer version of the identification model is right and, when R.B. has the relevant memories, he does not feel that the person who, in the past, experienced the remembered scenes was him. The claims make sense, too, if the object version of the model is correct, and R.B. does not feel that he is the person represented as being part of the remembered scene. Furthermore, in report 3, R.B. claims that the relevant scene did not feel like it was something that really had been 'a part of his life'. Along similar lines, R.B. claims, in report 5, that the scenes remembered did not feel as if they had 'happened to him'. And, in report 7, R.B. claims that he feels as if the scene is 'something he didn't experience'. One

---

[10] I am grateful to an anonymous referee for pointing out this ambiguity. The referee also suggests a further reading of the identification model according to which R.B. lacks the sense of being the person who undergoes a current experience, namely, the memory being expressed. As far as I can see, however, there is no evidence to suggest that R.B. lacks the sense of being the person who is the bearer of the memory.

350 THE OWNERSHIP OF MEMORIES

would certainly expect claims of this type if the experiencer version of the identification model were right, and R.B. did lack the sense of being the person who, in the past, experienced the remembered scenes. And, conversely, in those instances in which R.B. did enjoy the feeling of being the person who, in the past, experienced the remembered scenes, one would expect R.B. to claim, as he does in report 6, that he felt that the relevant scene 'was something 'I' had done and experienced', and that the scene felt like it was part of his life. These remarks in reports 3, 5, 6, and 7 fit within the object version of the identification model as well. If R.B. did lack the feeling of being the person who was experienced as being part of the remembered scenes, one would expect him to claim that he does not have the sense that the remembered scenes happened to him. And, in those instances in which R.B. did enjoy the feeling of being the person who was experienced as being part of the remembered scenes, one would expect R.B. to claim, as he does, that the scene felt like it was part of his life. On either version of the identification model, therefore, one can see the motivation for reading R.B. as saying that he lacks the sense of being identical with a remembered person in the past. However, the identification model of the sense of mineness faces a difficulty. For it seems to be in tension with a number of details in R.B.'s reports.[11]

Let us consider, first, the object version of the identification model. The view that R.B. does not have the sense of being identical with the person who was experienced as being part of the remembered scenes does not sit easily with some references that R.B. makes to himself while describing the content of his memories. In report 1, for example, R.B. refers to the remembered scene as a scene 'of me' at a certain beach, which does not seem to be neutral on who R.B. remembers to have experienced being at that beach in the past. In that report, R.B. seems to be describing a memory that presents a past perceptual experience of a scene (a scene that involves a beach in New London, and R.B.'s family in it) as having been his own experience. This is perhaps clearer in report 2, where he refers to a memory of 'having been' at MIT, and in report 3, where he refers to a memory of 'studying with my friends'. This kind of talk does not seem to be neutral on who R.B. remembers to have experienced being at MIT at the remembered time.

---

[11] Two anonymous referees are concerned that the objections raised against the identification model below are too reliant on the precise wording of R.B.'s reports. The thought is that perhaps we should not assume that R.B.'s reports are raw transcriptions of what it feels like to him to have those memories. I acknowledge that relying on first-person reports of mental states for investigating the phenomenology associated with those states is a methodology with some obvious limitations in pathological cases. But this worry cuts both ways. To the extent that it is problematic to rely on the details of R.B.'s reports for challenging the identification model of memory ownership, it is also problematic to make use of this type of data in support of the model. I take it that the project in which Klein, Nichols, and myself are all involved is that of finding a reading of R.B.'s reports which, overall, makes the most sense of the highest proportion of remarks in those reports. In order to pursue this project, it seems reasonable to trust R.B.'s comments as expressions of his memories, and not as expressions of beliefs to which he has arrived through inferences grounded on those memories (except, of course, where R.B.'s reports give us a clear reason to believe that he has performed such inferences).

THE ENDORSEMENT MODEL OF MEMORY OWNERSHIP   351

It does not seem to be neutral on who R.B. remembers to have experienced studying with his friends at that time either. Notice that R.B. does not claim that he remembers 'someone being at MIT', and he does not claim that he remembers 'someone studying with his friends'. And yet, one would expect him to use locutions of that kind if he did not feel that he was the person who experienced the scenes to which he refers in reports 2 and 3. Similarly, in report 7, R.B. claims to remember 'myself walking into the room and other things that I did and felt'. In this case too, R.B.'s references to himself give the impression that R.B.'s memory is presenting him with some past experiences and actions which appear to R.B. to have been his own.

Let us consider, now, the experiencer version of the identification model. The view that R.B. lacks the sense of being identical with the person who experienced the remembered scenes does not square with some references that R.B. makes to a phenomenology of mental time travel associated with his memories. In reports 3 and 4, for example, R.B. talks about 'reliving' and 're-running' a past experience in memory. This experience is described by R.B., in report 4, as involving 'a sense of being there, at MIT, in the lounge'. It is hard to make sense of this talk if the person who R.B. remembers to have experienced being at the study lounge at MIT, studying with R.B.'s friends, is not R.B. himself. If R.B. does lack the sense of being the person who originally experienced the scene at the MIT study lounge, then in what sense is R.B. reliving, or re-running, that scene when he has the relevant memory? After all, that scene is, by assumption, not remembered by R.B. as having been experienced by him in the first place. An analogous worry applies to R.B.'s talk of having 'a sense of being there'. If the identification model is correct, then one would expect R.B. to claim, in order to describe his memory of the scene at the study lounge, that his memory conveys a sense of someone being there; not a sense of being there. R.B.'s talk of having a sense of being there when he remembers the scene mentioned in reports 3 and 4, and his talk of reliving and re-running the experiences of that scene in memory, strongly suggests that R.B.'s memories do carry the feeling that he is the person who experienced the remembered scenes in the past.

What we need, then, is a reading of R.B.'s reports that, on the other hand, makes sense of R.B.'s remarks about the reported memories not being his own while, on the other hand, accommodating R.B.'s remarks about them being memories of himself as well as R.B.'s comments that the relevant memories involve an experience of reliving the remembered scenes. Let us turn, therefore, to a proposal that is aimed at satisfying these constraints.

4. The Endorsement Model of Memory Ownership

It seems clear that at least some of R.B.'s memories do lack some salient phenomenal feature that episodic memories normally enjoy. It also seems clear that, due to that fact, R.B. feels, in some sense, estranged or alienated from those memories.

Thus, if we manage to specify the form of estrangement that R.B. is experiencing, this case should provide us with some clues as to the nature of the sense of mineness for episodic memories that is present in the non-clinical population. The question, then, is what phenomenal feature is missing from some of R.B.'s memories; those memories which R.B. disowns.

Usually, when we think that one of our mental states is a memory of some state of affairs, then that state of affairs will appear to us as having been the case in the past and, accordingly, we will take ourselves to be remembering the relevant state of affairs. Thus, if I take myself to be having a memory of me giving a lecture while facing a theatre with some students in it, it will thereby seem to me as if, in the past, I was giving a lecture in a theatre with some students in it. And, likewise, it will seem to me as if I am remembering that I was giving such a lecture. This is, in fact, one of the characteristic ways in which the phenomenology of remembering tends to be similar to that of perceiving, and dissimilar to that of imagining. (Whereas those states of affairs that we take to be perceiving appear to us to be the case, those states of affairs that we take to be imagining do not appear to us to be the case.) Let us abbreviate the idea that a subject has the sense that the content of a memory that they are having matches the past by saying that the subject 'endorses' the memory. The suggestion that I wish to put forward is that R.B. does not endorse those memories to which he refers in reports 1–5 and 7, but he endorses those to which he refers in report 6; hence his disowning the former and claiming to own the latter. By contrast, in normal circumstances, we are aware of our episodic memories as being our own in that we have the sense that the content of those memories did take place in the past.[12] Let us abbreviate this view as the 'endorsement model' of the sense of mineness for episodic memories.

What reasons are there to think that the endorsement model of the sense of mineness is correct? In order to describe the experience of those memories that R.B. disowns, he uses two telling analogies; an analogy with the experience of imagination and an analogy with the experience of looking at a photograph. In reports 3 and 4, in which R.B. tries to describe what it is like for him to have a memory of the scene at the MIT study lounge, he compares his experience to the

---

[12] An anonymous referee raises the question of what it is for a subject to be aware of a mental state as a memory over and above being aware of the mental state as representing the past. The worry is that, unless there is such a distinction, it is hard to see why R.B. refers to his disowned memories as memories when he lacks the sense that the content of those memories matches the past. (As we will see in section 5, an analogous question should be raised for our awareness of phenomenal states of other types.) My own view is that memories represent themselves as having a certain causal history, that is, as originating in the subject's past experiences. For that reason, I am inclined to think that the awareness of a mental state as a memory is the awareness of it as originating in a past experience of the subject. The idea would be, then, that R.B. enjoys this awareness even though he lacks the awareness of the past experience as having been veridical. I, however, cannot elaborate this idea here for reasons of space. For details, see (Fernández 2006).

THE ENDORSEMENT MODEL OF MEMORY OWNERSHIP   353

feeling of imagining a scene that is being described by someone else.[13] Suppose that, when R.B. has a memory of the scene at the MIT study lounge, it does not feel to him as if the scene of him studying with his friends at that lounge really took place. Suppose that, by having an episodic memory of that scene, R.B. can picture being at the study lounge with his friends. And yet, when R.B. pictures that scene, the fact that he was there, studying with his friends, does not seem to R.B. to have actually happened. Then, it makes sense that he tries to express this experience by saying that having a memory of the scene at the study lounge feels like an episode of imagination. For if R.B. was imagining the scene as described by someone else, then R.B.'s relevant episode of imagination would certainly not present the scene to R.B. as having been the case.

R.B.'s other analogy is revealing as well. In report 1, in which R.B. tries to describe what it is like for him to have a memory of the scene at the beach in New London, he compares his experience to that of looking at a photograph; a photograph of someone else's vacation.[14] Suppose that, when R.B. has a memory of the scene at the beach in New London, it does not feel to him as if the scene actually happened. Then, it makes sense that he tries to express this experience by saying that having a memory of the scene at the beach in New London feels like looking at a photograph. For if R.B. was looking at a photograph of the scene, the scene would not appear to R.B. as having really happened. To be sure, R.B. would be able to visualize the scene by looking at the photograph. But visualizing the scene in this way would not convey to R.B. the sense that the scene being visualized had in fact taken place in the past.

The endorsement model of the sense of mineness, like the identification model, can account for why R.B. disowns some of his memories. Notice that if the endorsement model is right, then R.B. is aware of having certain memories, but he does not have the feeling that the scenes represented in those memories happened in the past. And if he does not have the feeling that the scenes represented happened in the past, then he should not have the feeling that he is remembering those scenes.[15] The suggestion, then, is that what R.B. is trying to express, by disowning some memories, is that he does not feel like he is recollecting some scenes despite having memories of those scenes. Thus, if R.B. does not feel like the scene of him and his family at the beach in New London really took place when he remembers it, it seems natural for him to claim that the remembered scene 'is not his memory'. For R.B. will not feel like he is remembering the scene at the beach

---

[13] I take it that this is also the experience to which R.B. is referring when, in report 7, he claims that the scene concerned feels like something he was told about by someone else.

[14] In (Klein 2012, 493), R.B. is cited, instead, as saying 'As if I am looking at a movie of someone else's vacation' in that report. Similar considerations to those that follow will apply whether R.B. actually used an analogy with the experience of looking at a photograph or he used an analogy with the experience of looking at a movie.

[15] Interestingly, Klein agrees that, when R.B. has an episodic memory that he disowns, having that memory is not experienced by him as an act of recollection (Klein 2015, 19).

354   THE OWNERSHIP OF MEMORIES

in virtue of having a memory of it. Similarly, if R.B. does not feel like the scene of him and his friends at the MIT study lounge did actually happen when he remembers the scene, then it seems natural for him to claim that the remembered scene is 'not his'. After all, R.B. will not feel like he is remembering the scene at the study lounge, even though he feels like he has a memory of it.

It is also no wonder that R.B. claims, with regards to some of the scenes which he has memories of, that they do not feel like they were something that really had been 'a part of his life', or that they do not feel as if they had 'happened to him'. That seems to be a natural way of expressing the odd feeling that the scenes are not real. The contrast that R.B. is drawing with those memories to which he refers in report 6 can also be accounted for if R.B. has managed to endorse the relevant memories. Suppose that what R.B. feels, for each of the memories that he claims to have come to 'own', is that the remembered action or experience did take place in the past. Then, it is not surprising that R.B. describes what it is like for him to have those memories by saying that, at that point, what he remembers seems to be something that he had indeed done and experienced; or by saying that what he remembers seems to have been part of his life, his past.

Unlike the identification model of the sense of mineness, however, the endorsement model can accommodate R.B.'s references to himself while he describes his memories in reports 1–3 and 7, as well as R.B.'s talk of 'reliving' and 're-running' a past experience in memory in reports 3 and 4. Suppose that R.B.'s memories represent him as having experienced certain scenes in the past even though, oddly enough, R.B. does not have the sense that the remembered scenes actually ever happened. Then, it makes sense that he refers to those memories as memories 'of him' at a certain beach, memories of 'having been at MIT' (as opposed to memories of 'someone being at MIT'), memories of 'studying with his friends' (as opposed to memories of 'someone studying with his friends') and memories 'of himself' walking into the room in reports 1, 2, 3, and 7 respectively. After all, R.B.'s memories do represent him as having experienced those scenes. It is just that, in virtue of having those memories, R.B. represents himself as having experienced those scenes in much the same way in which he would be representing himself as having experienced those scenes if R.B. was imagining that he experienced them in the past. Thus, the endorsement model allows us to take those references that R.B. makes to himself while describing the content of his memories in reports 1–3 and 7 at face value.

What about R.B.'s talk of 're-running' and 'reliving' the experience of being at the MIT study lounge with his friends, and his talk of having 'a sense of being there' in reports 3 and 4? Suppose that, when R.B. has a memory of the scene at the study lounge, R.B. does not have the sense that the scene actually ever happened. If R.B. has a memory of the scene at the study lounge, then the way in which he will picture the lounge in virtue of having his memory will seem to R.B. to be that in which he experienced the scene when he was present in the lounge at the time. In other words, when R.B. has a memory of the scene in the study lounge, it will seem to R.B. that his memory presents to him the objects in the lounge as having had those properties which R.B. originally perceived them to have. Thus, such-and-such friend will not only appear to R.B. to have been, let us say, sitting to his right when R.B. has his memory of the scene, but it will also seem to R.B. that this is where he originally perceived his friend to be when they were all sitting in the lounge. The table in the study lounge will not only appear to R.B. to have been, let us say, blue, but it will also seem to R.B. that this is the color he originally perceived the table to be when he was present at the lounge; and so on. This much seems to be part of what it is for a subject to have a memory of some scene. But if R.B. has a memory of the scene at the study lounge in this way, then it seems natural for R.B. to talk of having a sense of being there, and reliving the experience of being there, when he has a memory of the scene. After all, when R.B. has a memory of the scene, it will seem to R.B. that every object in the study lounge is represented in his memory as it first appeared to R.B. when he was there, at the lounge. It seems, therefore, that the reading of R.B.'s reports according to which he does not experience some of his memories as matching the past preserves the virtues of Klein and Nichols's interpretation of those reports while, at the same time, sidestepping its difficulties.

5. The Ownership of Phenomenal States

Let us take stock. We have examined patient R.B.'s disownment of some of his memories as a piece of evidence that suggests that the experience of a memory as being the subject's own is indeed a genuine experience. We have also been trying to determine how exactly R.B.'s reports, in which he disowns some of his memories, should be interpreted. And the proposed interpretation has been that, for each of those memories that R.B. disowns, R.B. lacks the sense that the content of that memory took place in the past; that it was real. With this proposed interpretation of patient R.B.'s reports, came a proposal about the nature of the sense of mineness for episodic memories more generally. The proposal has been that what it is for a subject to experience an episodic memory as being their own is for them to have a sense that the content of that memory did take place in the past. Where does this leave us with regards to our original question?

Our original question was why our awareness of our phenomenal states leads to the self-attribution of those states. This was not a question about our awareness of our episodic memories specifically. Thus, one might be worried that the case of patient R.B. does not give us enough reasons for believing in the experience of our phenomenal states as being our own; just a reason for believing in the experience of our memories as being our own. Similarly, one might be worried that the proposal that being aware of our episodic memories as our own consists in having

356 THE OWNERSHIP OF MEMORIES

the sense that those memories match the past does not have a wide enough scope. For it is unclear what this proposal tells us about what it is for us to be aware of our phenomenal states, more generally, as being our own. It seems that, unless we can offer some reasons for thinking that the justification of the sense of mineness for episodic memories offered in section 2, and the analysis of its nature offered in section 4, can be generalized to other types of phenomenal states, we will need to conclude that our progress with regards to our original question has been very limited indeed.

How could we justify, first of all, the existence of a sense of mineness in our awareness of our phenomenal states of types other than memory? One thought is that, given that the condition of disowned memory suggested that there is a sense of mineness associated with our awareness of our episodic memories, perhaps there are other pathological conditions in which the subject disowns some of their phenomenal states; conditions to which we could appeal in order to vindicate the sense of mineness. And, in fact, it does seem that we can find some disturbances of the relevant sort among the first rank symptoms of schizophrenia (Schneider 1959). In certain delusions, subjects with schizophrenia seem to be able to report some of their phenomenal states while, at the same time, disowning those states.[16] These are so-called 'passivity' symptoms such as the thought insertion delusion, and delusions of 'made' feelings, impulses, and actions. The following reports illustrate, respectively, delusions of thought insertion, delusions of made feelings, delusions of made impulses and delusions of made actions:

<u>Report 8</u>

As I walked along, I began to notice that the colors and shapes of everything around me were becoming very intense. And at some point, I began to realize that the houses I was passing were sending messages to me: *Look closely. You are special. You are especially bad. Look closely and you shall find. There are many things you must see. See. See.*

I didn't hear these words as literal sounds, as though the houses were talking and I were hearing them; instead, the words just came into my head—they were ideas I was having. Yet I instinctively knew they were not *my* ideas. They belonged to the houses, and the houses had put them in my head. (Saks 2007, 27)

<u>Report 9</u>

I cry, tears roll down my cheeks and I look unhappy, but inside I have a cold anger because they are using me in this way, and it is not me who is unhappy, but they are projecting unhappiness onto my brain. They project upon me laughter, for no

---

[16] The diagnostic manual of the American Psychiatric Association DSM-5 characterizes a delusion as 'a 'fixed belief that is not amenable to change in light of conflicting evidence' (2013, 87). I will assume this conception of delusions for the purposes of the present discussion.

reason, and you have no idea how terrible it is to laugh and look happy and know it is not you, but their emotions. (Mellor 1970, 17)

Report 10

The sudden impulse came over me that I must do it. It was not my feeling, it came into me from the X-ray department, That was why I was sent there for implants yesterday. It was nothing to do with me, they wanted it done. So I picked up the bottle and poured it in. It seemed all I could do. (Mellor 1970, 17)

Report 11

When I reach my hand for the comb it is my hand and arm which move, and my fingers pick up the pen, but I don't control them...I sit there watching them move, and they are quite independent, what they do is nothing to do with me...I am just a puppet who is manipulated by cosmic strings. When the strings are pulled my body moves and I cannot prevent it. (Mellor 1970, 18)

There is a certain analogy between, on the one hand, reports illustrating the four delusions above and, on the other hand, patient R.B.'s reports of disowned memory. Just like, in the disowned memory case, R.B. reports to remember things even though R.B. claims that the relevant memories are not his, in these delusions, patients claim to have thoughts, feelings and impulses which are not theirs, or they claim to be the proprietors of the bodies in which certain actions are taking place while, at the same time, rejecting the claim that they are the agents of those actions.[17]

The reason why this analogy is interesting concerns the issue of what methodology to adopt while reading reports 8–11. We approached the case of disowned memory by assuming that a charitable way of interpreting R.B.'s disownment of some of his memories is by attributing to R.B. the lack of a sense of mineness in his awareness of those memories. Similarly, then, it seems that a charitable way of reading reports of patients with the thought insertion delusion, and delusions of made feelings, impulses, and actions is by assuming that they, too, lack a sense of mineness in their awareness of the relevant states: It seems to be a natural way of reading report 8, in which the patient claims that a certain thought is not 'their idea'. It seems to be a reasonable way of reading report 9 as well, in which the patient claims that 'it is not them' who experiences a certain feeling. It appears to be a sensible way of reading report 10, in which the patient claims that the impulse was not 'their feeling'. And it also seems to be a plausible way of reading report 11, in which the patient claims that what happened in their disowned action is that 'their bodies' (as opposed to the patient themselves) moved. But if

---

[17] I do not mean to suggest that the sources of these conditions are also analogous. In R.B.'s case, for example, there seems to be no suggestion of any form of mental illness being present. The analogy that I am drawing only concerns the structure of the patients' reports.

358 THE OWNERSHIP OF MEMORIES

the reason why patients with the thought insertion delusion, and delusions of made feelings, impulses, and actions disown those states is that they are not aware of the relevant states as being theirs, then this diagnosis suggests that most of us, in the non-pathological condition, are indeed aware of our thoughts, feelings, impulses, and actions as being our own. It suggests, in other words, that the sense of mineness is a genuine feature of our awareness of our phenomenal states.

What about the concern that we are yet to find out what it is for us to be aware of our phenomenal states, and not only our episodic memories, as being our own? Things are more complicated regarding this concern. It seems, on the one hand, that there are some reasons for thinking that the endorsement model of memory ownership can be generalized to the ownership of phenomenal states of other types. But it also seems, on the other hand, that such a generalization will require additional conceptual resources and may, in any case, suffer from some limitations of scope.

The reason why it seems that the endorsement model can be generalized is that the notion of endorsement does not only apply to memories. It applies more generally, since endorsement is simply an experience wherein some phenomenal state is presented to the subject as fitting, merited, or appropriate. And such an experience can be associated with our awareness of phenomenal states other than memories. Which phenomenal states? Those phenomenal states that we regard as being subject to the reasons, or grounds, that we have in our possession. Thus, we can think of a subject as endorsing a thought of which they are aware when the subject finds reasons for regarding the content of that thought as being correct. Similarly, we can think of a subject as endorsing a feeling of which they are aware when the subject regards the circumstances in which they are as justifying, or warranting, the feeling. And, finally, we can think of a subject as endorsing either an impulse or an action of which they are aware when the subject finds reasons for regarding the goal of that impulse, or that action, as worth pursuing. For, in all of those cases, the subject will experience the relevant mental state as being appropriate in virtue of the fact that they experience finding reasons for occupying the state. This notion of endorsement allows us to put forward a generalized version of the endorsement model of ownership. According to the generalized version of the model, a subject is aware of their phenomenal states as being their own just in case the subject has the experience of endorsing those states; the experience of finding reasons for regarding them as being appropriate.[18] But what

---

[18] Since the relevant notion of endorsement does not apply to those mental states that we do not regard as being subject to reasons, the model cannot explain our experience of ownership for mental states such as episodes of imagination or dreams. I am grateful to an anonymous referee for pointing this out. The model cannot explain our experience of ownership regarding sensations, and regarding generalized emotions (that is, feeling happy as opposed to feeling happy about such-and-such thing), for the same reason. Whether this feature of the model is a limitation in scope or not will depend on whether there are in fact cases of disowned mental states of these types.

evidence is there to suggest that the experience of endorsing a phenomenal state is indeed the experience of the phenomenal state as being one's own?

The main reason is that the experience of endorsement seems to be the experience that has gone missing in those conditions that we have used to motivate the existence of a sense of mineness, namely, delusions of thought insertion, and delusions of made feelings, impulses, and actions.[19] The hypothesis that patients with the thought insertion delusion do not endorse their 'inserted' thoughts accounts for some references that patients make to those thoughts as being representationally neutral. The patient in report 8, for example, refers to their inserted thought as an 'idea'.[20] The expression suggests that the thought is not being experienced as the type of mental state that needs to match the world. After all, entertaining an idea will not bring with it the feeling that there are reasons for regarding the content of that idea as being correct. It seems, then, that if thought insertion patients experience their inserted thoughts as being representationally neutral, they will not find reasons for regarding the content of those thoughts as being correct; they will not endorse them. Furthermore, the hypothesis that patients with delusions of made feelings do not endorse their disowned feelings squares with the fact that, in report 9, the patient claims to behave as if they felt happy 'for no reason'. If the patient is not endorsing their feeling of happiness, then they are not regarding the feeling as warranted by the circumstances. And if they are not regarding the feeling as warranted by the circumstances, then you would expect them to claim that they find no reason for having the disowned feeling. Likewise, the hypothesis that patients with delusions of made impulses do not endorse their disowned impulses squares with the fact that, in report 10, the patient claims to have felt an impulse to pour the bottle because 'they wanted it done'. If the patient is not endorsing the impulse to pour the bottle, then you would expect the patient to say that someone else, and not themselves, wanted the bottle to be poured. For, in that scenario, the patient would not find reasons of their own that could motivate their impulse. And, finally, the hypothesis that patients with delusions of made actions do not endorse their disowned actions accounts for the fact that, in report 11, the patient claims to experience a bodily movement that 'has nothing to do with them'. If the patient is not endorsing the action to comb their hair, for example, then they are not regarding the state of affairs in which their hair has been combed as a goal to be pursued. But if they are not regarding that state of affairs as a goal to be pursued, then it is no wonder that the patient says that the combing action has nothing to do with them. After all,

---

[19] For a discussion of the idea that the experience of endorsement is missing in cases of disowned thoughts, see (Fernández 2010). The idea that it is missing in cases of disowned action is explored, for example, in (Graham and Stephens 2000).

[20] Other patients with thought insertion refer to their inserted thoughts as 'pictures' (Mellor 1970, 17) and 'pieces of information' (Hoerl 2001, 190).

in that scenario, the patient would not be able to produce any reasons which recommend the action of combing their hair.

The extension of the endorsement model for the ownership of memories to the ownership of thoughts, impulses, feelings, and actions, however, will require further work. Notice that, while making the case that the experience of endorsement has gone missing in delusions of thought insertion, and delusions of made feelings, impulses, and actions, I have been assuming that the relevant patients are aware of their non-endorsed thoughts as thoughts, of their non-endorsed feelings as feelings, of their non-endorsed impulses as impulses, and of their non-endorsed actions as actions. After all, what they claim to have is mental states of those types, and not something else. This means that, despite lacking the experience that the mental states of which they are aware are appropriate given the reasons they have for being in those states, these patients must have some kind of awareness of those states which has not been disturbed. What a complete generalization of the endorsement model requires, therefore, is an account of what this type of awareness amounts to. As it stands, the generalized account remains incomplete, even though there are reasons for thinking that the account can be developed in the direction of explaining our felt ownership of phenomenal states other than memories.

6. Conclusion

What all this means for our project in this chapter is that the advocate of the sense of mineness can make a case for the existence of such an experience, and they can offer an informative proposal about the nature of it, at least in the case of memories. This allows them to draw a distinction between two experiences that, arguably, are involved in our awareness of our memories. These are the experience of a memory as being instantiated, and the experience of the memory as being one's own. The advocate of the sense of mineness can use this distinction in order to, among other things, account for why our awareness of our memories leads to the self-attribution of those memories. We have also seen some reasons for thinking that, more generally, the distinction can be drawn for phenomenal states of other types, such as thoughts, feelings, impulses, and actions. If this is correct, then the advocate of the sense of mineness can also use the distinction to explain why our awareness of those states leads to their self-attribution.

However, even if the model of the sense of mineness for memories offered here can eventually be generalized with success, this will only be done at a cost; a cost that should be disclosed. The distinction drawn by the advocate of the sense of mineness seems to be, on reflection, a sort of double-edged sword. On the one hand, the distinction allows the advocate of the sense of mineness to account for a fact about the relation between inner awareness and the attribution of phenomenal states; a fact that others will have trouble explaining without the conceptual resource of the sense of mineness. But, on the other hand, the distinction also brings up a difficult question for the advocate of the sense of mineness; a question with which others will not need to concern themselves if they do not accept the existence of a sense of mineness. This is the question of why, in our awareness of our phenomenal states, the two experiences distinguished by the advocate of the sense of mineness should go together in the first instance. If our awareness of our phenomenal states does involve two different experiences, and not one, then why do those experiences go hand in hand in episodes of inner awareness?

The endorsement model of the sense of mineness does not yield an answer to this question, but it does indicate where such an answer may be found. Suppose that the sense of mineness associated with our awareness of our phenomenal states is the experience of endorsing those states. Then, the issue of why experiencing the occurrence of a phenomenal state tends to go together with experiencing the state as one's own is really the issue of why we endorse those phenomenal states that we are aware of having. If the endorsement model is correct, then the challenge for the advocate of the sense of mineness is to specify the function that the experience of endorsement is supposed to have in inner awareness. How manageable this challenge is for the advocate of the sense of mineness may ultimately depend on the commitments that the opponent of the sense of mineness will need to acquire in order to explain why we self-attribute those phenomenal states which are revealed to us in inner awareness.

References

American Psychiatric Association. (2013) *Diagnostic and Statistical Manual of Mental Disorders*, Fifth Edition (DSM-5). Washington, DC: American Psychiatric Association.

Bayne, T. (2008) 'The phenomenology of agency', *Philosophy Compass* 3: 1–21.

Bayne, T. and Montague, M. (2011) 'Cognitive phenomenology: An introduction', in T. Bayne and M. Montague (eds.), *Cognitive Phenomenology*. Oxford: Oxford University Press, 1–35.

Billon, A. and Kriegel, U. (2015) 'Jaspers' Dilemma: The psychopathological challenge to subjectivity theories of consciousness', in R. Gennaro (ed.), *Disturbed Consciousness*. Cambridge, MA: MIT Press, 29–54.

Fernández, J. (2010) 'Thought insertion and self-knowledge', *Mind & Language* 25: 66–88.

Fernández, J. (2006) 'The intentionality of memory', *Australasian Journal of Philosophy* 84: 39–57.

Gallagher, S. (2005) *How the Body Shapes the Mind*. Oxford: Oxford University Press.

Graham, G. and Stephens, L. (2000) *When Self-Consciousness Breaks: Alien Voices and Inserted Thoughts*. Cambridge, MA: MIT Press.

Hoerl, C. (2001) 'On thought insertion', *Philosophy, Psychiatry and Psychology* 8: 189–200.

Klein, S. (2015) 'What memory is', *WIREs Cogn Sci* 6: 1–38.

Klein, S. (2013) 'Making the case that episodic recollection is attributable to operations occurring at retrieval rather than to content stored in a dedicated subsystem of long-term memory', *Frontiers in Behavioural Neuroscience* 7: 1–14.

Klein, S. (2012) 'The self and its brain', *Social Cognition* 30: 474–518.

Klein, S. and Nichols, S. (2012) 'Memory and the sense of personal identity', *Mind* 121: 677–702.

Lichtenberg, G. (1990) *Aphorisms*, tr. R.J. Hollingdale. London: Penguin.

Mellor, C.S. (1970) 'First rank symptoms of schizophrenia', *The British Journal of Psychiatry* 117: 15–23.

Saks, E. (2007) *The Centre Cannot Hold: A Memoir of My Schizophrenia*. London: Virago.

Schneider, K. (1959) *Clinical Psychopathology*. New York: Grune & Stratton.

Tulving, E. (1972) 'Episodic and semantic memory', in W. Donaldson and E. Tulving (eds.), *Organization of Memory*. New York: Academic Press, 381–403.

Zahavi (2008) *Subjectivity and Selfhood: Investigating the First Person Perspective*. Cambridge, MA: MIT Press.

Analytic Index

Note: Tables and figures are indicated by an italic '*t*', '*f*', and notes are indicated by 'n.' following the page number.

For the benefit of digital users, indexed terms that span two pages (e.g., 52–53) may, on occasion, appear on only one of those pages.

acquaintance 58–9
agency 264–5
  agentive phenomenology 269–70, 279–82
  feeling of 18–19, 293, 296–7, 301–4, 306–8
  sense of 319, 321–3, 329–30, 331*f*,
    see also sense of ownership of action
Akins, K. 285, 287
Anscombe, E. 225–6, 226n.6, 271–2
apotemnophilia, *see* xenomelia
autoscopic phenomena 143, 151, 157–8
awareness
  peripheral *vs.* focal 183–4
  peripheral inner 87–8
  primitive 204–9
  self-awareness
    basic 19, 319, 329–32, 331*f*
    pre-reflective 192, 217–19

Barrett, D. 307–8
belief 172–3, 176, 180–1
  see also reasons and belief
Bermúdez, J.L. 149–50, 269, 271–4
Billon, A. 13–14, 90–2, 94–5, 152–3
  and Kriegel, U. 347nn.8–9
Blakemore, S. 135–6
Block, N. 3–5, 7–8, 172
body
  bodily sensation 250–1, 253–4
    location of 143, 148, 150–1, 251n.4, 255–6,
      258, 262–5, 269–70, 274–5, 278, 285
    and visual perception 260–1, 274–5
  schema 153–8, 261–6, 280–1, 286
    defensive body schema, *see* self-protection,
      protective body map
  significance 269–70, 281–6
  see also boundedness; connectedness; control,
    body; representation, body; sense of
    ownership, bodily
Bodyguard hypothesis 17–18, 270, 282–3, 286
boundedness 149–51, 153, 157–8, 255–6, 262
  boundaries 274–5, 278–82, 285
  sense of 148, 150, 158–9, 256, 259–62, 264–5

Boyle, M. 107–9
Brentano, F. 183

Capgras' syndrome 69
Chalmers, D. 231
cognitive impenetrability 272–4
Coliva, A. 16–17, 223–8, 231, 238
connectedness 149–50
consciousness
  abnormality 92–6
  access 39–42
  higher-order theories of 8, 35n.9, 208
  intentionalism about 170–1, 174–5, 177, 180–1
  phenomenal 1–5
control
  body 269–70, 280–2
  delusion of 14–15, 18–19, 132–7, 213–15,
    292, 301–3
corollary discharge 134–5
Cotard's syndrome 71–5

Dainton, B. 241–2, 337
Davidson, D. 99–100, 104
delusion, affective model of 299–301, 304–5
depersonalization 19, 56, 71–5, 90–2,
    276, 314–20
desire 14, 106, 114–18
  see also reasons and desire; self-attribution
    of desire
Donnellan, K. 239–40
Duncan, M. 9
Dugas, L. and Moutier, F. 317n.2, 334

egocentric
  space 278–9, 287
  see also representation, egocentric
emotion 18–19, 332–4, 336
  and intentionality 18–19, 293–5
  elicitation 295–7
  appraisal theory of 18–19, 296–7, 303–5, 308
  effects of 298–9
endorsement, sense of 322

364 ANALYTIC INDEX

evaluation 18–19, 305–9
experience 194–7, 198n.8, 199–200, 202,
    210–12, 216, 219, 229
  assymetry between first- and third-personal
    access to 12, 14, 38–42, 103–4,
    109, 112–13
  experiencing subject 193–5, 197–8, 201–2,
    205n.13, 209–11, 215, 217–18, 220–1
  reportability of 42–5
  unreflective 86, 90, 96
  see also property, experience property
    framework; representation of
    experience; self-attribution of
    experience; self-experience; sense of
    ownership of experiences

fact of ownership 145, 263–4
familiarity 283–5
Farrell and McClelland 4–5
'feel'
  affective reading 130–1
  epistemic reading 126–8
  sensory reading 127–8
feeling
  of alienation 301, 308
  of disownership 18–19, 301, 304
  of ownership 18–19, 269–73, 279, 293, 301,
    303–7, *see also* sense of ownership
  of passivity 301–2, 304
  see also mineness, feeling of; agency,
    feeling of
for-me-ness 15–16, 29–30, 30t, 179–89, 189f
full-body illusion 63–4, 143–4, 158–9

Gallagher, S. 36–8, 44–5
  and Zahavi, D. 4–5, 306–7
Gertler, B. 236–7
Guillot, M. 8–9, 8n.18, 12–13, 16, 50–1, 145,
  191n.1, 192nn.2–4, 216n.24, 319–20

Harman, G. 82
Helmholtz, H. von 134
Hill, C. 2
Howell, R., and Thompson, B. 6–7, 6n.13
Hume, D. 7, 83
Husserl, E. 260–1

imagination
  and memory 352–3
  first-person 330, 331f, 332
immunity to error through misidentification
  12, 16–17, 36–8, 224–5, 232–3, 243–5
  Simple Account 243–5
introspection 5–6, 87–8, 177–8, 182–4
  introspective data 14–15, 121–4, 131

Jaspers, K. 316–17, 320–1
judgment
  ease of 12, 42–5
  phenomenal 231–3

Klein, S., and Nichols, S. 19–20, 345, 347n.7,
  349, 350n.11, 353nn.14–15, 354–5
Kriegel, U. 4–5, 4n.9, 9, 39–42, 44–5, 87–8,
  101–2, 195–6, 199n.11, 202, 233, 244
  see also Zahavi and Kriegel; Billon and Kriegel

Levine, J. 3–5, 47n.27, 195–6, 233, 244

Martin, M. 147–8, 150–1, 256–61, 274–5, 278
McClelland, T. 10
McLaughlin, B.P. 299–301
memory
  disowned 19–20, 345–9, 356–8
  endorsement model of 19–20, 351–5, 358–61
  episodic 344n.3, 345, 348–9, 351–3, 353n.15,
    355–6, 358
  first-person 329–30, 331f, 332
  identification model of 19–20, 349–51, 353–4
  sense of ownership of 332
  see also imagination and memory
mineness 30–1, 30t, 50–4, 102, 180, 213–16,
  269–70
  feeling of 291, 294–5, 297, 299, 307–9
  function of 12–13, 60–3, 74–5
  lack of 316–20, 324–6, 329–30, 332–4, 336–7
  link 19, 104–5, 332–4
  malfunction of 12–13, 52–3, 56, 60–75
  nature of 334–7
  negative 14–15, 121
  positive 14–15, 121
  sense of 31–2, 31t
  unity of 326–7
myselfness 122–4
Moore, G.E. 7, 13–14, 83
  Moore's paradox 110n.10, 129

Nagel, T. 2–3, 6, 12, 46–7
narcissism 17–18, 284–7
No-Split 16–17, 225–7, 232, 239–43
Neander, K. 58–9

O'Conaill, D. 6, 9, 13–14

pain 275–8, 281, 283
Papineau, D. 236
parsimony principle 14–15, 121–5, 133, 138
Peacocke, C. 155–6, 172, 279, 286
perception 28–35
peripheral deafferentation 276, 280
perspectival fact 106–7

ANALYTIC INDEX   365

phantom limb 274–5, 278–9
phenomenal character, models of
 Salad model, the 185
 Tree model, the 185–7
 Circles model, the 187–8, 189*f*
phenomenal concept 16–17, 229–38, 240, 243
 phenomenal-causal 236–7, 241
 pure 229–32, 236
phenomenal contrast 12–13, 55–7, 181
 contrast-resistant phenomenal
  property 55, 57
phenomenality
 attitude-based 172–8, 184–8, 189*f*
 content-based 169–72
phenomenism 8
phenomenological tradition 78–9
phenomenology
 affective 17–18, 269–70, 281–7
 cognitive 176, 269–70, 273
presence 29, 278–9
projection 85–6
property
 content property 169–71, 173
 experience property framework 16, 193–4,
  196–7, 199, 210–11
 experiential property 193n.5, 194–5,
  198–202, 204–6, 210–11, 219–20
  pure 206–8
 phenomenal property 169–71, 173, 180
  in relation to content property 170–7, 180–1
  see also phenomenal contrast, contrast-
   resistant phenomenal property
 subject property framework 16, 193–4,
  196–9, 210–11

qualitative character 197–9, 198n.8, 201–2,
 210–11
 qualia 1–2, 4–5, 13–14

Real Guarantee, the 16–17, 227–8, 231, 238
realness 173–4
reasons
 and belief 106, 110–12
 and desire 116–18
 and judgment 111–12
 and experience 113
 responsiveness to 113–14
reflection 56–7, 90
reflexive rule 331
representation
 body 262–3, *see also* body, body schema
 egocentric 122
 nature of 58
 of experience 12–13, 58–60
 see also content property

Ribot, T. 317n.2, 324
rubber hand illusion 14–15, 124–32, 150–1,
  159–60, 272–5, 280–3, 285
Ryle, G. 99–100, 102, 104

Sartre, J.P. 7, 82, 86–7, 192n.2
Schear, J.K. 6–8
Sebastián, M.A. 9
self-attribution
 of experience 14, 35–8, 106–7, 113
 of judgment 110
 of desire 117
self-concept 16–17, 223–38, 240–4, 244n.32
self-experience 16–17, 223, 233–5, 237–8,
  240–3
self-knowledge 14, 54, 99–100, 104–7,
  109–10, 113
 deflationist accounts of 104–7
self-monitoring 134–8
self-protection 280–2, 287
 protective body map 17–18, 156–9, 281–7
 skin conductance response 280–4
self-tickling 135–6
sense field 257–61
sense of ownership, *see also* feeling of ownership
 bodily 15, 17–18, 60–4, 66, 69–70, 143–60,
  250–5, 269–70, 274–9, 281–8
 of action 60–2, 64, 330, *see also* agency
 of experiences 61, 64, 69–70, 74, 101–2,
  319–21, 323–4, 327, 329–32, 331*f*,
  see also mineness
 of memory, *see* memory, sense of ownership of
Shea, N. 229–30
Snowdon, P. 2
Soldati, G. 234–5
sole-object view 274–5
somatoparaphrenia 18–19, 143, 145, 150–3, 155,
  159, 233–4, 276–7, 279–80, 282–3, 285,
  292, 301, 303–4, 308
Stoljar, D. 2–3, 3n.4, 6n.13, 8nn.17–18
Strawson, G. 9
subjective character 3–5, 13–14, 78–82
 [subjective character]₁ 16, 191, 195–204,
  210–12, 215, 219–20
 [subjective character]₂ 16, 192, 203–4,
  210–12, 215, 219–20
 [subjective character]₃ 16, 192, 219–20
 deflationary view of 5–10, 12
 essence question about 1, 18–20
 existence question about 1, 14–15, 19
 explanation question about 1, 19
 function question about 1, 18–19
 peripheral 87
 robust view of 5–10, 12–17, 19
 thick 80–1, 84–6, 90–1

366 ANALYTIC INDEX

thought-insertion 18–20, 66–70, 73, 213–16, 292, 301, 304–5, 320–3, 356–60
tool use 154–5
transparency 13–16, 82–4, 107–10, 112–15, 176–8, 182, 184–5
  of experience 82–5
  of self 83–5
  rationalistic account of 110–15, 117
touch 257–8
Tye, M. 7, 171

Vignemont, F. de 153–7, 261–5

Williford, K. 8n.17, 9
Wolpert, D. 134

xenomelia 154–5, 276–7

Zahavi, D. 4–5, 4n.7, 9–10, 43–4, 88, 91, 102–4
  and Kriegel, U. 5, 6n.12, 10–11, 33–5, 45–6, 88–9, 103–6, 108–9, 113, 191n.1
  see also Gallagher, S., and Zahavi, D.